Politics in

THE
MIDDLE
EAST

*The Little, Brown Series
in Comparative Politics*

Under the Editorship of
GABRIEL A. ALMOND
JAMES S. COLEMAN
LUCIAN W. PYE

Politics in

THE
MIDDLE
EAST

SECOND EDITION

James A. Bill
Carl Leiden

University of Texas, Austin

Boston   Toronto
LITTLE, BROWN AND COMPANY

Library of Congress Cataloging in Publication Data

Bill, James A.
  Politics in the Middle East.

  (The Little, Brown series in comparative politics)
  Bibliography: p.
  Includes index.
  1. Near East — Politics and government — 1945–
I. Leiden, Carl. II. Title. III. Title: Middle East. IV. Series.
DS63.1.B54 1983   956′.04   83–13599
ISBN 0–316–09506–0

Library of Congress Catalog Card No. 83–13599

ISBN 0-316-09506-0

9 8 7 6 5 4 3 2 1

ALP

Published simultaneously in Canada
by Little, Brown & Company (Canada) Limited

Printed in the United States of America

CREDITS AND ACKNOWLEDGMENTS
Gabriel A. Almond and G. Bingham Powell, Jr. From Gabriel A. Almond
and G. Bingham Powell, Jr., *Comparative Politics: System, Process, and
Policy*, 2nd ed. Copyright © 1978 by Little, Brown and Company (Inc.).
Reprinted by permission. **Abba Eban.** From *The Jerusalem Post*, Interna-
tional Edition, No. 1137, 15–21 August 1982. Reprinted by permission.
Lord Kinross. From Lord Kinross, *Atatürk: The Rebirth of a Nation* (Lon-
don: Weidenfeld and Nicolson, 1964). Reprinted by permission of George
Weidenfeld and Nicolson Ltd. and William Morrow & Company, Inc.
Henry Kissinger. From *Years of Upheaval* by Henry Kissinger. Copyright
© 1982 by Henry A. Kissinger. Reprinted by permission of Little, Brown
and Company and the author. **The New York Times.** From the account of
Frank Sinatra's concert in Egypt, *The New York Times*, 28 September 1979.
© 1979 by The New York Times Company. Reprinted by permission. **Gen.
Mattityahu Peled.** From *The New York Times*, 30 December 1982. © 1982
by The New York Times Company. Reprinted by permission. **Lawrence
Rout and Steve Mufson.** From Lawrence Rout and Steve Mufson, "Mixed
Barrel: Possible Oil Price Drop Is Welcomed or Feared, Depending on
Outlook," *The Wall Street Journal*, 26 January 1983. Reprinted by per-
mission of The Wall Street Journal, © Dow Jones & Company, Inc. 1983.
All Rights Reserved. **Robert Springborg.** From Robert Springborg, "On the
Rise and Fall of Arab Isms," *Australian Outlook* 31 (1977). Copyright 1977
by The Australian Institute of International Affairs. Reprinted by per-
mission.

*To Tim, Rebecca, and Ann
and the Memory of Louise Stookey*

Preface

OVER THE PAST decade, much has happened in the Middle East. The Shah has fallen, to be succeeded by a revolutionary Muslim regime directed by mullahs. Islam has reasserted itself socially and politically throughout the region. Iran and Iraq have been fighting a bloody war. Oil has skyrocketed in price and, despite enormous economic pressures, OPEC continues its precarious existence. Sadat went to Jerusalem and then on to Camp David. The Israelis left Sinai but then invaded and occupied Lebanon. Battered and bloodied, the Palestinian people still struggle for their homeland. Leadership has changed in many Middle Eastern countries. The generals are back in control in Turkey, while in Afghanistan a native Communist regime governs nervously under the watchful eye of the occupying forces of the Soviet Union. There is one less king. But Faisal and Khalid of Saudi Arabia are also dead, as are Bhutto of Pakistan and Sadat of Egypt. By the time this book appears, others may have joined the ghostly parade.

A book that reaches a third edition must have satisfied someone, actually enough purchasers to convince publishers to continue making it commercially available. We are pleased about this; we hope that the present effort to revise the 1979 edition will prove to be as acceptable as the earlier editions were.

A comparison with the first edition will show considerable change in organization. We find ourselves compelled to discuss more of current issues than we did in the past. The danger in covering current issues is that any analysis of the Middle East is apt to become dated very quickly. But any text that does not treat at all the politics of revolution in the area or the pavane (sometimes resembling the tarantella) that Arabs and Israelis mutually and periodically engage in would be doing a disservice to the reader. Despite this, we have also tried to emphasize the continuing characteristics of the area and have made an effort to analyze the major issues and problems that dominate the Middle Eastern political scene. This edition includes a new chapter on the Persian Gulf and the challenge of revolutionary change there. Although we have revised and updated all chapters, the chapters on political development, leaders and change, the Arab-Israeli issue, and the politics of oil (Chapters I, V, VIII, and X) have been substantially altered.

The system of transliteration in this study generally follows the format used by the *International Journal of Middle East Studies*. We have decided to delete all diacritical marks with the exception of the *ayn* (') and the *hamza* (') when they appear in the middle of a word. This decision may upset a number of careful scholars of Middle Eastern history and linguistics. It is done, however, to assist students and non-area specialists who have expressed their reluctance to plow through numerous dots and dashes, which to them appear randomly sprinkled over the pages of the text. (It should even merit an enthusiastic hurrah from the typesetters.) Arabic, Persian, or Turkish words commonly used in English are spelled as they appear in *Webster's Third International Dictionary* or in *Webster's Geographical Dictionary*. Well-known proper names are presented as they appear in the English literature or as they have been transliterated by the individuals themselves, for example, Gamal Abdel Nasser, Anwar Sadat, Muhammad Reza Shah Pahlavi, King Farouk, Nuri al-Said, King Hussein, and Kemal Atatürk. This approach, of course, leads to occasional inconsistencies. In response we quote T. E. Lawrence, who, in the preface of his *Seven Pillars of Wisdom*, writes, "Arabic names won't go into English, exactly, for their consonants are not the same as ours and their vowels, like ours, vary from district to district. There are some 'scientific systems' of transliteration, helpful to people who know enough Arabic not to need helping, but a wash-out for the world."

Anyone who reads this book will know that we are not indebted to every author who has written on the Middle East. Many individuals, however, have been of great help. Over the years, scholars such as Vernon Aspaturian, Manfred Halpern, John Duke Anthony, Ervand Abrahamian, George Lenczow ski, Malcolm Kerr, Robert Springborg, William Royce, and the late T. Cuyler Young have all had a great impact on our thinking. More recently, we have benefited from the works of Dale Eickelman, Monte Palmer, Joseph Szyliowicz, Fereidun Fesharaki, Marvin Weinbaum, Ruhollah Ramazani, Nikki Keddie, J. C. Hurewitz, William Cleveland, John Esposito, Oles Smolansky, and John Peterson. Scholars and teachers such as John Damis, John Lorentz, Bruce Borthwick, Gene Garthwaite, Arthur Goldschmidt, Jerrold Green, Tareq Ismael, Yasumassa Kuroda, Phebe Marr, Eric Hooglund, Hossein Razi, Robert Young, Mark Ewig, and many others have used the book in the classroom or have offered comments and suggestions that have been especially useful. Don Peretz's, Michael Hudson's, Amir Ferdows's, and Frank Tachau's reviews of the first edition were stimulating and helpful. Specific expertise and assistance have also been provided by Jim Hitselberger, William Millward, Metin Heper, Steven Dorr, Jerry Obermyer, Hisham Sharabi, John Cummings, Arnold Leder, Othman Rawwaf, John Williams, Ali Jazayery, Joy Lough, Daniel Goodwin, Tawfic Farah, R. M. Burrell, Jacob Landau, Abdullah Galedary, and Kamal and Ali Ghaemi. Public servants and genuine authorities on the Middle East such as David Long, Philip Stoddard, Arthur Allen, Larraine Carter, John Limbert, George Harris, Alan Gilbert, and Stephen Grummon have also taught us much. Scholar-economists like A. J. Meyer and scholar-diplomats like James Akins have been consistently supportive. We also appreciate the support of Richard Ware and Antony Sullivan of the Earhart Foundation and of Barbro Ek of Harvard University.

Among our students of recent years, several have worked

with us on the various editions of this book and have forced us to discuss, defend, and revise our ideas. These include Nazar Al-Hasso, Salman Al-Khalifa, Tim Dickey, Thomas Hartwell, Pamela Kress, Ibrahim Natto, Muafa Tikriti, Munther Dajani, William Hickman, Mohammed Daoudi, David Fink, Blake Dominguez, Edgar Wright, Abbas Manafy, Ahmad Farokhpay, Clifford Gladstein, Robert Kitrinos, Manochehr Dorraj, and Farzin Sarrabi-Kia.

We wish to single out Robert W. Stookey for special gratitude. A meticulous and accomplished scholar of the Arab world, Bob Stookey has graciously and generously reviewed a number of the chapters of this edition; it is a better book because of it. Finally, we thank Gabriel Almond, the Editor of the Little, Brown series in comparative politics. Professor Almond has been an encouraging and supportive force throughout. The same is true of Will Ethridge and Don Palm of Little, Brown.

James A. Bill
Carl Leiden

Austin, Texas

Contents

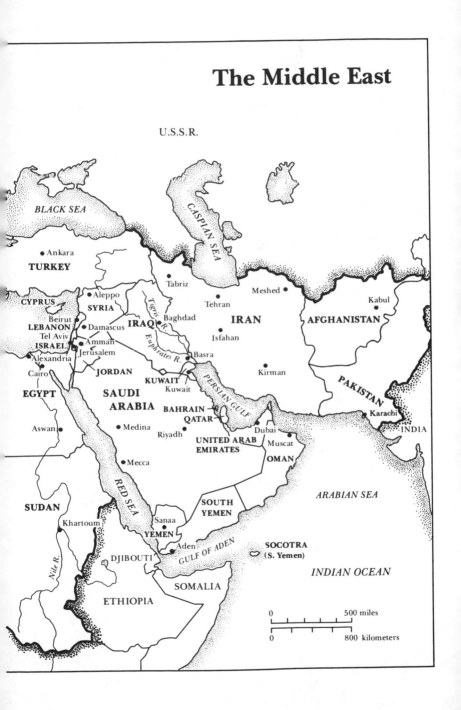

The Middle East

CHAPTER I

Political Development and the Challenge of Modernization

THE POLITICS OF turbulent change and revolutionary upheaval dominates the Middle East as mankind steadily approaches the year 2000. The dialectical clash between the challenging forces of modernity and the persistent strength of tradition is a fundamental reality in the region. Old human relationships and social structures are crumbling, while new systems remain to be formed. In the midst of such incoherence, many hold a vision of a promising but unknown future; others seek to return to a more familiar past. From Morocco and Algeria on the west to Afghanistan and Pakistan on the east, the peoples of the Middle East find themselves caught in a daily drama of economic hardship, political crisis, and personal insecurity in which survival remains the primary goal.

Politically, traditional rulers, revolutionary command councils, authoritarian military leaders, and religious governing elites live side by side. No form of government seems immune to coups and countercoups. Internal violence sparked by sociopolitical dissatisfaction and interregional warfare dominated by the persisting Arab-Israeli conflict have become an integral part of the scene. Lavish wealth exists alongside of abject poverty, both between and within socieities. Homeless Palestinians are scattered about the region, while militarily powerful Israel continues to expand its borders and influence.

1

The effects of the developmental challenge in the Middle East extend far beyond the confines of the area itself. The international impact of the oil embargo of 1973, the Lebanese civil war of 1975, the Iranian revolution of 1978–1979, the Soviet invasion of Afghanistan in 1979, and the Israeli attacks on Lebanon in 1982 are among the cases in point. The continuing impact of the message of revolutionary Iran and the broad appeal of the Islamic revival in the region will have a deep influence in the Third World throughout the 1980s.

At the level of everyday living, change is highly evident for ancient customs, and lifeways are under heavy siege. This is particularly true with respect to the related areas of occupation, transportation, recreation, and education. Stenographers and typists are rapidly replacing calligraphers and scribes; the carpet and metal industries have been transformed by the machine; and factories and assembly lines are taking the place of town workshops and cottage industry. In the realm of transportation, donkeys and camels have already lost their centuries-long domination to automobiles and trucks. Airplanes and airports are omnipresent. Throughout the Middle East, herdsmen and shepherds listen to transistor radios, and television sets now adorn village teahouses. The urban young increasingly flock to movie houses, dance halls, bowling alleys, pool halls, and ski resorts. The patterns of dress are also in a stage of interesting transition. Veiled women go about their shopping in tennis shoes, and street cleaners ply their trade in reasonable facsimiles of sport coats.

Countering this drive to modernity has been a growing trend to recapture important practices of the past. Throughout the region, there is a noticeable return to the veil by significant numbers of young women — women of all social classes. Middle Easterners seem to be increasingly engaged in a search for their roots. The resurgent strength of Islam must be viewed in this light. Social change in the Middle East therefore is marked by a curious and even bizarre blend of tradition and modernity. The jagged course of change has left in its wake a number of imbalances, inconsistencies, inequalities, and enigmas: discotheques and mosques, modern luxury hotels and squalid mud huts, nuclear energy programs and the fuel of animal droppings, F-16s and old rifles and daggers, palaces and tents, computerized libraries and omnipresent illiteracy.

Central to the entire problem of change as it is manifested in the Middle East are the related issues of modernization and political development. The revolution of modernization and the politics of development are two of the most critical problems confronting Middle Eastern peoples and cultures. It is here that they are caught in a grim struggle for survival, justice, and happiness. The extraordinary importance of these issues is perhaps matched only by the great difficulty involved in coming to grips intellectually with them. The following section will present some of the definitions and distinctions essential to any serious analysis of the processes of modernization and political development in the Middle East.

THE CHALLENGE OF MODERNIZATION

C. E. Black defines modernization as "the process by which historically evolved institutions are adapted to the rapidly changing functions that reflect the unprecedented increase in man's knowledge, permitting control over his environment, that accompanied the scientific revolution." [1] Dankwart Rustow writes that modernization is a process of "rapidly widening control over nature through closer cooperation among men." [2] And Marion J. Levy, in a major hypothesis in his work, asserts that "the greater the ratio of inanimate to animate sources of power and the greater the multiplication of effort as the effect of applications of tools, the greater is the degree of modernization." [3] Modernization is most concisely defined as the process by which man increasingly gains control over his environment.

The process of modernization has, of course, always occurred in every society. In the past, the wide variety of responses to environmental challenges produced some very disparate re-

[1] C. E. Black, *The Dynamics of Modernization* (New York: Harper and Row, 1966), p. 7.
[2] Dankwart A. Rustow, *A World of Nations: Problems of Political Modernization* (Washington, D.C.: The Brookings Institution, 1967), p. 3.
[3] Marion J. Levy, Jr., *Modernization and the Structure of Societies* (Princeton, N.J.: Princeton University Press, 1966), p. 35.

sults; this legacy is evident today in much of the developing world, including the Middle East. In the twentieth century, rapid communication not only facilitates the discovery that stages of modernization other than one's own are possible but also enables the tools and techniques of certain cultures to be transmitted to others.

Perhaps the most dramatic dimension of modernization is the technological revolution, which carries with it impressive trends in the areas of industrialization, economic development, and communication. In the Middle East, the constant physical transformations that seem to occur everywhere are outward evidence of technological development. Skyscrapers, highway grids, airports, hotels, dams, petrochemical plants, and steel mills continually sprout throughout the area. One author refers to this rapid change in the economic and material aspects of life as the "Edifice Complex."[4] Spurred by the discovery and exploitation of petroleum and natural gas, these economic and technological factors provide the driving force of modernization.

Closely related to technological advancement are the strides that have been made in education. The grip in which the clerics traditionally have held education in the Middle East has begun to be broken. Literacy programs multiply in the area, while the sheer numbers of school buildings and educational facilities increase at an amazing rate. The result of all this activity has been a heightened consciousness and an expanded scientific and technical knowledge. Acting as a catalyst to all this, of course, are technological forces such as advances in communications and the mass media, which provide the means by which information can be transmitted more quickly, effectively, and universally.

The developments in the Middle East in technology and education have a number of organizational and psychological implications. Organization is becoming more elaborate and specialized, and formal institutions are beginning to replace informal, personal administration. As values and expectations

---

[4] Norman Jacobs, *The Sociology of Development: Iran as an Asian Case Study* (New York: Frederick A. Praeger, 1966), p. 74.

become more secular, important shifts in attitudes are occuring. Traditional emphasis on the spiritual and magical waxes and wanes.

The patterns that constitute the modernization syndrome are mutually reinforcing. This reinforcement accelerates modernization even in societies in which resources are scarce and in which the population largely continues to follow traditional lifestyles. Technological progress promotes educational advancement, which in turn influences attitudes and values that are reflected in organizational settings. Moreover, value systems and organizational styles that are in a state of transformation are highly supportive of continuing and deepening technological and educational change. It is easy to see why modernization is a major obsession of the peoples of the Middle East.

Modernization is inevitable and omnipresent. In the words of Marion Levy, it is a "universal social solvent." [5] Those societies that are relatively more modernized have tended to be located in the West, and hence the process has sometimes been unfortunately referred to as Westernization. The inevitability and universality of modernization are products of the increasingly interdependent world in which we live. Although the societies in the Middle East will all struggle in one way or another to modernize, not all will succeed to the same degree. The unevenness of the success of modernization in the various Middle Eastern societies is in itself a source of tension and conflict.

Modernization is an unsettling, disruptive, painful process. The comforts of traditional habits are lost as these habits are uprooted. In modernizing societies, new processes and institutions seem always to be trapped in a state of becoming, and, as a result, the expected uncertainties of the past have given way to the more frightful and unknown insecurities of the present. In the Middle East, where most of the societies have seriously begun to modernize, any slowing or reversal of the process causes unprecedented stress. Yet the uneven supply of

---

[5] Marion J. Levy, Jr., *Modernization: Latecomers and Survivors* (New York and London: Basic Books, 1972).

national resources, the shortage of technical skills, and the weakness of political leadership are all severe impediments to continuing modernization. Modernization is a process in which expectations necessarily race beyond their satisfaction. However, satisfaction must never lag too far behind. In most Middle Eastern societies, the gap between sharpened aspirations and their attainment threatens to become a chasm. The consequent frustrations directly promote social upheaval and political unrest.

The direction and depth of the drive for modernization are determined largely within the political system. The political elites of the various Middle Eastern societies make the basic decisions that shape the strategies and programs of modernization. Much of the responsibility for the success and failure of policies of modernization resides in the political arena. Modernization in turn affects the capacity of the political system to respond to political challenges. For reasons such as these, the important issue of political development is closely interwoven with the problem of modernization.

THE CONCEPT OF POLITICAL DEVELOPMENT

One survey of the literature on development tallies ten different definitions of political development.[6] There is much confusion about the relationship between the concept of modernization and that of political development. Often the terms are treated as synonymous. In other instances, they are sharply distinguished from each other. In this study, we view the two processes as analytically distinct but actually interrelated. It is in this sense that we will study them in the Middle East.

Alfred Diamant writes that "political development is a process by which a political system acquires an increased capacity to sustain successfully and continuously new type of goals and de-

---

[6] Lucian W. Pye, *Aspects of Political Development* (Boston: Little, Brown and Co., 1966), pp. 33-45. For a penetrating analysis of the major intellectual attempts to confront the issue of development, see Leonard Binder's chapter, "The Crises of Political Development," in L. Binder *et al., Crises and Sequences in Political Development* (Princeton, N.J.: Princeton University Press, 1971), pp. 3-72.

mands and the creation of new types of organizations." [7] S. N. Eisenstadt provides a similar definition when he discusses a political system's ability to meet changing demands and then "to absorb them in terms of policy-making and to assure its own continuity in the face of continuous new demands and new forms of political organization." [8] Eisenstadt goes on to state that "the ability to deal with continuous changes in political demands is the crucial test of such sustained political development." [9] This concern for the capacity of a political system to meet new challenges is also evident in the Social Science Research Council Committee's work on development. The developmental capacity of politics "is a capacity not only to overcome the divisions and manage the tensions created by increased differentiation, but to respond to or contain the participatory and distributive demands generated by the imperatives of equality. It is also a capacity to innovate and manage continuous change." [10]

The last sentence above introduces a central dimension of our conceptualization of political development. The political system is not only a responsive, reactive mechanism in which demands and challenges are absorbed and digested; it is preeminently a system with a primacy and an autonomy that permits the introduction and generation of change. It is the political system that leads, guides, and directs. And it is in this system that the demands and programs of tomorrow often originate.[11] Manfred Halpern therefore defines political develop-

[7] Alfred Diamant, "The Nature of Political Development," in *Political Development and Social Change,* ed. Jason L. Finkle and Richard W. Gable (New York: John Wiley and Sons, 1966), p. 92.

[8] S. N. Eisenstadt, "Initial Institutional Patterns of Political Mobilization," *Civilizations* 12 (1962), reprinted in *Political Modernization,* ed. Claude E. Welch, Jr. (Belmont, Calif.: Wadsworth, 1967), p. 252.

[9] *Ibid.*

[10] James S. Coleman's words in Binder et al., *Crises and Sequences,* p. 78.

[11] This emphasis upon the political is especially critical in studying development in the Middle East. The Middle Eastern perception of change is oriented more to politics than to economics. In making this important point, C. A. O. van Nieuwenhuijze writes: "Intriguingly, the most conspicuous aspect in the Middle East is not the one that has virtually undisputed primacy in the Western perception of change, namely the economic aspects of material well-being. As it happens, this discrepancy in

ment as the "enduring capacity to generate and absorb persistent transformation."[12] Political development as it is discussed in this study involves the capacity of Middle Eastern political systems to initiate, absorb, and sustain continuous transformation.

Among the most important of the demands that the political system must foster and satisfy are the demands for equality of opportunity, political participation, and social justice.[13] These demands are much more difficult to meet than those derived directly from the economic and technological facets of life. The process of political development includes the capacity to provide more and more individuals with the power to improve their own positions in society on the basis of personal merit rather than personal connections. New groups and classes continually appear in society and must be brought effectively into the political process. Political development is a "process of admitting all groups and all interests, including newly recognized interests and new generations, into full political participation without disrupting the efficient working of the political system and without limiting the ability of the system to choose and pursue goals."[14] Finally, the rewards and priorities of the society need to be allocated and reallocated in a way that permits all to expect equal opportunity and to receive just treatment.

By defining political development in terms of a capacity to stimulate demands and to solve problems, one is able to avoid a number of ethnocentric problems that have long haunted developmental studies. The proclivity to define political de-

---

orientations has resulted in endless confusion and misunderstanding between on the one hand Middle Easterners with their development needs and on the other hand Western experts and observers with their development aid and advice. The two are, so to speak, on different wavelengths." See van Nieuwenhuijze, *Sociology of the Middle East: A Stocktaking and Interpretation* (Leiden, The Netherlands: E. J. Brill, 1971), pp. 773–774.

[12] Manfred Halpern, "The Rates and Costs of Political Development," *Annals* 358 (March 1965): 22.

[13] For a fine study of the politics of the Arab world that focuses on the concept of participation, see Michael C. Hudson, *Arab Politics: The Search for Legitimacy* (New Haven, Conn.: Yale University Press, 1978).

[14] This is Leonard Binder's view of the manner in which most liberal democrats in the West define political development. See Binder *et al.*, *Crises and Sequences,* p. 68.

velopment in terms of a Western-oriented view of democracy is one example of this ethnocentricity. Many "democratic" systems may not succeed in political development because of their inability to effectively absorb the changes occurring in the contemporary world. In the Middle East, Lebanon is a tragic case in point.

It is also possible that an authoritarian system that is able to overcome its inherent weaknesses concerning the issue of participation may succeed in political development. Using this definition of political development, it is possible to account for the developmental process as it existed in many ancient and traditional systems. Indeed, certain traditional Islamic societies were perhaps more highly developed politically than some contemporary Middle Eastern societies. This need not be surprising, since these traditional systems undoubtedly had much more limited demands placed upon them. To speak of political development as if it were something rare and unique to our modern age hinders our ability to understand the dynamics of change, since it distorts important historical realities.

The contemporary era, however, is fundamentally different from any earlier time because scientific advances and technological revolution have wrought unprecedented change. This change spreads rapidly because of the increasingly interdependent nature of the world. Modernization, or man's growing control over his environment, races onward at a breakneck pace. The impact of this modernization on the patterns of political development has been profound. Modernization and political development must be analyzed together.

THE DIALECTICS OF MODERNIZATION AND POLITICAL DEVELOPMENT

Partly to maximize their own power and authority, political elites may seek to generate and accelerate the processes of modernization within their societies. Although such efforts enlarge capacities to meet new challenges, they also help improve the standing of particular societies in the world of nations.[15]

15 J. P. Nettl and Roland Robertson go so far as to define modernization in terms of the search for technological equivalence among nation-states. See J. P. Nettl and Roland Robertson, *International Systems and the Modernization of Societies* (New York: Basic Books, 1968).

The unleashed forces of modernization, meanwhile, influence the behavior and policies of the elites. Leonard Binder writes that in Europe, "the overwhelmingly accepted view was that politics was essentially a response to the historical forces of modernization. Outside of Europe, the prevailing view has been the opposite. Politics is not a response to modernity, it must rather be the cause of modernity if modernity is to be achieved." [16] In this discussion, we view the processes as mutually interactive. Political elites forge modernization policies that strongly affect their future decision-making capacities.

Once modernization has begun, it tends to become a pervasive, persisting process. As a result, the political group that has stimulated and encouraged the modernizing movement often loses its ability to control and regulate the process. Demands increase and outstrip any capacity to cope with them. It is for this reason that political development is a highly problematic process. It cannot be assumed that because "modernization is taking place, political development also must be taking place." [17] It *can* be assumed that there will always be a gap between the demands that accompany modernization and the political system's ability to satisfy those demands. In this sense, it is easier to generate change than to absorb it.

Changes occasioned by the forces of modernization usually occur in the physical environment and are most dramatically evident in the areas of technology and economics. Impressive change here, however, does not necessarily signal basic alteration in the sociopolitical system. Traditional patterns of power and authority tend to resist fundamental change. Personal equality, political participation, and social justice are usually the last issues to be confronted. Political elites have vested interests in preserving ongoing political patterns. Yet if political development is to take place, it must involve a capacity for continuous change *especially* with respect to these social and political issues. No matter how much technological and economic progress may occur, there can be no political devel-

---

[16] Binder *et al.*, *Crises and Sequences,* pp. 15–16.
[17] Samuel P. Huntington, "Political Development and Political Decay," *World Politics* 17 (April 1965): 391.

FIGURE I.1 *The Development Process*

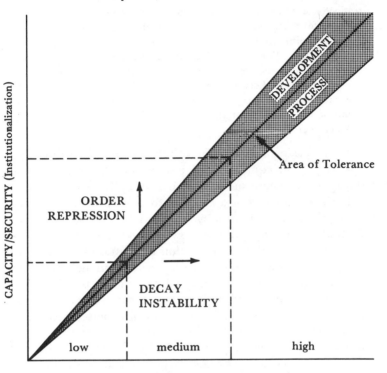

DEMANDS/LIBERTY (Participation)

opment without accompanying change in the power and authority structures.

The developmental process is driven by a dialectical dynamic that marks the relationship between demands and capacity. In more conventional terms, the struggle is one for both liberty and security. Figure I.1 provides a diagrammatic view of this process.

In their important study of comparative politics, Gabriel Almond and G. Bingham Powell identify liberty and security as two basic political goods that societies must provide. They point out that the provision of both of these goods has long been the classic dilemma of politics.

At the logical extremes, at least, there seem to be negative tradeoffs between liberty and security, and no ready ethical answer dictates the most appropriate balance between them.... At some point, liberty for some individuals threatens the security of others. The logical and ethical dilemma does not, however, obviate some very important empirical questions about the relationships between security and liberty.... For part of the problem of liberty concerns the use that citizens wish to make of it, and part of the problem of security concerns who shall enforce it.[18]

The increasing demand for liberty and related values such as participation, equality, and justice must be confronted in today's world. There must be either an enhanced capacity to satisfy these demands or a capacity to repress them. The satisfaction of demands is usually provided by increasing institutionalization and by effective new methods and style of rule. This often means the centralization and concentration of authority as ongoing relations are uprooted and new ones created. The forces of modernization, by providing political elites with more sophisticated techniques of control, can enhance their capacity to meet demands and to provide security. They also, however, can permit elites to stifle demands through repressive means. Calls for participation, equal opportunity, and justice can be smothered by "security" forces superbly equipped with the most modern technology. When this occurs, demands are confined and bottled up; they are not satisfied. Security through repression is often a harbinger of violence and upheaval. At the other extreme is a situation in which anarchy and chaos reign supreme. Here, the society explodes into fragments in the absence of effective institutions and guiding authority.

Almond and Powell investigate some of the conditions for a tradeoff between liberty and security by constructing a three-part typology of societies.[19] Society A is one in which the citizens enjoy substantial amounts of both liberty and security.

[18] Gabriel A. Almond and G. Bingham Powell, Jr., *Comparative Politics: System, Process, and Policy*, 2d ed. (Boston: Little, Brown and Co., 1978), pp. 411–412.

[19] *Ibid.*, pp. 412–415.

Such a society is usually culturally homogeneous and often lacks deep and divisive ethnic or religious cleavages. Although these societies are characterized by relatively low tension levels, there are short pendulum-like movements between an emphasis on liberty and an emphasis on security in these societies. In the Middle East, countries that tend to fall into this category include Egypt, Turkey, Israel, Tunisia, Libya, and Algeria. Algeria and Libya tilt more strongly in the direction of security, while Egypt and Tunisia are somewhat more sensitive to liberty.

Society B is one in which both ethnic and class tensions are so deeply embedded in the social body that the pendulum swings away from security, back through liberty, and ultimately into anarchy. "After a substantial amount of liberty appears, the society collapses at least temporarily into civil war, and security vanishes completely. Moreover, even with very great sacrifices of liberty, it may be impossible to attain high amounts of security." [20] The prototype of Society B is Lebanon, a society torn both vertically and horizontally by religious and class strife. Other Middle Eastern candidates for Society B status include Sudan, Syria, and Afghanistan. In the case of Syria, the constant specter of violent anarchy has caused the Alawite al-Assad regime to become preoccupied with security. This, then, brings us to the third type of society.

Society C is one in which coercion and repression are dominant. In its most extreme form, "the massive application of terror tactics — against even high-level officials in the government, not to mention millions of citizens — and a context of constant police and party intervention, complete censorship, and travel control destroys liberty, but provides little security. The uncontrolled actions of the regime itself undermine any security for its citizens." [21] Iran and Iraq are the Middle Eastern societies that most closely approximate the Society C type. Although there are fundamental differences in the political and ideological structures of these two countries, the leadership of both has opted to sacrifice liberty for tight and complete con-

[20] *Ibid.*, p. 413.
[21] *Ibid.*

trol from the center. Other examples, in descending order of applicability, include Pakistan, Saudi Arabia, Morocco, Oman, and Jordan.

The push and pull between the demands of the regime for control and the demands of the populace for freedom and participation is in a state of constant change. Societies move from one type to another. Algeria, for instance, was an extreme example of Society C when central control was enforced by the French, an outside power. After the revolution, it moved through a short chaotic Society B period, beginning when Ahmad Ben Bella was unable to consolidate control and continuing into the rule of Houari Boumedienne and Chadli Benjedid, whose regimes have delicately balanced popular demands and central authority. Although there is no doubt that control by the regime takes precedence over personal liberty in Algeria, there is nonetheless considerable emphasis on mass political participation, education, and social justice in the country.

There is also a continual shifting of emphasis within each type of society. In Iran under the rule of the Shah, periods of crushing oppression were interspersed with times of relative freedom. The early months of the revolution were months of moderation, but beginning in June of 1981 the Islamic Republic slipped into a stage of extremist politics as the religious regime engaged in an internal war against dedicated guerrilla opposition groups.

In Egypt, both Nasser and Sadat alternately tightened and relaxed their control. It was shortly after a sudden political crackdown that Sadat was assassinated on 6 October 1981. Although President Hosni Mubarak has generally relaxed control from the center, he has also resorted to sporadic repressive policies.

These examples indicate the delicate dialectic that lies at the core of the process of political development. Its outcome is shaped, however, within the larger field of modernization. It is this latter dynamic that can either retard or promote political development. Dramatic economic and technological growth increases the needs felt by the population. At the same time, such advancement strengthens the capacity of the political elite to exert influence and control. In order to muster the strength necessary to exploit scarce resources and to initiate effective planning programs, Middle Eastern elites have often relied upon authoritarian political methods. When they do this, they risk sliding into repressive and oppressive modes of behavior that fatally weaken their capacities for political development. Centralization and institutionalization may take complete precedence over participation. On the other hand, if the elites govern loosely and decentralization reigns supreme, they may also forfeit their developmental capacities as society breaks down into competing and conflicting ethnic, regional, and class-based cliques. As Figure I.1 indicates, the developmental process is a wobbly path between repressive rule and anarchical instability. The process is a delicate balance of capacity and demands. Increasing demands require an enhanced capacity to meet them. Development involves a constant push and pull between the two sides of this dialectic. Meanwhile, the fires of modernization continue to crackle. This complicates the developmental process by constantly altering and shifting balances, demands, responses, and capacities.

Any assessment of political development is made difficult by the accompanying processes of modernization that tend initially to suggest fundamental change. In fact, many traditional political systems are able to foster modernization while maintaining ongoing political patterns. In such systems, however, the basic sociopolitical demands usually outstrip the capacity to meet them, ultimately giving rise to revolutionary upheaval. A fundamental difficulty of Middle Eastern politics is the expanding gap between political demands for increased participation and justice and the ability to satisfy such demands. This situation is sometimes partially alleviated by a greater capacity to satisfy material demands, which are also vital to the population. In this arena, modernization plays a temporarily stabilizing role. In the long run, however, there must be an enduring capacity to satisfy continually and effectively the social and political needs of all groups and classes in society.[22]

22 We note here the extreme difficulty of developing an operational concept of political development. The assessment of capacity to generate

MODERNIZATION IN THE MIDDLE EAST

Nowhere in the world are the forces of modernization moving more rapidly than in the Middle East. Technological growth, industrial development, and the dramatic expansion of transportation, communication, and housing facilities are evident throughout the area.

Another visible sign of the modernizing process is the growth of military activity in the region. Such countries as Israel and Saudi Arabia are now among the world leaders in military expenditures. They are gathering some of the most sophisticated weapons that modern technology can produce. In terms of per capita military expenditure, Saudi Arabia, Israel, and Kuwait lead the world among those nations that spend $1 billion or more on such material.[23] Iran, Turkey, Iraq, Egypt, and Syria are also among the world's largest buyers of arms.

Quantitatively, gigantic advances have also been made in the social fields of health and education. Thousands of new school buildings, clinics, and hospitals have sprouted up throughout the countries of the Middle East. The number of students enrolled in primary, secondary, and higher education in sixteen selected Middle Eastern countries was less than 5 million in 1950; by 1965, this figure had more than tripled to over 16 million; in 1973 the number approached 27 million; and in 1978 the number was over 33 million — almost a sevenfold increase since 1950 (see Table I.1 for the detailed figures). In recent years, the education explosion has been especially evident at the college and university levels. In the five years

---

and absorb change is obviously more complex than the accumulation and interpretation of modernization data. Nevertheless, we do have some measures of this capacity, although perhaps crude ones. These include the analysis of power structures, authority relations, and political programs and policies.

[23] The figures for 1978 were $1,004, $839, and $613 per capita in Saudi Arabia, Israel, and Kuwait respectively. Comparative figures for the United States, the Soviet Union, and China, for example, were $499, $394, and $26 respectively. See Roger D. Hansen *et al.*, *U.S. Foreign Policy and the Third World: Agenda 1982*, published for the Overseas Development Council (New York: Praeger Publishers, 1982), pp. 220–221.

TABLE I.1 *Enrollment in Primary, Secondary, and Tertiary Levels of Education (in thousands) 1965–1978*

	Primary level			Secondary level			Tertiary level		
	1965	1973	1978	1965	1973	1978	1965	1973	1978[b]
Afghanistan	358	621	872	34	70	112	3.5	9.4	16.6
Algeria	1,358	2,409	2,976	95	384	852	8.1	30.1	61.8
Egypt	3,450	4,097	4,287	819	1,710	2,524	177.1	351.5	493.3
Iran	2,412	3,646	5,021	687	1,778	2,357	36.7	123.1	172.0
Iraq	978	1,409	2,460	241	405	846	28.4	65.5	96.2
Israel	450	527	568	66	149	190[a]	35.9	70.4	83.7
Jordan	295	353	431	99	126	231	3.2	8.2	17.2
Kuwait	50	94	117	29	60	129	.4	5.3	12.4
Lebanon	354	498	381	82	174	194[a]	20.3	44.3	78.6
Libya	190	489	587	23	107	151	1.9	9.6	15.1
Morocco	1,116	1,506	1,925	195	433	662	9.0	25.5	67.3
Saudi Arabia	261	571	753	24	148	287	1.9	14.9	43.8
Sudan	427	1,083	1,358	90	231	352	7.7	20.0	24.1
Syria	707	1,103	1,407	183	408	580	32.7	51.8	73.6
Tunisia	734	910	1,004	104	197	250	6.2	9.2	28.6
Yemen Arab Republic	69	179	255	2	14	25	—	1.0	4.1
Totals	13,209	19,495	24,402	2,723	6,494	7,385	373.0	839.8	1,287.9

Note: For detailed explanation of the data contained in this table, see the sources from which the data are drawn.

[a] Tentative estimate.

[b] In a number of cases, especially at the tertiary level, the figures provided are for the year 1977.

Sources: United Nations, Department of Economic and Social Affairs, *World Economic Survey, 1969–1970* (E/4942 ST/ECA/141) pp. 206–208. United Nations, *Statistical Yearbook 1975* (New York: United Nations, 1976), pp. 845–867. United Nations, UNESCO, *Statistical Yearbook 1980* (England: UNESCO, 1980), *passim*.

between 1973 and 1978, the number of students enrolled in higher education in these 16 Middle Eastern countries increased by over 50 percent.

The modernization boom has accelerated sharply since 1974, when a fourfold increase in the price of oil suddenly provided a huge pool of the resources essential to fuel modernization. In 1970, the petroleum revenues of the eight major Middle Eastern oil-producing countries was less than $6 billion. By 1974, the figure had ballooned to more than $82 billion. By 1980, Saudi Arabia alone was receiving over $100 billion in petroleum revenues. By the middle of 1982, Saudi Arabia had approximately $150 billion invested overseas, while Kuwait had $75 to $80 billion invested abroad.[24]

It is sometimes not realized that the Middle East is very rich in resources other than petroleum. Iran, for example, has the second largest reserves of natural gas in the world. Only the Soviet Union has more. Algeria and Saudi Arabia also possess huge reserves of this important resource. One of the world's richest deposits of copper has been discovered in Iran. Turkey is the international leader in wolfram production and the third largest producer of chromium. Both Turkey and Iraq have very large deposits of lignite and iron ore. Morocco accounts for more than 90 percent of the exports of phosphates in the world and is the world's fourth largest producer of cobalt. Tunisia, Jordan, and Egypt also have substantial phosphate reserves. Soviet-occupied Afghanistan has one of the largest iron deposits in the world but is very rich also in copper and chromium. As the oil revenues pour in, they will be used for the exploration and production of other valuable resources. Rapid modernization will be one of the persisting effects of this wealth of resources.

When one examines aggregate data and gross statistical indices, such as annual per capita gross national product (GNP) figures, the conclusions concerning modernization and development are somewhat distorted. Abu Dhabi, of the United Arab Emirates, for example, has a per capita GNP that is three

[24] A. J. Meyer, lecture delivered at the International University of Japan, Niigata, Japan, June 28, 1982.

times that of the United States. The per capita GNP of Kuwait is over five times that of the Soviet Union. In the early 1950s, Libya's per capita GNP was about $40; by 1974 that figure was approaching $5,000; in 1983, it was over $9,000. Iran's per capita GNP rose from less than $300 in 1960 to over $2,000 in 1980. Yet in all these societies the benefits of this wealth are very unevenly distributed. Quantitative measurements, no matter how impressive they may be, indicate very little about the qualitative effects of wealth and resources. In short, they do not address American political scientist Harold Lasswell's fundamental question: who gets what, when, and how? Surely, in any study of the modernization of society and politics, it is necessary to get some sense of how these benefits affect the society at large.

During the last few years, a group of scholars associated with the Overseas Development Council has been developing a new index designed to measure more than quantitative growth. Headed by Morris David Morris, a developmental economist with long experience in South Asian studies, this group has taken a significant step away from the emphasis on GNP. In discussing the need for this new measure, Dr. Morris writes:

> The traditional measure of national economic progress — the gross national product (GNP) and its component elements — cannot very satisfactorily measure the extent to which the human needs of individuals are being met, nor should it be expected to do so. There is no automatic policy relationship between any particular level or rate of growth of GNP and improvement in such indicators as life expectancy, death rates, infant mortality, literacy, etc. A nation's economic product at any particular level may be allocated in a variety of ways, both among areas of activities and among social groups; or national policies may emphasize the growth of military power and of sectors of the economy that do not contribute in any obvious way to improving the health and physical well-being of that country's people. Nor does the growth of average per capita GNP or personal disposable income necessarily improve the well-being of large portions of a country's population since that income may flow to social groups in very unequal proportions. The very poorest groups of the society may not benefit much, if at all, from rising incomes and some may even suffer de-

clines in real income. Moreover, even if rising incomes are shared with the poorest groups, there is no guarantee that these increases in income will be spent in ways that improve physical well-being.[25]

In response to these difficulties, Morris and his colleagues have carefully and conservatively constructed a new index known as the Physical Quality of Life Index (PQLI). This new measure is a composite of three indicators — life expectancy, infant mortality, and literacy rate. Each indicator is weighted equally, and all the problems of monetary measurement are avoided. The new index is also resistant to charges of ethnocentrism, since its major assumption — that people everywhere desire improvements in life expectancy, infant mortality, and literacy — does not in any way specify how these goals ought to be sought. Finally, the three indicators "do reflect distributional characteristics within countries, for countries cannot achieve high national averages of literacy, life expectancy, and infant mortality unless majorities of their populations are receiving the benefits of progress in each of these areas." [26] The theoretical range of the PQLI is 0 to 100.

Table I.2 presents the per capita GNP and PQLI for 23 Middle Eastern countries. It also indicates the mid-1981 population figures for each country, as well as the specific statistics that were used in calculating the PQLI: life expectancy at

[25] John W. Sewell *et al.*, *The United States and World Development: Agenda 1977,* published for the Overseas Development Council (New York: Praeger Publishers, 1977), p. 147.

[26] *Ibid.*, p. 152. The basic statement explaining the construction of the PQLI and its theoretical underpinnings is Morris David Morris, *Measuring the Condition of the World's Poor: The Physical Quality of Life Index,* published for the Overseas Development Council (New York: Pergamon Press, 1979). Professor Neil Richardson of the University of Wisconsin has helped us check the operational soundness of the PQLI by running some dummy data through the outlined procedure. The index appears to be conceptually and operationally sound. It is worth repeating, however, two points made by Morris David Morris. First, the PQLI is a limited measure that does not pretend to address the question of the social or psychological characteristics usually suggested by the phrase "quality of life." Second, the data upon which the index is based are not good. They are, however, the best that are available. This difficulty is surely not unique to these formulations. The quality of data is a problem that plagues all attempts at cross-national analysis.

TABLE I.2 *Modernization Indicators for Middle East Countries*

Country	Population mid-1981 (millions)	Per capita GNP, 1980 ($)	Physical Quality of Life Index (PQLI)	Life expectancy at birth	Infant mortality per 1,000 live births	Literacy (%)
Afghanistan	16.4	170	21	42	185	12
Algeria	19.3	1,920	48	56	127	35
Bahrain	.4	5,560	60	62	78	40
Egypt	43.5	580	54	55	90	44
Iran	39.8	2,030 a	57	58	112	50
Iraq	13.6	3,020	47	55	92	24
Israel	3.9	4,500	92	74	16	88
Jordan	3.3	1,420	63	56	97	70
Kuwait	1.4	22,840	77	70	39	60
Lebanon	3.2	1,740	75	65	45	68
Libya	3.1	8,640	52	55	130	50
Morocco	21.8	860	45	55	133	28
Oman	.9	4,380	33	47	142	20
Pakistan	88.9	300	40	52	142	24
Qatar	.2	26,080	46	55	138	34
Saudi Arabia	10.4	11,260	35	48	118	15
Sudan	19.6	470	32	46	141	20
Syria	9.3	1,340	64	62	81	53
Tunisia	6.6	1,310	59	57	123	62
Turkey	46.2	1,460	62	61	125	60
United Arab Emirates	1.0	30,070	65	60	65	56
Yemen Arab Republic	5.4	460	22	40	160	13
Yemen, Peoples Republic	2.0	420 a	30	44	170	27

a Tentative estimate.
Source: Adapted from Roger D. Hansen et al., *U.S. Foreign Policy and the Third World: Agenda 1982*, (New York: Praeger Publishers, 1982), pp. 160–171.

birth, infant mortality per thousand live births, and literacy rate. The data are instructive. The ten leading countries on the basis of per capita GNP standing are, in descending order, the United Arab Emirates, Qatar, Kuwait, Saudi Arabia, Libya, Bahrain, Israel, Oman, Iraq, and Iran. Using the PQLI as the standard, the ranking is quite different: Israel, Kuwait, Lebanon, the United Arab Emirates, Syria, Jordan, Turkey, Bahrain, Tunisia, and Iran. Only five countries that rank in the top ten on the GNP scale also appear among the PQLI leaders. The five that do not have done relatively poorly in the important area of resource distribution.

Qatar, which is second in per capita GNP, ranks only fifteenth on the PQLI. Oman, which is eighth in per capita GNP, places nineteenth on the PQLI. The important country of Saudi Arabia has a surprisingly weak record in the distribution of the fruits of modernization. This Kingdom, which is fourth in per capita GNP, is eighteenth in PQLI; only the two Yemens, Oman, the Sudan, and Afghanistan have weaker PQLIs. Libya, fifth in per capita GNP, ranks only twelfth according to the PQLI.

If one takes the major Middle Eastern countries in terms of resources, geographic size, and population,[27] then Syria, Turkey, Iran, Egypt, and Algeria have done the best according to the PQLI. As we shall see below, Turkey was the first Middle Eastern country to undergo deep social and political reforms, and Syria, Egypt, and Algeria have now had at least two decades of authoritarian leadership dedicated to distributive and mobilizational goals. Of these five countries, only Iran has had the huge petroleum reserves that are easily transformable to rich financial resources.

During the last half of the 1970s, the PQLI figures for nearly all countries in the Middle East increased. Only Lebanon, the Sudan, and the Yemen Arab Republic showed a decline in this important indicator. The figure for Lebanon dropped from 80 to 75; the Sudan's number fell one point from 33 to 32; and the Yemen Arab Republic's PQLI indicator declined from 27

[27] Our arbitrary cutoff point here is a population figure of at least 9 million persons.

to 22. The most dramatic increase occurred in the case of the United Arab Emirates, where the 1974 figure of 34 had increased to 65 by 1980. Other countries that show significant PQLI increases include Iran (38 to 57), Tunisia (44 to 59), Jordan (48 to 63), and Qatar (32 to 46).[28]

In comparing particular Middle Eastern countries with those of similar population size in other parts of the world on the basis of PQLI, we note the following results. Iraq has a PQLI of 47, while Chile's is 84; despite this, Chile's per capita GNP is less than that of Iraq ($2,160 compared to $3,020). Turkey and Thailand, with per capita GNPs of $1,460 and $670 respectively, have PQLIs of 62 and 75. Even more dramatic is the comparison of Morocco with Burma. Morocco's PQLI of 45 is 10 points less than that of Burma; yet the per capita GNP figures are $860 and $180 for Morocco and Burma respectively.

The Middle Eastern PQLI figures are higher than those of the countries of Black Africa. Ghana, for example, with a population similar to that of Iraq and Chile, has a PQLI of only 40. Ethiopia's PQLI of 20 falls far below that of either Iran or South Korea, countries roughly equivalent to Ethiopia in population. At the same time, however, the per capita GNP figures of these African countries are also very low. For Ghana and Ethiopia, the numbers are $420 and $140 respectively.

The patterns indicated in these comparisons of specific countries are also evident when we analyze per capita GNP and PQLI data for four regions of the Third World. Table I.3 presents the results of these regional comparisons, which are based on the average of individual county indices. The Middle East, with far and away the largest average per capita GNP, ranks a distant third behind South/Southeast Asia and Latin America in average PQLI. Only Africa has a lower PQLI average than the Middle East. Yet Africa also has a very low average per capita GNP. In order to compare the gap between per capita GNP and PQLI for the four regions, we have constructed what we term a Per Capita GNP-PQLI Ratio. This

---

28 In order to analyze these changes more completely, please compare the figures in Table I.2 with the figures provided in Table I.2 on p. 21 of the first edition of this book.

TABLE I.3   *Per Capita GNP and Physical Quality of Life Ratios:
The Third World*

	Average per capita GNP ($)	Average PQLI	Per capita GNP-PQLI ratio
South/Southeast Asia	1,072	63	17
Latin America	1,599	75	21
Africa	579	32	18
The Middle East	5,601	52	108

Note: The data contained in this table have been calculated on the basis of information provided in Roger D. Hansen *et al., U.S. Foreign Policy in the Third World: Agenda 1982* (New York: Praeger Publishers, 1982), pp. 160–171. The figures refer to 16 South/Southeast Asian countries, 19 Central and South American states (including Mexico but excluding Cuba), and 36 African countries (the North African states are herein considered part of the Middle East).

ratio is designed to give us a general idea of the comparative regional standing with respect to resource distribution.

The outstanding feature of Table I.3 is the extraordinary size of the gap between per capita GNP and PQLI in the Middle Eastern countries. The anomalies in the data presented here are so great when figured both linearly and curvilinearly that they can only suggest that for the year of record (1980) the Middle Eastern countries trail far behind the rest of the Third World in the distribution of key resources. The huge size of this gap is partially explained by time factors and lags, since it is to be expected that time is required before improvements can be registered in such PQLI indicators as life expectancy and literacy. The huge GNP gains in the Middle East have been recent, and it is of course much too soon to expect any noticeable increase in the PQLI. On the other hand, the infant mortality index should reflect improvement much sooner. In this case, the Middle Eastern countries still trail significantly behind both the South/Southeast Asian and Latin American countries. The average figures for infant mortality per thousand live births are 67, 86, and 111 for Latin America, South/Southeast Asia, and the Middle East respectively.

The gross data that measure modernization are very impressive indeed for the Middle East. This is particularly true of economic modernization. Between 1974 and 1980, for example, the per capita GNP of countries such as Saudi Arabia, Qatar, and the United Arab Emirates tripled. With respect to quantitative and qualitative progress in such areas of social modernization as health and education, the record is much less imposing. And within this context, quantitative progress far outstrips qualitative change. Education is a case in point. The sharp increases in school enrollment and the dramatic new availability of modern facilities and buildings have not been matched by equivalent progress in educational content. The principal conclusion of Joseph Szyliowicz's major study on education and modernization in the Middle East is precisely that the educational enterprise in Egypt, Turkey, and Iran "has demonstrated a remarkable ability to withstand efforts at reform and to absorb the impact of major external forces without changing." [29]

The bridge between modernization and political development concerns the problems of distribution, which themselves must be solved before quantitative growth can be transformed into qualitative progress. As the analysis of Physical Quality of Life Indices has indicated, the countries of the Middle East have not yet successfully met this challenge — a challenge that is above all else political in nature.

POLITICAL DEVELOPMENT IN THE MIDDLE EAST

Processes of modernization run far ahead of advances in political development in the Middle East. The capacity to generate and absorb persistent transformation varies widely from society to society. In all cases, however, the ability to fundamentally transform the basic power configurations has been the rarest form of political change. Even when nations have occasionally sought to do so, they have tended to lack the capacity in the face of a resistant and resilient tradition. Transformations in the economic system have come easiest, followed

[29] Joseph S. Szyliowicz, *Education and Modernization in the Middle East* (Ithaca, N.Y.: Cornell University Press, 1973), p. 454.

by alterations in the social system. Political development in the Middle East lags conspicuously.

Spurred by economic modernization and especially by social modernization, the capacity to *generate* change in the political realm has been increasing. By sponsoring advancements in the related fields of education and technology, Middle Eastern elites have been indirectly responsible for the burgeoning of indigenous professional middle classes. The members of these middle classes are among those calling loudest for political change and reform. In failing to address these demands, the political elites exhibit their unwillingness to absorb and institutionalize political transformation. This begets a situation in which expanding gaps, like bubbles, burst into one another. The gap between socioeconomic modernization and political development is increased by the capacity to generate transformation and the failure to absorb it.

Change dominates the history of Middle Eastern political systems. Transformation, or radical alteration of the underlying power and authority structure, has been considerably less in evidence.[30] The legitimating authority structure and the fundamental power patterns have consistently weathered changes of rulers, elites, and dynasties. The traditional political patterns of the Islamic Middle East survived by being in a state of constant movement. Continual modification and piecemeal revision effectively deterred system transformation. Political elites in the Middle East carefully implemented policies of both co-optation and coercion. Selective mobility and sporadic repression ensured the preservation of ongoing political patterns by introducing carefully apportioned doses of modifying change. These tactics and techniques still persist to a large degree in the contemporary Middle East. One leading scholar of the Arab world writes, therefore, that "the Arabs have not

[30] Transforming change is fundamental, radical change — change at the very roots of relationships and institutions. Modifying change, in contrast, is a reforming and revising process in which adjustments are continually made, leaving basic patterns unaltered. For a detailed discussion of these concepts and their relationship to political power and violence, see James A. Bill, "Political Violence and Political Change: A Conceptual Commentary," in *Violence as Politics: A Series of Original Essays,* eds. H. Hirsch and D. C. Perry (New York: Harper and Row, 1973), pp. 220–231.

yet experienced a political revolution under nationalism, i.e., a fundamental change that produced a new principle of authority, political organization and style of political life." [31]

Perhaps the most critical dimension of political development is participation. The demands of the population for an effective voice in important matters that affect their lives need to be confronted and satisfied. The literature on political development generally argues that participation is furthered by institutionalization and that formal institutions, such as political parties and parliaments, are the most effective instruments for building participation. The Middle Eastern experience provides some differing insights on this issue.

Political institutionalization has never been absent in the Middle East. Masses and elites were bound together by a number of important linkage structures, which included elaborate networks of intermediaries and middlemen composed of messengers, adjutants, clerics, secretaries, advisors, bureaucrats, and secret police. The existence of an informal assembly (the *majlis*) in the traditional Arab world enabled individuals from all walks of life to approach their leaders directly and personally for assistance and aid.[32] This kind of personalized institutionalization resulted in numerous lines of communication through the society. These provided channels through which demands and grievances moved upward to the political elite, while orders and policies poured downward to the middle and lower classes. This was the quality of political participation in traditional Middle Eastern politics. Grievances could often be aired and demands could be heard. The political elite, however, enjoyed the prerogative of action and redress. The petitioners lacked the institutional organization that could guarantee the satisfaction of their demands.

The coming of political parties and parliaments has seldom changed this form of participation. If anything, these new in-

31 P. J. Vatikiotis, *Conflict in the Middle East* (London: George Allen and Unwin, 1971), p. 25.

32 For an extremely illuminating article analyzing the informal politics of mediation in the Middle East, see Marvin G. Weinbaum, "Structure and Performance of Mediating Elites," in *Elites in the Middle East,* ed. I. William Zartman (New York: Praeger Publishers, 1980), pp. 154–195.

struments have served more as barriers to rather than channels of communication. Parties have often existed as loose collections of personal cliques that have penetrated little beyond the upper crust of society. In the upper crust, they have served largely as the instruments of powerful individuals and small elites. This phenomenon has been true even in Tunisia, whose Destourian Socialist Party is the most effective mass party organized at the grass roots level in the Islamic world. Like political parties, Middle Eastern legislatures tend to exist as Western-style institutions grafted to Middle Eastern political systems. In legislatures, however, participation is even less advanced than it is in the political parties. The legislatures often promote underrepresentation, pseudorepresentation, and misrepresentation.[33] In fact, they tend to extend participation little beyond the confines of the parliamentary body itself.

Political participation is a process whereby individuals engage in activity that impinges directly upon the national power and authority structure of society. This activity can be system-challenging or system-supportive. System-supportive participation exists when large numbers of individuals come to support an authority structure to which they have meaningful access and which represents their interests. As the process of participation develops and matures, the masses of people are continually brought into the decision-making process, primarily at the grass roots level of society. Increasing social and political demands emanating from the lower and middle classes accompany this entire movement. The political elite will persistently both encourage and meet these demands for expanding representation.

In the Middle East, the first important break with the past signaling the serious advance of political participation was the overthrow of a number of traditional monarchical regimes. Turkey and Egypt are the two most dramatic early examples of this kind of revolution. The Iranian revolution of 1978–

---

[33] For a rare but excellent analysis of voting behavior in the Middle East, see Jacob Landau, Ergun Özbudun, and Frank Tachau, eds., *Electoral Politics in the Middle East: Issues, Voters and Elites* (London: Croom-Helm, and Stanford, Calif.: Hoover Institution Press, 1980).

1979 represented a multiclass mass movement that overthrew the Pahlavi ruling elite. The Islamic Republic that replaced the Shah carefully and consistently stressed its commitment to the *mostaza'fin* (the deprived, downtrodden). Yet in all these cases, the issue of participation remains unresolved, as authoritarian rule from the center still predominates. The new regimes may be for the people but they are not always of the people.

Even revolutionary acts such as the Egyptian revolution of 1952 and the Iranian revolution 25 years later do not guarantee the institutionalization of political participation nor the beginning of political development. Traditional patterns and power resist change and persist. The trauma of political upheaval promotes destruction over construction. Capacity is weakened by a lack of resources. Crucial resources that do exist are drained away in emotion-charged international adventures. The festering Arab-Israeli issue has profoundly stunted the growth of political development both in Egypt and in the region as a whole. The Iran-Iraq war of the early 1980s has had the same effect on the political systems of these two countries. The existence of an attacking outside foe enables regimes to tighten arbitrary and authoritarian rule. Meanwhile human casualties, physical destruction, shattered morale, national insecurity, and political disillusionment — the inevitable by-products of such conflict — all combine to weaken developmental capacities.

The delicate dialectic between demands and capacity to meet them, between anarchy and repression, between participation and institutionalization, between liberty and security, is a particularly important issue in the Middle East. Demands increase dramatically as larger and larger groups of people seek political participation. Harried elites threatened by serious domestic and international problems struggle to maintain their own authority while at the same time striving to modernize their societies. Moderate authoritarianism begins to move in the direction of harsh repression as these elites gradually stifle demands. In the footrace between modernization and political development in the Middle East, modernization always runs out ahead. Manfred Halpern's "authoritarian road to democracy" [34] is in fact a narrow path fraught with peril and false exits.

Middle Eastern societies have adopted various and differing strategies for political development. The countries fall into four different categories on the basis of their policies of political development: democratic-populist, traditional-authoritarian, traditional-distributive, and authoritarian-distributive.[35]

The democratic-populist path of development stresses liberal democratic political values and provides relatively open participation through such institutions as parties, parliaments, and elections. Systems in this category are in wide retreat throughout the world, and the Middle East is no exception. In recent years, only Israel, Turkey, and Lebanon belonged in this category. Israel's relative success with this form of government stems partly from its ability to import a set of social and political patterns wholesale into the area. Turkey's democratic style survived through extraordinary measures including military intervention and takeovers in 1960 and 1971. In 1980, the military intervened again, and this time it has refused to go back to its barracks. A November 1982 election approved a new constitution that legitimized a military government with General Kenan Evren as president for a seven-year term.

The fragility of the democratic-populist model is best illustrated, however, by the continuing collapse of Lebanon beginning in 1975. Here, a feeble central government stood by helplessly as religious and class tensions erupted into a bitter and bloody civil war and as predatory neighbors such as Syria and Israel invaded and occupied the country.

In the traditional-authoritarian political system, "emphasis

[34] Manfred Halpern, *The Politics of Social Change in the Middle East and North Africa* (Princeton, N.J.: Princeton University Press, 1963), pp. 223–226.

[35] This taxonomy of political systems according to developmental strategies is a variation of that presented in Almond and Powell, *Comparative Politics,* pp. 372–390. The five Almond and Powell developmental strategies are termed democratic-populist, authoritarian-technocratic, authoritarian-technocratic-equalitarian, authoritarian-technocratic-mobilizational, and neo-traditional.

is placed on increasing the order-maintaining and economic-growth-facilitating capacities of the government." [36] Rule is of the most conservative traditional mode, and although economic dynamism is often present, the benefits tend to coagulate at the top. The monarchies of Jordan, Morocco, Oman, and Saudi Arabia, along with Numayri's Sudan, are examples of this kind of system. Security for the ruling house is the overwhelming obsession of the political strategists who direct these governments. Political participation is severely restricted, and all important decision making is monopolized by the central figures in the ruling establishment. Although these governments distribute in varying degrees the goods and services that they control, this is not a high priority on their political agendas. Thus, with the exception of Jordan, the traditional-authoritarian countries have extremely low PQLI ratings (see Table I.2). These systems are increasingly unstable and have been the scenes of numerous challenging incidents, including attempted assassinations, popular unrest, aborted military plots and coup attempts, and religious-inspired upheaval. The fall of Iran's Shah in the late 1970s demonstrates the precarious nature of all traditional-authoritarian political systems.

Bahrain, Kuwait, Qatar, and the United Arab Emirates fall into the traditional-distributive category. Although their systems are governed in much the same way as the major monarchies referred to above, these shaykhdoms are fundamentally different in their greater will and capacity to distribute their wealth through their respective populations. The average PQLI figure for these four shaykhdoms is 62, as opposed to an average of only 42 for the five traditional-authoritarian nation-states. This program of greater distribution is made possible by the enormous hydrocarbon wealth generally present in these small countries. In Abu Dhabi, the leading member of the United Arab Emirates, annual income from oil jumped from less than $1 billion in 1973 to over $15 billion in 1980. Citizens of Abu Dhabi are provided with everything from free schooling and health care to free housing. The same is true of Kuwait, where the citizens enjoy a welfare system unequaled anywhere. Amidst such wealth, the issue of political participation is less urgent. Despite this, in the wake of the Iranian revolution, the shaykhly families who govern these mini-states began long private debates and discussions concerning the issue of widening political participation. In March 1981, after almost five years of inactivity, elections were held again in Kuwait and a new National Assembly was formed.

Most Middle Eastern developmental strategies involve some kind of non-monarchical authoritarian leadership committed to the mobilization of the masses. This new form of authoritarianism (herein termed authoritarian-distributive) follows on the overthrow of traditional-authoritarian systems and stresses a very specific form of political participation. "Because people are mobilized in the implementation of policies formulated by the party elites, rather than in the making of policies, it is a form of mobilized or structured participation." [37] There are two categories of authoritarian-distributive systems, the radical modernizing model and the extremist Islamic model. Examples of the former include Algeria, Egypt, Iraq, Libya, and Syria. Post-Pahlavi Iran is the major example of the latter type. In all authoritarian-distributive systems, capacity takes precedence over freedom, although the relatively equitable distribution of goods and services is a major priority of this kind of rule. The major difference between traditional-authoritarian and authoritarian-distributive strategies concerns the question of distribution. There is in the latter model greater commitment both to political participation and social and economic development. The average PQLI figure for the authoritarian-distributive countries listed here is 54, a dozen points higher than the average for the traditional-authoritarian cases.

In the radical modernizing type of authoritarian-distributive systems, leaders are committed both to rapid modernization and to a broader distribution of the fruits of this modernization to the population in general. In this situation, the gap between modernization and political development increases

[37] *Ibid.,* p. 381.

as tiny governing elites concentrate political power in their own hands. Examples include Qaddafi's rule in Libya, Saddam Hussein in Iraq, Hafez al-Assad in Syria, and Hosni Mubarak in Egypt. The extremist Islamic model in Iran also witnesses authoritarian control at the center, where Ayatollah Khomeini and the leaders of the Islamic Republican Party direct the affairs of state. In this case, however, there has been a conscious and successful effort to slow significantly the processes of modernization. This in turn has narrowed the gap between modernization and political development, which has temporarily dampened the explosiveness of its dialectic. The model of revolutionary Iran is especially significant, since it has demonstrated considerable attractiveness and appeal throughout the region, where the revival and resurgence of Islam is everywhere evident.

The developmental struggle is always a grim one. In the Middle East, it has taken on a special urgency because of the accompanying intense and unsettling process of modernization. Gaps, divisions, imbalances, and inequalities are visible everywhere. In one area (Abu Dhabi), the annual per capita GNP approaches $35,000 per year, while in another country (Afghanistan) the figure is less than $200. Such imbalances are as common within countries as between them. In societies like Egypt, Turkey, and Tunisia, 60 percent of the national income has been monopolized by the top 20 percent of the population. In the traditional-authoritarian states, this distribution curve has been even more skewed. Meanwhile, the winds of modernization blow unevenly through the area.

The challenge of development is complicated by four further factors. First, no Middle Eastern society has yet found that it could relax in its quest for development. There are no plateaus and no end points in this journey. Both monarchs and their military-oriented successors have learned this lesson the hard way. Witness the fate of the Shah of Iran and of Anwar Sadat of Egypt. The religious leaders who have succeeded the Shah and the political descendants of Sadat will also have to face this reality.

Second, there is no particular political or ideological path that ensures success. As our typology of developmental strategies indicates, there are examples of failures in all categories. The democratic-populist model so much admired in the West was dealt a severe blow with the collapse of Lebanon in 1975 and the reversion of Turkey to military authoritarianism in 1980. The various authoritarian and traditional alternatives have a history of stifling oppression interlaced with continual plotting and coups. Middle Eastern political leaders must write their own prescriptions for development. Thus far, such prescriptions have been singularly unsuccessful.

The third complication concerns the historical and cultural backdrop against which developmental programs must occur. The traditional Islamic system was one of considerable dynamism, social mobility, and personalistic participation. The resurgent strength of Islam and its growing impact on the political process indicate the close relationship that must exist between Islam and the process of political development. The experiments in Pakistan, Saudi Arabia, and Iran demonstrate that the precise dimensions of this relationship have not yet been determined. At this point, Islam is more effective as an ideology of political opposition than as an ideology of political rule.

Finally, the issue of political development in the Middle East is complicated by interregional and international considerations. The Arab-Israeli conflict has already been mentioned. Both the competition between the United States and the Soviet Union and the international energy issue have also had profound effects upon the developmental problem. With some exceptions, the United States has tended to support the traditional-authoritarian regimes, while the Soviets have more often stood behind the authoritarian-distributive governments. The massive infusions of military aid into the region have complicated rather than alleviated the problem of political development. Not only has this activity deflected attention and resources away from the central issue of development, but it has also tended to strengthen the forces of security at the expense of liberty and participation.

In the Islamic Middle East, Turkey and Egypt have over the years been among the leaders in political development. Although both countries have witnessed many instances of social unrest and political instability, they both have middle-class regimes that have been relatively supportive of political participation. Despite the military takeover in Turkey in 1980 and the assassination of Anwar Sadat in 1981, neither country is ruled by terror. Algeria and Tunisia have also done relatively well in the developmental struggle. In Algeria, strong central control is balanced against genuine concern for the masses of people. This concern is reflected in a heavy emphasis on equal educational opportunity and in support for peasants and workers to manage their own farms and factories. The Destourian Socialist party in Tunisia is one of the few strong political party systems in the region. Both Algeria and Tunisia, however, face serious political problems. In Algeria, the strong central control is becoming less acceptable as economic problems deepen, and in Tunisia the Destourian Socialist party is increasingly seen as an instrument of political control and repression.

The other authoritarian-distributive regimes (Iraq, Syria, Libya) have been even less successful in political development. Iraq and Syria labor under the severe handicap of deep sectarian, ethnic, and ideological divisions. Although sensitive to the need for popular participation and social equality, the Libyan regime has not yet suceeded in seriously loosening its grip from the center as Mu'ammar Qaddafi clutches all the reins of power in his own hands. In Syria and Iraq, the political situation deteriorated significantly in the early 1980s as the leaders of these countries brutally transformed their regimes into virtual police states.

The families that rule the Persian Gulf shaykhdoms have tended to avoid political development. Because of their extraordinary wealth, however, they have a record of distribution in the social areas of health, education, and housing that is unrivaled anywhere. This distribution has disguised the absence of political participation and has cushioned popular discontent. Political control remains firmly in the hands of a few members of ruling families, who have shown little inclination to share it. Since the Iranian revolution, there has been a somewhat greater sensitivity to the need to broaden somewhat the base of political decision-making. In Bahrain, for example,

the progressive Minister of Foreign Affairs, Shaykh Muhammad bin Mubarak Al-Khalifa, has been a leading proponent
for increased modes of political participation both in Bahrain
and in the Gulf Cooperation Council community more generally. According to Shaykh Muhammad, the creation of National Consultative Assemblies is "a must." In his words, "The
more you share your problems with your own people, the
stronger you become." [38]

The most explosive developmental problems in the Islamic
Middle East exist in the major monarchies, i.e., the traditional-
authoritarian governments. Here, traditional power and authority relations persist alongside growing middle classes and
deeply religious lower-middle and lower classes whose members remain locked out of the corridors of power. Unlike their
tiny counterparts along the Persian Gulf, these monarchies,
with the partial exception of Saudi Arabia, do not have comprehensive social programs that can serve to alleviate the tensions arising from the increasing gap between economic modernization and political development. Jordan, Morocco, and
Oman lack the resources and revenues. Furthermore, these
traditional governments are plagued by visible and especially
severe strains of corruption. For these countries, the failure
to develop politically can only have violent and costly long-
term consequences.

The collapse of Lebanon and the fall of the Shah in Iran
contain many lessons with respect to the related issues of
modernization and political development. Perhaps the most
important of these is that an impressive record of modernization does not indicate that political development is also occurring.[39] Rather, modernization may hasten the destruction
of the political system by persistently widening the modern-
ization-political development gap. Impressive growth in Lebanon and in Iran in per capita GNP and even in the PQLI
had the further effect of lulling both political leaders and
political observers into a false sense of complacency. In both

[38] Personal interview, Manama, Bahrain, August 19, 1982.
[39] This is a theme in Malcolm Kerr's important article, "Rich and Poor
in the New Arab Order," *Journal of Arab Affairs* 1 (October 1981): 1–26.

countries, the deep group and class divisions were disguised by the deceptively successful environment of modernization. When Lebanon crumbled, it dealt a final blow to the theory supporting the democratic-populist road to development. The collapse of the Pahlavi dynasty in Iran severely weakened the argument of those who championed the traditional modernizing monarchical model of government.

All of these case studies indicate the complex delicacy of the related issues of modernization and political development in the Middle East. In a constantly changing situation, there are no obvious success stories and no developmental strategies proven to be successful. Many of the fundamental problems that now confront the Middle Eastern peoples are directly related to this situation. These problems will be analyzed in depth in the following chapters.

CHAPTER II

Islam and Politics

THE GREAT REVEALED religions all came into being in the Middle East. Its history is rich in religious wars and conquests. The storm center of the area today, Israel, was founded on the right of a religious people to return to ancestral pastures. It is not an exaggeration to say that no understanding of the complex political patterns of the area can be attempted without giving prior attention to its religious characteristics.

The contemporary Middle East is a crazy quilt of religions. Although Islam pervades most of the area, the Muslims differ among themselves in culture and orthodoxy. Furthermore, religious minorities are to be found in most Muslim countries. The Druze, a mystic heretical sect of Islam, inhabit the mountains of southern Lebanon and Syria and live in Israel as well. In the north of Syria are the Alawites, who maintain a mixture of Christian, Muslim, and pagan beliefs. The Alawites most closely resemble the Shi'ites with a special emphasis placed upon the charismatic personality of Ali, the son-in-law of the Prophet. (Syrian President Hafez al-Assad is an Alawite.) In 1973, the Alawites were formally recognized as part of the Shi'i community in Lebanon. Also in Lebanon are various Christian groups, notably the Maronites and the Greek Orthodox. Remnants of another minority, the Armenian Christians, are to be found in many parts of the Middle East. The few Assyrian Christians that are left live in Iraq, Iran, and eastern Syria. In Egypt is another Christian group, the Copts, numbering about 10 percent of the population. In southern Sudan, the people are racially (Black African) and religiously (often Christian) different from the Sudanese of the north, who are Arabs and Muslims. In Iran, there are the Zoroastrians and the Bahais (originally Babists), although neither group is very significant in numbers. The Israelis are, of course, largely Jews. But these Jews are by no means all identical; they range from the extreme orthodox to the agnostic. Indeed, the Israelis are compelled to consider as Jews, for the purpose of the Law of Return, many who are only nominally religious but who might suffer persecution in other countries for their "Jewishness." This brief list hardly exhausts the many religious groups that can be found in the Middle East. We shall later discuss the great split of Muslims into Shi'i and Sunni sects.

ISLAM

Most Middle Easterners are Muslim. Islam, however, is to be found outside the Middle East. There are large numbers of Muslims in Soviet Central Asia and in India, Bangladesh, and Indonesia; Islam is also rapidly gaining adherents and influence in Black Africa. Altogether Islam's members throughout the world now number more than 800 million.

It is the Middle Eastern Muslims that concern us here. What does it mean to be a Muslim in the Middle East? How does being a Muslim affect one's political life and the political life of one's community? And very particularly in this transitional age, how does the presence of the Islamic spirit influence the directions of political change? Is there a plasticity to Islam that has accommodated considerable modifying change over the centuries, while remaining resistant to ultimate transformations? Is there a new reassertion and resurgence of Islam?

Islam, which literally means the surrender of man to God (Allah), is one of the great religions of the world. The messages that became the essence of Islam were revealed to the prophet Muhammad beginning in A.D. 610. To become a Muslim takes but a simple affirmation of faith, repeating the *shahada*: There is no god but The God and Muhammad is the messenger of The God. The creed of Islam is simple, and although there is a voluminous, sophisticated literature on various aspects of Is-

lam, belief in the basic *shahada* is the main characteristic of
the mass of Muslims.

Muhammad brought his message to the Arabs of Mecca, the
"idolators," whose confused animistic and totemistic religious
practices were repugnant to him. He also hoped that Christian
and Jew would be attracted to his message; after all, he believed
that it was their God, as well as his, from whom the message
came.

The message, if we strictly count only what the Muslims term
the revelations, was the Quran.[1] It was probably not wholly re-
corded until after Muhammad's death; its language, the sacred
language, was Arabic. Muslims have always believed in the com-
pleteness of the Quran; it is not to be supplemented by recur-
rent messages. The Quran contains the principles of eternal
truth from which modern science or any other kind of knowledge (however much it may change in detail) must be derived.
Among the Quran's truths is a prescription for regulating the
political and social affairs of man. Islam makes no distinction
between the state and the realm of believers; in theory at least,
there is nothing to render unto Caesar. There is nowhere in
Islamic history, as there is in that of Christendom, any recourse
to a doctrine of "two swords" or any proliferation of a political
theory of the rights of a secular ruler against those of God.[2]

Conservatism forced the Arabs of Muhammad's time to resist his blandishments; it was only after he and his followers
had demonstrated a certain *baraka* ("heavenly blessing" or
"grace") in war and caravan raiding that great numbers of followers rallied to his cause. But however fervently his adherents
embraced the message of the Quran, they needed more direct
and personal counsel for the regulation of their daily lives.
Much of this is to be found in the Hadith, or the Traditions,
of the Prophet's life. What would Muhammad have said, or
done, in such and such a situation? Although every Muslim
concedes that Muhammad was only a man, nevertheless they

[1] W. Montgomery Watt, *Bell's Introduction to the Qur'ān* (Edinburgh:
Edinburgh University Press, 1970) is particularly useful here.
[2] See Muhammad Asad, *The Principles of State and Government in
Islam* (Berkeley, Calif.: University of California Press, 1961).

believe that his life was exemplary. Indeed it furnishes a guide for all good Muslims to follow.

On one crucial question, however, Muhammad offered no guidelines. Who would assume the role of the leader of the Muslim community upon the Prophet's death? The first caliph — a title originally signifying successor to the messenger — was Abu Bakr, Muhammad's father-in-law. He and the next three caliphs where chosen by the leading members of the Muslim community in Medina. These have come to be known as the Rightful Caliphs. The last of this group, Ali, the Prophet's son-in-law, was defeated in battle by Mu'awiya, one of the generals who disputed Ali's claim to the caliphate. Mu'awiya founded the Umayyad dynasty of caliphs by insisting that his son, Yazid, be accepted as his successor.

The early caliphs were wielders of power. Gradually they changed their role from the lesser one of acting as successor to Muhammad's spiritual leadership to that of being God's viceroy on earth, a viceroy that increasingly became a mundane monarch of immense power and authority. Ultimately, however, the strength of the caliphs waned, and, retaining only the symbolism of their position, they surrendered their power to ambitious generals and strongmen.

This development, which occurred over a period of several hundred years, resulted from the imposition of political necessities on a religious community. Muhammad himself was a superb politician, knowing when to persuade and when to coerce. In the process of establishing a new religion, he created a military machine and a semblance of political organization for an area extending far beyond Mecca and Medina. He outmaneuvered rivals and forced recalcitrant tribes to cooperate and accept his leadership. After his death, Islam spread rapidly into North Africa, Byzantium, and Persia. The maintenance and support of conquering armies, the control of their leaders, the supervision of the division of spoils, and the adjudication of disputes among followers and newly assimilated peoples — all of these required political leadership of a high order and the necessary administrative apparatus to give it substance. Without the powerful figures that some of the early caliphs became, the large Arab Muslim empire that once existed could

not have been created. With the firm establishment of a hereditary caliphate,[3] prestige and authority could be maintained
despite the gradual deterioration of the power of the caliph.
Power was assumed by those who could hold it. Often some
subordinate of the caliph with exceptional abilities and command of military force wielded great political influence.[4]

Muslims believe in one god, Allah, to the exclusion of all
others. In so professing their faith, they acknowledge the special historical role that Muhammad played as the messenger of
God. As a religion, Islam is relatively uncomplicated. Other
than the profession of faith, there is little that a Muslim is
obligated to do. He ought to make a contribution (*zakat*) to
the poor; he should at some time in his life make a pilgrimage
to Mecca (Hajj); he should ritually submit himself to prayer
five times a day; during one month (Ramadan) of his lunar
year, he must fast during the daylight hours. But it must be
noted that there is really no distinction between religious and
secular acts and obligations. The true Muslim state operates
under the *sharia,* that is, Muslim law as derived from the
Quran. Thus, the practicing Muslim finds himself immersed
in rules and practices, not as obligations of his religion per se,
but rather as obligations of a legal system that is the only conceivable one in Islam.

The political and social life of Muhammad's time did not
necessitate an elaborate system of law. The early Islamic law
reinforced some of the customary law of the Arabs of pre-

3 As Hitti points out, hereditary succession did not mean that sons always succeeded. Speaking of the Abbasids, he says, "of the first twenty-
four caliphs, whose reign covered almost two centuries and a half (750–
991), only six were immediately succeeded by a son." (Philip K. Hitti,
History of the Arabs, Seventh Edition [London: Macmillan and Co., 1961]
p. 318). But what the hereditary principle did mean was that succession
would occur within the family of the caliph. In the few modern Muslim
monarchies that remain, such as Saudi Arabia, the official crown princes
have more often been brothers than sons of the ruling monarchs.

4 By the middle of the ninth century, the Abbasid dynasty was in rapid
decline. Typical of the state to which the dynasty now fell was the rule
of the eunuch soldier Mu'nis al-Muzaffar, who deposed the caliph al-
Muqtadir in 932. In 945, the general Ahmad Ibn-Buwayh established a
dynasty of sultans that lasted for a century, independent of the caliphs,
whom the sultans created or destroyed at will. See Hitti, *History,* pp.
469–471.

Islamic times, but it also contained much that was new. It dealt largely with family matters and with the simpler forms of interpersonal relations. It spelled out the detailed circumstances of marriage and divorce; regulated the legitimation and custody of children; and, most important, specified in great detail the rules of inheritance. Penalties for a number of criminal delicts were also specified, but even the criminal law "did not exist in the technical sense of a comprehensive scheme of offences against the public order." [5] Even homicide, although "regulated in meticulous detail . . . was treated as a private and not as a public offence. For the rest the doctrine (of the criminal law) was largely confined to the exposition of six specific offences — illicit sexual relations, slanderous allegations of unchastity, theft, wine-drinking, armed robbery, and apostasy — in which the notion of man's obligations towards God predominated and which, because God himself had 'defined' the punishments therefore, were known as the *hadd* . . . offences." [6]

The sharia has always been subject to interpretation. When an entire body of legal scholars can agree on a certain interpretation, this consensus is called *ijma*. When the individual scholar (*mujtahid*) makes such an interpretation, it is termed *ijtihad*. And even today in Sunni Muslim countries an individual called a mufti will issue legal opinions, or *fatwas*, on the pressing questions of the day.[7] Such are the processes, although sometimes tortuous and slow, through which change is introduced.

Islam, like any great religion, has suffered heresies and splits. The main group of Muslims is called Sunni. A much smaller group, the Shi'ites, is largely found in Iraq, Iran, Pakistan, India, and Yemen. Theoretically, the Shi'ites are those who especially honor the person of Ali, the fourth caliph, and argue that the Imamate (religious leadership) of the Muslim community should descend through the family of Ali. More practically today Shi'ism is the blend of Islam with Persian culture.

[5] N. J. Coulson, *A History of Islamic Law* (Edinburgh: Edinburgh University Press, 1964), p. 124.

[6] *Ibid.*

[7] Birth control is one such problem. In general, religious authorities have supported family planning.

(The founder of the Safavid dynasty, Shah Isma'il, made it the state religion in the early sixteenth century.) It is by no means completely homogeneous. Well known today are the Isma'ilis (headed by the Agha Khan) and the Ahmadis (largely in Pakistan).

In Sunnism, the gates of ijtihad were closed in the ninth century; in Shi'ism, this power of interpretation is carried by mujtahids who by consensus of the religious leadership are those who are sufficiently endowed with Quranic knowledge, piety, and purity to interpret not only religious doctrine but on the higher levels, at any rate, serve as a conduit for communication with the occulterated Twelfth Imam. These higher levels are the ayatollahs, of whom Ayatollah Ruhollah Khomeini of Iran has been the most notorious in recent years. There are approximately 100 ayatollahs in Iran and perhaps a half-dozen grand ayatollahs, who are literally the manifestation of God on earth. Reduced to more mundane terms, Sunnism provides for no such glorification of religious leaders nor for the infallibility of their pronouncements, while Shi'ism does contain what amounts to the possibility of continuing guidance. While there are imams in Sunni Islam there are no Imams.[8]

More difficult to classify are the Sufis, the Islamic mystics. Sufism is not a sect, but rather the product of the apparent human need for a religion with more mysticism and color than are to be found in the normally austere practice of Islam. Philosophically, Sufism is monistic; organizationally, it is divided into a number of orders. In addition to the regular obligations of the Muslim, Sufis undertake still more, often a variety of spiritual invocations. The most famous Sufi was al-Ghazali (twelfth century), who was also one of the great Islamic philosophers. The Sufis themselves have generally eschewed political leadership, but they have widely influenced those who have exercised power. Hasan al-Banna, founder in 1928 of the puritanical Muslim Brotherhood, was strongly influenced by the

---

[8] For a superb discussion of the differences between Shi'i and Sunni Islam with respect to politics and authority, see Hamid Enayat, *Modern Islamic Political Thought* (Austin, Tex.: University of Texas Press, 1982).

Sufis in his youth. Most importantly, Sufism often serves as a retreat for the oppressed. It offers an escape from the world and one that can be shared vicariously with large numbers of ordinary people who have no other way of enduring the difficulties and agonies of lower-class life.

THE CONTEMPORARY ROLE OF RELIGION

The twentieth century has been one of great stress for all religions. Perhaps man, in the abstract, is scarcely less religious than he was earlier, but the forms of his worship have altered. If he is not more basically tolerant of the idiosyncrasies of others, he has found it necessary to come to terms with beliefs and practices foreign to his own. The rapid growth of communication and the dissemination of knowledge have forced a reexamination of much of tradition, including religion. Middle Eastern countries have, in varying degrees, become enamored of modernization. This process of modernization inevitably affects traditional religious practices and beliefs.

In attempting to assess the impact of outside challenges on Islam, it is important to understand that Islam has no formal organization. Since the abolition of the caliphate in Turkey in 1924, there has been no central symbolic figure of leadership. A Muslim's obligations are to God and not to any church or to any individual who purports to speak for God. (Note, however, our earlier comments on ayatollahs.) There are no priests or ministers as such. Some men claim, however, to be particularly learned in the intricacies of Islam. They may occupy certain political positions (mufti, qadi) or they may have different titles (shaykhs, mujtahids, mullahs). Collectively the leading figures of these are known as the *ulema*, and what organization Islam has resides in this body. Entrance to the group is sometimes by co-optation and sometimes by simple acceptance by others of a newcomer's right to speak with authority about religion. The individuals in the ulema are usually learned in such traditional subjects as philosophy, theology, rhetoric, law, and literature.

The ulema have, as much as any others, represented the forces of tradition in the otherwise rapidly changing Middle Eastern world. Relatively few members of the ulema have sought to accommodate the insistent secularization of the age. Most have tried to brake the changes that have occurred. They have often objected to the emancipation of women and to the liberalization of the marriage and divorce laws. They have not noticeably encouraged the growth of science. They have greatly influenced the creation of literature and art and in recent years the production and screening of motion pictures and television performances. They have demanded observance of the old practices: the daily ritual prayers, the pilgrimage, the fasting during Ramadan, and the dietary laws. They have generally struggled for the maintenance of an "Islamic state," an "Islamic constitution," and an "Islamic law."

In the face of the intractable challenges of modernization and industrialization, the members of the ulema continue to exert considerable influence throughout the Middle East. In Saudi Arabia, they attempt to check the government's impulses to introduce too much modernization and too rapid development. The secular ruling elite in Egypt increasingly takes the wishes of the shaykhs and religious leaders into consideration before it embarks upon new policies. The same is true in Pakistan. In Iran, the clerics in fact govern. For many Muslims there are no doubts; their lives are led as closely as possible in harmony with the Quranic precepts. For many others there are doubts tempered with feelings of guilt; they surrender to the pressures of the times, but they remain susceptible to religious nostalgia. There is also a small group that has cut all ties with the past and embraced the new secular age as fervently as possible.

One of the most appealing characteristics of the Muslim clerics is the fact that they have often effectively served as the protectors of the struggling masses. Although they have sometimes been portrayed as venal, selfish, and ignorant, the clerics have perhaps more often been sincere, honest, and intelligent. It has been the mullah in the countryside, for example, who has traditionally shielded the villager from oppressive and rapacious governmental agents. The mullah has been the one who has advised the peasant during times of travail and who has provided a modicum of education for the children of the masses. Throughout the history of Islam, the clerics have performed an invaluable social-welfare function. Even today in the Middle East, the practicing Muslim will turn to the cleric for protection and support against secular forces considered corrupt and oppressive. He finds it difficult to believe that individuals who have consistently extorted should suddenly become the standard-bearers of reform. Thus, when the mullah seeks to resist modernizing programs, he will do so more effectively because of the strong bonds of trust that he has often developed with the people themselves. This is one reason why some scholars strongly argue that reform must develop through traditional channels if it is to be at all effective.

Those who rule have much stake in the extent and direction of political change. Their commitment to religion is therefore important. Equally important is the degree to which the populace demands religious observance (and the resulting extent of the influence held by religious leaders).

(This phenomenon is well exemplified by modern Israel. Although it was founded as a haven for a religious minority, its leadership has been decidedly secular, and much of the middle class remains alienated from religious orthodoxy. Yet it is impossible to describe the politics of Israel, or its daily life, without considerable reference to the role of its religious functionaries and their organizations. The operation of taxis on the Sabbath, the serving of nonkosher food on the steamship line, even the delineation of what is a Jew — many things like these have forced compromises from a government that needs parliamentary support from the relatively small, but politically potent, religious parties.)

In the Muslim countries, to varying degrees of course, there remain the pervasive demands of the religious community. A Nasser finds it necessary to make the pilgrimage or to keep photographs of his wife out of the press (although his successor, Anwar Sadat, did not choose to be so conservative). The rector of al-Azhar, the great religious university in Cairo, declaims on the length of women's skirts. A mufti issues a fatwa on the acceptability of birth control. In Saudi Arabia in the fall of 1982, even the worldly King Fahd took time off from a busy schedule to make the Hajj and to spend several days in private consultation and meditation with the leading members

of the ulema in Mecca. In every Middle Eastern country, political and social change must accommodate itself to the religious consciousness of the country's inhabitants and to the
vested interests of its clerical class.

RELIGIOUS REFORM

Islam has been altered through time and has adjusted itself
to changing conditions. This has been true not only in the
modern period but throughout its history.

The Muslim world was in decline by the time of the Crusades, and although there was glory in the Fatimids (Egypt),
the Safavids (Iran), the Moghuls (India), and the Ottomans
(Turkey) during later periods, it was in every case a glory that
had been achieved in traditional terms. Strong leaders — Salah
al-Din, Shah Abbas I, Akbar, Süleyman — by military prowess,
shrewd alliances, and political acumen, as well as good fortune,
managed to build impressive dynasties. Such dynasties might
have survived if all of the leaders had been of the caliber of
these. In the case of the Ottomans at least, survival was accompanied by other changes. Competent administrative processes
were created, and mechanisms for handling the diverse problems of empire came into being. Yet almost all of this was
done within a traditional framework. No challenge to any of
these empires from within or without occurred in any but these
traditional terms.[9] It was only with Napoleon's conquest of
Egypt in 1798 that tradition in the Middle East, including
religious tradition, was severely challenged.

As is so often the case, it was military defeat that dramatized
the need to change some aspects of the traditional system. The
immense and successful challenge of the West — young, brash,
and unbelieving — forced, for the Muslim world, a painful
introspection that has now lasted nearly two centuries. The
direct challenge to Islam itself began in the nineteenth cen-

[9] This is not precisely true with respect to Akbar and the Moghuls in
India. The Moghuls were Muslim rulers of heterogeneous peoples of differing religious beliefs (notably Hindus); many of their practices and
innovations could hardly be said to have been traditional. Akbar himself
had religious beliefs that transcended Islam and were certainly heretical
by all ordinary standards. See S. M. Ikram, *Muslim Civilization in India*
(New York: Columbia University Press, 1964).

tury, although Islam is undergoing the most traumatic changes now, in the last quarter of the twentieth century.

Religious reform in the nineteenth century began with the attempt to answer the simple question: How is it that power, skills, and material comforts have come to those who reject Islam, the right path to the life of man in God? (Such questions were posed even in the columns of popular newspapers, and readers would reply with their own suggestions.) The alternative answers were not many: (1) the right path was in fact wrong; (2) the proper life of man is not to be defined in terms of power and material comforts; and (3) somehow man has misinterpreted and misunderstood God's word. The third attitude was the most palatable to many of the deeply religious shaykhs of the nineteenth century.

It was this view that characterized the position of Jamal al-Din al-Afghani, the most prominent of the reformers of that period:

> The chief aim of Jamal al-Din in all his untiring efforts and ceaseless agitation, was the accomplishment of the unification of all Muslim peoples under one Islamic government, over which the one Supreme Caliph should bear undisputed rule, as in the glorious days of Islam before its power had been dissipated in endless dissensions and divisions, and the Muslim lands had lapsed into ignorance and helplessness, to become the prey of western aggression. The present decadent condition of Muslim countries weighed heavily upon him. He believed that if these countries were once freed from the incubus of foreign domination or interference, and Islam itself reformed and adapted to the demands of present-day conditions, the Muslim peoples would be able to work out for themselves a new and glorious order of affairs, without dependence on, or imitation of, European nations. To him, the religion of Islam was, in all essentials, a world religion and thoroughly capable, by reason of its inner spiritual force, of adaptation to the changing conditions of every age.[10]

---

[10] Charles C. Adams, *Islam and Modernism in Egypt* (London: Oxford University Press, 1933), p. 13. As phrased, this resembles Hasan al-Banna's program. There is indeed a philosophic connection from al-Afghani to Abduh to Rashid Rida to al-Banna; Rashid Rida was the biographer of Abduh, the editor of *Al-Manar*, and a distinguished Islamic publicist.

Al-Afghani's view was clear enough: Islam is not wrong. It is the perfect prescription for the attainment of happiness for man in God. This means the achievement of material prosperity; it certainly means the victory of Muslims over unbelievers in whatever conflicts are generated. But reality was not like this. Therefore, the only possible explanation was that man, in spite of proper guidance, had turned aside and gone astray. His loss of power was his punishment for leaving the *sunna,* or "true path."

It was obvious that many Muslims were not living in accordance with the Quran. Political leaders were often lax. Their personal lives were frequently caricatures of the good Muslim life. They often led their people into activities, conflicts, and acts that had never been countenanced in the Quran or by the Prophet. The solution to this was to admonish people to live better lives, and when necessary to use whatever political resources were required to achieve behavior more in keeping with Muslim belief. Al-Afghani did not hesitate to suggest extreme measures. For recalcitrant rulers his remedy might even be the assassin's touch: Nasir al-Din Shah of Iran was felled by one of al-Afghani's followers in 1896.[11]

It was also apparent that men were not aware of what the Quran really meant. People subjected themselves too readily to traditional formulas without contemplating their essential meaning. It was al-Afghani's follower, Muhammad Abduh, who was perhaps most famous for this point of view. He blamed most of all the religious leader who merely and blindly repeated old views. A leading shaykh from al-Azhar, a judge, and finally mufti of Egypt — and throughout his adult life an indefatigable agitator and writer — Abduh was the leading religious reformer of modern Egyptian history. His fatwas, while mufti, were famed for their liberality. "Two of these fatwas are best known: one declaring it lawful for Muslims to eat the flesh of animals slain by Jews and Christians; the other declaring it likewise lawful for Muslims to deposit their money in

11 "Jamal once said ... 'No reforms can be hoped for till six or seven heads are cut off' " (Adams, *Islam and Modernism,* p. 14). Adams also points out that Jamal's followers in Egypt had discussed at considerable length the prospects of assassinating Isma'il Pasha.

the Postal Savings Banks where it would draw interest." [12] More typical, but equally famous, were his views on polygamy. Because the Quran does not endorse, although it permits, the luxury of as many as four wives to a husband, and because it specifically enjoins husbands to treat their wives equally, Abduh chose to interpret the Quranic statements as an indirect, but nonetheless clear, prohibition of polygamy. His grounds: that it is clearly impossible for a man to treat his wives equally. Abduh was struck with the fact that the powerful nations of his day did not permit overt polygamy.

In India, Muhammad Iqbal, who wrote magnificent poetry in Urdu, attempted to find in his *Six Lectures on the Reconstruction of Religious Thought in Islam*[13] the basis for all of modern science. For example, he argued that the Quranic verse that speaks of the light (*nur*) of the world was equivalent to Einstein's assumption that the speed of light was constant (invariant) under all tranformations.

It is not fair to ridicule these attempts. They were made by men who combined a religious faith with a knowledge of the modern world. If the attempt, at an earlier date, was worthy of a Thomas Aquinas, it was an equally worthy enterprise for a modern Muslim philosopher. But twentieth-century times, buffeted about by incredible transformations, are not equivalent to the time of the thirteenth-century *Summa Theologica*. An Abduh or an Iqbal can contribute to the ferment of thought and can lay the groundwork for later behavioral changes, but he cannot alone carry the burden of reform. This task belongs to the political leader.

Because Islam is so entwined with everyday life, any kind of social reform must produce religious reform as well. Most of the well-known Middle Eastern reformers of the twentieth century have been primarily social reformers, and most of these would have denied any intention to alter Islam. In fact, however, they have altered it profoundly. We cannot exhaustively examine their efforts. (The legal and constitutional reformers of the nineteenth century — such as Midhat Pasha of

12 *Ibid.*, p. 80.
13 London: Oxford University Press, 1934.

Turkey[14] — would have to be included here.) But something must be said of the efforts of such individuals as Kemal Atatürk (Turkey), Reza Shah (Iran), Gamal Abdel Nasser (Egypt), Abdul Karim Kassem (Iraq), and Habib Bourguiba (Tunisia). These individuals are similar largely in that they produced religious change in very practical ways.

Kemal Atatürk is the most famous of the twentieth-century Middle Eastern social reformers. Finding power in the Turkey of the post-First World War period, Atatürk rid it of its enemies, reestablished a viable government, and set about implementing a major program of social and political reform. He was virtually unique among reformers in admitting his atheism, and he struck at religious institutions in many ways.[15] The last caliph in Islam, Abdülmecid, was deposed in 1924, perhaps because Atatürk felt that the sources of political reaction were primarily religious in nature. In 1925, the fez, a rather ersatz religious symbol, was banned in public, along with other religious garb. The monasteries and retreats were taken over and religious orders were abolished in the same year. Of that act, Kemal had this to say:

> To seek help from the dead is a disgrace to a civilized community.... What can be the objects of the existing brotherhoods (*tarikat*) other than to secure the well-being, in worldly and moral life, of those who follow them? I flatly refuse to believe that today, in the luminous presence of science, knowledge, and civilization in all its aspects, there exist, in the civilized community of Turkey, men so primitive as to seek their material and moral well-being from the guidance of one or another *şeyh* [*shaykh*]. Gentlemen, you and the whole nation must know, and know well, that the Republic of Turkey cannot be the land of *şeyhs*, dervishes, disciples, and lay brothers. The straightest, truest Way (*tarikat*) is the way of civilization. To be a man, it is enough to do what civilization requires. The heads of the brotherhoods will understand this truth I have uttered in all its

---

[14] See Robert Devereux, *The First Ottoman Constitutional Period* (Baltimore, Md.: John Hopkins Press, 1963).

[15] It is only fair to say that a number of Turkish specialists deny Atatürk's atheism. See N. Berkes, *The Development of Secularism in Turkey* (Montreal: McGill University Press, 1964).

clarity, and will of their own accord at once close their convents, and accept the fact that their disciples have at last come of age.[16]

In 1926, a form of the Swiss civil code was adopted and the sharia abolished; in the process, "polygamy, repudiation — all the ancient bars to the freedom and dignity of women — were abolished. In their place came civil marriage and divorce, with equal rights for both parties. Most shocking of all, to Muslim opinion, the marriage of a Muslim woman to a non-Muslim man became legally possible, and all adults were given the legal right to change their religion at will."[17] In 1927, the Arabic alphabet was superseded by a Latinized one. This is of importance because Arabic is the language of the Quran. Even the call to prayer in the mosque was now to be in Turkish, not Arabic.

Of course, not all people were enthusiastic about these changes, and in the countryside many resisted them. In any event, not all of this frantic attack on the Islamic institution survived Atatürk's death in 1938; in later years the ill-fated Democratic party and its successor party, the Justice party, sounded a responsive chord in the rural areas through their promises to treat religion more favorably. Yet the role of religion in Turkey will never again be quite the same.

As important as Atatürk's direct attack on religion was his political nationalist revolution of "Turkey for the Turks." Religion stood in the way of his modernizing Turkey economically and politically; the country would have to adjust to the new exigencies. At the same time, Atatürk was so successfull in freeing Turkey from the disabilities of the First World War and in giving it dignity and stability that many Turks were generally willing to accept the antireligious tone of many of his acts. One remaining legacy: While the Pakistani consti-

[16] Quoted from Bernard Lewis, *The Emergence of Modern Turkey,* 2d ed. (London: Oxford University Press, 1968), pp. 410–411.

[17] *Ibid.,* p. 273. See A. J. Arberry, "Law," Chapter 21 in *Religion in the Middle East,* vol. 2 (Cambridge: Cambridge University Press, 1969), for an up-to-date discussion of the problem of mixed marriages in Muslim countries. A fairly typical practice in Egypt is that the non-Muslim male goes through a sham declaration of conversion to Islam.

tution proudly proclaims an Islamic state, in Turkey the post-Kemalist constitutions have maintained a rigidly secular character.

In the 1920s, the example of Atatürk was emulated less enthusiastically, as well as less successfully, by Reza Shah Pahlavi in Iran and also by Amanullah Shah in Afghanistan. Neither had the political or personal resources of Kemal. Reza Shah was much more interested in introducing economic improvements than in social and political reforms. Amanullah Shah was even more of a dilettante in reform — he was much impressed, during several trips to Europe in the 1920s, with the trappings of Western affluence — and he was always careful to insist upon his devotion to Islamic principles. But such insistence did not save him from overthrow in 1929.

In later years, men rose to political leadership because of their commitment to such policies as military modernization and militant nationalism. Certainly, men like Habib Bourguiba or Ahmad Ben Bella had not come to power because of any attachment to religious orthodoxy. Though it may be necessary to refrain from overt actions against religion, most of these contemporary political leaders have initiated or supported decisions that have seriously undermined the traditional religion.

One of the issues that contemporary political leaders have had to confront is the position of women in society. In Egypt and other progressive Islamic countries, divorces are now easier for a woman to obtain. Although the inequity still favors the male, his privileges are more difficult to come by. Despite considerable opposition, Bourguiba in Tunisia for a time officially discouraged the fasting during Ramadan (typically, activities in Muslim countries come to a standstill for this month, when fasting is obligatory during the daylight hours) by opening restaurants during the day and closing them at night, and by treating the fasting period as just another month. The bedrock of Muslim law, the congeries of regulations on inheritance, underwent alteration in Iraq during Kassem's tenure. *Waqf* (endowments) reform has been initiated almost everywhere except in the most traditional of Islamic states; of Egypt, Gabriel Baer has said, "Waqf reform has been perhaps the most successful part of the Egyptian land reform."[18] This reform resembles the confiscation of church property and lands in the West and has seriously affected the funding of traditional religious activities. And it was a former minister of waqfs, Dr. Muhammad Hussein al-Zahabi, who was murdered by religious extremists in Egypt in the summer of 1977.

It is sometimes argued that reform proceeds too rapidly. Y. Linant de Bellefonds has said:

> The legislator must proceed, even towards ... a modest objective, with caution. He must not advance too far ahead of the social evolution of his country, otherwise he runs the risk of being obliged to retrace his steps and to return, crestfallen, to the system which he had pressed to abolish. Witness the case of Libya. The Libyan law of Judicial Organization of 20 September 1954 abolished there the jurisdiction of personal status and the civil courts became competent in all matters and with regard to all litigants, whatever might be their religion. The reform was premature. The people (especially the Muslim litigant) soon missed the simplicity of the qādi's court, to which they had been accustomed and which seemed to them superior to the complexities of civil justice. In order, therefore, not to offend public opinion, the new law of Judicial Organization of 18 December 1958 re-established the duality of jurisdictions in all matters concerning personal status. The Libyan reform had lasted for exactly four years.[19]

It has been argued, on the contrary, that because of the resilient nature of Islam, rapid and radical alterations are necessary in order to insure the retention of any change whatsoever. Rather than an accumulating adsorption of change in the Islamic context, it is perhaps essential that genuine absorption be required. This can be effected only by massive and sharp transformations.

The twentieth century is a secular age. The very location of the Middle East, the resources (notably oil) that it possesses, as well as the resources it requires — all of these and other factors push the area into increased contacts with a world re-

---

[18] *Studies in the Social History of Modern Egypt* (Chicago: University of Chicago Press, 1969), p. 92.
[19] Quoted in Arberry, *Religion in the Middle East*, vol. 2, pp. 457–458.

ligiously alien. It seems very probable that Islam will undergo severe readjustments because of these contacts and pressures.

Interestingly enough, the Israeli Jews face a somewhat similar readjustment. One thesis with respect to the future of Judaism in Israel is compounded by Georges Friedmann in his *Fin du Peuple Juif?* [20] in which he argues that, to the degree that Israel becomes a viable political and cultural entity in the Middle East, to that degree will the traditional Judaism that sustained the Jews throughout the centuries be abandoned. A similar thesis could be constructed for the broader world of Islam.

RELIGIOUS REACTION

Not all response to modern pressures has produced a desire for reform. Some Muslims argue that indeed man has gone astray by not following the prescriptions of God. What is needed is not new interpretations of old principles, but more rigorous adherence to what has already been revealed to be the true path. This view can be termed religious reaction.

The history of Islam has contained an element of reaction virtually from its inception. As early as 657, in the struggle between Ali and Mu'awiyah, a group called the Kharijites deserted Ali on the grounds that, in agreeing to arbitrate his differences with Mu'awiyah over his claim to the caliphate, he was not following the Quran literally. The remnants of this movement were still in existence by the time of the Crusades. In the thirteenth and fourteenth centuries, the most conservative voice was that of Ahmad Ibn Taymiyyah. Phillip Hitti says of him that he "bowed to no authority other than the Koran . . . and lifted his voice high against innovation, saint worship, vows and pilgrimage to shrines." [21] His influence in the eighteenth century inspired Muhammad Ibn Abd al-Wahhab, who was determined to cleanse the "corrupt" Islam of his day, "to purge it and restore it to its primitive strictness." [22] What came from all of this was the Wahhabi move-

---

[20] Paris: Editions Gallimard, 1965.
[21] Phillip Hitti, *History*, p. 689.
[22] *Ibid.*, p. 740.

ment, largely centered in the Arabian peninsula, and which has survived to contemporary times.

By far the most prominent and interesting of the Islamic puritanical movements has been the Muslim Brotherhood. It was founded in Ismailia, Egypt, in 1928 by a schoolteacher named Hasan al-Banna. Al-Banna had incredible organizational talents and mesmeric appeal. He gradually put together what was in fact a highly popular and aggressive political movement. Al-Banna himself always denied that his movement was anything but one of dedicated Muslims who wanted to return to the life of a purer, earlier period. But in the 1930s and 1940s in Egypt — which was affected by the world depression and later by the Second World War, a British occupation, a corrupt government, and a rising Zionism in neighboring Palestine — an atmosphere developed in which almost any popular movement became political. The Muslim Brotherhood attempted to force the government to mend its ways, and ultimately the secret cadres of the movement resorted to violent techniques, including assassination, to gain their ends. From the mid-1940s to the late 1940s, they assassinated two prime ministers of Egypt, Ahmad Mahir Pasha and Nuqrashi Pasha. It was the latter event, in December 1948, that prompted the government to resort to assassination in return, and in February 1949 Hasan al-Banna was gunned down in the streets.

After al-Banna's death, the Brotherhood was rent by discord. In 1952 the revolution came, but the Muslim Brothers were not able to gain from this event. To Nasser and the young officers who made up his junta, competition from the Brotherhood could not be allowed. A Brother attempted to shoot President Nasser in 1954; since then, the Brotherhood has been outlawed in Egypt.

The appeal of the Brotherhood splashed beyond Egyptian frontiers into Syria, Iraq, and Saudi Arabia. In Egypt itself, it remains a secret organization that everyone knows about and many support. A weekly journal is published by the Brotherhood and is widely distributed.

Another modern force in Egypt has been the *Takfir Wal Hijira* ("repentence from sin and retreat"). Led by Ahmed Mustapha Shukri, the members of this group believed in a return to the pure life of the past and the rejection of much that is modern. They considered themselves particularly the enemies of President Sadat and mounted a terrorist campaign to gain attention and perhaps force the government into concessions. By murdering in July 1977 the former waqf minister, Dr. Zahabi, they pushed the Egyptian government to vigorous retaliation. Hundreds were arrested; about fifty were tried by military court and five were sentenced to death in November. This group is typical of religious extremism in Egypt, which has almost always been accompanied by terrorism. Sadat was himself assassinated in October 1981 by a group led by a Lieutenant Islambouli and described officially as "fundamentalist." Although trials were held that resulted in executions, the exact nature of the criminal conspiracy has not been made public. It must be said that Sadat was, at the end of his life, at the storm center of a struggle involving a large number of Muslim and Coptic (Christian) leaders, many of whom were jailed. It was not simply a small reactionary group that opposed Sadat but a large percentage of the religious community. Large numbers of these groups continue to be active in Egypt. In September 1982, the Mubarak government discovered a major clandestine Muslim opposition group dedicated to the overthrow of the regime. Over 300 members of this organization, known as the al-Jihad group, were put on trial in December 1982. The Egyptian government charged the accused with seeking to establish an Islamic "Iran-style" government in Egypt and in other Arab countries.

In other Muslim countries, there are a variety of organizations resembling the Muslim Brotherhood. Usually they are insignificant. More important is the Fidayan-i Islam in Iran. In the late 1940s and early 1950s, this religious teaching organization wielded considerable coercive influence in Iran. Elaborately organized in the form of an inner cell of 50 to 60 members surrounded by two concentric circles of membership totaling approximately one thousand dedicated individuals, the Fidayan-i Islam was directly implicated in the assassination of important Iranian political figures, including Prime Minister Razmara in 1951. In Syria, religious murders (often of Alawites by Muslims) have continued into the early 1980s. And in Israel, too, there are minor pockets of reactionary Judaism. It is, of course, not necessarily religion itself that is reactionary. Rather, some of its adherents make it so by their desire to return to some earlier day.

What are the reasons for this kind of reaction? A surprising number of young, middle-class individuals have been drawn to the ranks of the Muslim Brotherhood. It was not, and probably is not today, simply a repository of religious fanatics. There are, of course, those individuals who are drawn to a movement by expediency, just as there are those who assuage nostalgic guilt by supporting a religious posture that they find increasingly uncomfortable. There are also individuals who are genuinely bewildered, and who no doubt wonder whether the secular age that they have entered is truly right. These persons have often become alienated from a system that they see as corrupt, unjust, and venal. And there are the fanatics. But the large numbers who have supported some of these movements belie the assertion that all the members can be characterized as fanatics. The feelings of insecurity, the trauma of discovering a self in the political and social innovations of the times, an embryonic suspicion at least of the world outside of Islam (the *Dar al-Harb*) — all of these help explain the seeming need of many people of all descriptions to lose themselves in religious reaction.

Part of this return to Islam is a reaction against repeated political defeats and humiliations. In the words of one educated, middle-class Egyptian woman,

> Really, I wonder what people expect us to do. Nasser put us under Russia's armpit. The Russians didn't want to help us; they wanted to dominate us. Then we were lied to and put in the 1967 War. Then Sadat comes and turns to America. The Americans didn't want to help us; they exploited our longing for peace to make us give concessions to their pet dog, Israel, and humiliate us. And the prices went up and the thieves made fortunes and we said "that's capitalism." And our rich "Arab brothers"; did they want to help us? Did they care about all we had suffered for thirty years for the "Arab Nation"? No, they

wanted to measure out their *riyals* and their *dinars* and keep
Egyptian boys fighting for Palestine. To whom shall we turn
for help, if not to God? In Him alone I will put my trust! [23]

The problems have been compounded by the increasing disillusionment with the West and the East and their particular
paths to modernity. Both American and Soviet models become
increasingly unacceptable to the masses of Muslim believers
who first began to become deeply disillusioned in the 1960s
and 1970s. Mohamed Heikal describes this disillusionment in
the following words:

> They turned away too from foreign idols. All the indications at
> this time were that western capitalism was in a state of disinte-
> gration. People read daily of growing drug addiction, of hippies
> and "flower-people," of sexual promiscuity and the collapse of
> what Arabs still regarded as the basic unit of society, the family.
> They read of Watergate and the activities of the CIA, of kid-
> nappings and riots. It ceased to be a sign of emancipation to
> wear blue jeans, open a Wimpy stall in Cairo or drink Coca-
> Cola. Nor did Moscow and communism look any more attrac-
> tive than the West. Revelations about Stalin's rule had de-
> stroyed the credibility of communism as a political system; the
> invasion of Czechoslovakia destroyed Russia's credibility as a
> benevolent protector of smaller nations.[24]

In Egypt, this soul-searching had begun in earnest after the
traumatic 1967 defeat in the June war. "As always happens in
history, when forward movement becomes impossible people
begin to look towards the past, and it was to religion that
Egyptians turned for consolation after the military defeat." [25]

A word must be added about new groupings of religious
"fighters," emanating from recent Iran and Afghanistan. In
both countries they have taken the name *mujahidin* ("crusaders"). Although their behavior is much the same in both

---

[23] Quoted in John Alden Williams, "Veiling in Egypt as a Political and
Social Phenomenon," in *Islam and Development: Religion and Sociopolitical Change*, John L. Esposito, ed. (Syracuse, N.Y.: Syracuse University Press, 1980), p. 83.
[24] Mohamed Heikal, *Iran: The Untold Story* (New York: Pantheon
Books, 1981), p. 126.
[25] *Ibid.*, p. 127.

countries, their origins and beliefs are quite different. In Afghanistan, the mujahidin were almost certainly a rural reaction to the Marxist modernizing efforts of the Kabul government and to the colonizing invasion of the Soviet Union itself. These are the fighters that oppose Soviet troops in Afghanistan today. In Iran, on the other hand, they have been an urban reaction to the direction taken by Ayatollah Khomeini's followers. Many but not all of the Iranian mujahidin combine piety with quasi-Marxist convictions. One result is that among the Iranian Mujahidin-i Khalq is an enthusiasm for an Islam that is heretically different. Many argue that Khomeini does not know what Islam is all about. These groups are difficult to classify and their future is uncertain.

ISLAM AND MODERNIZATION

Modernization, which involves man's increasing control over his environment, does not mean the same thing to all of those who consider themselves to be modernizers. For many, it indicates little more than the gaudy possession of air-conditioned hotels, jetports, casinos, and cinemas. To others, it means the physical and frequently counterproductive existence of sophisticated military systems, or even such things as dams and macadamized highways. But one thing does characterize the modernizing nation. There is deep dissatisfaction with the existing political, social, and economic systems. The standard of living is too low. Educational skills are too few. Frustrations are too many. To the leaders in modernization, what they lack is seemingly possessed by others. The process of modernization generally becomes one of emulating as many of the outward features of these other peoples as possible. Ideologically, it may seem necessary to couch these desires in such indigenous terms as Turkish nationalism or Arab socialism.

How does Islam in its contemporary setting affect this drive for modernization? Equally important is the question of how Islam is affected by modernization. Perhaps the term *modernization* can itself provide insight into these questions. This is not the first time in history that societies have undergone confrontation with other "advanced" societies and have learned to accommodate to them. Every such confrontation was, in a sense, a clash or contact with modernization. Examples abound: The Romans were modernized by the Greeks (as were the Macedonians by their southern and eastern neighbors), the Gauls and Britons by the Romans, and the New World by the French, English, and Spanish. Islam was, of course, originally quite Arab — although it is evident that Muhammad wove many strands of Christian and Jewish doctrine into his revelations — but even by the time of the second caliph, Umar, it had had major contacts with the Egyptians (who could not then be termed Arab), the Byzantines, and the Persians.

In religious terms, these contacts were with Christians of varying hue, with Zoroastrians, and with pockets of Jews. But in a broader cultural sense, these contacts were between the relatively simple and primitive Arab society and the vastly more complex and sophisticated societies of the periphery. Although basic acceptance of Islam followed Arab conquests, the religion, as well as the cultural behavior, of its original followers were gradually adjusted to views and attitudes held by those who had been conquered.

Islamic culture then, as it had emerged by the time of the Abbasids (749–1258), was already an amalgam of other cultures. This is to suggest that Islam at least has had a tradition of confrontation with other cultures and a tradition of accommodation to them. This was true in North Africa and Spain; it was equally true in both the conquest of the Byzantine possessions and the subsequent fraternization with its empire for several centuries. During the Crusades, the Christian princes (of, for example, Antioch, Jerusalem, and Tyre) resembled the Muslim amirs who opposed them. Persia became Muslim but absorbed its conquerors; later the Mongols (many of whom were Christians) and Turks (representing lesser cultures in their periods of history) passed on still further contributions to the Islamic culture.

Actually, all societies are an amalgam of the traditional and the modern. Few societies can live and prosper when one heavily overbalances the other. In general (although the truth of this varies from region to region), Islam has demonstrated a vital blend of these ingredients in its history.

It is interesting that in Black Africa the greater proportion of conversions are to Islam, not to Christianity.[26] The Christian missionary is usually less accommodating than the Muslim, and less willing to accept traditional features of a society alien to him. It is also true that in the history of the holy places in Jerusalem the most generous and tolerant of the rulers with respect to the followers of other religions were the Muslims; the least tolerant were the Christians.

Islam has been incredibly resilient to the pressures of an outside, and sometimes hostile, world. This has been particularly true of Shi'ism. In Sunnism, the body of law is theoretically complete and unchangeable. Shi'ism, on the other hand, teaches that the law is always alive and changing. Through the chain of Imams that stretches to this very day, Shi'i Islam is continuously able to interpret and account for the new and the different. This is precisely the key role of the mujtahids, "who can practice ijtihad or exercise their opinion in questions of Law. They are living interpreters of the Law who interpret it in the absence of the Imam and in his name."[27] One learned mujtahid explains this ability of Shi'ism to adapt dynamically to new circumstances by writing, "What deserves attention is the unique process by which the institution of ijtihad can adapt, scientifically, the basic principles of Islam to everyday problems of Life. Since it always can apply the principles of Islam to the everyday problems of life of the people, the scholastic group (mujtahids) believes that there is no contradiction between modernity of life and religious inclination in the country."[28]

In Shi'i communities, the mujtahids have the immensely significant role of controlling and channeling change. In Shi'i Iran, for example, the success of programs of social change initiated by the secular authorities depended in the past to a large degree upon the position taken by the mujtahids. In contemporary Iran it hardly needs stating that the influence

[26] See James Kritzeck and William H. Lewis, eds., *Islam in Africa* (New York: Van Nostrand-Reinhold Co., 1969).

[27] Seyyed Hossein Nasr, *Ideals and Realities of Islam* (London: George Allen and Unwin, 1966), pp. 104–105.

[28] Mehdi Haeri, "Islam and the State in Iran," unpublished mimeographed paper, p. 7.

of the mujtahids is paramount. Moreover they have slowed significantly the process of modernization.

Islam has in the past always managed to respond to the challenges of change in a wide variety of ways. Certainly it will respond to the contemporary processes of modernization, although it is difficult to ascertain exactly what form this response will take. The ulema will make sporadic pronouncements that will liberalize the role of women, support land reform programs, encourage economic reorganization, facilitate the growth of a new literature, and make it possible for Muslims to participate in the broad stream of world culture. (We state this in early 1983, in the face of events in Iran and elsewhere. The Middle East taken as a whole will continue to modernize.) The religious leaders will do this, however, in a manner that will make modernization palatable to Islamic doctrine. At times, they will be forced to follow the lead of politically perceptive leaders who have their own reasons for mobilizing popular support for their programs of modernization. The shape that modernization takes in the Middle East will, to a large degree, be the result of "creative tensions which have so often crackled between the religious and the political establishments." [29]

Modernization will, in fact, progress to the degree that mass support for it can be generated; this in turn is a function of the spread of communications. Modernization will proceed as money for its objects is raised and priorities for its effectuation are sorted out. Support for modernization is often, but not always, self-generating; once the material benefits of modernization become evident, rationalization will follow. The problem becomes one of finding a government strong enough to catalyze its beginnings and one imaginative enough to select wisely among competing priorities. If Islam is not overtly denounced — indeed, some effort may well be spent to placate its functionaries and laud its virtues — there may be small reaction from a citizenry eager to find a way to reconcile tradi-

[29] Charles F. Gallagher, *Contemporary Islam: The Plateau of Particularism* (American Universities Field Staff: Reports Service, Southeast Asia Series, vol. 15, no. 2, 1966), p. 2.

tion with the glitter of something new. It is easier for this to happen in the city than in the village, and among individuals prosperous enough to share the bounties of a world culture. But eventually it will spread throughout the area.

(Islam is not alone in facing modernization. Christianity is likewise encountering it. The Roman Catholic church, for example, faces enormous issues emanating from a changing society in a world culture. The beginnings of concessions on celibacy, birth control, and divorce represent the degree to which this church has already gone to pacify its critics and mollify its friends. There is no reason to believe that Islam will prove any less malleable. Although one could not say that modernization is aided by Islam in any real way, Islam will have to adjust to modernization.)

The political process in the Middle East differs in a number of ways from that in the West. It is less often open, and the formal channels of political influence tend to be fewer in number and less effective. Though associational politics are rarer, those of the clique are more commonplace. All this affects the role that religion plays with respect to politics.

Islamic religious leaders have rarely been very well organized. To be sure, they have shared this weakness in most states of the Middle East with professional men, workers, and others whose strength in the West is a function of their organization at work. But Islam has never had a hierarchy, and seldom have its functionaries been able to forestall public policy except through the influence of individual leadership.[30] It has been difficult for Muslim leaders qua Muslims to play a political role. Even when they have had the desire to do so, they have often lacked the technical resources to do so. Often there is no party system, and when there is, it is rigidly controlled. In Israel, by contrast, religious leaders have sometimes organized their own party formations and have, as a consequence, been able to exert enormous political leverage. In most Mus-

---

[30] Certainly, a good example of the power of traditional religious leadership was the boycott of the foreign tobacco concession in Iran in the late nineteenth century. The full story is told in Nikki R. Keddie, *Religion and Rebellion in Iran, the Tobacco Protest of 1891–1892* (London: Frank Cass and Co., 1966).

lim societies, on the other hand, such opportunities are less obvious. Political parties in the Islamic world tend to be constellations of personal groupings. Although the groups themselves may exert considerable influence, the parties exist largely as facades. Whatever power religious leaders exert is wielded through these personal groups and not through more formal party organizations.

The religious leader is compelled to fall back upon traditional and highly personal, informal means of disseminating his views and influencing opinion. These are the Friday sermon, informal discussions within the confines of the mosque, and religious writings and pronouncements. On occasion, these traditional modes of communication have been sufficient to generate political activity on the part of followers. But compared with the secular leader — who has available to him such facilities as radio, television, newspapers, billboards, and motion pictures — the religious leader has few means of influencing opinion. Although the religious may indeed use these same facilities, they do so at the sufferance of the secular authorities. It is interesting that those religious movements that have held political strength (the Muslim Brotherhood, for example) have had to emulate the secular system in organizational style, fund raising, and opinion formation. For all its denunciation of modernity, the Muslim Brotherhood equipped itself with the latest model printing presses and other gadgetry.

Although the fall of the Shah in 1979 was hastened by a wide variety of opposition groups, it would be foolish to deny the unexpected power of the clergy and the catalyzing leadership of Ayatollah Khomeini. But even Khomeini sent his messages to Iran (from Paris) in the form of tape recordings and, once in power, did not eschew the modern technologies of opinion formation. Iran remains an exceptional case — Pakistan is not at all the same — in which religious leadership was able to pull a government and a system down and install, if jerry-built, a form of Islamic government. Its fate is currently uncertain, but no one can gainsay the incredible achievements of the Iranian clergy, which was, it might be said, just as fragmented as those in other Muslim states.

Even where moderately open party systems have not prevented their entry, overt religious parties have not been greatly successful. In Israel, there is nothing to prevent the growth of the religious party itself; indeed, the nature of the electoral law encourages the formation of splinter parties. Although religious parties have influence beyond their numbers because party coalitions in the Knesset invariably need their support, they have had no broad-scale appeal among the masses.

There does not seem to be a way for "Islam," without an organized hierarchy, and without great fortune in political opportunity, to carry on effective political activity except through sporadic, and usually face-to-face, attempts to influence. It is important to be clear here. Islamic influence and control are strongest when maintaining the status quo in a backward community — in a Yemen or an Oman, for example — where Islam does not have to compete with a political authority possessing facilities disproportionate to its own. In an industrializing nation, the gap between political and religious authority in facilities for dissemination of opinions becomes progressively greater. In time it is possible to imagine a reconstituted religious authority competing on more equal terms, but this can come about only after the first fever of modernization has passed.

We must certainly append some comment on what passes for the "revival of Islamic fundamentalism." [31] The trauma of Iran has not only frightened many westerners but many Muslims in the Middle East as well. Pakistan under General Zia seems to some to be on the same course and Sadat, it will be remembered, was killed by religious fundamentalists. There seems to be a *revival* of something in the Muslim world and *fundamentalist* best describes its characteristics. This revivalism can be seen throughout the Islamic world.

In the North African countries of Morocco, Algeria, and Tunisia, there has been considerable Islamic fundamentalist activity ever since 1978. This has occurred despite the quite

[31] See Roy R. Anderson, Robert F. Seibert and Jon G. Wagner "The Islamic Revival and the Islamic Republic," Chapter 12 of *Politics and Change in the Middle East: Sources of Conflict and Accommodation* (Englewood Cliffs, N.J.: Prentice-Hall, 1982). This is one of the few of the newer texts that at least gives some prominence to this question.

different ideologies that mark the political systems in these three countries. In Morocco, Muslim fundamentalists have participated in anti-regime demonstrations in 1978, 1979, and in June 1981. Islamic opposition leaders in Morocco include the influential Abdel Salem Yassin and the exiled radical Muhammad al-Basri. In Algeria, there has been a dramatic growth in unofficial, private mosques and from these centers the Algerian imams criticize the government. In November and December of 1982, the Algerian regime arrested nearly 1,000 members of the Islamic movement there, including elderly respected imams such as Shaykh Abdel Latif Soltani and Shaykh Ahmad Sahnun. In 1981, the Islamic Tendency Movement was established in Tunisia. When the leaders of this movement criticized the government, they were arrested and jailed, along with over 100 other fundamentalists.

This revival or reassertion of Islam, with all of its political implications, does not necessarily indicate a reversal of the processes of modernization. After all, a foreign observer, particularly in 1980, might conclude from studying the United States that it was in the throes of religious revivalism. Several thousand people are married by Reverend Moon in a mass ceremony; Billy Graham still packs stadiums with people seeking faith; Jerry Falwell and his political action committees are busy going after political backsliders; prayer in the public schoolroom is being urged in Congress; and all over America the forces of creationism are fighting those of evolution. Yet modernization continues. Scientific advances and technological breakthroughs remain in great evidence. In the Middle East, the forces of modernization are being reexamined and the leaders who propagate them are being questioned. But, as even the case of Iran demonstrates, the surging, militant Islam must come to some accommodation with the modern world.

The impact of Islamic reassertion in the Middle East is profoundly political in nature. It is the lower and middle classes who are tightly embracing Islam, which is increasingly becoming an ideology of the oppressed and the disaffected. These are the people who have the deepest grievances and who are now making the greatest demands. They do so in the name of a reassertive and redirected Islam. This Islamic message challenges unpopular, unrepresentative regimes whether they be conservative, moderate, or radical in political approach. In this sense, King Hassan in Morocco, President Hosni Mubarak in Egypt, and President Chadli Benjedid of Algeria all face the growing force of populist Muslim fundamentalism.

JUDAISM IN THE MIDDLE EAST

The ancestral home of the Jews was in Palestine (Canaan), from which they were generally expelled by the Romans in the second century. The result was the Diaspora, in which Jews were dispersed over most of the Western world. There was to be no real return until the twentieth century.

The term *Sephardim* was given to those exiles who originally lived in Spain and Portugal, and *Ashkenazim* to those whose roots were in Central and Eastern Europe. More recently, the former has come to mean simply the Oriental Jew and the latter the European Jew. There was, of course, a dispersal of Jews that antedates Rome and certainly preceded the Muslim conquests of the seventh and later centuries. After the rise of Islam, the Jewish communities within the Arabian peninsula proper gradually faded, with the exception of the community in Yemen.

Throughout North Africa, however, and in the peripheral Arab territories (Iraq, Syria, Palestine), as well as in Turkey, Iran, and Afghanistan, there were sizeable Jewish communities that had flourished for centuries. Flourishing in many cases meant merely surviving. Nevertheless, both before and after the rise of Islam, many Jews engaged in professions and occupations that were discouraged for Christians and/or Muslims (for example, moneylending and goldsmithing). Generally, the Jews were not discriminated against, although from time to time they were forced to wear distinctive clothing. The principle was established by Samuel in the third century "that where it does not conflict with Judaism's religious demands, the civil law of the country in which Jews are living must be considered religiously binding for the Jew." [32] In any case, the Jewish minority rarely gave its hosts any trouble.

[32] Jakob J. Petuchowski, "Judaism Today," in Arberry, *Religion in the Middle East*, vol. 1, p. 5.

Those Jewish communities in French North Africa suffered some disabilities with the departure of the French in the early 1960s. This was particularly true in Algeria, but Morocco and Tunisia, as moderate states on the Arab-Israeli dispute, were much more congenial to the survival of a Jewish minority. Jews continue to live in Turkey, Iran, and Afghanistan. The once-prosperous community in Egypt, numbering 75,000 as recently as 1950,[33] for a time all but disappeared. It may perhaps regain some of its vitality with the Egyptian-Israeli rapprochement. Jews in Syria and Iraq suffered considerable harassment, and most left for Israel. In Yemen, a community of Jews existed probably from the time of the destruction of the first Temple.[34] With a few exceptions, this entire community removed to Israel between 1948 and 1962. At the end of the Second World War, perhaps a million Jews lived in the Middle East other than in Palestine; today probably less than 20 percent remain.[35]

Consequently, among the Middle Eastern states, Judaism is of importance today only in Israel. However, we must briefly ask two questions: How resilient has Judaism been over the centuries? To what degree does it aid or impede modernization in Israel?

We can state in general that a religious minority, particularly when it suffers persecution, tends toward the conservation of its traditional principles. Reform in such a situation becomes compromise with those who seek to destroy the oppressed religion. Although Judaism had undergone many alterations prior to 1948, these alterations largely occurred during those times when, and in those places where, the Jewish community had become large enough to acquire confidence and free enough to indulge in reform. This meant, for example, Germany (reform here was associated with such names as Abraham Geiger, Samuel Holdheim, Zacharias Frankel, and Samson

[33] H. Z. Hirschberg, "The Oriental Jewish Communities," in Arberry, *Religion in the Middle East,* vol. 1, p. 215.

[34] See S. D. Goitein, "The Jews of Yemen," in Arberry, *Religion in the Middle East,* vol. 1, pp. 226–235.

[35] Estimate based on H. Z. Hirschberg, "The Oriental Jewish Communities," p. 223.

Hirsch) and the United States (Isaac Wise, Solomon Schechter, and Mordecai M. Kaplan) in the nineteenth and twentieth centuries.[36]

As Jakob J. Petuchowski has said, "German Judaism provided the ideologies and the religious reforms which enabled the Western Jew, qua Jew, to enter the world of modernity. Russian Judaism maintained the reservoir of traditional Jewish existence. But it was in America that the Judaisms of West and East were given an unhindered opportunity to test their mettle and their ability to adapt themselves to unprecedented circumstances." [37] The Yemeni Jews can be said to illustrate the relatively unchanging nature of a very small minority living without encouragement from or much contact with the outside world. They supported little reform.

Judaism has displayed a resilience, conservative in adversity but reformist under favorable circumstances. The existence of Israel has, of course, given Jews a majority status for the first time in many centuries. Jews can now live, at least in Israel, without constant contact with the sources of anti-Semitism. This has led an observer, Georges Friedmann, to suggest in his *Fin du Peuple Juif?* that Judaism under such unfamiliar conditions may suffer all sorts of alterations, including perhaps its own destruction.

Israel had indeed faced two very practical problems: 1. political survival in the midst of a hostile Arab community; and 2. the creation of a suitable environment for the preservation and nourishment of a number of diverse cultural strains of Judaism. Whatever religious homogeneity is achieved will reflect these two forces. Idiosyncratic religion will have to give way to the practical exigencies of cultural and political survival. This problem is even more acute for the Jews than it is for the Muslims.

Although some Israeli Jews are so extreme as to deny the legitimacy of Israel itself, and although successive Israeli governments have had to live with the political pressures emanating from their need for parliamentary support from the small,

[36] Jakob J. Petuchowski, "Judaism Today," *passim.*
[37] *Ibid.*, p. 37.

religious parties, there seems little doubt that Judaism in Israel is undergoing considerable change. The nature of Israel has forced technological modernization upon it, regardless of what otherwise might have happened. The same process has produced great changes in the role of women and the cultural standards of the past. Prime Minister Golda Meir was not the only Israeli woman to have occupied what in the Middle East is a man's position. The very diversity of the Israeli population, containing every degree of cultural backwardness and sophistication, has given it all the characteristics of a melting pot. Judaism is the one thing most Israelis have in common, but it is a Judaism that is itself changing. In the broad sense, the Judaism of Israel cannot be considered a serious impediment to modernizing tendencies. Israel is, of course, unique in that it was formed solely as a religious haven for one particular people. The normal concepts of religious toleration and freedom must be reinterpreted within this context.

OTHER MIDDLE EASTERN RELIGIOUS FORCES

Religions other than Islam and Judaism (and the latter only in Israel) are of relatively little consequence in the contemporary Middle East. Nowhere are the other religious groups a majority, not even the Christians in Lebanon. And only in Lebanon do Christians play a major role in politics.

In the Middle East, Christian communities have had to adopt the characteristics of minorities. They have become unbending and unresponsive. Everywhere without authority, except again Lebanon, and with survival their main concern, Middle Eastern Christians have not been overly eager to adapt. Nevertheless, secularism has swept into these communities. Christianity is hardly an obstacle to modernization, but this is because it has no power with which to obstruct. Surely these characteristics apply to the Copts in Egypt, who number approximately five million in a total population of 44 million. Even the Muslims recognize that the Copts are pure Egyptians and that there cannot be any thought of expelling them. But the Revolution in 1952 did nothing to favor them; they had greater opportunities under the old regime. They are discriminated against in all sorts of small and subtle ways. They are virtually powerless, and most of their energies are spent in trying to survive in an environment generally unsympathetic to them.[38]

The same is true of Bahaism and Zoroastrianism in Iran. The former still remains theoretically aggressive in expansion. Zoroastrianism is but a relic of its former glory and clings precariously to its diminished population. Bahaism in particular has been under strong pressure from the Islamic government in Iran. There are no reliable statistics on deaths or disabilities, but there have been many Bahais who have emigrated.

Everywhere religion has some impact upon the political process. In general, modernizing societies, such as those in the Middle East, are characterized by strong patterns of religious influence. As societies change — and in particular, as their political processes change — their religious patterns also change. Nothing is stable. Although it is difficult to predict the dimensions of all of these interacting changes, it is necessary in any analysis of political behavior to understand the religious context.

[38] In 1977, the Coptic community in Egypt (and overseas) was thrown into a frenzy by publicized draft legislation that called for the death penalty for apostasy from Islam. With the current resurgence of religious extremism in Egypt, such concern could be well founded. In this instance, President Sadat gave strong reassurances to the Copts and had the offending legislation altered. It is of interest that President Sadat, in his trials with the foreign ministry — losing two foreign ministers in a year — utilized the services of Professor Butros Ghali as acting foreign minister. Butros Ghali is a Copt. He remains in the foreign ministry today. Yet in 1983 the Egyptian Coptic Patriarch remained under arrest. For the Copts, life in Egypt is a troubled one.

CHAPTER III

The Genes of Politics:
Groups, Classes, and Families

IN THE MIDDLE EAST, individuals express their social and political demands through membership in various groups. These collectivities range from family units to class aggregations, from recreational groupings to religious affiliations, from personal cliques to political associations.[1] Middle Eastern societies contain a kaleidoscopic array of overlapping and interlocking groups in contant flux. Individuals maintain membership in a large number of groups. In so doing, they build webs of personal connections that constitute the basic sinews of the social system.

Group formations dominate the vertical dimension of stratification as family, friendship, ethnic, religious, professional, recreational, and political groups and cliques exist in a state of continual interaction. The social and political systems resemble mosaics composed of a "limitless crisscross of groups."[2] Yet

[1] For purposes of our analysis, a *group* is defined as a collectivity of individuals who interact in varying degrees in pursuance of a common interest or goal. This definition is broad enough to include aggregations exhibiting a wide variety of organizational styles, yet narrow enough to exclude collectivities of individuals who neither interact nor share similar goals.

[2] This is Arthur F. Bentley's phrase. See Bentley, *The Process of Government* (Cambridge, Mass.: Harvard University Press, Belknap Press, 1967), p. 204.

this web of fluctuating groups is not a seamless one. Differing levels of power, wealth, and prestige indicate a system of stratification the lines of which cut horizontally across other group configurations. In this sense, family, tribal, and religious groups, for example, are embedded within a structure of inter-related classes.

The key political dimensions of power and authority are shaped in the Middle East largely by the prevailing group and class structure. Political demands and policies are filtered through a complex prism of group formations, and this prism leaves its own imprint upon the political process. Although a changing political system tends to alter the social structure, political changes are often the result of a shifting social structure. The politics of development and modernization are profoundly influenced by the patterns and processes that mark group and class relationships.

In all societies, social structure strongly influences the political process. The patterns of group interaction, however, vary considerably from one area of the world to another. Distinctive characteristics mark the styles of group and class interaction in Islamic cultures and Middle Eastern societies. Some of these patterns are congruent with patterns in other societies; some of them are not. The Middle Eastern patterns are the subject of our analysis.

GROUP STRUCTURE: VERTICAL STRATIFICATION

In the East persons were more trusted than institutions.
      T. E. Lawrence, Seven Pillars of Wisdom

The Middle Easterner belongs to a number of groups that vary greatly in their membership, goals, and modes of organization. These groups also differ considerably in their capacity to further the interests of their membership. On the basis of organizational style, groups in the Middle East can be divided into two major categories, formal and informal.[3]

---

[3] The terms *formal* and *informal* risk exposing us to the criticism of ethnocentricity. For the viewpoint of many non-Westerners, even informal groups have form and can therefore be considered formal. We use the term *informal*, however, to refer to an unofficial, fluid, personalistic, and relatively covert type of group structure.

Formal groups are corporate collectivities that are officially organized and visibly operating. Membership is always clearly defined, and the members have specific and sharply differentiated roles. In our group taxonomy, formal groups include both associational and institutional structures.[4] Associational groups are highly organized structures that are formed for the articulation of a specific interest. Examples include trade unions, business organizations, civic clubs, and ethnic, religious, professional, and political associations. Institutional groups exist primarily to perform a certain function but also act to present and pursue their own interests. Although officially organized, like associational groups, they generally operate somewhat more loosely. Institutional groups are usually governmental bodies and include legislatures, bureaucracies, armies, and political parties. Formal groups always maintain a corporate apparatus that includes officials and functionaries, each of whom has a clearly defined responsibility.

Informal groups are noncorporate, unofficially organized collectivities that articulate their interests in a relatively diffuse manner. This category includes kinship, status, and regional groups, as well as anomic aggregations that tend to form spontaneously, such as rioting crowds and demonstrations. Most often, however, informal groups are cliques, factions, or coteries. They are highly personalistic in character and take shape on the basis of constantly fluctuating ties and relations among individuals. The personalistic and amorphous nature of informal groups enables them to maintain a degree of fluidity and flexibility that is absent in the more rigid formal types of groups.

Patterns of Group Interaction. Political associations that have been able to take effective action have been conspicuously

[4] Associational and institutional interest groups are part of an important typology of groups developed by Gabriel Almond in his comparative study of political systems. For the original presentation of this schema, see Gabriel A. Almond and James S. Coleman, eds., *The Politics of the Developing Areas* (Princeton, N.J.: Princeton University Press, 1960), pp. 33–38; Gabriel A. Almond and G. Bingham Powell, Jr., *Comparative Politics: A Developmental Approach* (Boston: Little, Brown and Co., 1966), pp. 74–78; and Gabriel A. Almond and G. Bingham Powell, Jr., *Comparative Politics: System, Process, and Policy,* 2d ed. (Boston: Little, Brown and Co., 1978), pp. 169–176. The 1978 study places a noticeably stronger emphasis upon nonassociational, informal groups.

absent in the social history of the Islamic Middle East. Even economic associational groups have been of limited significance, despite the appearance and growth of trade union organizations during this century. Nor does the mere existence of associational groups necessarily indicate that they play an active role in the sociopolitical life of the area. Often they exist only as empty organizational shells while their functions are performed by other structures. This generalization is, of course, more applicable to certain Middle Eastern countries than to others. In Morocco, Algeria, Turkey, and Bahrain, labor unions not only exist but occasionally have had an appreciable impact upon political processes. In Iran and Iraq, on the other hand, the existence of modest union organization has been more a facade than a force. In still other countries, such as Saudi Arabia and Oman, there are no trade union organizations.

Institutional groups hold a more central position in Middle Eastern political history than do associational groups. Although parliaments and political parties are recently established institutional groups, bureaucracies and armies are institutional groups of a more ancient vintage. Thus, while associations are generally twentieth-century phenomena in the Middle East, certain institutional groups have roots that extend back to pre-Islamic days. These groups, however, have tended to be large, sprawling conglomerations composed of personal cliques, familial networks, and regional factions. The Middle Eastern military today is indeed often analyzed in terms of various officer cliques, while the bureaucracies are best understood as systems of administrative factions.

Associational and institutional groups that have played a critical role in Western political systems have been considerably less significant in the Middle Eastern context. The dominant group structure in the Islamic world has been the informal group.[5] Group organization hardens around particular individuals and kinship structures. Small, shifting clusters of individuals form cliques that resemble one another only in their personalistic, informal, fragmented mode of organization. Key

[5] As we will see in Chapter IV, informality is one of the major characteristics of patrimonial social and political systems.

political decisions are made in the context of this kind of group. Formal groups exist either as extraneous facades or as general structures within which small, informal groups carry out their important activities. Informal groups penetrate and many times suffuse the more formal aggregations. Decisions attributable to the formal organization may in fact be the product of a parasitical informal group within it.

In local Moroccan politics, for example, political parties are perceived by the people "as amalgamations of individuals bound together by a multiplicity of different personal ties rather than by any all-pervasive organizational structure or ideological commitment...." [6] In Lebanon, "loyalty to patrons, relatives or nonrelatives, takes precedence over loyalty to labor unions." [7] In national Iranian politics, the *majlis,* or parliament, "masks a fluctuating and fractionating network of personal cliques, and it is here where decisions are made and business is transacted." [8] The army in such countries as Iraq and Syria has been described as a "collection of factions" because its officers are deeply involved in politics.[9] The situation is excellently summarized by Clifford Geertz: "Structure after structure — family, village, clan, class, sect, army, party, elite, state — turns out when more narrowly looked at to be an *ad hoc* constellation of miniature systems of power, a cloud of unstable micropolitics, which compete, ally, gather strength, and very soon overextended, fragment again." [10]

[6] Lawrence Rosen, "Rural Political Process and National Political Structure in Morocco," in *Rural Politics and Social Change in the Middle East,* ed. by Richard Antoun and Iliya Harik (Bloomington: Indiana University Press, 1972), p. 299. One scholar of Middle Eastern sociology goes so far as to posit the "uselessness" of the concept of political party in the Middle Eastern context. See C. A. O. van Nieuwenhuijze, *Sociology of the Middle East: A Stocktaking and Interpretation* (Leiden, The Netherlands: E. J. Brill, 1971), p. 497.

[7] Fuad I. Khuri, "The Changing Class Structure in Lebanon," *Middle East Journal* 23 (Winter 1969):40.

[8] James A. Bill, "The Politics of Legislative Monarchy: The Iranian Majlis," in *Comparative Legislative Systems,* ed. by Herbert Hirsch and M. Donald Hancock (New York: The Free Press, 1971), p. 365.

[9] See P. J. Vatikiotis, *Conflict in the Middle East* (London: George Allen and Unwin, 1971), p. 108.

[10] Clifford Geertz, "In Search of North Africa," *New York Review of Books* 16 (22 April 1971), p. 20, as quoted in Dale F. Eickelman, "Is There an Islamic City? The Making of a Quarter in a Moroccan Town," *International Journal of Middle East Studies* 5 (June 1974):280.

The growth of effective formal groups in the Middle East has been stunted by a number of interrelated factors. These are the technical, social, economic, and political conditions of organization. The formation of a viable formal group structure requires a certain kind of organizational skill, a minimal level of trust and cooperation, a considerable pool of funds for equipment and staffing, and a willingness on the part of political elites to tolerate the existence of such groups. In Middle Eastern societies, these conditions of organization are seldom all present at once. Social and political demands, therefore, are formulated and presented in a much different organizational environment. Groups are necessarily more limited in size in order to maximize trust and cooperative endeavor. Group members protect the private and secret nature of their proceedings in order to strengthen their position against both rival groups and the national political regime. Individuals attempt to retain the greatest possible personal freedom, so that they may move in and out of groups depending upon their perception of their own best interests. This in turn promotes considerable fluidity and fragmentation, since group memberships continually change in a manner that defies any rigidity, officiality, or formal routinization.

Besides these negative reasons for the lack of effective formal groups in the Middle East, there are a number of positive explanations. Small, informal groups are able to attain their common goals readily enough to preclude the need for larger groups. Over the centuries in the Islamic world, these small groups have simply proven to be more efficient and effective structures than larger groups. Recent research by economists and political scientists who work with "collective good" theory casts serious doubt on the assumption that it is rational for individual members of a large group to work to achieve the collective good of that group.[11] Instead, it is argued that the individual who fails to contribute to the large group will still stand to share in the reward once the group's goal is attained. In large groups, it may well be that an individual's effort will

11 For the basic presentation of this theoretical approach, see Mancur Olson, Jr., *The Logic of Collective Action: Public Goods and the Theory of Groups* (New York: Schocken Books, 1968).

make no perceptible difference in the attainment of the group's goal. In this situation, the rational individual will not contribute his efforts. Such is the case in most associational and institutional groups.

In a smaller group, each individual's efforts are more likely to make a difference in attaining the group's goal. And in such a group the individual will be much more susceptible to the pressures of other group members, who can further cooperation through mutual personal persuasion. In Middle Eastern social history, where action groups have been not only small but highly personalistic, this has been especially true. In such societies, there is much doubt about the efficacy of membership in, or attachment to, large or mass institutional groups. Personal ties based upon kinship, friendship, and religious and regional affiliation have been among the best means of insuring effective individual effort.[12]

One further reason for the emphasis on personal ties in the Islamic Middle East has been a belief that nobility and generosity of manner are virtues. Individuals in Islamic culture who believed in these virtues joined various brotherhoods and guilds that incorporated characteristics of both formal and informal organization. These guilds and brotherhoods have been important political aggregations throughout the history of the Islamic world. The Islamic guild, for example, has generally represented the interests of the lower-class and lower-middle-class members of society. It "was a spontaneous development from below, created, not in response to a State need, but to the social requirements of the labouring masses themselves. Save

---

[12] Ibn Khaldun's theory of social solidarity (*asabiyya*) proposes that *asabiyya* is critical to successful group activity and ultimately to civilization. *Asabiyya* is the cement of human relations and is based first upon common ancestry and eventually upon common interest and life experience. *Asabiyya* was most easily developed in small, informal, and highly personalistic groups. As Muhsin Mahdi writes: "Solidarity comes into being as a result of common ancestry, but it is usually sustained by external factors: the feeling of relatedness is dictated by the necessity of cooperation and self-defense." (Muhsin Mahdi, *Ibn Khaldūn's Philosophy of History* [London: George Allen and Unwin, 1957], p. 197.) See Ibn Khaldun's own writings about group formation in the Islamic world in *The Muqaddimah: An Introduction to History*, trans. by Franz Rosenthal (Princeton, N.J.: Princeton University Press, 1967).

for one brief period, the Islamic guilds have maintained either an open hostility to the State, or an attitude of sullen mistrust, which the public authorities, political and ecclesiastical, have always returned." [13]

The early craft guilds closely resembled Byzantine structures and were organized on the basis of a common craft or skill. With the passage of time, and particularly following the rise of the Qarmatian (Carmathian) movement during the ninth to the twelfth centuries,[14] the guilds became deeply infused with a moral and often mystical spirit. This contributed greatly to organizational cohesion and inspired the members to dedicate themselves to furthering group goals. Although the various guilds and brotherhoods had differing organizational emphases, they generally blended formal and informal characteristics. On the one hand, they exhibited such formal accoutrements of organization as elaborate ceremonial activity and a rigid internal hierarchy. On the other hand, they were intensely personalistic and highly secretive. The term *tariqa* ("brotherhood" or "order") literally means a "way" or "path" and refers to a mode of conduct, not to a formal association.[15] Thus, in the Middle Eastern context, even structures as corporate as guilds have an element of informality that renders them a highly diversified composite of organizational types. Like the

[13] Bernard Lewis, "The Islamic Guilds," *Economic History Review* 8 (1937):35–36. The research of Gabriel Baer indicates that the craft guilds were both more formally organized and more closely linked to the government than is commonly thought. Baer's arguments, however, are most applicable to guild structures after the eighteenth century. And the brotherhoods were always better examples than the guilds of the type of informal group that existed in opposition to governmental power. The state was better able to infiltrate and control guild structures than brotherhood organizations. For Baer's conclusions concerning Turkish guilds, see "The Administrative, Economic, and Social Functions of Turkish Guilds," *International Journal of Middle East Studies* 1 (January 1970):28–50.

[14] This was a great liberal movement that swept through the Muslim world, advocating social reform in general and justice and equality in particular. The movement appealed to all classes, sects, and religions but found special acceptance among the artisans, skilled, and semiskilled workers. See L. Massignon, "Karmatians," *The Encyclopaedia of Islam*, 4 vols. (Leiden, The Netherlands: E. J. Brill, 1927), Vol. 2:767–772.

[15] This point is made in Fazlur Rahman, *Islam* (Garden City, N.Y.: Anchor Books, 1968), pp. 189–190, and in Morroe Berger, *Islam in Egypt Today* (Cambridge: Cambridge University Press, 1970), p. 67.

familial group, which we will discuss below, the guild manages to span the formal-informal dichotomy.

Since activity of informal groups is herein considered the most dominant form of group politics in the Middle East, the following discussion will emphasize this type of group rather than associational and institutional groups. This does not mean that we choose to ignore the latter but rather that we will accord them an emphasis somewhat more commensurate with the political influence they wield in the area of our investigation. To state it quite baldly, a Middle Eastern legislature, for example, is much less important as a decision-making apparatus than are the informal groups that penetrate it, control it, and most importantly, survive it.

The Politics of Informal Groups. Informal groups, usually referred to as cliques or factions, are a fundamental unit of political action in many societies. In contrast to northern European and North American societies, where formal groups play a prominent role, the informal group is dominant in southern European, North African, Middle Eastern, and Latin American cultures.

It is true that wherever human beings are gathered, they will develop informal groups. Thus, in American society there are many obvious manifestations of informal-group politics. But even within the United States, the tendency to organize informal rather than formal groups differs in strength from one area of the country to another. In the South and the Southwest, nonassociational groups are prevalent. This once led an observer to characterize the state of Louisiana as "the westernmost of the Arab states." [16] Generally, however, the American political process places relatively less emphasis upon informal groups and relatively more upon such aggregates as trade unions, legislatures, and political parties. This is not the case in much of the world. Studies of Brazil, India, Burma, Taiwan, Japan, and Italy, for example, impressively show that informal-

---

[16] For reference to this memorable quote, see T. Harry Williams, *Huey Long* (New York: Bantam Books, 1970), p. 194.

and nonassociational-group politics are dominant in these societies.[17]

The gradual recognition of the critical role that informal groups play in the less industrialized world has been recently accompanied by preliminary analysis, by a small number of scholars of contemporary Middle Eastern political systems, emphasizing this phenomenon. Amal Vinogradov and John Waterbury, for example, introduce the term *security group* to refer to a factional group that "is the maximal unit in which there is some predictability in the exercise of power and authority."[18] Clement H. Moore discusses what he terms *contingent interest groups* that cut across associational interest groups and serve as "gatekeepers" for North African political systems. According to Moore, "examples of contingent interest groups range from sets of Algerian cousins and fellow maquisards or a Moroccan family of notables to professional veto groups or a handful of individuals out to convince Bourguiba that Ben Salah's Plan is a menace."[19]

The most crucial units of interest aggregation in the Middle East remain informal groups. In Iraq this kind of collectivity is referred to as a *shilla* or *jama'at,* and in Saudi Arabia the term most often used is *bashka*. The Egyptians also use the word *shilla* to refer to a group of approximately two to twelve members who socialize together and who work to help one another advance politically and economically. A slightly more

[17] A growing number of political scientists, heavily influenced by the patron-client analysis of anthropologists, now stress the important connection between personalistic group structures and politics in the developing world. These studies contain much that is relevant to the Middle East. See, for example, René Lemarchand and Keith Legg, "Political Clientelism and Development," *Comparative Politics* 4 (January 1972):148–178; James C. Scott, "Patron-Client Politics and Political Change in Southeast Asia," *American Political Science Review* 67 (March 1973):103–127; and Arthur J. Lerman, "National Elite and Local Politician in Taiwan," *American Political Science Review* 71 (December 1977):1406–1422. See also Gabriel A. Almond and G. Bingham Powell, Jr., *Comparative Politics: System, Process, and Policy*, pp. 170–174, 201–205.

[18] Amal Vinogradov and John Waterbury, "Situations of Contested Legitimacy in Morocco: An Alternative Framework," *Comparative Studies in Society and History* 13 (January 1971):34.

[19] Clement Henry Moore, *Politics in North Africa: Algeria, Morocco, and Tunisia* (Boston: Little, Brown and Co., 1970), pp. 201–202.

diffuse Egyptian informal group is the *dufaa,* or old-boy network. The *dufaa* (literally "pushing out") is often the general
structure from which the more tightly knit *shillas* are formed.
In Kuwait, the *diwaniya* is an informal gathering where males
meet to discuss and determine important political questions.[20]
Other words in the Arab world that carry the idea of cliques
and factions, but that sometimes also indicate a higher level of
formality, include *kutal* and *fi'at.* In Iran, the sociopolitical
system is backed by a gigantic network of informal, personalistic cliques referred to as *dawrahs* ("circles"). Afghan group dynamics are dominated by loose factional aggregates referred to
as either *dastahs* ("handfuls of individuals") or *girdabs* ("little
whirlpools"). One of the most important of the informal groups
in Turkey is the personal collectivity based on *hemşeri* ("from
the same region") relations. The hemşerilik is a group that
forms and re-forms as fellow villagers and "hometowners" aggregate to assist one another with social, economic, occupational, and political aims.[21] In Egypt, the same kind of group
formation prevails in the *baladiyya,* which is in fact a kind of
informal, expanded-family group.[22]

The juxtaposition of informal groups with formal political
associations is seen in the case of Bahrain, an archipelago off
the coast of Saudi Arabia, just west of the Qatar peninsula. An
early modernizer, Bahrain is the oldest petroleum-producing
state in the Persian Gulf and had already established a girls'
school in 1928. Strikes and labor unrest have occurred in this
small shaykhdom ever since the mid-1950s. Ruled absolutely by
the al-Khalifa family, this country has nonetheless had notable
experience with municipal and national consultative bodies.

[20] The political significance of the *diwaniya* in Kuwait is discussed by
Tawfic E. Farah and Faisal Al-Salem in their excellent paper, "Size,
Affluence, and Efficacy: Regime Effectiveness in Kuwait," delivered at the
Annual Meeting of the Midwest Political Science Association, Chicago,
20 April 1978.

[21] For an excellent analysis of the critical importance of *hemşeri* relations in Turkey, see Allen Dubetsky, "Kinship, Primordial Ties, and Factory Organization in Turkey: An Anthropological View," *International
Journal of Middle Eastern Studies* 7 (July 1976):433–451.

[22] See Mona Sedky, "Groups in Alexandria, Egypt," *Social Research* 22
(1955):441–450.

But the actual politics of Bahrain have taken place within an extensive network of clubs (*nawadi*) and societies (*jam'iyyat*). Numbering approximately one hundred, these informal groups, "whose memberships include a majority of Bahrain's elite public, have played the essential functions performed by political parties in other political systems." [23] Ostensibly organized for social, professional, and recreational purposes, these clubs are often intensely political. The 250-member al-Arabi Club, for example, is composed of educated workers who push for nationalistic and democratic goals. The Alumni Club, on the other hand, is oriented more toward the elite and consists of college-educated intellectuals from both the middle and upper classes. It is the establishment's liberal conscience. These kinds of informal groups in Bahrain coexist both with formal organizations and with the ruling family, whose tentacles reach deep down into the club network. The National Assembly first convened in December 1974 was dissolved 20 months later; the clubs persist.

Informal-group activity in the Middle East has manifested itself in a myriad of ways. Ranging from tiny dyads that plug in and out of one another depending upon mutual needs to enormously complex coalitions based on kinship, these groups have little in common besides their personal, informal nature. Personal homes have served as locations for the meetings of the more exclusive of the groups, while mosques, coffeehouses, teahouses, common rooms, and bazaar shops have served as meeting places for the more inclusive of the groups. Informal groups operating in these kinds of settings constantly relay information through the various societies. It is largely on the basis of this information that personal and political decisions are made. And, it may be added, it is in precisely such groups and such settings that middle-grade army officers sometimes decide to intervene in the political affairs of their countries. The same

---

[23] Emile Nakhleh, *Bahrain: Political Development in a Modernizing Society* (Lexington, Mass.: Lexington Books, 1976), p. 41. Most of the information in this paragraph is drawn from the Nakhleh book. For an important more recent study of Bahraini society and politics, see Fuad Khuri, *Tribe and State in Bahrain: The Transformation of Social and Political Authority in an Arab State* (Chicago: University of Chicago Press, 1980).

is even more true of the religious leaders, as is evidenced by the organization of the opposition against the Shah in Iran in 1977–1978.

One of the important characteristics of informal-group politics is an intense and pervasive spirit of personalism. The fundamental social and political ties tend to be personal in nature.[24] In moving into a wide variety of informal groups the individual strives to broaden his range of personal contacts in order to gain representation on as many fronts as possible. What determines the Middle Easterner's power and influence "is not the fact that he holds a certain office or even that that office affords certain opportunities for personal aggrandizement but the extent and success with which he as an individual is able to cumulate a wide range of personal ties, to display to others a number of highly valued personal characteristics, and . . . to merge them into a larger framework of political importance reaching up to the very highest government levels."[25] In this kind of environment, individuals develop great skill at personal persuasion as they seek their political goals. Decision making is determined by personal push and pull, as is interestingly indicated by the Turkish expression *torpil* and the Iranian term *parti*. While the personal element tends to be obliterated in formal groups, the informal group manages to preserve and promote this characteristic.

The personal nature of group politics in the Middle East is exemplified well by the Lebanese *zu'ama* system (singular: *za'im*). In the Lebanese context, the za'im is an informal group leader whose followers support him on the basis of personal loyalty and personal rewards. The personal power of the za'im is rooted in local and regional communities and is buttressed by the fact that the leader and his followers share a common religion or sect. Among the important za'ama families are the Frangiehs (Maronites), the Jumblatts (Druze), the Shihabs (Sunnites), and the al-As'ads (Shi'ites). Leaders with names such as these have been present for years in the national political in-

---

[24] See Chapter IV for a detailed discussion of personalism in the Middle Eastern variant of patrimonial politics.

[25] Rosen, "Rural Political Process," p. 216.

stitutions of Lebanon. When the Maronite leader and Lebanese president-elect Bashir Gemayel was assassinated in 1982,
he was replaced in his presidential position by his brother, Amin
Gemayel. The strength of the family ties of the zu'ama system
is very great indeed. This helps explain the bitterness and
depth of the blood feuds that have marked Lebanese politics
in recent years.

At the level of the informal group, the argument that Middle
Eastern politics is basically nonideological is quite convincing.
Commitments are more often to individuals and family units
than to ideas. The precedence of personal ties over ideology
is seen in the striking examples of family units that contain
within themselves all shades of political and professional commitment. Such families are able to transcend regime changes
and even revolution. The Marei family in Egypt is a case in
point.

The father, Ahmad Marci, was a well-to-do supporter of the
old regime, a member of the Wafd party, and a parliamentary
deputy. During the Nasserite revolution, the influence of the
family remained intact. One brother (and the patriarch of the
family today), Hassan Marei, was appointed minister of commerce and industry in 1954. Another brother, Sayyid Marei, the
most powerful member of the family over the years, had served
as a member of Parliament for six years during King Farouk's
rule. Under Nasser, Seyyid was minister of agriculture for many
years and an important official in the Arab Socialist Union. A
third brother, Marei Marei, served as director of the chemical
organization during the Nasser period. During these years, the
Marei family had the added connection of their more radical
cousin, Ali Sabry, a former member of the Free Officers,
secretary-general of the Arab Socialist Union, and one of Nasser's five premiers. Despite Sabry's removal from power by
President Anwar Sadat in May 1971 and his subsequent imprisonment, the Marei brothers survived well.

During the Sadat period, Hassan Marei remained influential
in the industrial community while Marei Marei held a director-
ship in a state holding company. In 1974, Marei Marei took
charge of the very lucrative economic relationships between
Egypt and Iran. In September 1971, Sadat appointed the

ubiquitous Sayyid Marei deputy premier and minister of agriculture. In October 1974, Sayyid became speaker of the assembly and four years later he settled in as presidential advisor to President Sadat himself. The Marei-Sadat relationship was cemented by the 1975 marriage of Sayyid Marei's son Hassan to Sadat's daughter Noha. Thus, Robert Springborg concludes that the first loyalty of "the Mareis and most other Egyptians is to the family itself, and political ideology is not sufficiently compelling to undermine primordial family ties." [26]

This pattern of family tenacity and ideological malleability has also prevailed in such countries as Iran, Iraq, Lebanon, and Morocco. Even the leading families of the very conservative shaykhdoms of the Persian Gulf have had members who have espoused radical causes. Shaykh Saqr bin Sultan, who ruled Sharjah between 1951 and 1965, is a notable example. Saqr, a strong Arab nationalist with Nasserist sympathies and a dislike for the British, was deposed in 1965, primarily for these reasons. In 1972, he returned from exile in Cairo and failed in an attempt to regain the throne.

An informal group "is like a cluster of bees round a queen bee. If the queen is damaged they quickly find another to cluster around." [27] The exigencies of politics require an individual to shift positions periodically in order to maintain as much manipulative leeway as possible. The informal group itself will often switch goals and alter the ideas that brought its membership together. Such changes, of course, always mean that a certain percentage of the membership will be lost, but this is one important by-product of the fluidity of this type of group. Individuals retain the capacity to circulate among a host of collectivities, depending on what they consider to be in their own interests. Coalitions are fragile and alliances fleeting in such

[26] Robert Springborg, *Family, Power, and Politics in Egypt* (Philadelphia: University of Pennsylvania Press, 1982), p. 75. The information on the Marei family has been drawn from this source. Springborg's book is superb and stands as the finest available study of family and informal politics in the Middle East.

[27] This statement was made concerning informal-group politics in India. See B. D. Graham, "The Succession of Factional Systems in the Uttar Pradesh Congress Party, 1937–1966," in *Local-Level Politics: Social and Cultural Perspectives*, Marc J. Swartz, ed. (Chicago: Aldine, 1968), p. 355.

social and political systems. Even the strongest social cement, personal ties, can be easily cracked. Yet the adhesive quality remains, so that the relationship can be reestablished whenever the winds of fortune dictate that it be reestablished. This plasticity of informal-group politics promotes a systematic stability that is not often recognized with regard to the Middle East.

Informal groups in the Middle East are characterized by alternating fission and fusion. "It is always possible to divide them, to prevent powerful coalitions from forming, for their solidarity, of course, is inversely proportional to their breadth. Hence political showdowns rarely occur." [28] Although tension, conflict, and competition infuse this network of "many-stranded coalitions," [29] the overall group system persists and prevails. The tension promotes balance. "Equilibrium in conflict is not achieved by both or all sides desisting from conflict but rather in both or all sides persisting in conflict. . . . The best defense of a security group lies in keeping up steady pressure against its rivals short of attack." [30] This principle of counterbalancing in group politics is prevalent throughout the Islamic Middle East, although it manifests itself somewhat differently from one society to another. In the traditional countries of the Gulf and Morocco, it helps foster systemic fluidity and flexibility. In Lebanon, on the other hand, it froze into a more rigid pattern, in which groups directly confronted one another; there, the more common pattern of many sides balancing against one another gave way to confrontations between two sides. The fragility of this situation became all too clear in April 1975, when the society exploded into bloody civil war.

This network of floating factions could not persist without a sturdier group backing to help anchor it in the social structure. Individuals require a more reliable vehicle than factions and cliques to defend their interests and to achieve their goals.

28 Moore, *Politics in North Africa,* p. 202.

29 This phrase is borrowed from Eric Wolf, *Peasants* (Englewood Cliffs, N.J.: Prentice-Hall, 1966), and is quoted in Khuri, "Changing Class Structure," p. 35.

30 Vinogradov and Waterbury, "Situations of Contested Legitimacy," p. 35.

In the Middle East, this mechanism is the kinship group in general and the family in particular.

The Primordial Group Nexus: The Family. Kinship units are a very special kind of informal group. The family, which is the basic unit and building block of groups in the Middle East, retains characteristics that render it more rigid and formal than most factional and nonassociational groups. Although the lines of association that mark personal cliques and political factions appear and disappear with amazing rapidity, true kinship relations are much more difficult to create and destroy. Ties of kinship remain in existence whether or not political actors choose to recognize them. Since family networks are virtually impossible to rupture or break, they provide the element of permanence needed to offset the impermanence of the other informal groups. Family groupings are the linchpins of the system of group interaction in the Middle East. Indeed, lineage patterns are "the invisible skeleton of the community." [31] Yet this skeleton contains the moving force of the community. In the words of Dale Eickelman; "Kinship relationships should be treated as something which people make and with which they accomplish things." [32]

The traditional Middle Eastern family unit is an extended family, usually consisting of a man, his wife (or wives), his unmarried sons and daughters, and his married sons and their wives and children. In the contemporary urban Middle East, the institution of the extended family is increasingly giving way to the nuclear family, which includes only the husband, wife, and children. Family groups, whether extended or nuclear, are consciously and carefully shaped. Marriage patterns are critical, since they determine the direction in which the family group will move. The most distinctive traditional trait of Middle Eastern marriage is the preferred mariage of a man and his father's brother's daughter (*bint 'amm*). This paternal first

[31] This phrase is John Gulick's. See Gulick, *Social Structure and Culture Change in a Lebanese Village* (New York: Wenner-Gren Foundation, 1955), p. 104.

[32] Dale F. Eickelman, *The Middle East: An Anthropological Approach* (Englewood Cliffs, N.J.: Prentice-Hall, 1981), p. 134.

cousin marriage was designed to strengthen important blood ties and to solidify a constantly expanding family unit. An endogamous marriage pattern such as this one has significant political implications. In the Middle East, it enabled family heads to enlist the critical support of their brothers and their brothers' sons. In societies deeply torn by divisions and cleavages, this minimal unit of coalition was a relatively effective action group. Few family clusters could afford the internecine conflict that might otherwise have occurred between brothers, nephews, and cousins.[33]

Every individual in the Middle East thus begins with membership in one important informal group, the family. This group seeks to magnify its kinship ties in at least three different ways. First, contacts are strengthened and regular communication is maintained with as many blood relatives as is practically possible. Even when there is great geographic and genealogical distance separating kinfolk, family members seldom hesitate to approach one another for needed economic and political assistance. In Egypt, for example, "while members of the descent group may not socialize regularly with one another, and may indeed be quite distant genealogically speaking, they have no compunction about asking their kin and affines for economic and political favors." [34]

The second way in which family ties are expanded in the Middle East is by the very broad and flexible definition of kinship. The Afghan concept of *qawm*, for example, defines actual kinship on the basis of deep social and political cooperation among those who live in the same area. Somewhat the same applies in Morocco, where the term *qaraba* or "closeness" is expressed as a blood tie "even when no demonstrable ties exist, because however such ties are valued in practice, they are considered permanent and cannot be broken." [35] Also, kinship ties

33 For excellent discussions of the marriage patterns of Middle Eastern families, see Raphael Patai, *Golden River to Golden Road: Society, Culture, and Change in the Middle East*, 3d ed. (Philadelphia: University of Pennsylvania Press, 1969), pp. 135–176, and Eickelman, *The Middle East*, pp. 105–134.

34 Springborg, *Family, Power, and Politics*, p. 54.

35 Eickelman, *The Middle East*, p. 109.

are often fictitiously manufactured in an attempt to enhance the influence of a particular individual or group. The most common examples of fictive kinship are elaborate arguments that purport to document one's direct descent from the family of the Prophet Muhammad.

Finally, family contacts are broadened by the incorporation into the kinship group of new individuals and other families through marriage. This is why in the Middle East, "arranging marriages is a highly serious matter, like waging war or making big business deals." [36] The process by which two families are brought together through intermarriage is described by Robert Springborg as "family nesting." "Family nesting occurs when two families, tied together through marriage, reinforce that connection through a series of social, economic, and political exchanges." [37] The branches of the family trees in the forests of Middle Eastern society and politics are filled with family nests. In Egypt, the Marei family discussed above nests with other powerful kinship units such as the Muhieddin, Sabry, Shamsi, Abaza, Mashour, and Elwan families. The Mareis have even nested with the Sadat family. Springborg concludes here that ". . . it is by nesting with other families that the descent group of the Mareis performs the greatest services for its members. The sheer number of family members involved in these nests, and the scope of their various economic and political activities, provides a complex of opportunities for the exchange of economic and political favors." [38] During the periods of Farouk, Nasser, and Sadat in Egypt, families with whom the Mareis nested were among those that exerted most economic and political influence in the country.

For the family group to remain strong, its members must maintain a continually updated knowledge of the intricate kinship structure to which they belong. In the Ottoman system, for example, "every member of the clan kept a genealogical

[36] Hildred Geertz, "The Meanings in Family Ties," in *Meaning and Order in Moroccan Society*, ed. by C. Geertz, H. Geertz, and L. Rosen (New York: Cambridge University Press, 1979), p. 363 as quoted in Eickelman, *The Middle East*, p. 124.

[37] Springborg, *Family, Power, and Politics*, p. 73.

[38] *Ibid.*, p. 88.

map in his head to orient him in his relations with others." [39] In Turkey, the situation is one "of everyone having to know very precisely to what extended family, to what kin village, to what lineage, to what clan, to what clan federation and to what principality or khanate he belongs." [40] This awareness of precisely where one stands with regard to other group members contributes greatly to group solidarity, and ultimately to the capacity to attain group objectives. Strands of kinship serve, at the very least, as relatively permanent lines of access among group members. It is in the individual's self-interest to be familiar with as many of these connections as possible.

Like all other group formations in the Middle East, the kinship group (whether family, tribe, or clan) is internally divided and fragmented. Intrafamilial tensions, quarrels, and feuds are common in Islamic cultures. Yet within the nuclear family, the divisions are not as deep, nor are the tensions as intense, as they are outside the family. More important, the kinship group presents a united front against outside competitors. Fragmented collectivities gain solidarity and cohesion through the pressure exerted by external rival forces. In this system of balancing opposition, the family unit always fares best. This is because the kinship group is the most cohesive and tenacious of the Middle Eastern group formations.

In addition to being both a biological and an economic unit, the family is very much a political aggregation. Family members support one another in their drives to attain important goals and to improve their respective power and authority positions in the particular community or society. "As a unit in terms of authority, it [the family] is the base line for traditional social organization. The traditional authority pattern of the Middle East along with the traditional social structure, pivots around the kinship principle." [41]

---

[39] Şerif Mardin, "Historical Determinants of Stratification: Social Class and Class Conciousness in Turkey" (Paper prepared for the Comparative Bureaucracy Seminar, Massachusetts Institute of Technology, Spring 1966), p. 19.

[40] *Ibid.*

[41] Van Nieuwenhuijze, *Sociology of the Middle East*, p. 388. Patai writes that "the political systems in the Middle East either grew out of the

Besides providing support for its members attaining political goals, the kinship group is politically relevant in many other ways. It serves, for example, as the staging ground from which individuals can move on to membership in other groups, both formal and informal. The family, in fact, determines much of its members' participation in other collectivities. Such informal groups as personal cliques and political factions have fathers, sons, brothers, nephews, cousins, and in-laws strategically sprinkled throughout them in patterns that tend to benefit the particular family unit. As often as not, a single family is represented in rival political factions, parties, or movements. Thus, although informal group membership cuts across kinship lines, it is also true that the filaments of kinship cut across the boundaries of cliques and factions. A major function of distributing family members among various other groups is the construction and maintenance of channels of communication among these groups, whether they be rivals or allies.

The ligaments of kinship bind the system of groups into a working whole. They run through rival collectivities, thus softening tensions. And, through membership in both formal and informal groups, blood relatives and in-laws help bind these two major organizational types together. Family members in such institutions as bureaucracies and parliaments are in close touch with relatives who are members of cliques and factions. Decisions made in one of the contexts are directly influenced by what occurs in the other.

Morocco has sometimes been referred to as the kingdom of cousins, and monarchical Iran was frequently called the country of one thousand families. Observers have labelled Farouk's Egypt as the land of two thousand families and contemporary Pakistan as the country of sixty families. The intricacies of family relationships explain a great deal about the orientations, formation, and behavior of political elites in the Mid-

---

lineage structure and retained its characteristics or, if they had no lineage basis, artificially assumed what can be called a lineage camouflage." Patai, *Golden River*, p. 430.

dle East. The more traditional the society, the more useful kinship analysis will be in understanding it. In all the Middle Eastern countries, however, patterns of kinship and marriage are valuable in understanding the structure of power and authority. Those societies that are developing politically and modernizing relatively rapidly may have a relatively large number of ruling families, as well as a high rate of familial mobility. A study of such family structures can explain much about national elites and the political processes of the societies under investigation. Selected examples follow.

In the three decades prior to 1958, the Iraqi political elite represented a tight cluster of families. The core of the elite included such families as the al-Saids, the al-Askaris, the Kannas, and the Kamals. The famous Nuri al-Said held the post of prime minister 14 times and that of minister 29 times! Ja'far al-Askari, who was assassinated in 1936, was prime minister twice and minister eight times. Nuri al-Said and Ja'far al-Askari married each other's sisters. Tahsin al-Askari followed in the footsteps of his assassinated brother, Ja'far, when in 1942 he assumed two ministerial positions. He was the brother-in-law of Ibrahim Kamal, who was himself a cabinet minister twice. Another al-Askari brother, Abd al-Hadi, married his daughter to Khalil Kanna, who held ministerial posts six different times. Two of Khalil Kanna's brothers were members of the Iraqi parliament.[42]

The Iraqi revolution of 1958 did not destroy the political power of the families. The Ba'thist regime of strongman Saddam Hussein al-Takriti is dominated by Saddam and his relatives from the town of Takrit. In the early 1980s, Saddam's two leading intelligence and security chiefs were his half-brothers Barzan Ibrahim al-Takriti and Watban Ibrahim al-Takriti. Saddam himself was the foster son, nephew, and son-in-law of Khayrallah al-Tulfah, the longtime governor of Baghdad. Iraqi minister of defense Adnan Khayrallah al-Tufah

---

42 This information is drawn from Nazar T. Al-Hasso's excellent Ph.D. dissertation. See Al-Hasso, "Administrative Politics in the Middle East: The Case of Monarchical Iraq, 1920–1958" (Ph.D. diss., The University of Texas, Austin, Texas, 1976).

is the son of Khayrallah and the cousin and brother-in-law of Saddam. This is only a tiny piece of the family web of power that still ruled in Iraq in 1983. In the words of a leading scholar of Iraqi politics, the Takritis' power is so great that "it would not be going too far to say that the Takrītīs' rule through the Ba'th party, rather than the Ba'th party through the Takrītīs." [43]

In the Shah's Iran, national politics were dominated by family considerations, since the political elite that clustered around the ruling Pahlavi family came from a small number of families. Among the most influential of the elite families in Pahlavi Iran were the following: Alam, Diba, Qaragozlu, Esfandiari, Ardalan, Bayat, Sami'i, Farmanfarmaian, Akbar, Bushehri, Jahanbani, and Emami. The ties among key members of these families were easily as close as the ties among the families in Iraq. Long-time minister of culture Mehrdad Pahlbod was the husband of Princess Shams, a sister of Muhammad Reza Shah. Former major general Minbashian was the brother of Pahlbod (formerly Ezzatullah Minbashian). The influential Senator Bushehri was the father of the husband of powerful Princess Ashraf, the twin sister of the Shah. Former air force commander Muhammad Khatami was married to the Shah's sister Fatima. Ardeshir Zahedi, Iranian ambassador to the United States, was once married to the Shah's daughter Shahnaz. During the last years of the Shah's rule, there were 40 national elite families that dominated the economic and political systems in Iran.

Despite the shattering nature of the Iranian revolution of 1978–1979, political influence in the Islamic Republic has tended to follow the primordial lines of kinship and family. The strands of kinship about which power and influence coagulate extend outward from the person of Ayatollah Ruhollah Khomeini himself. One of Khomeini's daughters, for example, was married to the now-deceased Ayatollah Esh-

---

[43] Hanna Batatu, *The Old Social Classes and the Revolutionary Movements of Iraq* (Princeton, N.J.: Princeton University Press, 1978), p. 1088. This important book documents in detail the family and kinship relationships that undergird the Iraqi political system. (See especially pp. 1073–1110).

raqi; they in turn had three daughters, all married to individuals who played important political roles in the early days of the Islamic Republic. These three officials were former Plan Organization head, Minister of Oil, and Majlis deputy Ali Akbar Moinfar, former Minister of Post, Telephone, and Telegraph Engineer Qandi, and former Deputy Minister of Oil Bushehri. In another part of the same network, Ayatollah Khomeini's brother-in-law is Ayatollah Hussein Ali Montazeri, the man chosen by Khomeini himself to be his successor. Montazeri's son, Muhammad, was a powerful if erratic force and Majlis deputy in revolutionary Iran before his assassination in June 1979. A daughter of Ayatollah Montazeri was married to the late Ali Qoddusi, the Iranian prosecutor-general after the revolution. Finally, Khomeini's own son, Ahmad, has been an extremely important political broker ever since the revolution.[44]

Family connections loom even larger in the shaykhdoms of the Persian Gulf, where the core of the political elite always consists of members of the ruling family. Other members of the elite are almost always drawn from other wealthy, aristocratic families. Political decision making in Saudi Arabia, Kuwait, Qatar, Oman, the United Arab Emirates, and Bahrain is monopolized by the ruling families in these countries. In Bahrain, where political and economic decision making is dominated by Shaykh Isa bin Salman Al-Khalifa and his brother, Shaykh Khalifa bin Salman Al-Khalifa, the names of the leading families such as Kanu, Fakhru, Shirawi, and Mu'ayyid are well known. The following anecdote illustrates that, in Bahrain, family is more important than any formal governing body. While in the marketplace in 1973, an elderly Bahraini was told to go vote in the elections for the Constitutional Assembly. The old man looked around and asked, "Who owns that building?" "A Kanu," he was told. "And who owns this one?" "A Mu'ayyid," was the response. "And this third one?" "Shaykh Khalifa." The old man then asked, "Will the elections change any of this?"[45] The right family connec-

44 Much of the information in this paragraph has been drawn from an article that appeared in *Iran Times*, February 6, 1981, p. 9. In Persian.
45 This story is presented in Nakhleh, *Bahrain*, p. 129 n.

tions remain an important passport to the elite in much of the Middle East.

Political revolution and economic modernization have hardly lessened the role of the family group in government. It is true that the form of family organization has changed considerably and that kinship relations now crystallize in new ways. The most evident change of this sort is the transfer from the extended to the nuclear family style of household. This change, however, has not fundamentally altered the important role that kinship relations play in the political process. Fuad Khuri writes that "the change from the extended family subculture to that of the nuclear family does not imply the loss of family ties and duties. Family ties and duties, no doubt, continue, but in new forms." [46] The physical living arrangements of the family may be changing, but its sociopolitical demands and supports remain essentially the same.

The Power of Women: A Case Study of Informal Politics. When one examines the informal nature of group politics in the Middle East, a number of previously overlooked and underemphasized dimensions of the political game suddenly come into sharper focus. Persons who were formerly considered peripheral to political decision making take on a more central and critical significance. This is precisely the case in cultures where there is no sharp distinction between the private and the public spheres or where key community and national decisions are made in less viable, informal settings by individuals often considered peripheral to politics. An important case in point is the Middle Eastern woman. Studying the woman's role in society can provoke new insights into the kinds of actors and actresses who play out the political drama, and can indicate both the importance of informal politics and the special place that family relationships have in Middle Eastern politics.

For years, Middle Eastern women have been stereotyped as an oppressed and passive group who have been hidden by veils and whose lives have been dominated by men. Western writers in particular have presented the Muslim woman as someone

[46] Khuri, "Changing Class Structure," p. 38.

held captive in the kitchen or harem while her husband frolics personally and protects politically a system of polygamy that rationalizes female servitude. Quotations from the Quran and the relative absence of female actresses on the public political stage have often led outsiders to believe that the woman in Islamic society has been little more than a personal and political cipher. This perspective has been reinforced by Middle Eastern historians and chroniclers who have traditionally downplayed the role of women in their writings. And essayists, both male and female, have distorted the historical position of women in the Middle East as one means of attempting to improve their position today.

In stressing the formal, public, and institutional aspects of political behavior at the expense of the private and informal aspects, Western analysts have overlooked precisely those individuals who dominate the private and informal aspects. In the Middle East, women are important political forces because of their critical position in the webs of informal relationships that make up the private realm. In the crucial world of informal, private groups, they have been more than the homemakers. They have also been "the matchmakers and the peacemakers." [47] As anthropologist Emrys Peters puts it,

> The pivotal points in any field of power in this, a superficially dominant patrilineal, patrilocal and patriarchal society where the male ethos is vulgar in its brash prominence, are the women. What holds men together, what knots the cords of alliances are not men themselves, but the women who depart from their natal household to take up residence elsewhere with a man, and who, in this critical position, communicate one group to another.[48]

[47] We are indebted to Gerald J. Obermeyer for this phrase.

[48] Emrys Peters, "Consequences of the Segregation of the Sexes Among the Arabs" (Paper delivered at the Mediterranean Social Science Council Conference, Athens, 1966), p. 15. This important observation has been quoted by such scholars as Cynthia Nelson and Carla Makhlouf, whose works are among the few that stress the political power of women in the Middle East. Anthropologically inclined analysts have been much more sensitive to this power than have political scientists. Two further examples are Elizabeth Warnock Fernea, who has done field work in Iraq, Egypt, and Morocco, and Lois Grant Beck, who has worked in Iran. Cynthia Nelson's field observations come from Egypt, and Carla Makhlouf's from Yemen.

This quotation refers to only one of the ways in which Middle Eastern women shape political events at all levels of the societies in which they live.

In both the traditional and the modern Middle East, women have exerted political influence through the wide variety of roles that they have played. Perhaps the most important of these roles have been natal and marital kinship roles. Such natal roles as daughter, sister, cousin, aunt, mother, and grandmother and such marital roles as wife and mother-in-law have been politically strategic throughout Islamic history. The special relationship between mother and son is particularly relevant to our understanding of Middle Eastern political events. As we shall see in the examples discussed below, only the role of wife has been more important in the female repertoire of political roles. One knowledgeable observer writes that "it is hardly surprising that the relationship to the mother is preferred to the paternal one, and that every patriarchal society is condemned to be matriarchal on the edges. On the edges? Not at all! It is a question here of the depths of existence." [49]

Other roles in which Muslim women have exerted influence in the political arena include such diverse traditional callings as prostitute, concubine, entertainer, servant, religious leader, soothsayer, and advisor. More modern roles, such as career woman and politician-stateswoman, are becoming more important with time. Female revolutionaries and terrorists are also visible and increasingly important.

Among the tools that Middle Eastern women have used to exert influence are such resources as wealth, beauty, intelligence, and information, as well as both psychological and physical coercion. They have often converted the very signs of their oppression into formidable offensive weapons that have enabled them to secure their interests. Excellent examples of

[49] A. Bouhdiba, "The Child and the Mother in Arab-Muslim Society," in *Psychological Dimensions of Near Eastern Studies*, ed. by L. Carl Brown and Norman Itzkowitz (Princeton, N.J.: Darwin Press, 1977), p. 133. For another fine discussion of the power of the mother and mother-in-law in Muslim society, see Fatima Mernissi, *Beyond the Veil: Male-Female Dynamics in a Modern Muslim Society* (Cambridge, Mass.: Schenkman Publishing Co., 1975), pp. 69–79.

such weapons are the harem and the veil that segregate the sexes. The conventional wisdom is that it is the women who are excluded from the male world, but, as one scholar has recently written: "One can venture to assert that it is in fact the men who are excluded from the female world, as much, if not more, than females are excluded from that of man." [50] This researcher goes on to give a number of examples of how much easier it is for women to penetrate men's gatherings than for males to participate in those of women.

A survey of Middle Eastern political history indicates the important contributions that women have made to the political process. From the very foundation of Islam, women have been critical political forces. Indeed, as we shall see in Chapter IV, there is little doubt that the Prophet Muhammad could not have succeeded in his mission without the indispensable support of his first wife, Khadija. Other women who helped shape the early social system of Islam were Muhammad's wife A'isha and his daughter Fatima. Fatima's sister-in-law Zaynab was also a powerful force in early Islamic history, as were the wives of the various imams who were the direct descendants of Fatima and her husband Ali.

The political role of women in the famous Umayyad and Abbasid caliphates is little known. In both instances, it was critical. This was especially true during the golden age of the cosmopolitan Abbasid dynasty in the late eighth and early ninth centuries. At a time when Europe was plunged into its Dark Ages and when Charlemagne and his lords "were re-

---

[50] Carla Makhlouf, *Changing Veils: Women and Modernisation in North Yemen* (Austin, Tex.: University of Texas Press, 1979). This study contains fascinating material showing how the veil has traditionally provided Middle Eastern women with a mobile form of security and anonymity, and has even facilitated the expression of aggressiveness. More than religious fervor is involved in the return to the veil in the early 1980s by numerous liberated young women in countries such as Egypt. For a fine study of a Muslim culture (Tuareg), in which the males are the veiled ones, see Robert F. Murphy, "Social Distance and the Veil," in *Peoples and Cultures of the Middle East*, ed. Louise E. Sweet (Garden City, N.Y.: Natural History Press, 1970), vol. 1, pp. 290–314. On the informal power of women among the Tuareg, see R. V. C. Bodley, *The Soundless Sahara* (London: Robert Hale Limited, 1968), p. 82.

portedly dabbling with the art of writing their names," [51] the powerful Abbasids ruling out of Baghdad were debating philosophic texts and making gigantic intellectual strides in medicine, astronomy, mathematics, and the arts. The glory and grandeur of this period are captured in romantically imaginative terms in *The Thousand Nights and a Night,* and such rulers of the period as Harun al-Rashid (786–809) and his brilliant son the caliph al-Ma'mun (813–833) are among the most renowned of Eastern rulers. Names such as Umm Salama, Khayzuran, and Zubayda, however, are considerably less known, even among scholars of the area. Umm Salama was the wife of Abu al-Abbas and thus served as a critical link between the two dynasties. A strong personality, she directed her husband's affairs and he "took no decisive measure without Umm Salamah's advice and approval." [52]

Khayzuran was the favorite wife of the third Abbasid caliph, Muhammad al-Mahdi; she was also the mother of the fourth and fifth caliphs, Musa al-Hadi and Harun al-Rashid. A slave girl born in Yemen, she received an excellent education and caught the eye of the caliph al-Mansur, who brought her to the court, where his son al-Mahdi married her. For 30 years, during the reigns of three caliphs, her political power was enormous. Her agents and secretaries were spread throughout the empire; she intervened directly in the administration of justice; she influenced the rise and fall of the caliph's closest advisors; she financed the construction of public works; and she directed the succession of kings. It was Khayzuran who held the system together and ensured the smooth transition of kings both upon the death of her husband and then again when her eldest son, al-Hadi, passed away. Khayzuran was an owner of extensive property, and, next to her illustrious son Harun al-Rashid, she was the wealthiest person in the Muslim world of her day. In describing Khayzuran's role during the caliphates of her two sons, one writer succinctly summarizes

[51] Philip K. Hitti, *The Near East in History* (Princeton, N.J.: D. Van Nostrand Co., 1961), p. 244.

[52] Nabia Abbott, *Two Queens of Baghdad* (Chicago: University of Chicago Press, 1946), p. 11.

her position: "The ambitious mother travels in state on the imperial highway of power." [53]

Better known in the annals of Islamic history than Khayzuran is her niece Zubayda, the wife of Harun al-Rashid. One of the greatest builders of public works in Islamic history, Zubayda is remembered particularly for sponsoring the construction of over ten miles of complex aqueducts leading into Mecca. She spent over 75 million dinars in digging the Mushshash Spring in that holy city — a spectacular feat in any age. Like Khayzuran, Zubayda was intimately involved in all the important political issues of the time. She had influence over judges, police officials, and military generals, not to mention her husband. The observation that "Zubaidah had (complete) control over Hārūn's mind and did with him as she pleased" [54] is perhaps only a slight exaggeration. In the succession battle between her son Muhammad Amin and al-Ma'mun, she played a critical role in Amin's victory. Zubayda was a major force also in turning Harun against the powerful Persian Barmecids, who had directed the political fortunes of the Abbasid dynasty more than any other family. Indirectly, but very effectively, she helped bring about their destruction. Although less aggressive than Khayzuran, Zubayda nonetheless left her imprint even more deeply in the sands of Abbasid social and political history.

Moving chronologically onward and geographically southward, we come to the Sulayhid dynasty, which ruled in South Arabia from 1037 to 1138. This Shi'ite dynasty made its capital in Sanaa and later in the Dhu Jibla of today's Yemen. The Sulayhi "educated their daughters to the same standards as their menfolk, instilled in them the same moral and political principles, and made them their equals in astuteness, ability, and judgement." [55] The greatest of the Sulayhid queens was Urwa bint Ahmad al-Sulayhi, who upon her husband al-

---

[53] *Ibid.*, p. 132.
[54] F. Wustenfeld, *Die Chroniken der Stadt Mekka*, vol. 3, p. 15 as quoted in Abbott, *Two Queens*, p. 256.
[55] Robert W. Stookey, *Yemen: The Politics of the Yemen Arab Republic* (Boulder, Colo.: Westview Press, 1978), p. 67.

Mukarram's death in 1084 took complete command and ruled for 53 years. A woman of great political acumen, Queen Urwa ruled the Sulayhid state by judiciously emphasizing tactics of compromise, personal maneuver, and the wise appointment of assistants and advisors. Urwa's political success is perhaps largely attributable to the training she received under the direction of another woman, Queen Asma, the wife of the founder of the Sulayhid dynasty.

The Ottoman Empire, which boasts a political history that extended from the thirteenth to the twentieth centuries, is a much more significant example of an Islamic system in which women wielded political power. The Ottoman style, however, is more similar to the Abbasid style of indirect kinship control than to the Sulayhid style of direct rule by a queen. Although one can select any particular sultan and discover in association with him a number of women active in the central decision-making process, we will cut into Ottoman history at perhaps its best-known period of grandeur, the reign of Süleyman I the Lawgiver (1520–1566). Süleyman was known for his legal promulgations and his empire for its architectural creations, naval strength, and military expansion deep into Europe. Surrounding Süleyman were three women of particular note — his mother, Hafsa Hatun, and his wives, Hurrem Sultan and Gulbahar Hatun. Their political influence was great, especially in controlling the sultan and the grand vazir, the most important administrative official in the Ottoman system. Of these three women, the most powerful was Hurrem Sultan, a former Russian slave girl known in the West as Roxelana. It was she who convinced Süleyman to let her live with him in the seraglio, "where she obtained complete ascendancy over the Sultan and ruled supreme in the harēm until her death in 1558." [56]

Hafsa Hatun and Hurrem Sultan formed an alliance of convenience to expel one grand vazir and to appoint another

[56] N. M. Penzer, *The Harēm* (Philadelphia: J. B. Lippincott, 1937), p. 186. There are many sources that describe this period of Ottoman history. For an excellent example, see Stanford Shaw, *History of the Ottoman Empire and Modern Turkey*, vol. 1 (Cambridge: Cambridge University Press, 1976), pp. 87–111.

early in the reign of Süleyman. The new vazir, Ibrahim Pasha, felt indebted to Hafsa Hatun for his position and was careful to do her bidding. Meanwhile, he was independently linked to Süleyman himself, who permitted the vazir practically to run the empire. Ibrahim Pasha in the process became one of the most powerful of the grand vazirs in Ottoman history. An extraordinarily ambitious person politically, Hurrem Sultan saw the vazir as her major competitor and sought to destroy him. When her mother-in-law died in 1534, she moved quickly against the vazir. The now exposed Ibrahim Pasha found an ally in Süleyman's first wife, Gulbahar Hatun, who was anxious that her son Mustafa become the heir apparent. Hurrem Sultan, with her own sons' interests at heart, gathered other supporters (including the French ambassador) and was able to prevail in the struggle. In 1536, Ibrahim Pasha lost not only his job but also his life.

Hurrem Sultan then succeeded in getting her eldest son Mehmet named as heir to the throne. With his untimely death, however, Gulbahar Hatun, with the assistance of the new vazir, Hadim Süleyman Pasha, finally placed her son Mustafa in the coveted position. But Hurrem Sultan's power was not to be denied, and she forced this vazir into exile. And she now saw that someone more reliable got the post. Her own son-in-law, Rustem Pasha, became vazir. This new alliance resulted in the execution of Gulbahar Hatun's son Mustafa. When there was a revolt in 1555, partially against this execution, Hurrem Sultan's son Bayizat successfully put it down. When Hurrem Sultan died in 1558, she had pretty well determined that one of her sons would become the next sultan. Her son Selim succeeded Süleyman to the throne in 1566 and ruled for eight years as Sultan Selim II. Selim's wife Nurbanu Sultan in fact ruled the empire during his reign. During the rule of her own son, Sultan Murad III, she shared political power with her daughter-in-law, Safriyah Sultan. And so it continued. It is small wonder that the Ottoman empire during the sixteenth and seventeenth centuries has come to be historically known as the Sultanate of Woman (*Kadinlar Sultanati*). (For a diagrammatic representation of the women of Süleyman the Lawgiver's reign, see Figure III.1.)

FIGURE III.1   *The Women of Süleyman the Lawgiver's Reign*

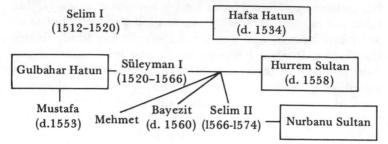

The names of the women in the system appear in boxes.

Early in this century, women played an important part in the various constitutional and revolutionary movements that swept across the Middle East. An excellent case in point is Halide Edib Adivar, a leading Turkish intellectual, nationalist, and supporter of Mustafa Kemal's movement for independence. Born in 1883, she was educated at the American College for Girls and then began writing and speaking for liberal causes. Her inspired public speeches in support of the nationalist revolution earned her national and even international fame. Her statement that "governments are our enemies, peoples are our friends, and the just revolt of our hearts our strength" became the rallying cry of Turkish nationalists.[57] Halide Edib Adivar actually served in Kemal's army as a corporal, a sergeant, and a sergeant major.

Women also played a critical role in the Iranian constitutional movement from 1905 to 1911. They organized themselves into informal meeting groups (*anjumans*) and did not hesitate to take to the streets in support of their political ideals. When the newly established parliament (*majlis*) faced extinction in 1911, a large group of women marched on the building:

> Three hundred women surrounded the entrance to the *Majlis*, or Parliament, recently formed, and demanded admission. A few only were admitted. They walked in closely veiled, but when

[57] Elizabeth Warnock Fernea and Basima Qattan Bezirgan, eds., *Middle Eastern Muslim Women Speak* (Austin, Tex.: The University of Texas Press, 1977), p. 189.

they found themselves in the assembly they tore their veils aside, and said that their intention was to kill their husbands, their sons and themselves if the liberty and dignity of Persia were not firmly upheld. They offered their money and jewels, saying: "We are women and cannot fight, but we can give to our country." They had their own places of assembly where they discussed these matters, and they used the Press, and personal influence was largely exerted.[58]

As time has passed, Muslim women have assumed a more direct and dramatic role in Middle Eastern politics. In the Algerian war of independence, women were an important part of the resistance and did everything from hiding fugitives to throwing bombs. National heroine Jamilah Buhrayd, for example, rather than becoming a seamstress, became a revolutionary and was eventually shot, after having been imprisoned and tortured by the French. Young women have been very conspicuous in the Palestine guerrilla movement. Leila Khaled, for example, gained international notoriety when she was captured as part of a four-plane hijacking operation in September 1970. In May 1972, two young Arab women, former nursing students, participated in the hijacking of a Sabena Boeing 707 to Lod Airport in Israel. There are many other examples. One observer writes: "Mostly young and often educated in the West — France, England, the United States — the Palestinian girl fedayeen have a better political understanding than their male counterparts. Indeed, they are more the material from which real revolutionaries are made. Proportionate to their numbers they have caused the Israelis more trouble than have their male comrades." [59]

Women were also key participants in the revolutionary struggle in Aden. According to one knowledgeable source, there were 250 hard-core women guerrillas involved in the independence movement there. One of them, Nagwa Makkawi,

---

[58] C. Colliver Rice, *Persian Women in Their Ways* (London: Seeley, Service and Co., 1923), p. 270. For an even more dramatic description of this event, see W. Morgan Shuster, *The Strangling of Persia* (New York: Century Co., 1912), p. 198.

[59] John Laffin, *Fedayeen: The Arab-Israeli Dilemma* (New York: Free Press, 1973), p. 138.

was so famous (or infamous) that when the British captured her, they paraded her through the streets on a tank. She later became the first female ambassador for the People's Democratic Republic of Yemen.[60]

This revolutionary role of Muslim women in influencing Middle Eastern politics is only one of many more direct and formal ways that they now exert power. As their legal rights expand and as they gain greater stature in the formal governmental arena, they are conspicuously acquiring political authority. Women's movements are present in the Middle East, and women are slowly taking their places in government bureaucracies. In so doing, however, they have not relinquished their traditional influence in the informal sphere of power. It is as part of the informal group or family that women continue to operate most effectively.

In Pahlavi Iran, Empress Farah Diba did not confine herself to social work and charitable causes. Although she headed nearly 40 different social organizations, she was also involved in political issues. In the latter half of the 1970s, the Empress was the Shah's last important line to reality and was the only person left among his advisors who could take issue with his decisions. Towards the end, the Shah refused to take the advice of his wife seriously. If he had, the political outcome in Iran might possibly have been different.

In Tunisia, Wassila bin Amar, the wife of President Bourguiba, has long been embroiled in national politics. Her advice and opinions often shaped the course of events in that country. In November 1977, she visited President Sadat in Cairo to indicate her country's support for his direct approach to peace in the Middle East. Jihan Sadat, the wife of the assassinated Egyptian president, was an important force in Egyptian society and politics. Amina al-Said, one of Egypt's leading female journalists, once stated that Mrs. Sadat "conceives of herself as a woman, an Egyptian woman first, and the President's wife second." [61]

---

[60] John Duke Anthony, lecture delivered at the University of Texas, Austin, Texas, 22 July 1977.

[61] Deborah Mason, "Egypt's First Lady," *Christian Science Monitor*, 18 December 1974, p. 5.

In the shaykhdoms along the Persian Gulf, women have in recent years also been influential politically. In both Abu Dhabi and Dubai, the two leading countries in the United Arab Emirates, the mothers of Shaykh Zayid and Shaykh Rashid converted their royal motherhood directly into political clout. Zayid's mother was the real power broker in Abu Dhabi until her death in the early 1970s. Rashid's mother, Hussah bint al-Murr, "is widely acknowledged as having been the real power in the shaykhdom for most of the first half of this century. Once, during an armed conflict with neighboring Sharjah, she is said to have charged her husband and sons with indifference and to have led the local forces in defense of Dubay herself." [62] Today, Shaykh Zayid's wife, Shaykha Fatima, exerts important social and political influence in Abu Dhabi.

Muslim women in the Middle East have never enjoyed legal equality with men and have suffered discrimination in many areas of existence. Any study of the formal scaffolding of the social and political systems clearly demonstrates their lack of authority. This lack of authority has been reinforced in recent years by the reassertion of Islamic fundamentalism throughout the region. The lack of authority, however, is not the same as the lack of power. Middle Eastern women have never been powerless. Indeed, they have played a pervasive and persistent part in shaping political decisions and determining political events ever since the time when the widow Khadija married and then materially and psychologically supported the young man Muhammad. Only by analyzing politics at the informal level does one begin to understand and appreciate the significance of women to the entire political process.

Our brief survey of Middle Eastern women in politics yields several general observations. First, women throughout Muslim history have had a more profound impact upon political events than is generally thought. Second, this political power has usually been wielded indirectly and informally through men. Natal and marital relationships have often been the most

[62] John Duke Anthony, *Arab States of the Lower Gulf* (Washington, D.C.: The Middle East Institute, 1975), pp. 156, 158. We are indebted to Dr. Anthony, who has explained the role of women in the Persian Gulf to us in private correspondence.

critical ones here. Third, there has been a movement over the past several decades among Middle Eastern women for legal equality and social and political rights. Although this movement has been slowed significantly in recent years by the resurgence of Islamic fundamentalism, it is still very much alive, even in the most traditional of countries such as Saudi Arabia. In the Middle East, women's liberation is a drive not so much to acquire power as to add authority to power: Why must women's political influence be indirect and confined to the informal arena? Fourth, this drive for authority has not, however, displaced the power and position of women in the traditional realm of informal groups. Middle Eastern women after all are quite sensitive to the fact that this is the main decision-making arena. That is why Algerian heroine Jamilah Buhrayd states: "It's true we don't find as many women in politics as men, but women have always imposed their views in a quieter way without public fuss." [63]

CLASS STRUCTURE: HORIZONTAL STRATIFICATION

> *It is He who has made us the inheritors of the earth, who has elevated us one above the other by degrees in order to help us experience His gifts.*
>
> *Quran, Chapter 6, Verse 165*

Although informal groups and networks must be taken into account in any study of Middle Eastern politics, the political process is not played out in a seamless web of interacting groups. The above case studies, for example, indicate that it is only women of the upper class who in fact influence the national polity. The masses of women (like the masses of men) have little if anything to say about major political decisions. By emphasizing only the group dimension, we suggest that group pluralism promotes equality. What is left out of the equation is the issue of horizontal stratification. Slashing across the web of groups are lines of stratification that profoundly affect not only the group dynamics discussed above but also the entire political process of the Middle East. Şerif Mardin cogently summarizes this point when he writes that

---

[63] Fernea and Bezirgan, *Middle Eastern Women Speak*, p. 261.

although membership in a kinship group "raised the expectations of a less prestigious member of the group that he could rise in society, the fact that he belonged to a well-recognized stratum led to frustrations as regards the actual capacity to rise in society." [64]

G. E. von Grunebaum once wrote that "the Muslim's personal equality with his fellows in the faith which is guaranteed, so to speak, by his right to a direct relationship with his Lord does in no way preclude elaborate social stratification within the community of Islam." [65] The group network and communalism discussed above cloak a system of horizontal stratification in which Middle Eastern societies break down into a fairly small number of interrelated classes.[66] A class structure always involves entities in superior and subordinate positions. The overall hierarchy of classes is founded upon the unequal possession of one of the fundamental values of social and political life. In the sociological literature, class is most often defined according to one of three different emphases: wealth, status, and power. An individual's place in a social class is determined by his or her position with respect to one of these characteristics. Although all three determinants are interrelated in the sense that the possession of one may strongly affect the acquisition of another, the question of which is the basic criterion remains open. In this volume on the Middle East, we define class in terms of power and employment position.[67]

---

[64] Mardin, "Historical Determinants," p. 4.

[65] Gustave E. von Grunebaum, *Medieval Islam: A Study in Cultural Orientation*, 2nd ed. (Chicago: University of Chicago Press, 1961), p. 170.

[66] For an important recent study in which "class" is the basic tool of analysis, see Ervand Abrahamian, *Iran Between Two Revolutions* (Princeton, N.J.: Princeton University Press, 1982).

[67] For two explicit attempts to discuss class analysis as it applies to Middle Eastern society and politics, see Jacques Berque, "L'Idée des Classes dans L'Histoire Contemporaine des Arabes," *Cahiers Internationaux de Sociologie* 38 (1965):169–184; and James A. Bill, "Class Analysis and the Dialectics of Modernization in the Middle East," *International Journal of Middle East Studies* 3 (October 1972):417–434. The latter article provides the conceptual and theoretical underpinnings for the linkage of class and power.

Class and Power in the Middle East. For our purposes, power refers to one's ability to shape and control the behavior of others.[68] This ability may rest as much upon indirect personal maneuvering and verbal persuasion as upon direct threat, coercive demand, or economic inducement. The basis of power may be located in the political, economic, social, educational, religious, or psychological systems. Because Islam is a way of life that involves all of these dimensions, power relations in Islamic societies usually involve a subtly integrated complex of factors. One Islamic scholar writes, for example, that "political influence, military power, administrative rank, wealth, birth, and schooling, in every possible combination, strengthened or counteracted one another in assigning a given individual his place in society." [69] Wealth is but one of a number of important variables that determine one's position in the class structure. Material resources have seldom been enough to enable individuals consistently to attain their goals. Personal contacts, social manipulation, saintly ancestry, mystical strength, familial solidarity, higher education, political maneuvering, and an innate sense of timing are all crucial ingredients that help determine one's class standing.

Among the more common, if seldom recognized, dimensions of power that have been instrumental in shaping the formation of Middle Eastern class structure are:

1. exchange transactions in which one person convinces others to accede to his wishes by rewarding them for so doing;

2. informational exchanges that involve dispensing and withholding information of varying degrees of value;

3. decisional situations in which one person controls the decision-making environment and thus the decisions made therein;

---

[68] This definition of power is slightly broader than those provided by scholars who have chosen to reword Max Weber's original definition. In our view. a power relation can involve more than getting someone to do what he or she would not otherwise do. It can be a reinforcing pattern whereby one individual encourages another to continue behaving in a certain way, or it may simply be a case of one person's causing another to translate a predisposition into action.

[69] Von Grunebaum, *Medieval Islam*, p. 212.

4. debt-inflicting relationships in which one does favors for others with the confident expectation that they will someday be returned;

5. overt deference behavior by which one person gains the trust of another and thus makes the temporarily more powerful person vulnerable;

6. bargaining interactions that occur in environments of doubt, and rest upon such techniques as the bluff and the compromise;

7. kinship patterns in which family members strive to assist one another to improve their relative positions in the class structure;

8. modes of misrepresentation that distort reality in a manner designed to shift the balance of interpersonal influence.

The exchange transaction is the simplest and most direct means of exerting power; it is a major pattern in all societies.[70] It is most often expressed as financial dealings, which range all the way from salary transactions to bribery payments. In the Middle East, a disproportionately high percentage of exchange transactions occur in noneconomic terms, since the objects of exchange include personal loyalty, political service, religious approval, and reliable information. Informational exchanges are critical in societies where informality cloaks the exercise of power and where decisions are made within personalistic networks. Indeed, information is a valuable commodity in the Middle East, since it can be used both offensively and defensively. Political elites constantly seek information concerning the actual and potential opposition forces in their societies. Individuals and groups in the middle and lower classes both hoard and barter information in order to improve their own positions in the social structure.

Another dimension of the power syndrome is the phenomenon of "nondecision making," whereby superordinately situated individuals control the behavior of subordinates through the manipulation and control of the environment in which the

---

[70] For a theoretical exploration of the various facets of exchange transactions, see Peter Blau, *Exchange and Power in Social Life* (New York: John Wiley and Co., 1964).

latter must operate.[71] An example of this phenomenon in the Middle East is the executive control of parliaments and political parties. Decisions tend to be made in the parliaments and parties according to what the deputies believe the will of the ruler or military junta would be. It is not necessary that there be any communication between the leadership and the representative. If deputies do not correctly anticipate what the ruler wants and do not act accordingly, they may find themselves politically unemployed; or, as happened in the mid-1970s in Bahrain and Kuwait, the rulers simply dissolve the parliamentary bodies themselves. Control is thus built into the structure of the system in a less than obvious manner. Learning how to interact in this kind of system is essential to the determination of one's class standing.

One of the most distinctive facets of power relations in Middle Eastern society is debt infliction. In the Muslim community of North Africa, "every act requires some form of reciprocation as an inherent aspect of its very nature: Every act creates an obligation or expresses a right held." [72] Those upon whom debts are inflicted are put into a disadvantageous position of dependence. It is in this sense that Fredrik Barth describes the mechanism as it manifests itself in the Swat Valley in Pakistan. The relationship to political power is unmistakable here, since even "gift-giving and hospitality are potent means of controlling others. . . ." [73] As one Lebanese citizen puts it, gifts are "the lubricants of social interaction." [74]

Deference, which is part of the somewhat extravagant patterns of courtesy and politeness that obtain in the Middle East, can be used effectively to balance highly uneven personal relationships. When properly displayed, deference can loosen the

[71] See Peter Bachrach and Morton S. Baratz's classic discussion of the "nondecision-making process" in "Two Faces of Power," *American Political Science Review* 56 (December 1962):947–952.

[72] Lawrence Rosen, "Muslim-Jewish Relations in a Moroccan City," *International Journal of Middle East Studies* 3 (October 1972):438.

[73] Fredrik Barth, *Political Leadership among Swat Pathans* (London: Athlone Press, 1959), p. 79.

[74] This is reported in Fuad I. Khuri, *From Village to Suburb: Order and Change in Greater Beirut* (Chicago: University of Chicago Press, 1975), p. 86.

control of the more powerful actor over the less powerful individual. Deferential behavior can stimulate a false sense of security in the superior person in any relationship, thus heightening his or her vulnerability. It was in this spirit that the Ziyarid prince Kai Ka'us Ibn Iskandar wrote his son that "if you are being fattened by someone, you may expect very quickly to be slaughtered by him. . . ." [75]

Another context in which power exchange occurs in the Middle East is bargaining, in which the actors in fact agree to disagree. Each side in the encounter uses a wide variety of persuasive techniques in order to further his or her interests. The outcome of the confrontation remains in doubt until the very end of the process, when one side indicates a willingness to accept the terms of the other. An individual who is able to use an effective blend of candor and the bluff, as in bargaining, can greatly enhance his or her position in the social and political hierarchy.

The final two tactics of control and influence have to do with kinship ties and modes of misrepresentation. As we noted earlier, the family is the most cohesive unit in Middle Eastern society. As such, it is least susceptible to radical change and most reliable as a unit of personal and group support. The mobility of one family member affects the potential mobility of the whole family. Entire families often move up in the class structure. They are also downwardly mobile. Because of the centrality of the family in determining one's position in the power structure, individuals constantly seek to attach themselves to rising or already prominent families. This is usually accomplished through marriage, but it is also often done through the invention of fictive kinship ties. This is only one of the forms of misrepresentation designed to help improve one's class position. To exaggerate and falsely embroider reality at propitious times is a technique more frowned upon in the West than in the Middle East, where such behavior often deflects conflict and prevents violent confrontation. It also is a

---

[75] Kai Ka'us Ibn Iskandar, *A Mirror for Princes* (The Qābūs-nāma), trans. Reuben Levy (London: Cresset Press, 1951), p. 191.

dimension of influence that must be considered when explaining class membership and class conflict.

The Middle Eastern Class System. There is one further consideration in analyzing power relations in the Middle East. Throughout Islamic history, a person's power position has been closely intertwined with his occupational skill. Mode of employment to a large degree determined an individual's capacity to utilize the techniques and to operate effectively in the environment discussed above. An individual was best able to wield power using skills and talents he already possessed. The military, cleric, and bureaucratic occupations provided their practitioners with unusual opportunities to strengthen and improve their positions in the class structure through informed use of the coercive, religious, and political dimensions of power. The intimate connection between power and employment was a direct result of the development of Islamic social history and the Prophet Muhammad's early strictures concerning the occupational bases of the community of Islam. One of the earliest foundations for stratification was the assignment of the believers "to a more or less definite hierarchy of professions." [76] For purposes of the following empirical analysis of horizontal stratification in the Middle East, we define classes as the largest aggregates of individuals united by similar modes of employment and maintaining similar power positions in society.

Classical Islamic thinkers have presented views of horizontal stratification that range from two-class to eight-class hierarchies. According to the criteria developed above, the traditional Middle Eastern Islamic social structure consisted of seven interrelated classes: the upper (ruling) class, the bureaucratic middle class, the bourgeois middle class, the cleric middle class, the traditional working class, the peasant class, and the nomadic class. This schema includes one upper, three middle, and three lower classes. This designation of upper, middle, and lower refers to the general power categories, while the more specific labels are assigned on the basis of both power and employment.

[76] Von Grunebaum, *Medieval Islam*, p. 177.

The nomenclature of each class indicates its employment function.

The upper class in the traditional Islamic social structure represented a tiny percentage of the population, usually less than 2 percent. The upper class was a ruling class, since it possessed a monopoly of the instruments of both power and authority in society. This class was composed of the elites that rested at the very apex of the governmental, landholding, religious, tribal, military, and business pyramids of influence. The rulers and the networks of ruling families were at the core of the upper class. Also included were the military leaders, the large native landlords, the highest-level bureaucrats (the vazirs, for example), the leadership of the ulema who supported the system, the tribal chieftains and khans, and the wealthiest merchants and business entrepreneurs. This ruling class exhibited exclusive and inclusive characteristics that tended to balance one another out, ultimately stabilizing membership size. In most cases, a single member of this class had a number of power-laden functions. For example, a member of the ruling family was often at the same time a military leader and a large landlord. The tribal nobility maintained large landholdings and were often among the highest-ranking military officials. In this way, wealth, influence, and coercive power reinforced one another and strengthened one's class position. This helped to narrow upper-class membership. On the other hand, the kinship mechanism tended to expand the size of the upper class while at the same time linking this class to the various middle classes. The extended family ties of a ruler, vazir, or landlord brought new waves of individuals into ruling-class ranks. Indeed, one of the best ways even today to understand ruling classes in Middle Eastern societies is to analyze the structures of leading families.

Ruling classes in the contemporary Islamic Middle East are shaped by the lines of kinship along which power flows. Family ties and intermarriage patterns help solidify an inherently fragmented and fissured upper class. The lack of any strong class consciousness, at least among the ruling class, is partially compensated for by a kind of interfamilial and intrafamilial consciousness. Although studies show that family membership in

Middle Eastern upper classes is relatively unstable, there are indications that a small number of families remain in upper-class ranks over time. The informality of family structure in many ways mirrors the character of the upper class, which is also relatively fluid. In an impressive study of the upper class ("patriciate") of Muslim Nishapur from the tenth to the twelfth century, Richard Bulliet writes that "the reality of the patriciate consisted in individuals and families who knew each other and recognized each other as being above the ordinary run of people. There was no formal membership in the patriciate." [77] In sum, the upper class in Islamic history has been a complex of leading clerics, generals, vazirs, khans, and merchant kings familially and informally bound together round the person of the ruler and his family. By virtue of its advantageous power position, this ruling class directs the political system of society.

The bureaucratic middle class has been the most powerful of the three traditional middle classes. Its membership is composed of the mass of governmental employees who staff the administrative system. Possessing a minimum of traditional education, these individuals are the scribes, accountants, recorders, and bureaucratic functionaries of the traditional Middle Eastern society. Like the ruling class, this middle class is rather loosely and informally organized. Although in many Islamic societies there were families that came to be known as bureautic families, kinship ties are not as important as class indicators here as they are in the upper class.

In our concentric circles of class and power, the bureaucratic middle class most closely rings the ruling class. It is an important intermediary class that translates the directives of the ruling class into action. This administering class appears to be almost an appendage to the upper class because of its many points of contact with the upper class. Owing to this proximity, the bureaucratic middle class has more often served the interests of the ruling class than those of the other middle and lower classes. While maintaining an important power of its own, this

---

[77] Richard W. Bulliet, *The Patricians of Nishapur: A Study in Medieval Islamic Social History* (Cambridge, Mass.: Harvard University Press, 1972), p. 86.

class traditionally saw its interests as bound up with those of the upper class. The proximity to power always held out to the bureaucratic middle class the possibility of movement into upper-class ranks.

Located approximately between the bureaucratic and cleric middle classes is the bourgeois middle class, which is a class of businessmen, merchants, and traders. The symbol and center of activity of this class is the bazaar, or *suq*. As an individual, the merchant or trader has relatively little economic power and virtually no political influence. As a class, however, this bourgeoisie has considerable political power. When ruling-class policies have seriously endangered the interests of commerce and the life styles of the merchant, the bazaar has often become the heart of opposition to the regime in power. It was out of the ranks of the bourgeoisie that Islam itself developed as a community and civilization. And throughout the history of Islam, a number of social and religious movements have sprung up from this class in opposition to the prevailing political order.

There are three reasons why the merchants and tradesmen have been able to give birth to opposition movements. In the first place, the members of this class managed to institutionalize their traditional informal patterns of interaction in a system of guilds and brotherhoods. Secondly, their organizational apparatus had a semblance of ideology, which helped provide a rationalization for their activities. This ideology was composed of various folk and mystic Islamic beliefs. Finally, this kind of organizational and ideological framework linked the business middle class with important elements in both the cleric middle class and the traditional working class. The suqs and bazaars were the meeting place for merchant, cleric, and artisan.

The cleric middle class, which is composed of the lower and intermediate ranks of the ulema, is the third traditional middle class. The members of this class enjoy neither the political influence of the bureaucrats nor the wealth of the businessmen. They have, however, possessed important religio-psychological influence over those members of society who have been practicing Muslims. They also have controlled the educational system through their role as teachers and directors of the traditional educational institutions (*maktabs* and *madrasas*). The constituency of the clerics has been largely concentrated within the lower classes, and because of this, the interests of the cleric middle class have been closely entwined with those below them in the social structure.

The three traditional middle classes were closely related to one another in a number of ways. The members of all these classes were the products of the same educational system — a system that was directed by the ulema and that stressed reading, writing, religious law, rhetoric, and the Quran. The educational method used was rote memorization. One result of this was that all traditional middle-class individuals had a similar value system, largely conservative. This meant that these classes rebelled only under very special circumstances, consisting of either a severe and adverse disruption of business conditions or a series of policies by the ruling class that abrogated and contradicted the tenets of Islam. Usually both these conditions had to come about simultaneously in order for these middle classes to move to active opposition. And even then, the bureaucratic middle class seldom participated.

The bulk of the population of all Middle Eastern societies falls into the three lower classes, consisting of workers, peasants, and nomads. Ideally, Islam commands that the community treat the poor and least powerful with compassion. The giving of alms is one of the acts that all the faithful are expected to consistently practice. In describing the class structure of Islamic communities, Imam Ali, son-in-law of the Prophet, said of the lower clases: "Lowest of all are the afflicted and the poor who are the unfortunate and the suffering. They are always the broken-hearted and the weary." [78] In fact, however, the situation of the lower classes has been little improved by such words of sympathy and ideals of charitable assistance. The harsher realities of class structure are reflected in another scheme of classification presented by the Abbasid courtier Yahya al-Fazl. He divides society into four classes and then

[78] Imam Ali, Farman to Malik Ashtar, governor of Egypt, *Sukhanan-i Ali* [The words of Ali], trans. by Javad Fazil (Tehran, 1966), p. 242. In Persian.

writes that "the remainder are filthy refuse, a torrent of scum, base cattle, none of whom thinks of anything but his food and sleep." [79]

Most of the members of the lower class belong to the peasant class. In preponderantly agricultural societies, these are the individuals who work the land under a variety of arrangements that only alter the degree of their poverty, dependence, disease, and ignorance. The peasant class, located at the very bottom of the social structure, has very little power and is thus exposed to exploitation by all the other classes in society. For the individual peasant, this usually means abuse at the hands of landlord, merchant, and government official. Peasants have also often suffered from manipulation by the clerics and from the raids of tribesmen. The situation of the nomadic lower class is not much better than that of the peasants. The tribal masses have existed in a state of subjection to a hierarchy of khans and have had to struggle to make a living from an often inhospitable land. Because of a modicum of natural freedom and their occasional importance as military forces, the tribesmen have been a cut above the peasant in the power structure.

The traditional working class includes such groups as servants, manual laborers, craftsmen, and artisans. In the Middle East, this class has been as much a rural as an urban phenomenon. Like the members of the other lower classes, these workers have earned their livelihood through the use of their physical skills. Working with their hands, they have been scorned by the middle and upper classes. The members of this class have often joined guilds and brotherhoods; accordingly, they have enjoyed some organizational protection. This has placed the traditional working class in the best power position among the lower classes.

The traditional class structure in the Islamic Middle East is still in place to a large extent in contemporary Middle Eastern society. There have been, however, a number of obvious changes that have largely resulted from the forces of modernization discussed in Chapter I. Land reform programs, coupled with the

---

[79] Ibn al-Faqih, *Kitab al-Buldan*, as quoted in Reuben Levy, *The Social Structure of Islam* (Cambridge: Cambridge University Press, 1957), p. 67.

increasing emphasis upon industrialization, have caused a shift-ing of the bases of power of the ruling class. Land ownership, which was an important upper-class power credential for cen-turies, has given way to industrial investment in the form of contracting, banking, export-import trade, and business con-cessions of all kinds. The traditional middle classes have grown in size relative to the upper and lower classes, with the bour-geois middle class expanding at an especially rapid rate. No-madic tribes are slowly being forced to settle, and as a result are grudgingly blending into the peasantry. Strong rural-to-urban migration patterns have resulted in the mushrooming growth of shanty towns and the appearance of an unemployed proletariat that continues to expand along the edges of the major cities. This last change is a dramatic one, since it repre-sents the appearance of an important modern addition to the centuries-old class structure.

The relatively recent appearance of two new classes is a sig-nificant break with the past patterns of horizontal stratification in the area. Both an industrial working class and a professional middle class have emerged as definite formations in the second half of this century. Both classes are the products of the acceler-ating process of modernization, and their roots trace back to the growth of large industry and the development of modern systems of education in the Afro-Asian world.

Industrialization and urbanization have been the major catalysts for the appearance of the new urban industrial work-ing class. Census data indicate that this class still represents a very small proportion in the various Middle Eastern countries, but that it is growing at a rapid pace. The growing masses of unemployed migrants referred to above are a ready pool of unskilled and semiskilled labor for new industry. This new lower class is more powerful than the traditional lower classes because of its strategic and visible location in the large cities as well as its growing social awareness. The industrial working class, however, has barely begun to realize its potential as a social and political force. This is not the case with the second and more recent class formation.

The Professional Middle Class. The forces of modernization and the acceleration of accompanying social change have given rise to the formation of a new middle class in the Middle East.[80] This class, which we here term the professional middle class, is one whose members derive their power from skills obtained through a modern higher education. Many members of the new class seek to advance themselves through their professional skills and talents rather than through the use of wealth and personal connections, two resources that most of them lack in any case. The professional middle class is not a bourgeois middle class, since its members earn their livelihoods less through ownership of property or entrepreneurship in business than through salaries, technical fees, scholarships, and professional activities. This class is composed of white-collar workers engaged in technical, professional, cultural, and administrative occupations. Its membership is drawn largely from such groups as teachers, bureaucrats, professors, students, technocrats, engineers, physicians, writers, artists, journalists, and middle-ranking army officers. Among the army officers, we must include political leaders such as Gamal Abdel Nasser of Egypt, Houari Boumediene of Algeria, Mu'ammar Qaddafi of Libya, Hafez al-Assad of Syria, and Ja'far Numayri of Sudan. All rose to power on the wave of the aspirations of the new middle class.

Although the professional middle class is not a class of intellectuals, it may be properly termed an intelligentsia, since it composes the intellectual elite in society. Unlike the educated members of the ruling class, who enjoy the twin privileges of great wealth and political authority, the members of the professional middle class have little other than their education to fall back on. Whereas the members of the traditional middle classes rested their power on the older educational system, dominated by religion, the individuals in the new middle class draw their influence from the modern educational system. And this is what makes them an increasingly indispensable segment of society. Modernization results in constantly accelerated demands for qualified physicians, engineers, technocrats, teachers, and sol-

[80] For the pioneering study of this class, see Manfred Halpern, *The Politics of Social Change in the Middle East and North Africa* (Princeton, N.J.: Princeton University Press, 1963). For an analysis of this class as it challenged the Shah's regime in Iran, see James Alban Bill, *The Politics of Iran: Groups, Classes and Modernization* (Columbus, Ohio: Charles E. Merrill, 1972).

diers. Economic and industrial development guarantees the growth of the new middle class.

In Turkey, Egypt, Libya, and Tunisia, members of the professional middle class have come to hold political power and have begun to implement developmental programs with varying degrees of success. In Iraq, Syria, Algeria, and Sudan, individuals from the new middle class have taken political control but have failed to solve the problem of division and discord among groups and classes. This failure has severely retarded political development and modernization. In Morocco, Saudi Arabia, Jordan, and the various Gulf shaykhdoms, the professional intelligentsia remains largely locked out of the political arena.[81] In Morocco and Jordan, where this class is a relatively large one, a number of its members have moved into the political elite as the result of a calculated policy of co-optation on the part of the ruling class. All in all, membership in the professional middle class throughout the Islamic Middle East is rapidly approaching 10 to 12 percent of the population.

The professional middle class is a threat to the traditional sociopolitical system in the Middle East. Many of its members decry the old network of personalism, favoritism, nepotism, and influence wielding that continues in many cases to suffocate their own opportunities to move forward on the basis of technical skills and professional merit. What makes this class such a serious threat to the traditional social structure is not so much that all its members are agents of modernization but that some of its members demand political development. The latter refuse to relate to the ruling class in terms of subservience and deference. Instead, they demand a share of political authority and promise to uproot the power relations upon which the authority structure rests.

The professional middle class is composed of many individuals whose goals include a transformation of power relations and the authority structure. Many of them prefer professionalism to personalism, justice to wealth, intellectual freedom to

---

[81] For a discussion of the appearance of the professional middle class in Saudi Arabia, see William A. Rugh, "Emergence of a New Middle Class in Saudi Arabia," *Middle East Journal* 27 (Winter 1973):7–20.

imposed stability, and effective political participation to political co-optation. Even in Saudi Arabia, when this kind of individual seeks "a role in the economy, he typically places a higher value on the prestige or dignity of the job than on its monetary reward." [82] In Lebanon, the new middle class is very weak economically. "But in no sense should this detract from its vital role as carrier of new skills, ideologies, and styles of life. And this is certainly more relevant to its role as an agent of modernization." [83] It was shortly after the Egyptian coup in 1952 that Ahmad Baha'eddine wrote that this new middle class was "the greatest hope we have for progress." [84]

The professional middle class has seldom borne out such hope, however, as it has not been as much a force for development as might have been expected. Besides the extraordinary strength of the traditional political system, there are other reasons why the new middle class has failed to implement much deep-seated change.

Like every other social unit in the Middle East, this class is torn by internal divisions and tensions. These divisions are along the lines of kinship, ethnicity, religion, occupation, social origins, geography (urban and rural), and university background. All of these divisions in turn affect the individual's orientations toward modernization and political development. It is concerning the latter that the new middle class remains most deeply divided. The influence of those who would uproot the traditional patterns of power and authority tends to be nullified by those who seek to preserve the traditional processes in order to improve their own positions in the system. This

---

[82] *Ibid.*, p. 22.

[83] Samir Khalaf, "Urbanization and Urbanism in Beirut: Some Preliminary Results" (Paper prepared for delivery at the Twenty-first Annual Near East Conference, Princeton, N.J., 9–10 April 1970), p. 37. This paper documents the important appearance of a new professional middle class in the Hamra district of Beirut. See also Samir Khalaf and Per Kongstad, *Hamra of Beirut: A Case of Rapid Urbanization* (Leiden, The Netherlands: E. J. Brill, 1973).

[84] Ahmad Baha'eddine, "Al-iqta'iyyun wal-ra'smaliyyun wal-muthaqqafun" [Feudalists, capitalists, and intellectuals] in *Rose Al-Yussif*, no. 1353 (17 May 1954), as quoted in Anouar Abdel-Malek, *Egypt: Military Society*, trans. Charles Lam Markmann (New York: Vintage Books, 1968), p. 178.

group usually supports modernization at the expense of political development. These are the maneuverers in the new middle class who survive by manipulation without imbuing it with the civility and courteous charm that was the hallmark of the aristocrats of the older generation. It is this segment of the professional middle class that is readily corruptible. In a stirring indictment of this group within the intelligentsia, one novelist writes: "Every country east of the Mediterranean is torn to bits by ever-competing jealous politicos coming to power by some kind of inheritance.... But I can envisage the day when these countries will be even worse, torn by degree-holders more self-interested and sycophantic than their predecessors, and far, far less charitable. If you think the sheikh grinds the faces of his tribesmen you should wait and see the Ph.D. grind the faces of all and sundry, without even a touch of the magnanimity we pride ourselves on." [85]

The professional middle class remains crippled in its challenge to traditional sociopolitical relations in the Middle East. The deep fissures throughout the class are intentionally deepened by the ruling class in order to weaken the cohesiveness of this challenging unit. The political elite encourages and supports those elements in the new class that are most susceptible to the blandishments of bribery and personal aggrandizement.

The new middle class carries another major weakness. It is separated from the lower class masses by an enormous social and cultural gap. An engineer or physician with a modern higher education has separated himself from the illiterate citizens that make up the majority of his own people. Often educated in universities of the West, multilingual in speech, fashionably chic in dress, secular in thought and belief, the professional represents the antithesis of the illiterate, suspicious, suffering, and deeply religious peasant. This division became most apparent in the Middle East in Iran after the revolution, when the masses turned to the religious leaders and tradition and away from the secular intelligentsia.

[85] Jabra I. Jabra, *Hunters in a Narrow Street* (London, 1960), as quoted in *A Middle East Reader*, ed. by Irene L. Gendzier (New York: Pegasus, 1969), p. 114.

Today, the members of the professional middle class find themselves increasingly swimming against the tides of Islamic fundamentalism. Although they are still dedicated to the transformation of traditional patrimonial rule, there is no longer any guarantee that they are destined to become the leaders of the new political systems. The fact that the religious leaders, with their mass constituency, have hijacked the Iranian revolution is an indication that the professional middle class may no longer be the political force of the future in the Middle East. Growing members of this class are returning to Islam as part of a general search for their dignity, roots, and personal heritage. In such times, the possession of a professional skill gained abroad can sometimes be as much as a detriment as an advantage.

Despite all this, the professional middle class continues to grow. A few voices within the class continue to clamor for radical social and political change. And because the ruling class desperately needs the skills and talents of these individuals in order to implement their programs of modernization, the uprooters are slowly improving their power positions. On the basic issues of power and authority relations, the ruling class grudgingly gives ground while working to preserve the ongoing class structure from the challenges presented by the new class. Regardless of who ultimately takes control of future revolutions in the region, the professionals, technicians, and scientists will remain an indispensable part of society. In Iran, even the regime of Ayatollah Khomeini has required skilled technicians in the oil fields, talented physicians in the hospitals, competent planners and managers in the bureaucracy, and capable pilots and officers in the military.

The Dynamics of Group-Class Interaction. The dynamics of Middle Eastern social structure develop out of an integrated system of both vertical and horizontal stratification. The overall social structure might best be viewed as an intricate web of groups that is partially partitioned by class lines. Group and class structures relate to each other reciprocally, and it is this reciprocity that builds coherence into the sociopolitical system. The multistranded sinews of group relations bind the class structure together by crisscrossing class cleavages. Ethnic, tribal, religious, and military groups, for example, often draw their membership from several different classes. Here class distinctions are somewhat softened by common group affiliation. At the same time, group relations and formations are molded and shaped to a considerable degree by class. Groups are often structured along class lines, and their memberships remain confined within the boundaries of a single class. Family units, for example, tend to belong to a single class. Certainly, class divisions serve to retard individual and group mobility.

Class conflict in the Middle East is a muted phenomenon. There are three major reasons for this, and all of them relate to the impact of vertical stratification. First, the existence of a wide variety of important intraclass groups in the Middle East renders class units relatively diffuse. Fissures within classes are numerous and deep enough to weaken class cohesion and to retard class consciousness. Loyalty to primordial groups such as the family takes precedence over loyalty to class. Second, the plethora of groups with multiclass membership promotes interclass communication and draws together individuals from differing classes on the basis of shared group goals. As we have pointed out above, this helps to integrate the class structure and therefore to mellow class conflict. Third, the group structure provides a system of mobility channels through which individuals can rise and fall in the class hierarchy. This constant individual movement across class lines lessens the harsh impact of class confrontation.

The pages of Middle Eastern history are dotted with dramatic examples of individual and group mobility. As one writer puts it, in the Middle East "one can be a liar in the morning, a vizir in the evening, and perhaps hanged on the following day." [86] Stretching vertically through the class structure are a number of shifting ladders of group configurations that, although unsteady and unpredictable, nonetheless can be negotiated by enterprising individuals. Many of the rungs of such ladders are difficult to discern because of the informal and con-

---

[86] Vincent Monteil, *Morocco* (New York: Viking Press, 1964), p. 141, as quoted in Rosen, "Rural Political Process," p. 223.

cealed nature of their formation. Informal groups are, in general, the most reliable of the groups that span class divisions. Examples of groups that connect the middle and upper classes include military officer cliques, mystic orders, high administrative caucuses, and interfamilial marriage clusters. Let us examing the last example in more depth.

Nuclear families more often tend to be intraclass groups than do extended families, since the latter include a larger number of individuals, each striving to improve his own position in the social system. But once one member of either a nuclear or an extended family is able to improve his class standing, he subsequently acts as a force that helps to propel other family members forward in the power structure. At the very minimum, the individual in the higher class will be able to protect and defend his family's interests. Always, however, when familial membership is spread among classes, it acts as a brake upon class tension and conflict. A more significant aspect of family-group structure in relation to class interaction is the mechanism of interfamilial marriage. In the Middle East, the marriage of two individuals is better described as the union of two families. When the marriage partners are of different social classes, entire family clusters develop relatively tight interclass relationships. Indeed, it is very common and increasingly possible for individuals of middle-class background to search consciously for a mate who comes from a powerful upper-class family.

Many members of the middle-class intelligentsia attempt to improve their power positions by marrying into the ruling class. Some pursue this strategy in a very calculating manner. Others are torn between their commitment to merit and achievement and their desire to gain enough political leverage to enable them to implement their social and political ideas. Practically all of them are forced to rely upon familial connections at many junctures in their professional and political lives. To the more professionally competent and politically radical among them, this is unpalatable business, and many are visibly embarrassed by the fact that they either belong to the ruling class or have married into it. Middle-class professionals thus find themselves in the unenviable position of denigrating their familial ties while at the same time being forced to use these ties in order to survive and advance in society. This kind of pressured compromise is another factor reducing the effectiveness of their class as a revolutionizing force. In terms of this discussion, it represents a method whereby the challenging middle class is bound to the ruling class. Family clusters cut across class lines and then serve as bridges for the upwardly mobile members of the kinship group.

Groups, then, are much more fluid collectivities than classes in the Middle East because they have much greater ranges of mobility. A class can improve its position only by rather limited incremental movements. The ruling class will always be the upper class, and so it is down the line. By definition, classes must always remain in a power hierarchy. Individuals and groups, on the other hand, can rise dramatically or fall meteorically within the social structure. The great movement of individuals and groups increases flexibility in a class structure that would otherwise be fragile and much more susceptible to upheaval and radical change.

The social structure described above is a formidable obstacle to the processes of modernization and political development that are under way in the Middle East. The traditional social system refuses to be torn, and the basic power and authority relations that make up this system are extraordinarily difficult to uproot. Since class conflict, often the agent of transformation, is neutralized, change involves chipping away at pieces of the mosaic. This modifying change seldom disturbs the underlying network of power relations that is the basis for the group and class structure of Middle Eastern societies.

The situation analyzed above varies considerably from one Middle Eastern society to another. Some societies, for example, are relatively congenial to modernization and political development. In these societies, the lines of horizontal stratification are only weakly intersected by communal cleavages. As a result, the traditional social structure is more easily torn, because class configurations are more cohesive internally and more bared to conflict externally. In Turkey, Tunisia, and Egypt, for example, the natural lines of class conflict and power confrontation are relatively infrequently intersected by ethnic, religious, and tribal divisions. In such countries as Syria and Iraq, on the other hand, communalism and the many vertical strands of stratification soften class confrontation and invest the traditional system with a stability nourished by a vast interlocking network of competing groups.

Much can be explained about the outbreak of the Lebanese civil war when it is recognized that the lines separating ethnic and religious groups had come to coincide more and more closely with class lines. The groups lost their cross-cutting character and gradually reinforced the explosive class divisions. In other words, the vertical structure of stratification gradually collapsed until it became a reinforcing part of the system of conflicting classes. The Lebanese upper class was dominated by Christian Arabs, while the lower class was overwhelmingly Muslim. Although there was some noticeable overlap, this had become less the case with time. When the explosion came, therefore, it was fueled by both group and class conflict. The presence of the Palestinians, a highly politicized appendage to the Lebanese lower class, only exacerbated the struggle. When group and class lines begin to coincide in the Middle East, the system begins to lose its balanced stability. Violent conflict is often the result, and the consequent changes can either accelerate or retard development. In Chapters IV and V, we will examine those individuals who do most to determine the directions these changes will take.

CHAPTER IV

The Politics of Patrimonial Leadership

AN IMPORTANT COMPONENT of the politics of power and change in the Middle East is the issue of political leadership. Although societies are composed of an interrelated network of groups and classes, there is always one group of individuals who have a disproportionate amount of power and political influence. Sometimes referred to as the political elite, this group of leaders to a large degree shapes the political style and molds the political system of a society. In this chapter, we shall analyze the social characteristics and political methodology of Muslim leadership. In the process, it is also important for us to understand how individuals are recruited into leadership positions.[1]

Middle Eastern political leaders vary considerably from country to country. As the last stronghold of absolute monarchy in the world, the Middle East is the home of four major kingdoms

---

[1] The growing scholarly interest in Middle Eastern leadership patterns is seen in the publication of several collections of articles analyzing the political elites of various Middle Eastern countries. See George Lenczowski, ed., *Political Elites in the Middle East* (Washington, D.C.: American Enterprise Institute, 1975); Frank Tachau, ed., *Political Elites and Political Development in the Middle East* (Cambridge, Mass.: Schenkman Publishing Co., 1975); I. William Zartman, ed., *Elites in the Middle East* (New York: Praeger Publishers, 1980); and I. William Zartman *et al.*, *Political Elites in Arab North Africa* (New York: Longman, 1982).

and ten mini-monarchies located along the Persian Gulf. In order of ruling experience, the major monarchs include the following: King Hussein of Jordan, King Hassan of Morocco, Sultan Qabus of Oman, and King Fahd of Saudi Arabia. The other countries are almost all governed by modern authoritarian leaders, most of whom came to power as the result of a military coup or national war of independence. In Iran, a form of Islamic authoritarianism and fundamentalism was born in 1979 and remains alive today. Besides these types of authoritarian control, more representative structures exist in Israel and, to a lesser degree these days, in Turkey.

Despite all the differences that separate Middle Eastern leaders and elites, there are in the Muslim world a number of deep-seated and persisting similarities in rule. These similarities, which are the subject of this chapter, have existed throughout Islamic history and can be traced to the days of the Prophet Muhammad, himself the model par excellence of political leadership.

The processes of leadership in the Islamic Middle East have been both represented and shaped by the life of Muhammad. Through the establishment of a new world community in the seventh century, the Prophet combined the roles of messenger of God and leader of men. Today, throughout the Islamic world, millions of Muslims continue to pattern their lives after his. It is not surprising, therefore, that twentieth-century Muslim political leaders often have styles and use strategies that are very similar to those instituted by the Prophet Muhammad in Arabia some 1,400 years ago.

The very success of Muhammad as a political leader is one of the reasons that he remains a shadowy, distorted, and even frightening figure to many Westerners. In the pantheon of truly great world leaders, the Prophet has been the one most maligned by Western writers, who have for centuries found him an extremely difficult figure to interpret sympathetically. He has been presented in Western literature as a thug, sorcerer, sex fiend, murderer, and epileptic, and even as a defrocked Roman Catholic priest. The ridiculous extreme of this perspective is seen in Guibert de Nogent's statement that Muhammad died "through excessive drunkenness and that his corpse was eaten by pigs on a dung-hill, explaining why the flesh of this animal and wine are prohibited." [2]

Dante's and Voltaire's views on the subject were only slightly more enlightened than those of de Nogent, and Diderot stated that Muhammad was "the greatest friend of woman and the greatest enemy of sober reason who ever lived." [3] Even Edward Gibbon and Washington Irving, whose writings about Muhammad were more objective, could not but view him negatively in the end. In concluding *Mahomet and His Successors*, Irving says that Muhammad had "mental hallucinations," which "continued more or less to bewilder him with a species of monomania to the end of his career, and that he died in the delusive belief of his mission as a prophet." [4]

These views of Muhammad undoubtedly result from ignorance and from insecurity because of the threat that his mission carried for the Western world. After all, Islam has been the only major non-Western, non-Christian movement that both posed a genuine political threat and provided an attractive alternative civilization while challenging Christendom on its own soil. Today, our understanding of the genius of Muhammad's leadership as well as of the patterns of rule of the contemporary leaders of Islamic countries remains sketchy and superficial. The fact that partisan Muslim scholars have tended to view Muhammad idealistically, defensively, and uncritically has not helped to improve this situation. In this chapter, we will attempt to avoid both extremes by analyzing Muhammad primarily and objectively as a political leader. By beginning our analysis with the general patterns of rule that Muhammad generated, we hope to be better able to understand the more recent political leaders to be discussed in chapter 5.

MUHAMMAD: THE POLITICS OF A PROPHET

The Prophet Muhammad was born in Mecca in 570. Social and political life was then dominated by the interaction be-

---

[2] Emile Dermenghem, *The Life of Mahomet* (London: George Routledge and Sons, 1930), p. 119.

[3] Tor Andrae, *Mohammed: The Man and His Faith* (New York: Barnes and Noble, 1936), p. 175.

[4] Irving, *Mahomet and His Successors*, vol. 1 (New York: G. P. Putnam's Sons, 1893), p. 491.

tween clans and tribes, and desert nomads were gradually moving into a more settled world of commerce and trade. This was a time of transition marked by continual feuds among clans and by intense commercial rivalry. The Prophet's personal environment was also unstable; by the time he was six, he had lost both of his parents. Muhammad was raised first by his grandfather and then by his uncle Abu Talib, who was the head of the clan of Hashim. Although little is actually known about his early life, it is safe to assume that he worked in menial positions related mainly to commerce and caravans. During his first 25 years, Muhammad gained firsthand experience and knowledge of the business, religion, and politics of the day. We know that he traveled to Syria and was in constant touch with peoples throughout that part of the world.

As an orphan and a member of one of the declining clans of the Quraysh tribe, Muhammad lacked many of the resources and contacts necessary to develop any important influence of his own. The first turning point in his life was, therefore, his marriage to the wealthy and twice-widowed Khadija. For the next two decades, Muhammad lived in the community as a prosperous and influential businessman. During this time, he acquired contacts and influence that were to be of fundamental importance to him in his role as prophet and preacher.

In about 610, Muhammad began receiving revelations, and shortly thereafter he began preaching in Mecca and presenting himself as a prophet. Although there were many Christians and Jews in Arabia at that time, most of the peoples were pagans and worshipped many gods. Muhammad preached the greatness and goodness of one God and emphasized the Judeo-Christian prophetic tradition. Few Meccans, however, chose to follow him. His earliest converts included his wife Khadija, his cousin Ali, his adopted son Zayd Ibn Haritha, and a respected and prominent Meccan, Abu Bakr.

As Muhammad continued his preaching and teaching, opposition to him grew. The reasons were many. He threatened the established economic and political order of the day, including the handsome income of the Meccans as custodians of the pagan shrines in their city. In a climate of escalating commerce and preoccupation with profit, his teachings emphasized the illusory nature of material wealth while encouraging such virtues as generosity, charity, and compassion. His criticism of the obsession for material gain was especially provoking, since he had made his own fortune in commerce. By striking at the idea of accumulating wealth, the Prophet was delivering a frontal attack on the Meccan lifestyle. Besides presenting an economic challenge, Muhammad posed a serious political threat to the leaders of Mecca. By questioning the economic basis of society and attacking the established order, the Prophet could only weaken the existing system. By attracting followers and building a community of his own, he offered the possibility of an alternative order. It is small wonder that the political leaders and influential persons in Meccan society became his dogged enemies. Muhammad's following was dominated by the young, the poor, and the dispossessed.

Despite this strong opposition, the Prophet was able to build the core of his Muslim movement while in Mecca. He received most of his revelations and gathered his original followers there during a decade of intense missionary activity. There are two basic reasons why this was possible. First, Muhammad was relatively discreet and diplomatic about his activities. His first efforts were directed toward those in whom he had most trust, such as close relatives, fellow clansmen, and intimate friends.[5] At times, important converts were brought into the community through marriage. This was the case with Uthman, a wealthy merchant who married a daughter of Muhammad's. Outside of this intimate circle of family and friends, attention was directed to those individuals who were most prone to conversion because of their peculiar position in society. D. S. Margoliouth writes, for example, that "Abu Bakr probably was aware that women are more amenable to conversion than men, resident foreigners than natives, slaves than freemen, persons in distress than persons in prosperity and affluence." [6]

---

[5] One of the Prophet's very first converts was Abu Bakr, an influential Meccan cloth merchant. He was an extremely valuable ally and possessed a "readiness to follow the fortunes of some one else with complete and blind devotion, never questioning nor looking back; to have believed much was with him a reason for believing more. Mohammad, a shrewd judge of man, perceived this quality and used it." D. S. Margoliouth, *Mohammed and The Rise of Islam,* 3d ed. (New York: G. P. Putnam's Sons, 1905), pp. 83–84.

[6] *Ibid.*, p. 97.

A number of slaves were among the first to embrace the teachings of Muhammad. Finally, the meetings and activities of the first Muslims were carried out very quietly and unostentatiously. They took place in informal settings and personal homes, where they would not invite direct confrontation and public condemnation. The most famous site of this kind was the home of al-Arqam, where Muhammad could usually be found during the day and where his followers came and went at their convenience. From the very earliest days of its development, therefore, Islam has been what has been described as a "secret society." [7]

The second explanation for the Prophet's ability to survive in Mecca concerns the clan politics of the time. Each clan had learned that, in the interests of self-preservation, individual clan members had to be protected from all threats emanating from outside the clan. An individual could rely deeply on the support and protection of his fellow clansmen. Muhammad's clan, headed by his uncle Abu Talib, stood by him and provided him with a protective umbrella against his powerful opponents. Unable to penetrate this kind of clan unity, the opposition managed to institute a policy of isolating and boycotting Muhammad's entire clan. But in this system of seventh-century politics, even the boycott failed and was abandoned after two years.

The Prophet was able to continue his activities in Mecca as long as his own clan shielded him. However, with the death of Abu Talib in 619, and the accession of Abu Lahab as head of the Hashim clan, Muhammad lost his clan's protective support. In the same year, his wife Khadija died and he was gradually forced out of Mecca. After numerous hardships, he fled to Medina in 622 in what is known in history as the *hijra* ("Hegira"). He was welcomed in Medina, a city torn by interclan strife and an economic competitor of Mecca. It is generally argued that the Medinans saw in Muhammad a leader who could serve as an effective and objective mediator between the constantly warring factions in their city. At the same time, they felt that the enemy of Mecca would serve them as a

7 See *ibid.*, pp. 83–117.

friend, and that Meccan hegemony in the area would in this way be weakened.

The significance of the hijra to Islamic political development cannot be overemphasized. It marked the beginning of the end of parochial clan politics and the origination of the *umma,* or "community." Clan divisions were to lose their meaning as clans were absorbed into a new religion and a new way of life. The community now had a "religious base" and could be described as a kind of "supertribe." [8] It was during his residence in Medina that Muhammad came to practice the style of leadership that formed the great Islamic community. During these last ten years of his life, he consolidated his position in Medina, defeated and took control of Mecca, converted numerous Arabian tribes and clans to his cause, and began a campaign of expansion that was to continue and spread long after his death.

Crucial to the success of Muhammad in Medina were his military campaigns, which escalated through time. Initially, they were confined to small *razzias,* or "raids," against Meccan commercial caravans. Although these campaigns had very limited success in terms of capture and booty, they served the important purpose of binding together individuals of different clans and backgrounds in a common cause. It was nearly two years before a Meccan caravan was actually captured. Through the constant camaraderie in the relatively safe enterprise of caravan raiding, the followers of Muhammad gradually developed an esprit de corps that enabled them to defeat the Meccans in the critical battles that were to follow. In this regard, it is instructive to note that the extraordinarily significant battle of Badr in 624 developed out of an intended caravan raid. In this battle, the Prophet's forces decisively defeated the Meccans and killed more than a dozen of their most important leaders. One year later, Muhammad's forces fought a large attacking Meccan expedition to a standstill in the battle of Uhud. In this encounter, the Prophet himself played an important part in the fighting. Finally, in 627 Muhammad and

[8] W. Montgomery Watt, *Muhammad: Prophet and Statesman* (London: Oxford University Press, 1961), pp. 94–95.

his community withstood a two-week siege of Medina. This was the last great effort by the Meccans to defeat the new community.

At Medina, the Prophet built solidarity into the community in a variety of ways. Besides the numerous military campaigns directed against a common enemy, there were other catalysts to unity. Those clans in Medina that adamantly opposed Muhammad politically and ideologically were either expelled or destroyed. Preeminent among these opposition groups were the three Jewish clans of Qaynuqa, Nadir, and Qurayza. Scattered cases of political assassination also indicate that Muhammad condoned the use of this kind of force against particularly disruptive and resistant personalities.[9] This kind of civil violence was, however, engaged in only as a last resort. The emphasis was upon conversion and reconciliation. A primary means of accomplishing reconciliation was the web of intermarriage that not only bound the Emigrants (original Muslims from Mecca) closer together, but also helped bind the Emigrants to the Helpers (Medinan Muslims).

The most outstanding example of the Prophet's flair for consolidation by compromise and reconciliation is the Treaty of Hudaybiya, which was negotiated in 628. Muhammad decided to make a pilgrimage to Mecca and was accompanied by some 1,500 men. The Meccans, who doubted his intentions and suspected a military invasion, prepared to fight. Muhammad camped at al-Hudaybiya on the outskirts of Mecca and from there entered into negotiations with the Meccans. In the end, an agreement was reached whereby the Prophet and his men were to return to Medina. They had permission, however, to return in the following year and carry out their pilgrimage. Another point in the treaty provided for a ten-year nonaggression pact between the Muslims and the Meccans. Despite strong pressures from numerous individuals in his own entourage who considered the expedition a failure, Muhammad

---

9 An example was the poet Ka'b Ibn al-Ashraf, who continually and bitingly attacked Muhammad and the Muslims. He went so far as to travel from Medina to Mecca, where he attacked the Muslim community in his poetry. He was assassinated in A.D. 624.

returned to Medina. In so doing, he was implementing a brilliant policy of diplomatic tact that insured the peaceful conquest of Mecca two years later. The treaty convinced the Meccans that the Prophet was a reasonable man, that he did not want conflict, and that he did not plan to destroy Mecca. The journey to Hudaybiya was a political move, not a religious pilgrimage.

When the Prophet Muhammad died in 632, he left behind a community of peoples that was to expand and become one of the great civilizations of history. Tribes and clans, cities and empires were drawn together and unified under the ideology of Islam. The political acumen and astute leadership of Muhammad were instrumental in making this possible. These and other qualities of the Prophet have been noted and imitated by Muslims for centuries; Muhammad is the ideal model for all Believers. The reasons are not only that he was the Seal of the Prophets, the Mirror of the Almighty, and the Founder of Islam, but also that he was intensely human. Unlike Christ, Muhammad was not considered divine. One leading Islamic scholar writes that the Prophet "married, had a household, was a father and moreover he was ruler and judge and had also to fight many wars in which he had to undergo painful ordeals." [10] In the words of another analyst: "It is a likeable characteristic of Mohammad that he never claimed perfection or infallibility, but always admitted frankly that he was guilty of shortcomings and mistakes like other men." [11] He lived, in short, as a convincing and believable model after whom all Muslims could pattern their lives.

The Course of Compromise. Muhammad was born into a world of interpersonal feuding, factional strife, and tribal conflict. The political system was an atomistic one in which families and clans survived by remaining in a constant state of embattlement against other families and clans. The lines of confrontation that crisscrossed the system were drawn so

[10] Seyyed Hossein Nasr, *Ideals and Realities of Islam* (London: George Allen and Unwin, 1966), p. 69.
[11] Andrae, *Mohammed,* p. 179.

rigidly that there was little room for flexible policies of retreat and advance. This was an era of the blood feud, punitive reprisal, and the *lex talionis* ("law of retaliation"). It was into this climate of division and distrust that the Prophet carried the strategy and spirit of compromise. This was, of course, essential if social integration and political unity were to be achieved at all. The need to unite was a fundamental issue in the Middle East then, and it remains a basic issue in the Middle East today. A leader's political success rests to a great extent upon his ability to integrate and unite the divided and fragmented groups that compose society. An indispensable tool to the implementation of this kind of program is a strategy of political flexibility and compromise.

Muhammad's willingness to compromise is particularly noteworthy because of the climate of feuding in which it occurred. One of the most dramatic demonstrations of this talent is, of course, the Treaty of Hudaybiya referred to earlier. This is one demonstration of the manner in which age-old hatreds and animosities were overcome. After twenty years of struggle with the Meccans, the Prophet returned victorious to Mecca in the year 630. "There, at a moment when the very people who had caused untold hardships and trials for the Prophet, were completely subdued by him, instead of thinking of vengeance, which was certainly his due, he forgave them." [12] Although many Islamic scholars tend to explain this forbearance in terms of the great nobility, generosity, and compassion of the Prophet, it can also be analyzed as one in a long series of wise political policies. It is significant, however, that the moral virtue of compassion and the political strategy of compromise were inseparably linked in the career of Muhammad. This again shows the intimate relation between the sociopolitical activity of the Prophet and the ideology of Islam.

Throughout his political career, Muhammad tried to soften confrontation and to gain strength and unity by bargaining. Thus, he and his followers entered numerous marriage pacts with both actual and potential opposition forces. And many tribes joined the Muslim community as a result of the Proph-

[12] Nasr, *Ideals and Realities*, pp. 71–72.

et's long and peaceful march to Tabuk on the Gulf of Aqaba in 630. When Muhammad dispatched two missions to Yemen, he told the leaders of both missions: "Make it easy and do not make it too difficult. Be the carriers of good tidings, and do not cause disaffection." [13] Resort to violence and warfare occurred only after other avenues to agreement had been closed.

The success of tribal societies in developing a relatively respected and influential place in the world community is almost directly proportional to their ability to overcome internal dissension and to resist external encroachment. The clans or tribes in Middle Eastern history that have formed the basis for national communities or international empires have been precisely those that have been able to overlook past conflicts and to weld themselves into political units seeking common goals. The will and capacity to compromise at critical junctures is an essential element in this process of integration. The Prophet's style of political leadership included this ingredient.

The Character of Charisma. The Prophet Muhammad viewed himself "as a man who had been given a special commission by God." [14] Although he was thoroughly human, he was not an ordinary human. He was the messenger and prophet of God, and his spiritual teachings were bound up in his social and political life. According to German sociologist Max Weber, a charismatic indivdual is one who "is set apart from ordinary men and treated as endowed with supernatural, superhuman, or at least specifically exceptional powers or qualities." [15] A charismatic leader is one who possesses a special grace and whose followers are irresistibly drawn to him because of this grace. There is a sensed otherworldly quality that engenders in others trust, commitment, and a willingness to follow. In Islam, there is an important concept that is remarkably similar to the idea of charisma. This is the concept *baraka*,

[13] Hasan al-Karmi, "The Prophet Muhammad and the Spirit of Compromise," *Islamic Quarterly* 8 (July and December 1964):90.

[14] Watt, *Muhammad*, p. 15.

[15] Max Weber, *The Theory of Social and Economic Organization* (New York: Oxford University Press, 1947), p. 358.

which is a special blessing of divine origin. "God can implant an emanation of *baraka* in the person of his prophets and saints: Muhammad and his descendants are especially endowed therewith. These sacred personages, in their turn, may communicate the effluvia of their supernatural potential to ordinary men. . . ." [16] In contemporary political analysis, the term *charismatic* has come to be applied so loosely and indiscriminately that it has lost the force of its original meaning. If one stands by the Weberian definition, however, genuinely charismatic leaders have been rather rare in world history. Despite the exclusiveness of this definition, the Prophet Muhammad remains an outstanding case of the charismatic leader and may in fact be the prototype of this rare kind of personality.

All of Muhammad's personal, social, and political activities carried a deep spiritual significance. As a prophet and receptacle of revelation, he held an extraordinary position in the eyes of his followers. The teachings and tenets of Islam became the ideology of his rule, and all aspects of community life were regulated by this ideology. Muhammad's charisma was derived from his role as prophet of God and publicizer of the word of God. As a result, his position as political leader had an extremely solid ideological foundation. Members of the Islamic community, because they were Muslims, considered Muhammad to be the temporal, social, political, and religious leader of society. Muhammad "had been marked out from his early youth, even from his birth, by supernatural signs and qualities." [17] He was a charismatic personality in the full sense of that term.

One of the basic principles of political leadership is that a leader be able to justify his special position by developing a supporting system of ideas and ideals. This kind of ideology may bear little relation to the hard realities of politics and society, but it can play a crucial role in enabling a leader to maintain his rule and to institute effective policies. Muhammad emerges as a model of success in this regard, since the

---

[16] G. S. Colin, "Baraka," *The Encyclopedia of Islam,* new ed. (London: Luzac and Co., 1960), Vol. 1:1032.

[17] Watt, *Muhammad,* p. 2.

divine and the human, and the spiritual and the material, are inextricably entwined in his message. Muslims did not think of questioning his authority in the community. Thus, he stands in great contrast to numerous contemporary Muslim leaders, who assiduously attempt to build supportive ideologies only on the basis of flimsy and fabricated relationships to Islam or to the Prophet himself.

Much of the appeal of Muhammad's ideological message undoubtedly derived from the social and political content of that message. Islam called for equality, compassion, and unity in a world dominated by inequality, self-aggrandizement, and disunity. In its stress upon equality and simplicity, it appealed to the downtrodden masses. And Muhammad himself lived what he preached. Thus, even Edward Gibbon could write: "The good sense of Mohammed despised the pomp of royalty; the apostle of God submitted to the menial offices of the family; he kindled the fire, swept the floor, milked the ewes, and mended with his own hands his shoes and his woollen garment." [18] In its emphasis upon unity and integration, on the other hand, Islam offered much to the middle and upper strata in society. As the prophet who announced this message and as a leader who lived by it, Muhammad charismatically built the foundation of a civilization.

The Politics of Personalism. Another pattern of politics that enabled the Prophet Muhammad to gain and consolidate a strong leadership position in the nascent Islamic community was the pervasive pattern of personalism. In societies where clans and kinship groups were the key social and political realities of life, personal ties were the basic channels of power and influence. By analyzing and exploiting the intricate web of personal relations that existed in seventh-century Arabia, Muhammad and his associates were better able to form their

[18] Gibbon, *Decline and Fall of the Roman Empire,* (New York: The Modern Library, 1932), Vol. 3:116. No matter what their ultimate judgment concerning Muhammad might be, well-known Western interpreters of world history are united in their recognition of the simple and spartan life that he led. Besides Gibbon, Toynbee and Durant also comment specifically about this facet of Muhammad's life.

new community. Abu Bakr's expertise as a genealogist, which is emphasized in many sources, is highly significant when viewed in this light. As Muhammad's chief advisor, Abu Bakr continually used his deep knowledge of the complex relations of kinship, as well as of the factions and feuding, that marked the society of the day.

One of the major means of consolidation and integration for the Prophet was the manipulation of this personal web through marriage. For Muhammad, "many of his marriages were political ones which, in the prevalent social structure of Arabia, guaranteed the *consolidation* of the newly founded Muslim community. Multiple marriage, for him, as is true of Islam in general, was not so much enjoyment as responsibility and a means of *integration* of the newly founded society." [19] Muhammad married at least nine times, and one could argue that all of his marriages, even the union with Khadija, were political in nature. W. Montgomery Watt writes that for a "poor orphan" to make his way, "the one possibility was to find a rich woman to marry him, so that he could, as it were, enter into a business partnership with her." [20] It was through marriage that the Prophet hardened the nucleus of his community, while softening the resistance of those outside the community.

The central leadership of the Islamic community was tightly bound together through marriage, since the Prophet developed family ties with those among his closest followers who were later to become the first four caliphs (see Figure IV.1). Muhammad himself married A'isha and Hafsa, who were the daughters of Abu Bakr and Umar, respectively. At the same

[19] Nasr, *Ideals and Realities*, p. 70. Italics ours.

[20] Watt, *Muhammad*, p. 10. Watt cannot seem to emphasize enough the importance of the political motive in the Prophet's various marriages. In this study alone, he makes the argument in eight separate places. See pp. 10–12, 79, 102–103, 131, 155–157, 195, 206, 233. In another study Watt writes that "all Muhammad's own marriages can be seen to have a tendency to promote friendly relations in the political sphere." See Watt, *Muhammad at Medina* (Oxford: Clarendon Press, 1956), p. 287. Although, like Watt, we have stressed the political dimensions of Muhammad's marriages, we do not mean to deny the human and personal motives that were also obviously involved.

FIGURE IV.1   *Consolidation by Marriage: The Core of the Community*

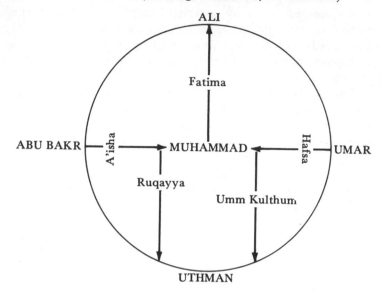

time, he married three of his own daughters to Uthman and
Ali. Ali married Fatima, and Uthman first wedded Ruqayya
and then upon her death renewed this important tie by marrying her sister Umm Kulthum.[21] The concern for holding the
community together can also be seen in the tendency for leading Muslims to marry the widows of those members of the
community who died or were killed in battle. Four of the
Prophet's wives, for example, were widows of prominent early
Muslims. Three of these Muslims had been killed in the important conflicts at Badr and Uhud.

The second category of marriages involved those that were
contracted with members of potential or actual opposition
forces. Many personal ties were developed with tribal groups
throughout Arabia by means of this mechanism. Muhammad
himself married three women who were the daughters of non-
Muslim tribal notables. In each case, the marriage neutralized
much political tension. The most important personal ties es-

---

[21] Ali also married a granddaughter of Muhammad's while Umar married both a granddaughter of Muhammad's and a daughter of Ali's.

tablished through wedlock, however, were those involving the opposition in Mecca. By marrying the daughter of the influential Meccan leader Abu Sufyan, and then one year later wedding the sister-in-law of the new head of the Meccan clan of Hashim, al-Abbas, Muhammad managed to establish intimate personal ties that were crucial to his tranquil conquest of Mecca. This two-pronged policy of developing personal relations both to strengthen an ongoing alliance and to absorb opposition forces is reflected in a split that occurred among Muhammad's wives. The wives divided into two factions — those who had come from within the Muslim community itself and those whose original roots had been in the opposition clans in Mecca.[22]

The original Muslim community functioned politically solely on the basis of personalities and personalism. In this sense, it differed very little from the pre-Islamic style of tribal and clan politics. Ruling institutions such as formal administrative organizations were unknown. The Prophet appointed specific individuals to lead military campaigns, diplomatic expeditions, and economic missions, depending upon the exigencies of the moment. As we have seen in the case of the marriage mechanism, this political personalism had real advantages. Not the least of these was the introduction of a degree of social and political flexibility, which is crucial in the construction of a new social and political system.

The Unity of the Community. Through the interrelated patterns of compromise, charisma, and personalism, the Prophet Muhammad was able to build integrative patterns into a system otherwise prone to disintegration. Through a universal message delivered by a charismatic leader, peoples of widely differing background were attracted to a single community. This process of integration and consolidation is the main principle of Muhammad's message, for, as Seyyed Hossein Nasr has written, "Unity is the alpha and omega of Islam." [23] Muham-

22 W. Montgomery Watt, " 'Ā'ishā Bint Abī Bakr," *The Encyclopedia of Islam,* new ed. (London: Luzac and Co., 1960), Vol. 1:308.
23 Nasr, *Ideals and Realities,* p. 29.

mad's charisma was an integrating force that intertwined the spiritual with the material and combined the social, the religious, and the political. The leader himself exhibited an internal unity by combining such virtues as compassion and strength, and this in turn strengthened his charismatic appeal.[24] The ideology professed by a charismatic personality was a key ingredient in sealing the fissures and rifts that characterized the social structure. The more practical political policies of compromise and personalism as adopted and implemented by Muhammad then enabled him to confront on a daily basis the centrifugal social tendencies. The capacity to compromise dulled old antagonisms and hatreds in a way that allowed policies of personalism to acquire new meaning. Personal ties could now signal a kind of cooperation and conciliation that more often than not led to conversion and consolidation. These three qualities of compromise, charisma, and personalism, were the key elements in the Prophet Muhammad's style of leadership.

PATTERNS OF PATRIMONIALISM IN THE MIDDLE EAST

> *My good Pasha, the will of the people emanates from my will!*
>
> *King Farouk of Egypt* [25]

In his important analysis and typology of traditional political systems, Max Weber includes two types that he labels patriarchal and patrimonial systems.[26] The patriarchal system is the core of all traditional systems and is generally confined to household kinship groups. In this kind of system, the authority relation is one that binds master and family. The head

---

[24] For an interesting discussion of this point, see Frithjof Schuon, *Understanding Islam* (London: George Allen and Unwin, 1963), pp. 87–105.

[25] As quoted in P. J. Vatikiotis, *The Egyptian Army in Politics: Pattern for New Nations?* (Bloomington, Ind.: Indiana University Press, 1961), p. 39.

[26] A third type is the feudal system, which was the dominant traditional system in Western societies. For the presentation of Weber's analysis of patriarchal and patrimonial politics, see Weber, *The Theory of Social and Economic Organization*, pp. 341–358; and Reinhard Bendix, *Max Weber: An Intellectual Portrait* (Garden City, N.Y.: Doubleday and Co., 1962), pp. 330–360.

of the household "has no administrative staff and no machinery to enforce his will.... The members of the household stand in an entirely personal relation to him. They obey him and he commands them in the belief that his right and their duty are part of an inviolable order that has the sanctity of immemorial tradition. Originally the efficacy of this belief depended on the fear of magical evils that would befall the innovator and the community that condoned a breach of custom." [27] The patrimonial system, on the other hand, is one in which an identifiable administrative structure develops and spreads throughout the particular society or empire. The tasks of government become more specialized, complex, and elaborate. As a result, the ruler's relation with the ruled tends to be filtered through a huge network of bureaucrats. Owing to the introduction of a more complex and differentiated administrative apparatus, the emphasis on the mysterious and the magical becomes somewhat softened.

The literature that has attempted to discuss and utilize this Weberian typology has greatly overemphasized the differences between the patriarchal and patrimonial forms of rule. This has resulted in a misplaced preoccupation with such issues as specialization of roles and differentiation of structures. The key to understanding the traditional processes of leadership is the fundamental human relations that bind ruler and ruled. These were shaped in the patriarchal environment and were hardened and routinized in the patrimonial system. In essence, the patrimonial form of rule represents little more than an extension and expansion of the patriarchal system. The relations that bind ruler and ruled, leader and led, master and servant, and king and subject are fundamentally the same in both Weberian categories. Reinhard Bendix defines patrimonial rule, therefore, as "an extension of the ruler's household in which the relation between the ruler and his officials remains on the basis of paternal authority and filial dependence." [28]

In most Islamic societies, patrimonial patterns of leadership

27 Bendix, *Max Weber*, pp. 330–331.
28 *Ibid.*, p. 360.

have been dominant. The particular manifestation of patrimonial rule that has marked these societies is referred to by Manfred Halpern as a "relationship of emanation." The politics of emanation involves an "encounter in which one treats the other solely as an extension of one's self. The other accepts the denial of his own separate identity because of the mysterious and overwhelming power of the source of this emanation — a yielding which is rewarded with total security." [29] When the Spanish Ummayad caliph Abd al-Rahman al-Nasir died at the turn of the tenth century after fifty years of rule, he was publicly eulogized in terms that capture the basic meaning of rule by emanation: "The souls of the people were absorbed in his soul: when he died they died also." [30] There is little doubt that this caliph possessed baraka in abundance. In the Islamic world, where religion and politics have always been inseparable, shahs, sultans, and shaykhs have tended to rule in a paternal, patriarchal, and patrimonial manner. Government has been personal, and both civil and military bureaucracies have been little more than extensions of the leader. In the cases of the Ottoman, Safavid, and Moghul empires, the royal household developed into a huge administrative octopus, with the leader as head and the leader's gigantic retinue of personal servants and confidants as tentacles. In patrimonial politics, "bureaucratic recruitment and advances are based on personal confidence and not on objective qualifications; they reflect the more or less precarious balance reached by the prince in his effort to create and maintain a bureaucracy completely dependent upon his power. In each case, the position of the patrimonial bureaucrat must remain what it originally was — an

---

[29] Halpern, "Four Contrasting Repertories of Human Relations in Islam," *Psychological Dimensions of Near Eastern Studies,* ed. by L. Carl Brown and Norman Itzkowitz (Princeton, N.J.: Darwin Press, 1977), p. 64. In this article, Halpern sensitively explores the significance of the politics of emanation to the Middle Eastern peoples and political systems. We have chosen to emphasize his conceptualization of emanation as the central pattern in patrimonialism.

[30] Lisan al-Din Ibn Khatib, [Book of works by leading authors concerning those accepted as kings of Islam] (Rabat, Morocco: New Press, 1934), p. 44. In Arabic.

emanation of his relation of purely personal submission to the Lord. . . ." [31]

In the patrimonial Middle East, the sovereign is located at the center of the political system. He is surrounded by advisers, ministers, military leaders, personal secretaries, and confidants. The one thing that all members of this inner circle share is unquestioned personal loyalty to the leader. This is best indicated by their continual reflection of the will and personality of that leader. These individuals may relate submissively and passively to the leader, but they do not relate in this way to their own peers and followers. Here, they are caught up in the most intense manipulations and machinations possible.[32] The reason for this, of course, is that a minister who relates passively to a monarch on one level is the central source of leadership on another level. Therefore, within his own ministry, he may be the emanating influence, and his subordinates (deputy ministers, director generals, and so on) survive by remaining passive before him. Although the vertical relations tend to be one-sided, the horizontal patterns are characterized by balanced rivalry. Those of relatively equal power and authority are locked in constant conflict and struggle. This conflict can occur only below the level of the sovereign, since the sovereign has no equals in a patrimonial context. This kind of division and rivalry is constantly being sharpened by the competition among the rivals to demonstrate the greatest loyalty and submission to the leader. The leader, in turn, encourages and manipulates this competition. The traditional politics of patrimonial leadership in the Middle East, therefore, tends to consist of chains of vertical emanation and horizontal competition that cut through the sociopolitical fabric (see Figure IV.2).

In the patrimonial style of Middle Eastern leadership, the leader becomes the fount of all important ideas and strategies. Policies and programs emanate from him. New ideas and sug-

---

[31] Magali Sarfatti, *Spanish Bureaucratic-Patrimonialism in America*, Politics of Modernization Series, no. 1 (Berkeley, Calif.: University of California Institute of International Studies, 1966), p. 8.

[32] The Watergate incident indicates that this situation is not unique to the Middle East.

FIGURE IV.2   *Patrimonial Leadership*

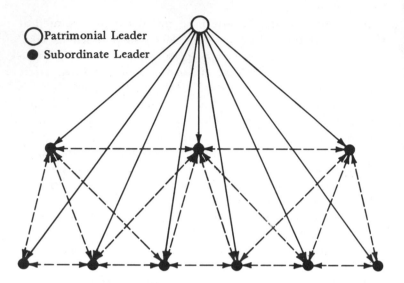

○ Patrimonial Leader
● Subordinate Leader

gestions that others might have must somehow be submitted
to the leader, who may propose them as his own. Historically,
the Middle Eastern political landscape is littered with individuals who attempted and failed to project themselves into the
political limelight through their own ideas and ambitions.
Often, they were the very closest confidants of the leader himself; by staking claim to their own political ground, they challenged the very relation of emanation and hastened their own
inevitable political demises. This is precisely what happened
when Abbasid caliph Harun al-Rashid in 803 disposed of his
powerful Barmecid friend and advisor Ja'far ibn Yahya and
imprisoned the other members of Ja'far's family. Numerous
similar examples exist in both Ottoman and Persian history.

We have already mentioned how Süleyman the Lawgiver
suddenly turned on his intimate friend the vazir Ibrahim
Pasha in 1536. The most famous example of a leader turning
against an independent-minded subordinate in Persian history
occurred in the mid-nineteenth century during the rule of the
Qajar dynasty (1779–1925). Nasir al-Din Shah, who ruled Iran
for half a century, gave the orders that led to the dismissal and

death of his strong-willed and illustrious minister Mirza Taqi Khan Amir Kabir. Mirza Taqi Khan has gone down in Persian history as that country's greatest reformer and most beloved prime minister. Because of this man's brilliance and dramatic administrative programs, the young shah's light only flickered until Mirza Taqi Khan was disposed of in 1851, after having served only three years in the post. As we shall see in Chapter V, there are many contemporary examples of this pattern.

The nearer individuals are to the patrimonial leader, the more likely they are to have their ideas accepted and put into practice by the leader. In such a personal system of politics, physical nearness to the leader is an especially significant variable in explaining the distribution of power and influence. It would be wrong to assume that in a patrimonial system those who surround the leader have no influence at all. They always exert a subtle and passive influence, largely by having their ideas absorbed into those of the leader. In such a system, "advisers" never demand, seldom suggest, and only advise when advice is actively sought. They more often applaud than appraise. Although their influence on the leader may be sporadic, their influence on everyone else will usually be very intense. The closer an adviser is to the leader, the more influential he will be both with the ruler and with the people.[33]

Middle Eastern societies have been governed by authoritarian patrimonial systems throughout most of history. Islam fostered patrimonial patterns both through its ideals and in reality. The entire philosophical framework that evolved with Islam stressed relations of emanation. The term *Islam* itself means submission, and Islam demands that all believers perfect their acceptance and reflection of the Almighty. The Prophet

---

[33] Because of the continual competition and wielding of influence that occur at all levels of Islamic society, the intricate but effective manner in which subordinates can have their ideas incorporated into those of the ruler, and the constant challenging of particular relations of emanation by those who wish to assert their own power, we cannot characterize Islamic leadership as either "Oriental despotism," to use Wittfogel's term, or "sultanism," to use Max Weber's term. As we shall see, the informal, bargaining, and balancing nature of Middle Eastern politics contradicts such an emphasis on absolute authority, total power, and hardened hierarchy.

Muhammad is the prototype of the leader linked in the chain of emanation, since he is the one who relates the material to the spiritual. Muhammad represents perfect passivity before God and perfect activity before man. He was the mirror who reflected the word of God, and "he saw nothing except in God and through God." [34] In his relations with man, however, the Prophet lived a most vigorous social, political, and religious life, since he traded, fought, judged, and ruled. He was "that warrior on horseback who halts before the mountain of Truth, passive towards the Divine Will, active towards the world. . . ." [35] As Muhammad modeled his life after the Divine, millions of Muslims labor to model their lives after his. The Prophet's community in Medina was a patrimony infused with the charisma of a special leader.

The intermeshing of religion and politics in Islam has meant that political leaders have often had the opportunity to present themselves as linked directly to God. This has helped invest them with a mysterious and otherworldly aura that has allowed them to be exalted as models to be imitated and followed by the people. This is one reason why political leaders in Islamic societies have historically attempted to trace their ancestry back to the family of the Prophet. The only innate aristocracy in Islamic civilization consists of those individuals in the community who are related to the family of the Prophet Muhammad.

The personal rivalry that has always been central to patrimonial society has led to numerous schisms and divisions within the Islamic community. What has marked all of these splinter movements, however, has been their tendency to reform themselves by placing extreme emphasis upon leadership by emanation. Part of the reason for this is the need for any political movement playing the role of challenger to legitimate its existence and its claims. This must be done as convincingly and dramatically as possible. All Shi'i societies have exhibited the patrimonial rule by emanation in its most pronounced

---

[34] Nasr, *Ideals and Realities*, p. 84.
[35] *Ibid.*, p. 9

form.[36] This is seen in the significant figure of the Imam, who is the leader par excellence in the Shi'i community.

Ali was the first Imam, and he has been succeeded by other imams, their number varying with the different sects. The critical point here is that the imam is not selected by the community, but succeeds by virtue of divine appointment, or *nass*. The imam is the vicegerent of God, and the line of imams consists of a divinely fashioned chain of emanation that is unquestioned in the minds of the believers. Whereas the Sunni caliph is an ordinary mortal, the Shi'i imams exist in a state of permanent grace that renders them infallible, impeccable, and immaculate.[37] The imam is the one who rules by the will of God and in the name of God. In the Iranian version of Shi'i Islam, the twelfth and last Imam has gone into hiding and is meanwhile represented by the important cleric leaders known as *mujtahids*. According to strict Shi'i doctrine, as representatives of the Hidden Imam, these mujtahids are the major sources of interpretation for all social, political, and religious affairs. The shahs, however, traditionally attempted to lock themselves into the legitimizing tradition of the imams. Historically, much of Iranian politics revolved about the relationship between the mujtahids and shahs as they competed for legitimacy by emanation. In the Iranian revolution of 1978–1979, the mujtahids finally triumphed and ultimately took direct control of the political system of the country.

Muhammad's early community was organized according to patrimonial principles. The Prophet stood at the head of the sociopolitical household, and personal ties and relations knit the entire community together. These relations were made particularly binding by the fact that most of the main leaders and followers were brought into the Prophet's own familial household. The dynamics of Muhammad's leadership that

---

[36] For an exceptionally fine analysis of the Fatimid caliphate, which emphasizes the theoretical aspects of patrimonial patterns of emanation, see P. J. Vatikiotis, *The Fatimid Theory of State* (Lahore, Pakistan: Orientalia Publishers, 1957).

[37] Professor Martin B. Dickson of Princeton University has clarified this particular point for us.

have been briefly sketched above highlight these patterns. Muhammad's charismatic personality and his relation to the Divine enabled individuals such as Abu Bakr to become absorbed in his affairs and to accept his leadership completely. The special charismatic nature of the Prophet's rule by emanation overcame much of the intracommunity dissension and conflict endemic to systems of patrimonial politics. It was when Muhammad died that all of these submerged dissensions broke to the surface and schisms became common.

The patrimonial leaders who succeeded the Prophet found relations of emanation less persuasive and effective. This became more and more the case as dynastic heads became further removed from the days of Muhammad's rule. Islamic history, therefore, is replete with examples of leaders at all levels and in all communities who made dramatic efforts to strengthen the patrimonial patterns by infusing new life into increasingly unbelievable relations of emanation. This was done in two complementary ways: (1) the original charismatic leaders to which the new leaders were attached were accorded supernatural status; and (2) a proclaimed leader attempted to build a special relation between himself and the earlier prototype.

In the first case, the leaders in early Islam are glorified and purified until in some instances they appear to have possessed godly qualities. This has been particularly true in the case of Ali, the fourth caliph and son-in-law of the Prophet. In the second instance, communities develop around individuals who claim to be special representatives or messengers either of these early patrimonial heroes or even of God himself. Saints and holy personages play an important role in Middle Eastern politics and society. One scholar writes, for example, that "the most characteristic social institution of North African religious life is the saint, the holy personage. As Islam does not enjoin celibacy, saints proliferate and form lineages and dynasties." [38]

---

[38] Ernest Gellner, "Sanctity, Puritanism, Secularisation and Nationalism in North Africa: A Case Study," mimeographed (n.p., n.d.), p. 1. See also Gellner's fine study, *Saints of the Atlas* (Chicago: University of Chicago Press, 1969).

Mahdis, marabouts, and imams have formed political movements of great influence in the Middle East. The Moroccan marabouts were the major force shaping the social and political systems in large areas of North Africa until the end of the nineteenth century.[39] In a patrimonial political system, the basic patterns, which often shatter and disintegrate, have traditionally been reknitted through the appearance of a new leader claiming either special supernatural power or a special relation with those who are believed to have had such power.

Patterns of leadership in the Middle East have been highly congruent from institution to institution and from community to community. In the family, school, guild, and government, patrimonialism prevails. Much of the reason for this is the influence of Islam, which penetrates all aspects of a believer's life. In patriarchal or patrimonial societies, the patriarch is the main social and political reality. He is the model, the guide, the innovator, the planner, the mediator, the chastiser, and the protector. The community wraps itself around the leader, who governs through a constantly expanding web of personal relations. Within the family, which is the basic social unit in the Middle East, the father is the unrivaled leader. The situation is best summarized as follows: "The Muslim family has remained patriarchal, and the head of it maintains his authority... down to the last day of his life." [40] Traditionally, wives and children have been little more than extensions of the will of the father, whose authority is in his own opinion "natural and divine." [41] One Middle Eastern writer refers to a "blind reverence" that the father receives from his children, who relate to him "as if fearing a mysterious super-

[39] Dale Eickelman tells this story well. He defines marabouts as persons "to whom is attributed a special relation toward God which makes them particularly well placed to serve as intermediaries with the supernatural and to communicate God's grace (*baraka*) to their clients." See Eickelman, *Moroccan Islam* (Austin, Tex.: The University of Texas Press, 1976), p. 6.

[40] Maurice Gaudefroy-Demombynes, *Muslim Institutions* (London: George Allen and Unwin, 1961), p. 128.

[41] Cyrus Parham, "Divine Authority of a Persian Father," mimeographed (n.p., n.d.) p. 1.

human force." [42] The personal tension that is built into patrimonial systems is dramatically evident in the family, where sibling rivalry takes a particularly intense form. Brother competes against brother, and various shifting alliances are formed as mothers, children, cousins, grandparents, aunts, and uncles are pulled into the continual competition and conflict. The father or leader tends to promote rather than to alleviate this kind of rivalry.

In educational and occupational settings, the roles and styles of leadership are essentially the same as those that mark the family and the government. The master-apprentice, teacher-student, and shaykh-*murid* ("brotherhood disciple") relations are patterns of superordination and subordination in which the follower's existence is an extension of the leader's being. The teacher-student relation is, in fact, somewhat closer to the father-son relation than to the patterns found in guild and brotherhood organizations. The latter have preserved much more of the otherworldly quality that serves to strengthen the bonds of emanation. This quality has been gradually lost in the educational system as the religious direction of education has given way to secular control. The basic pattern, however, can still be seen in almost any Middle Eastern classroom, where the teacher's person is deferred to and the teacher's word is memorized. In the environment of guilds and brotherhoods, deference becomes devotion, and shaykhs, who are the leaders, command a charismatic control that is generally absent in familial, governmental, and formal educational institutions. In the case of Sufi orders or brotherhoods, "all authority and allocation of authority positions in the hierarchy lie within the purview of the Sheikh, and the subordinates derive their statuses from him." [43] Those who are closest to the shaykh's person have the greatest influence in the order. Therefore, the personal secretaries and attendants of the shaykh are extremely important figures in these organizations. They are, of course, entirely devoted to and dependent upon the leader. In describ-

---

[42] *Ibid.,* p. 2.
[43] Michael Gilsenan, "The Sufi Orders and the Modern World," mimeographed (n.p., 29 September 1967), pp. 7–8.

ing this kind of relation between a private secretary and the shaykh in a contemporary Egyptian brotherhood, one member explained that the secretary does not even go to sleep "until the Sheikh tells him to." [44]

Patrimonialism has been the dominant pattern of leadership in Middle Eastern politics for centuries. The strength of this pattern has fluctuated greatly, depending upon the leader, dynasty, society, and era. Patrimonialism was most evident in the heyday of the shahs and sultans. The politics of patrimonial leadership as manifested in the Middle East reflects six major characteristics: personalism, proximity, informality, balanced conflict, military prowess, and religious rationalization.

Personalism. Patrimonial society rests upon personal relationships. The community or society is essentially an enlarged household, and the personal ties that dominate in the household are the model for the ties in any other patrimonial unit. Middle Eastern societies and political systems grew out of tribal constellations, and the personalism that prevailed in the family and the clan has had a pervasive and protracted influence. The Middle Eastern leader has led by virtue of his personal relations with his followers. Formal organizations and institutions have seldom effectively intervened. Even when institutions such as formal bureaucracies have developed and expanded, the real business of ruling and political decision making has resided in personal networks. These networks tend to hold together groups of people, and it is through these networks that the leader has attempted to establish as wide a range of contacts as possible.

In order to rule in this kind of setting, it is essential that the leader gather and retain as much personal information about others in the network as possible. One famous eleventh-century manual on the conduct of kingship advises the prince, "never omit to inform yourself of the doings of others...," [45] and tells the king that "it is your duty not to be ignorant of

---

44 *Ibid.*, p. 45.
45 Kai Ka'us Ibn Iskandar, *A Mirror for Princes (The Qabus-nama)*, trans. by Reuben Levy (London: Cresset Press, 1951), p. 194.

conditions in your realm, of the circumstances of your people or those of your soldiers. More particularly you must be vigilant concerning the doings of your vizier. He should not be able to swallow a drink of water without your knowing it...." [46] In this setting, the art of genealogy and the knowledge of friendship relations are serious political pursuits.

The prevalence of personalism is best seen in the great Islamic dynastic systems, where the rulers built gigantic households around their own persons. A more formal bureaucratic state organization also evolved in these systems in answer to the pressure to administer the large political empires. A distinguished Islamic scholar summarizes this situation as follows: "Throughout the whole system of the Eastern Muslim political organization there runs like a red thread the division of all the organs of administration into two main categories, the dargah (palace) and diwan (chancery)." [47] In the Iranian Safavid system, the royal household was referred to as the *khassah* and the state bureaucracy was known as the *divan*. In the Turkish Ottoman system, the division was between the "imperial household" and the "central administration." In traditional Islamic polities, the royal household has been the crucial arena of politics, since it has consistently dominated the state bureaucracy proper. This has occurred not only because of the superior concentration of power within the royal household, but also because the personalities of the palace have infiltrated the state bureaucracy. Hence, the royal household, which is organized around the person of the king, has in turn wrapped around itself the formal bureaucracy, which expands with the growth of the political unit itself.

The actual transition from a completely personal pattern of leadership to one with bureaucratic and institutional appendages occurred mainly during the rule of the Abbasids (749–1258). This represented, in Weber's terms, a movement from a patriarchal to a patrimonial stage. The Abbasid leaders built an elaborate administrative system that included the

---

[46] *Ibid.*, p. 235.
[47] V. V. Barthold, *Turkestan Down to the Mongol Invasion*, 2d ed. (London: Oxford University Press, 1928), p. 227.

office of *vazir* ("prime minister") and more than a dozen large organizational boards that were in turn composed of numerous departments.[48] Despite this bureaucracy, personal relations dominated the system, and the court staff remained the critical force. This dependence of the more formal state bureaucracy upon the person of the king is seen in the role of the vazir himself. Although the vazir usually headed the state bureaucracy in these political systems, he did so as the personal servant of the king and as a leading member of the royal household. It was the *person* of the vazir, not the *office* of vazir, that was the important political consideration.

This traditional style of political rule has carried over into contemporary Middle Eastern politics to a surprisingly large degree. Personalism predominates in such societies as Morocco, Jordan, Saudi Arabia, Yemen, and the shaykhdoms that still have traditional authoritarian leaders. In other Middle Eastern countries, the personal dimension of leadership prevails more at the subnational level, in such institutions as the family, the school, and the guild. In all of these societies, however, patrimonial personalism continues to shape leadership processes, although it is more and more submerged beneath the growing facade of formal institutions and bureaucratic machinery. Contemporary Middle Eastern political monarchs constantly describe their societies as large families and emphasize their own special positions as heads or fathers of these families. It is in this spirit that King Hassan of Morocco speaks about "the innate nature of Our family, characterized by its profound wisdom, its great nobility, and the solid communion which unites us ultimately to our people." [49]

Proximity. Patrimonial leadership attaches particular significance to physical proximity. Regardless of occupational designation or formal title, those who live closest to the leader regularly hold major political positions in the traditional Middle

---

[48] Vazir is most closely translated as prime minister. It is sometimes transliterated as vizir or vizier.

[49] John Waterbury, *The Commander of the Faithful: The Moroccan Political Elite — A Study in Segmented Politics* (New York: Columbia University Press, 1970), p. 150.

Eastern system. Zayd Ibn Haritha, who was a black slave adopted by Muhammad and Khadija and brought into their household, illustrates the power of proximity. Because he was the Prophet's adopted son, and despite his having been a slave, Zayd became one of the leading figures in early Muslim history. Throughout Islamic history, slaves have risen to great influence, and one of the most powerful Islamic political systems was built by a dynasty whose kings were once slaves. These were the Mamluks; the word *mamluk* itself means "owned" or "possessed." They were originally slaves who had served as bodyguards to the Ayyubid dynastic leaders. Proximity to leadership has meant that slaves, cooks, musicians, and stable keepers have often been able to exert great political power in traditional Muslim societies. In the dying days of King Farouk's reign in contemporary Egypt, his barber had such power.

Although proximity is a consideration relevant to any political system, it assumes special importance in those societies where leadership is built on a far-flung network of personal relations. Here, those closest to the *person* of the leader tend always to be the most influential. In patrimonial politics these are often, in the first instance, such family members as brothers, wives, mothers, and uncles. Those who marry into the leader's family and become in-laws also become potential centers of great influence. The special personal ties and ideal position of proximity that relatives of the leader hold often mean that when the pattern of emanation is broken, it is broken within this familial core. If anyone makes direct suggestions to the patrimonial leader, or questions or criticizes him, it is almost always a member of the ruling family. Certainly, it is from this source that new ideas are most likely to be entertained and absorbed. In an extended household administration, or patrimonial system, those in the core household or nuclear family will play major roles in political decision making. Western discussions and condemnations of nepotism, ascription, and favoritism must be reevaluated in light of the general structure of patrimonial politics.

Proximity counts most in systems where decision making is highly centralized, highly personal, and highly informal. In nonpatrimonial systems, decision making tends to be more equally distributed throughout the society. And such systems also have formal and associational channels that carry the influence and ideas of those distant from the centers of political decision making to the leader. In the patrimonial Middle East, the most effective way to submit a request or present a petition is to get as close as possible to the leader. The closer an individual is to the center of the personal web of politics, the more likely he is to share in decision making and to have his interests served. It is for this reason that there is constant and unrelenting pressure toward the center of power in traditional patrimonial politics. The leader is always being pressed in upon by individuals who attempt to be in his presence as often and as long as possible. At the same time, those closest to him, such as his advisers, ministers, and confidants, attempt to resist and control the flow of others to this precious territory. In *A Mirror for Princes,* Muslim vazirs are warned, "wherever the king goes, accompany him; do not leave him alone. . . ." [50]

It is proximity rather than professional merit or occupational position that explains why gardeners, cobblers, barbers, and physicians have moved into positions of great influence in Islamic politics. The patrimonial leader has more often sought the advice and counsel of these individuals than of any others, and at times such service personnel have eventually replaced their masters and become political leaders in their own right. It is not surprising, therefore, that even in the contemporary Middle East, political leaders rely heavily upon their personal attendants for advice and information. The last Shah of Iran, for example, said that he relied upon his valet and gardener when he needed "proper information." [51] Those nearest to the person of the leader serve to filter demands and requests, act as information bearers and receptacles of advice, and stand as influential intermediaries between the leader and his masses of followers. Where power is personal and politics are patrimonial, the issue of proximity is critical. The concept of the "inner circle" is particularly relevant to Middle Eastern politics.

[50] Iskandar, *A Mirror for Princes*, p. 214.
[51] E. A. Bayne, *Persian Kingship in Transition* (New York: American Universities Field Staff, 1968), p. 235.

Informality. Personal politics tends to be informal politics in the sense that the most important leaders are often those who are not bound by formal contracts or limited by institutional constraints. Even those leaders who visibly combine power and authority have consistently operated in highly personal settings rather than in well-defined and formal organizations.

In today's bedouin society, the great importance of the informal leadership structure is still in the person of the *rajal khayr,* or "good man." In the Ayshaybat tribe in western Egypt, this person is more influential than the *aqila,* in whom resides the contractual authority of the tribe. The aqila is, in other words, the formal leader. The rajal khayr is a cultural and political broker who has the loyalty and friendship of the people as well as the attention of high regional government officials, who prefer to work through him. As G. J. Obermeyer writes in an excellent case study of bedouin leadership: "The power of the 'āqila is limited by the very structure of the role. The role of the rajal khair, being less institutionalized and structured, is less confined with respect to the kind and amount of influence the role-player might exert." [52]

Political decision making in the Middle East has been marked by behind-the-scenes planning and negotiation. Leaders have seldom occupied themselves with the establishment of formal political institutions such as parliaments and parties. Where such formal institutions have been constructed, they have been rationalizing gestures more than seriously conceived political organizations. Once in existence, formal bodies have had relatively little impact upon a leader's political activities.

Informal patterns of control and authority have been responsible for a great deal of uncertainty in the decision-making environment. Middle Eastern political processes reflect a high level of intrigue and counter-intrigue as leaders at various levels maneuver in secret and semisecret settings. It is partially because of this emphasis on secrecy and organizational infor-

[52] Obermeyer, "Leadership and Transition in Bedouin Society: A Case Study," *The Desert and the Sown,* ed. by Cynthia Nelson (Berkeley, Calif.: University of California Institute of International Studies, 1973), p. 164.

mality that rumors have always been an important political phenomenon in the Middle East. Secrecy and uncertainty breed speculation, and the ability to uncover decisions and deals is an important political resource.

The propensity for informal organization that has marked Middle Eastern social life is most evident in the numerous secret and informal groups. These include secret orders and societies, religious brotherhoods, underground minority organizations, political cliques and *anjumans*, informal coffeehouse groups, Sufi meetings, ritualistic religious gatherings, regular meetings of extended families, royal social circles and *khalvats*, and bureaucratic and parliamentary factions.[53] This style of social organization has been a critical factor in the development of patrimonial patterns of leadership and has been discussed more fully in the preceding chapter.

Middle Eastern leaders have tended to operate as the centers of webs of personal relationships in which the lines of power and authority are indistinct and constantly changing. Spheres of political authority overlap. Hence, there is always doubt concerning who is closest to the leader and who influenced what decision. With the possible exception of the national political leader, there is even question about *who* the leader really is. Often the most influential political actors remain in the background, where they are members of the family, the harem, or friendship circles. In Middle Eastern politics, an informal personal organization has tended to rest behind the formal institutional organization. Oftentimes, observers are confused because of the presence of the identifiable leader at the center of both organizations and the presence of certain advisors and confidants in both.

This environment of informality has carried several political advantages for the patrimonial leader. It has provided him with an unusually flexible system, since lines of authority and responsibility tend to be fluid and blurred. In such a system, it is difficult for opposition forces to concentrate because targets

---

53 *Anjumans* are usually translated as "societies." *Khalvat* was a term used in Iran to refer to a regular social gathering of the shah and his closest male advisors.

are neither stable nor well defined. At the same time, the leader enjoys a broad capacity to intervene in governmental affairs and to move subordinates around with ease. Since there are no clearly defined responsibilities, and since hard and fast assignments are nonexistent, the patrimonial leader can interpret spheres of authority in almost any way he chooses. Those individuals who are most apt to challenge the leader find themselves severely crippled in this informal environment. They lack institutional foundations and formal legal supports that they can cling to, and therefore find themselves highly dependent upon the personal whim and will of the leader. Informal politics tend to conceal the merit of aspiring statesmen, and as a result these statesmen are seldom able to build the popularity necessary for the crystallization of opposition to the leader. Finally, informality builds distrust between and among those who are relatively influential in the system. Individuals report confidentially and personally to the leader, and this often involves statements about the activities and ambitions of other political figures. Such an informal and semisecret pattern of politics enables the leader to engender a great deal of division and distrust among his subordinates. This division has been institutionalized as overlapping lines of authority by which officials exert control in one another's area of expertise.

In patrimonial leadership, visibility and formality have been subordinated to personalism and covert organization. This characteristic has provided Middle Eastern leaders with a maximum amount of maneuverability and a minimum degree of accountability. Even in the contemporary Middle East of complex and sophisticated organization charts, the business of politics is negotiated outside of and in spite of these instruments. Political blueprints such as constitutions and fundamental laws heavily mask the actual patterns and processes by which political leaders make decisions and protect their interests.

Balanced Conflict. The patrimonial leader in the Middle East has ruled on the foundation of pervasive division and personal rivalry. In the Middle Eastern context, the dictum "divide and rule" takes on special meaning. Cutting through all levels in the Islamic system is a built-in rivalry that marks interpersonal, intergroup, and interclass relations. The leader who seeks to divide and rule, therefore, has an ideal social system within which to operate. Rivalry is institutionalized in the system, and the traditional ruler had only to encourage processes that were already at work. This is why unity is the most sought-after and least achieved goal in Islamic history.

Personal rivalry has so permeated the Middle Eastern social structure that it manifests itself in institutions all the way from the family to the national bureaucracy. In Egyptian village society, for example, intense sibling rivalry is considered essential to a child's growth. Parents continually sharpen and intensify rivalry among their children. This is done in numerous dramatic ways, including labeling the children with names that invite conflict. In one Egyptian family, for example, the elder brother was called "the stupid one," while the younger brother was nicknamed "the clever one." [54] In a study of Lebanese village life, it was found that fewer than half of the children sampled could name three persons they considered friends. The reasons for this reported scarcity of friendship relations were explained in terms of grudges, feuds, and rivalries.[55] The oft-quoted Arab proverb "I against my brother, my brother and I against my cousin, my cousin and I against the stranger" describes this general pattern very well.

At the national political level, the same pattern is evident in the way that leaders and rulers play their advisors and subordinates off against one another. The contemporary rulers of Morocco, Jordan, and Saudi Arabia have become especially adept in this skill and largely owe their continued existence as powerful monarchs to it. In Iran after the revolution, Ayatollah Khomeini shrewdly remained above conflicting factions. From here he played political groups off against one another, e.g. the radical leftists against the fundamentalists on the right. By splintering the potential opposition forces and at the same time

---

[54] Hammed Ammar, *Growing Up in an Egyptian Village* (New York: Octagon Books, 1966), p. 110.

[55] Judith R. Williams, *The Youth of Haouch El Harimi: A Lebanese Village*, Harvard Middle East Monograph Series, vol. 20 (Cambridge, Mass.: Harvard University Press, 1968), pp. 91–92.

standing above them as supreme arbiter, several Middle Eastern leaders have managed to maintain firm control in the political arena. Any concentration of skill, energy, or power is immediately shattered through leadership tactics of division and redivision. In the traditional Abbasid, Ottoman, Safavid, and Moghul administrative systems, the most important and influential political functions were constantly divided and redistributed among larger and larger numbers of officials. When a political figure became particularly influential, his title and function were given to a second and rival administrator, and influence was thus divided and shared. Tension was thereby instilled into the particular political sphere, and the personal power of the individual in control of this sphere was substantially lessened, if not halved.

The politics of rivalry and conflict not only served to buttress leadership positions but also reinforced systemic stability. The tension was balanced in such a way that overwhelming concentrations of power seldom developed outside the sphere of the national political ruler. Manfred Halpern analyzes the Islamic system in terms of its "ability to convert tensions into balances" and its capacity to bind society together "through conflict no less than through collaboration." [56] In contemporary Morocco, "all seek to maintain in the midst of the group that tension which is life, that variety that is solidarity." [57] The Moroccan monarch operates a system in which "no group may be permitted to become too strong, and to counter hegemonic tendencies life is breathed into rival groups." [58] In Iran, the former Shah created a stable balance of tension in which ministers, courtiers, security agents, military leaders, industrialists, and clerics were systematically divided against one another at all levels. The last four kings of Saudi Arabia have promoted the distrust and animosity that mark the relationships between many of their half-brothers, while at another level the national

[56] Manfred Halpern, *The Politics of Social Change in the Middle East and North Africa* (Princeton, N.J.: Princeton University Press, 1963), pp. 10, 18.

[57] Jacques Berque, *Structures Sociales du Haut-Atlas* (Paris, 1955), p. 449, as quoted in Waterbury, *The Commander of the Faithful*, p. 61.

[58] Waterbury, *The Commander of the Faithful*, p. 148.

guard stands in direct rivalry with the regular army. The Nassers, Bourguibas, Saddam Husseins, Qaddafis, and al-Assads have also promoted rivalry. In the Middle East, political leaders have traditionally expended much of their energies in manipulating personal networks of stabilizing tensions. A premium has been placed upon a leader's ability to sense the location of threatening power concentrations and then to splinter those concentrations either by heightening existing divisions or by fostering new personal rivalries.

Military Prowess. Max Weber writes that "with the development of a purely personal administrative staff, *especially a military force* under the control of the chief, traditional authority tends to develop into 'patrimonialism.'" [59] The key to patrimonial politics is the existence of a military force that is at the personal disposal of the leader. Within the Islamic world, this consideration has been a central one. Here, among the most highly respected qualities of leadership are personal bravery and physical courage. Islamic scholars present "combativeness" as one of the three great characteristics of the Prophet Muhammad.[60] The famous Islamic leaders are known and remembered for their bravery in battle and their victory in military campaigns. The warrior hero is a deeply admired figure in Middle Eastern history. Leaders who have been able to conduct themselves well on the field of battle have always had an extreme advantage in the arena of domestic politics.[61]

This emphasis on physical courage and military prowess is to be expected in a culture that developed out of a tribal context, and in which tribes continue to play a prominent social and political role. Throughout the Middle East today groups still exist that follow the Shi'i path or worship Ali primarily because of his personal courage and valor, which are summed

[59] Weber, *The Theory of Social and Economic Organization*, p. 347. Emphasis ours.

[60] See, for example, Nasr, *Ideals and Realities*, p. 73; and Schuon, *Understanding Islam*, p. 88.

[61] The reverse is also true, since failure in combat is as much a moral as a physical blow to Islamic leaders and societies. The impact of the Arab-Israeli conflict, for example, must be interpreted in this light.

up in his titles Lion of God and Sword of Islam.[62] This inspiration has been key to the fighting commitment of the young Iranian soldiers who died in large numbers in the war with Iraq in the early 1980s.

The emphasis upon personal courage and valor runs deep throughout Middle Eastern society. Bravery is so highly esteemed that it carries favorable moral connotations. The Arabic word *shaja'a,* which is also commonly used in Persian, implies a personal bravery that is especially infused with virtue and uprightness. It implies a kind of chivalrous courage. Throughout Middle Eastern history, the personally brave and physically courageous have had about them an aura of knightliness. Combativeness and chivalry could not be separated. Local champions such as *pahlavans* not only had tremendous physical strength but also were exceptionally kind, generous, and noble. Islamic guilds and brotherhoods traditionally supported and promoted ideals of physical and moral courage. Military valor and success, therefore, have invested Islamic leaders with additional strength and appeal in the eyes of their followers.

Military force was a major factor in the rise to and maintenance of power for Middle Eastern political leaders. "The struggles for succession were mostly settled by civil war and by coup d'etat, with the outcome generally as closely related to the structure of the military command as to the prevailing political environment." [63] A strong and effective military force has also been an important tool enabling a ruler to continue to rule. And a leader who has had several successful foreign military campaigns to his credit has been more effective in preserving his domestic rule. The deep patterns of division and discord described above persistently threaten to shatter the system and to destroy the ruler in the process. One scholar stresses the fact that "a patrimonial system is characterized by constant tension

[62] One of the authors (Bill) had the opportunity to live for a short time with the Qashqa'i tribesmen in southern Iran in 1967. The Islamic leader most admired and respected by these tribesmen is Ali, who is worshipped because of his virtues of personal courage and bravery.

[63] J. C. Hurewitz, *Middle East Politics: The Military Dimension* (New York: Frederick A. Praeger, 1969), p. 20.

between centripetal and centrifugal forces." [64] The patrimonial leader's key instrument in encouraging and buttressing the centripetal forces is his military organization. While promoting tension and discord in particular areas throughout the system, the patrimonial leader must at the same time guard against having balances become imbalances and rivals unite in a common front against him. It is only his military that can enable him to salvage his position and his life in such circumstances.

Despite its importance, the military organization is subject to the same patterns and pressures that characterize other institutions in patrimonial settings. The leader or ruler attempts to control the military as an emanation of his own will and personality and usually assumes the title Commander-in-Chief or Commander of the Faithful. The military forces are his "personal instrument." [65] The centrality of the leader in military matters can be seen diagrammatically in the Middle Eastern "battle order" described by Ibn Khaldun.[66] Surrounded by his closest confidants, the ruler stands at the center of his forces. The latter consist of four armies, situated at the front and rear and on the right and left flanks of the leader.

Throughout the history of the Middle East, the characteristics of personalism, proximity, informality, and balanced rivalry also infiltrated the military organization. Only the most trusted relatives and confidants were appointed military leaders. Those closest to the ruler, such as bodyguards and armed retainers, were recruited among slaves, orphans, and prisoners, and as a result maintained no entangling alliances or loyalties outside of their relation to the leader. It was essential that they be completely subsumed in the shadow of the ruler, to whom they owed everything. To insure this kind of absolute loyalty and submission, the mechanism of balanced rivalry is seen in perhaps its most critical manifestation in the arena of the armed forces. Different military leaders and different military bodies have existed in constant tension with one another and have served

[64] Robert H. Jackson, "Social Structure and Political Change in Ethiopia and Liberia," *Comparative Political Studies* 3 (April 1960):38.

[65] Bendix, *Max Weber*, p. 344.

[66] Ibn Khaldun, *The Muqaddimah*, trans. by Franz Rosenthal (Princeton, N.J.: Princeton University Press, 1967), p. 225.

as watchdogs of one another. Sometimes these intramilitary divisions reflected tribal cleavages; sometimes entirely new tribes were created both to strengthen loyalty and to serve as armed checks against other military units.

The modern Middle East has its authentic military heroes. For the Turks, Atatürk was the great hero of the First World War. Abdul Aziz Ibn Saud was the illustrious warrior king in Saudi Arabia; his son Saud was renowned for his physical courage in battle. King Hussein of Jordan has demonstrated that same courage on numerous occasions. Both Gamal Abdel Nasser and General Naguib, the titular leader of the 1952 Egyptian coup, had distinguished records in the fighting in Palestine.

There is bound to be a close connection between military upheaval and the turnover of political leaders. The proliferation of military coups that continues to mark Middle Eastern politics represents the failure of leaders and rulers to establish viable patrimonial patterns with respect to the military. The challenge to leadership has come not so much from the society at large as from within the military itself. When leadership rests so heavily upon the military reed, then it must be prepared to fall whenever that reed breaks.

Religious Rationalization. Islam provided the patrimonial leader with an ideology that buttressed and strengthened the political patterns by which he ruled. Chains of emanation are more firmly fashioned when they lead to the Almighty, and Islamic leaders have traditionally endeavored to demonstrate their own linkages with God and his Prophet Muhammad. Although actual theocratic leadership died with the Prophet in 632, Islamic leaders ever since have sought to be theocratic leaders. As time passed, this tendency became more and more pronounced, while theocratic leadership became less and less credible. The political meaning of the word *caliph* was gradually transformed from "deputy of the emissary of God" to "God's representative on earth." [67] The Islamic political leaders, who had at one time been considered the Prophet's depu-

---

[67] V. V. Barthold, "Caliph and Sultan," *The Islamic Quarterly* 7 (July and December, 1963), pp. 124–125.

ties, later became known as God's deputies. Even the concept of *sultan,* which developed a connotation of secular as opposed to religious authority, soon made the linkage with the Divine. This occurred when the actual sultan began referring to himself as the Shadow of God.[68] The concept of *imam* has been the best example of leadership related directly to the Divine, for unlike the caliph and the sultan, the imam has always been considered the infallible vicegerent of God. Despite the various titles and personalities involved, however, the Middle Eastern style of patrimonial leadership has usually meant the conscious establishment of some form of linkage between the leader and the Divine.

This pattern has provided political leaders with a rationalization and justification for their positions. It has been argued that "stiff religious cement" has been the strength of the patrimonial system of rule.[69] In one of the classic studies of politics, Gaetano Mosca analyzes the traditional strength of the Turkish nation in the following terms: "The Turkish peasants in Rumelia and Anatolia believed sincerely and deeply in Islam, in the Prophet, in the sultan as the Prophet's vicar, and the beliefs for which they were asked to make the utmost sacrifices were the beliefs that ordinarily filled their lives and made up their moral and intellectual worlds." [70] In a smoothly functioning system of leadership by emanation, to challenge the leader often meant nothing less than to challenge the rule of God. It is for this reason that political rebellion took the form of religious schisms and that the challenging political figures stressed their own special relation to the Almighty.

The Politics of Patrimonial Recruitment: General Observations. Contrary to what is often thought, the ranks of Middle Eastern political leadership are relatively permeable. Within certain patrimonial limits, vertical mobility is possible, and outsiders are often able to penetrate elite circles. In such sys-

---

[68] *Ibid.,* p. 130.
[69] Gaetano Mosca, *The Ruling Class,* trans. Hannah D. Kahn (New York: McGraw-Hill Book Co., 1939), p. 345.
[70] *Ibid.,* p. 108.

tems, the personalistic networks of leadership can be penetrated, especially on the basis of family, kinship, and friendship
relations. As Almond and Powell point out: "Perhaps the oldest and most traditional means of access to political elites is
personal connection. By personal connection channels we mean
the use of family, school, local, and social ties as instruments
for contacting political elites." [71] In the Middle East, the determination of who is to move in or out of the elite is often
still determined by these factors.

Built into and stretching throughout these webs of personal
connections are three broader channels of mobility. These are
the military, bureaucratic, and religious channels, and it is
through them that most individuals have made their entrance
into the political elite. Although the personalistic-patrimonial
factors discussed above decidedly influence who moves through
these channels, the very existence of the channels has helped
to institutionalize mobility.

The Middle Eastern patrimonial system of leadership remains largely intact today. There are, however, a number of
strong recruitment considerations that increasingly influence
leadership composition. The most important of them are professional skill, talent, and merit. Political elites have been
driven, because of the forces of modernization, to recruit individuals who have technical and professional competence. Ministries of health are increasingly headed by medical doctors and
health administrators; national petroleum companies are directed by better and better qualified petroleum engineers, geologists, and economists; national educational systems are
guided by Middle Eastern specialists in the field of education.
A look through the curriculum vitae of the representatives of
various countries in the Organization of Petroleum Exporting
Countries (OPEC) is one good way of documenting this trend.
Even in the most traditional of patrimonial systems, such as
Saudi Arabia and Abu Dhabi, the educated technocrats have
moved into decision-making positions. In the late 1970s, for

[71] Gabriel A. Almond and G. Bingham Powell, Jr., *Comparative Politics: System, Process, and Policy* 2d ed. (Boston: Little, Brown and Co.,
1978), p. 178.

example, the Saudi cabinet had more American-trained Ph.D.s than did the United States cabinet. In Abu Dhabi, where professionally trained talent is admittedly scarce, Shaykh Zayid and his royal advisors imported a bright and dedicated French-educated Algerian, Mahmoud Hamra-Krouha, to build and direct the Abu Dhabi National Oil Company (ADNOC). The members of the professional middle class, to use the terminology introduced in Chapter III, are inexorably moving into the ranks of political leadership in the Middle East.

Despite the changes in some of the qualifications necessary for entry into the elites, there are impressive indications that patrimonialism prevails.

First, recruitment processes are personally and firmly controlled from the center of the system. This is as true in the authoritarian-distributive systems of Algeria and Iraq as it is in such traditional-authoritarian systems as those of Jordan and Morocco. In all of these systems the considerations of political loyalty, personal connections, and complete central control remain at least as important in determining entry into the elite as those of professional expertise, personal merit, and institutional position.

The second sign of patrimonial persistence in the Middle East concerns the directional flow of the recruitment patterns. In their recent analysis of the politics of recruitment into the elite, Almond and Powell stress that the political party is the most common contemporary channel of recruitment.[72] This has not been the case in Middle Eastern patrimonial politics. Although political parties exist in most of the societies, political leaders are not generally recruited from the parties. Instead, the parties (as well as the legislatures) are headed by individuals who are already national political leaders. The patrimonial head selects the party leadership from among proven confidants, advisers, or ministers. In several Middle Eastern systems, party positions (whether leadership or rank-and-file) more often reflect a move out of than a move into the national political elite. Parties and legislatures many times serve as the political dump-

---

[72] *Ibid.*, pp. 123–126.

ing grounds for former members of the elite who have fallen from favor in the patrimonial establishment.

The continued strength of patrimonialism in the Middle East has meant that the personalistic networks that are directed from the center have a profound effect on both the shape of the political system and that system's capacity to confront the problems of modernization and political development. The patrimonial leaders and the political elites that surround them play a disproportionate role in determining the future of their societies. Although their policies at one level may be very similar from society to society, at another level there are striking differences. In some societies, the traditional webs of patrimonialism operate today just as they have for centuries; in other societies, these webs have begun to be torn and are unraveling in differing ways. In Chapter V we will examine a number of case studies of Middle Eastern patrimonial leaders with special focus upon the differing ways that they have coped with the challenge of change.

CHAPTER V

The Politics of Leaders and Change

THE POLICIES WHEREBY Middle Eastern societies have confronted the challenge of change have been determined to a large extent by political leaders. As we have seen in Chapter IV, the political processes of patrimonial systems are shaped around the patrimonial leader, who plays a disproportionate role in the decision-making process. The centrality of the national political leader assures him a critical position in confronting the important related issues of modernization and political development. The leader's tactics and strategies in this regard have far-reaching consequences for the political system and for the peoples of the society concerned.

Throughout Middle Eastern history, leaders have held a wide variety of attitudes toward change. In many cases, the political leadership has been determined to resist any forces of change. In other cases, Middle Eastern leaders have taken a more flexible stance and have attempted to meet the challenge through programs of reform and revision. Their strategy has been to forestall major transformations by promoting continual incremental adjustments. In still other instances, leaders have on occasion pursued revolutionary goals that involve radical social and political change. In all these cases, however, the leader has maintained a special position: he has controlled the instruments of persuasion and coercion that are essential to the implementation of any of these policies.

In this chapter, our analysis will emphasize Middle Eastern political leaders who have in this century chosen to promote various programs of change. Modernization has been a goal shared by all of these leaders. Political development, however, has not been so generally favored. We will analyze three pairs of leaders from three major Middle Eastern countries. These are Mustafa Kemal Atatürk and Ismet İnönü of Turkey, Reza Shah and Muhammad Reza Shah Pahlavi of Iran, and Gamal Abdel Nasser and Anwar Sadat of Egypt.

Before discussing these leaders, it is perhaps best to devote a few paragraphs to the more traditional Middle Eastern leader. It is against this backdrop of traditional leadership that the more modern and often more progressive leaders have operated. In all of our case studies, traditional patrimonial styles and tactics have still been very much in evidence.

TWENTIETH-CENTURY TRADITIONAL LEADERS

Twentieth-century Middle Eastern political history has been largely dominated by a number of colorful traditional leaders who did much to shape the destinies of their nations. In most cases, they resisted change and as a result became its victims. Some were hopelessly corrupt and venal in their personal and political lives; others were models of integrity, whose lifestyles were simple and ascetic. All failed in one way or another to understand a world of new challenges and new forces. Among the least impressive of these leaders are King Farouk of Egypt, Regent Abd al-Ilah of Iraq, Sultan Mehmet V and Sultan Mehmet VI of Turkey, Shaykh Shakhbut of Abu Dhabi, and Sultan Said bin Taymur of Oman. Traditional leaders of considerably more talent and integrity include King Idris of Libya, Zahir Shah of Afghanistan, King Abdullah of Jordan, King Muhammad V of Morocco, and especially, King Abdul Aziz Ibn Saud of Saudi Arabia.

Sultan Said bin Taymur ruled Oman for 38 years (1932–1970). Although he was educated at a British school in India, the Sultan spent nearly four decades walling himself and his country in against the forces of change. Even after oil was discovered in Oman, he steadfastly refused to expend his resources on development programs. During his rule, no tractors were allowed in the sultanate; the occasional importation of an automobile had to be personally approved by the Sultan himself; religious taxes were collected in the provinces in Maria Theresa dollars as late as the 1960s; houses could be rebuilt only from the actual material with which they were originally constructed; women were forbidden to accompany their husbands abroad; and Omanis educated abroad were not allowed to return to work in their own country.

Sultan Said was opposed to education, financial expenditure, and modernization in his country. He felt that the British lost India because they had educated the people, and he therefore decided to close the only three primary schools in Oman, just before he was deposed in 1970. He considered the schools to be hotbeds of Communism. The Sultan ruled supreme and kept his people in fear and subjection. The channels of access and personal contact that were such an essential part of Islamic patrimonial politics were destroyed by this traditional leader, who promoted only slavery and repression in his system. After 1958, he kept himself in isolation in the coastal city of Salala. His officials, working in an atmosphere "made even more oppressive by his absence, one might describe it as disembodiment, in Salala," [1] made no decisions. Sultan Said even locked up his son Qabus (the present ruler of Oman) when Qabus returned to Oman in 1966 after receiving a British education at Sandhurst.

British annoyance with and embarrassment by the old Sultan led to his overthrow in July 1970. His demise was inevitable; his long period of reactionary rule had resulted in a guerrilla war that broke out in the province of Dhofar. By 1970, the opposition forces had taken most of Dhofar and were even shelling Sultan Said's palace. He had been consistent in his determined opposition to any kind of change or innovation. Because of British support and his geographic position in what

---

[1] Ian Skeet, *Muscat and Oman: The End of an Era* (London: Faber and Faber, 1974), p. 168. Most of the material in this section has been drawn from Skeet's informed and entertaining book or from Fred Halliday, *Arabia Without Sultans* (New York: Vintage Books, 1974), pp. 277–315. An excellent scholarly study of Omani politics is J. E. Peterson, *Oman in the Twentieth Century* (London: Croom Helm, 1978).

were then the backwaters of the Middle East, he made this policy stick for a surprisingly long time. But in the end he failed. As Ian Skeet presciently wrote before the Sultan's fall, his kind of policy "is just plugging the holes in the barbed wire round the country's borders; one day the barbed wire will be rolled aside, and none of the Sultan's restrictions will help him one iota." [2]

If Sultan Said is one of the least successful traditional leaders in the Middle East of this century, King Abdul Aziz Ibn Saud is one of the most successful. Ibn Saud's style of leadership very closely approximated that of the classical model analyzed in Chapter IV. Born in 1880 in Central Arabia, Ibn Saud grew up in an environment of vigorous conflict among clans and political anarchy. In 1901, he was a banished youth whose clan was ruled by its enemies and whose immediate family was in exile in Kuwait. By 1934, he had conquered the territories of Najd, Hasa, Hijaz, and Asir and had welded them together into one political unit known as the Kingdom of Saudi Arabia. In so doing, he had healed the rifts within his own family, defeated or co-opted the other clans, taken Hasa from the Turks, and conquered Mecca and Hijaz at the expense of the Hashemite King Hussein (the great-grandfather of the present King Hussein of Jordan).

Abdul Aziz Ibn Saud ruled personally, informally, and patriarchally. He ran his kingdom as a gigantic personal household, which it in fact very nearly was. Ibn Saud had an estimated three hundred wives in his lifetime, as well as large numbers of concubines and slave girls. In 1955, it was estimated that there was one prince for every 5,000 persons in Saudi Arabia.[3] Like the Prophet Muhammad, after whom he patterned his life, Ibn Saud used marriage as an important political tool. Through the years, he married into all the leading tribal families in Najd. His links with the Sudairi family, from which four of his wives came, were especially strong; these wives bore

[2] Skeet, *Muscat and Oman*, p. 196.
[3] H. St. John Philby, *Sa'udi Arabia* (London: Ernest Benn, 1955), p. 298. The writings of Philby are invaluable sources on the politics of Saudi Arabia; he speaks on the basis of 35 years in residence at the Saudi court.

fifteen of his sons. Today, King Fahd is the most influential of seven full brothers who are the sons of Ibn Saud and Hussa bint Ahmad al-Sudairi.

In this setting, Ibn Saud balanced rivalries and directed the personal and political fortunes of all of the other main actors in the system. He made it his business to stay informed. "He had a deep knowledge of his people, their friendships and inter-marriages, their blood feuds and causes of quarrel, so that he could play the one against the other." [4] He never allowed power to concentrate at any point in the system other than at his own feet. He once stated; "Two things I will not stomach: firstly a rebel (*marij*); and secondly the feigned loyalty of two persons inwardly leagued against me." [5] Ibn Saud was also famous for his accessibility and approachability. Quite unlike Sultan Said, he spent several hours each day listening to the complaints and problems of his people.

Finally, Ibn Saud was a great warrior. The first thirty years of his leadership were a time of constant warfare. It was during this period that he became a legend as he personally developed military strategy, recruited his soldiers, and led them into bat-tle. At the end of these three decades of military struggle and political consolidation, Ibn Saud carried the marks of a dozen wounds, all attesting to the central role he played in the busi-ness of physical combat.

Although he founded a country and forged a following of disparate peoples into a nation, he stumbled when confronted with the challenges of modernization and political develop-ment. Between the time when oil was discovered at Jebel Dhahran in 1938 and when he died in 1953, Iban Saud clung desperately to tradition. As a result, he was unable to cope effectively with the new forces and demands that burst upon him and his society. He did not think to concern himself with widening the base of political participation; he watched social and economic gaps widen among his people; he could not or would not stem the tide of peculation, corruption, and waste

[4] H. C. Armstrong, *Lord of Arabia* (Beirut: Khayyat's, 1944), p. 111.
[5] H. St. John Philby, *Arabian Jubilee* (London: Robert Hale, 1954), p. 106.

that washed through his kingdom; he did little to build health and educational facilities. These tasks were only taken up later by his successors, Faisal, Khalid, and the current King Fahd.

Still, Abdul Aziz Ibn Saud was the greatest traditional leader of this century. He combined wit and physical courage with personal charisma and deep religious beliefs to consolidate a people and build a nation.[6]

The political leaders discussed in the following sections tried to move out ahead in their societies and directly confront the forces of modernization. The one who did this earliest and most dramatically was a Turk born only a year before the great Ibn Saud. He came to be known as Atatürk.

ATATÜRK: THE REVOLUTIONARY FATHER OF TURKEY

The modern Turkish state owes its political form and indeed its very existence to one remarkable military and political leader — Atatürk. First called Mustafa, he was given the additional name of Kemal ("perfection") by an instructor in secondary school. After his victory over the Greeks at Sakarya in 1921, the Grand National Assembly at Ankara gave him the title of Ghazi ("victor"). In 1934, the Assembly bestowed on him the surname Atatürk, or Father of the Turks. In this book, we will refer to him both as Kemal and as Atatürk.

Kemal was born in Salonika in Macedonia in 1881. His family was of the very lowest echelons of the middle class. His father, a onetime low-ranking civil servant, was a failure in both the timber business and the salt trade and died when Kemal was only eleven. A direct and often rebellious person, Kemal was thrown out of one school before he settled into a military education that included military prep school in Salonika, a military academy at Monastir, and finally the War College and the Staff College at Constantinople. In 1905, he graduated from the Staff College as a captain in the sultan's army. On his final examination and in his personnel file, the following assessment was reportedly written: "A brilliant student officer, difficult in

---

[6] For our detailed analysis of the patrimonial politics of Abdul Aziz Ibn Saud, see J. A. Bill and C. Leiden, *The Middle East: Politics and Power* (Boston: Allyn and Bacon, 1974), pp. 125–133.

temperament, precise and technically a perfectionist, politically unstable." [7] Shortly after graduation, Kemal was arrested and imprisoned for plotting against the ruling authorities.

Kemal was born into a world of transition in which ancient social and political institutions were crumbling. The once powerful Ottoman Empire was on its last legs. On all its borders, the empire was besieged by various ethnic minority groups who fought to separate themselves from the system. Meanwhile, liberal ideas from the West were breeding dissatisfaction among the empire's educated and middle-class populations. It is thus not accidental that the Young Turk movement was born and nurtured in the westernmost sector of the empire. Macedonians were conspicuous among the revolutionaries.

The sultanate in Constantinople was corrupt and venal, and its policies were increasingly unpopular. When pushed, Sultan Abdul Hamid had declared some reforms, only to repeal them when pressures were relaxed. In 1876, he agreed to a constitution providing for the establishment of a consultative assembly; in 1877, he dissolved the assembly; in 1896, a major coup attempt failed. Meanwhile, political opposition had spread everywhere and had become deeply rooted even within the sultan's own armed forces. Kemal was one of the most disenchanted of the young officers who saw their decrepit system crumbling around them. A fierce nationalist, he determined from the beginning that the Turkish nation had to be reformed, strengthened, and regenerated.

After a few months in jail, Kemal was posted to the Fifth Army in Damascus, where he immediately began to establish political opposition societies among his military colleagues on the Syrian front. His Vatan ("Fatherland") Society was soon swallowed up by the Young Turks' Committee of Union and Progress, which on 23 July 1908 forced the sultan to restore the constitution and recall his consultative assembly. Between 1908 and the outbreak of World War I in 1914, Kemal floated on

---

[7] Ray Brock, *Ghost on Horseback: The Incredible Atatürk* (Boston: Little, Brown and Co., 1954), p. 21. Although this book tends towards the sensational and owes too much to the fertile imagination of the author, it makes interesting reading and succeeds in capturing the colorfully human nature of Kemal.

the fringes of the Young Turks in a relationship marked by mutual distrust. Although his military skills were used by Enver Pasha and the other leaders during this time, he was carefully kept out of the corridors of power. "He was a realist, who thought in terms not of gestures but of action, thoughtfully conceived, scientifically planned and systematically executed. Too many of those whom he saw around him, and who were pretending to govern the country, were men of words, of undigested feelings and vague ideas." [8]

Although Kemal personally opposed the Turkish alliance with Germany in World War I, he earned his place in military history for his brilliant defense in 1915 at Gallipoli, where the Turks repelled a major Allied offensive spearheaded by the finest soldiers of the British Empire. Poorly armed and outnumbered, the Turkish troops under Kemal successfully held off the seasoned Australian, New Zealand, and British troops who desperately fought to break through to the Dardanelles and to clear the way to Constantinople. During this nine-month siege and bitter fighting, Kemal proved himself to be not only a brilliant military tactician but also an inspiration to his soldiers. He moved constantly among his men in the front trenches and miraculously survived a direct hit in his chest when shrapnel shattered the watch in his breast pocket. As he told his outgunned Fifty-Seventh Regiment: "I don't order you to attack, I order you to die, others troops and commanders can come and take our places." [9] The men of the Fifty-Seventh did die for their leader and for their country. Kemal somehow survived; he had taken the first major step toward becoming the Father of the Turks.

The Allies' victory in 1918 ended the Young Turks' ascendancy and forced their leaders into exile. The British appearance in Constantinople and a subsequent Greek movement into Smyrna were shocking and unacceptable events for Turk-

[8] Lord Kinross, *Atatürk: The Rebirth of a Nation* (London: Weidenfeld and Nicolson, 1964), p. 44. This remains the best biography of Atatürk. For a fine article-length study, see Dankwart A. Rustow's own analysis in his edited volume *Philosophers and Kings: Studies in Leadership* (New York: George Braziller, 1970), pp. 208–247.

[9] Kinross, *Atatürk*, p. 76.

ish patriots. Kemal left for Anatolia, where he began an opposition independence movement. In 1919, he organized congresses at Erzerum and Sivas, where delegates drafted and ratified a national pact legitimizing their movement. Turkey was in upheaval. During the next four years, Kemal put the pieces of the country back together. The task was a formidable one, since in the process he had to organize a political and military force that would not only hang together but also be strong enough to defeat the tribes and brigands in Anatolia; repulse and drive a major invading Greek force from the heart of Turkey; maneuver the British and Russians out of the area; and replace the Sultan's government, still claiming legitimacy in Constantinople, with a new nationalist government, resident in Ankara.

In three and a half years of brutal but brilliant military campaigns and pressure-packed political infighting, Kemal somehow accomplished all these goals. In November 1922, he proclaimed the abolition of the sultanate; in October 1923, Turkey was declared a republic and Kemal became its first president; and in March 1924, the caliphate was abolished. Kemal was president of Turkey until his death in 1938.

During his 15 years as president, Atatürk did not choose to rest on his military laurels. Instead, he began a program of social, cultural, and political modernization that shook the country to its roots. His program struck at the foundation of the conservative religious culture of the day and stressed national, secular, and modern goals. In a characteristic style, he directly and publicly attacked the very symbols of the old system by outlawing the fez, condemning the veil, and reforming the alphabet. He introduced such changes by personally initiating them in the very heart of the most conservative areas of Turkey.

These shattering changes in important symbols were accompanied by major reforms in the fields of administration, eduaction, and law. One of Atatürk's most important contributions was the successful establishment of an independent and effective judiciary. The programs of reform were backed by an international policy that was astutely conceived and implemented. This foreign policy was based on a premise stressing the consolidation of national power, not the expansion of national boundaries. It also emphasized the necessity of avoiding international entanglements such as the one that contributed to the disaster of World War I. It was Atatürk who established the policy that enabled Ismet Inönü to keep Turkey out of the Second World War. Despite tremendous pressures, Turkey did not take a formal position until February 1945, when it declared war on the Axis powers.[10]

Atatürk was not a liberal democrat. He was an authoritarian ruler who exercised power bluntly and forcefully. In his own words, "I don't act for public opinion. I act for the nation and for my own satisfaction." [11] He had climbed the ladder of power by himself and had survived everything from several serious illnesses[12] and difficult military campaigns to political plots and assassination attempts. When he finally reached a position of national political power, he did not hesitate to take severe measures against those whom he considered threats to himself or to his programs. The major example of this occurred when in 1926 Kemal used an abortive plot against his life as a rationale for imprisoning, exiling, or executing those he considered members of a serious political opposition. Among them were several of his oldest comrades and closest friends who had stood behind him in the difficult years in Anatolia. Many of these individuals were liberal thinkers who had begun to resist his personal, arbitrary rule. As Kâzim Karabekir, a trusted military leader whose assistance was crucial to Kemal's success in Anatolia, put it, "I am in favour of the Republic, but I am against personal rule." [13]

[10] For Atatürk and his successors as makers of foreign policy, see Metin Tamkoç's excellent book *The Warrior Diplomats* (Salt Lake City: University of Utah Press, 1976).

[11] Kinross, *Atatürk*, p. xvii.

[12] Physical ailments plagued Kemal throughout his life, yet he conquered these problems just as he overcame the social and political problems that confronted him. Besides sustaining a minor battle wound and some broken ribs, he survived two major attacks of malaria, three severe cases of influenza, a debilitating ear infection, and kidney problems that tormented him for 25 years. As a young man, he contracted gonorrhea, the effects of which were lasting. He died of cirrhosis of the liver and complications thereof.

[13] Kinross, *Atatürk*, p. 382.

LIFE OF ATATÜRK: MAJOR EVENTS

1881	Born in Salonika
1893	Enters military secondary school in Salonika; given added name Kemal
1899	Enters War College in Constantinople
1905	Graduates from Staff College with rank of captain
1908	Young Turk revolution
1914	Beginning of World War I; Turkey signs secret alliance with Germany; Russia, Britain, and France declare war on Turkey
1915	Kemal distinguishes himself at Gallipoli
1919	Leaves for Anatolia; issues declaration of independence; calls nationalist congresses at Sivas and Erzerum
1921	Defeats the invading Greeks at Battle of Sakarya
1922	Proclaims abolition of the sultanate
1923	Founds the Republican Peoples' Party; becomes president of the Turkish Republic
1924	Abolishes the caliphate
1926	Trials and suppression of opposition at Izmir and Ankara
1934	Takes name of Atatürk; women given the right to vote in parliamentary elections and to become members of parliament
1938	Dies in Istanbul

Yet there is another side to the story. Kemal was always scrupulously careful to seek legitimation for his actions and to base them upon legal principles emanating from the people or their representatives. Even as a rebel, he insisted on congresses and constitutional pacts that would provide political legitimacy for his movement. He also campaigned hard among the people and created a major and lasting political party, the Republican People's Party. He twice experimented with a two-party system but gave it up when it proved unworkable. Atatürk once admitted that he was a dictator yet went on to point out: "But I have not had pyramids built in my honour like the Pharaohs of Egypt. I did not make people work for my sake, threatening them with whips when I wanted an idea to be accepted by the country. I first called a congress, I debated the situation with the people, I carried out my plans only after taking authority

from the people."[14] His may not have always been a government by the people, but it was in many ways a government for
the people.[15]

Patterns of Rule. Atatürk was one of the more colorful of
the political leaders of this century. He was a man of imposing appearance, with peculiarly striking eyes. "Wide-set beneath the broad brow and the eyebrows that curled upwards
like whiskers, they gleamed with a cold steady challenging
light, for ever fixing, observing, reflecting, appraising, moreover uncannily capable of swivelling two ways at once so that
they seemed to see both upwards and downwards, before and
behind."[16]

Kemal's personal life was almost completely uninhibited. He
drank and gambled incessantly; and he enjoyed the company
and entertainment provided by women and spent a good part
of his life in cafes, hotels, brothels, and other similar settings.
During the critical early years of his political opposition both
to the sultan and to the young Turks, these personal activities
led the establishment forces to underestimate the danger that
he posed to them. At the same time, Kemal used these informal
gatherings to discuss social and political issues and to gather
information that passed through these grapevines. Just as Ismet
Inönü was able to convert his physical liability of near-deafness
into a political asset, Kemal's personal habits were not complete liabilities to him. A French writer wrote at the time that
Turkey was governed by one drunkard, one deaf man, and
three hundred deaf-mutes (the assembly deputies). When he
heard this, Kemal responded, "The man is mistaken. Turkey
is governed by one drunkard."[17]

Atatürk's political style and strategy in many ways sharply
broke with traditional Middle Eastern patterns. Although he

[14] *Ibid.*, p. 438.
[15] This terminology is Kemal Karpat's, as presented in his study *Turkey's Politics: The Transition to Multi-Party Politics* (Princeton, N.J.:
Princeton University Press, 1959), pp. 50–51. It is quoted in the writings
of Metin Heper.
[16] Kinross, *Atatürk,* p. 163.
[17] *Ibid.,* p. 261

would on occasion use the *hocas* (clerics) to legitimize a particular political move, he refused to use Islam as any kind of overarching ideology. Quite to the contrary, he had a strong personal aversion to religion and sought to smash its influence. Much is written about his charismatic personality, and he indeed had many of the extraordinary attributes of a charismatic leader. This can be seen even today in Turkey, where the anniversaries of his death are national mourning days, and where thousands upon thousands of Turkish citizens from all walks of life continue to file past his mausoleum in Ankara. But Atatürk was little impressed by his own charisma. He was often annoyed, for example, when other dignitaries would fawn over him. He once became so irritated when the mayor of a city he was visiting insisted on waiting on him in person at the dinner table that he snapped, "For God's sake, sit down! Are you a waiter, or the mayor of this city?" [18] Atatürk institutionalized and routinized his charisma by building organizations, such as the Republican People's Party, that would transcend the existence of one man. This is why one leading authority on Turkish politics writes that one might call Atatürk "an organization man thrown into a charismatic situation." [19]

Although Kemal learned to play his subordinates one against the other and on occasion to maneuver clandestinely and personalistically, he was essentially very direct. In the context of Turkish politics of the day, this directness often seemed crude, brutal, and even stupid. As his major biographer writes, "He detested the shifts and evasions of the oblique approach to Oriental politics, the circumlocutions and imprecisions of its thought and speech. He liked to speak his mind directly, to call spades spades. His outspokenness indeed not only infuriated his enemies but, on occasion, embarrassed his friends." [20] Nor did Kemal really play favorites with friends and relatives. One of the major reasons he divorced his wife, Latife, was that she continually interfered in matters of national politics. Finally, Atatürk was not in the least interested in amassing a

[18] *Ibid.,* p. 368.
[19] Rustow, *Philosophers and Kings,* p. 212.
[20] Kinross, *Atatürk,* p. 45.

fortune for himself and his family. Although he lived comfortably, he was by no means financially corrupt. His life style was in fact quite modest.

Atatürk was above all a realist. He understood power and people and had an unusual ability to bridge the gap between ideal and reality. He used idealists and dreamers, but he never trusted them. He considered them much more dangerous than the small-time politicians who lacked vision. Atatürk himself was both a visionary and a hard, experienced political realist.

Champion of Change or Camouflaged Conservative? A number of excellent social and political analyses of the Atatürk period make rather compelling arguments that Kemal's programs and policies were in essence conservative and nonrevolutionary. Although this school admits that dramatic changes were initiated in the cultural and religious systems of Turkey, the question at issue is that of social structure. Atatürk's programs and policies were initiated without basically altering the traditional class structure. Special care was taken to avoid upsetting the local landlords and aristocracy that controlled power throughout the country. Those at the bottom of the power structure witnessed very little change in their standard of living. If anything, the peasants' standard of living became worse during Kemalist rule. Land reform, for example, was almost completely ignored during Kemal's lifetime. In his important analysis of this question, Arnold Leder supports the following statement with cogent reasoning and convincing evidence.

> From its earliest days in the Turkish War of Independence when it sought the cooperation of the local notables in the countryside, the Kemalist movement became a collaborative movement. The nationalist struggle led by the Kemalists was fought against foreign enemies and not against a particular social class. The Kemalists did not undertake radical change in Turkey's social structure. In fact, they established a tacit alliance with the traditional elites in the countryside. This alliance was reflected in Kemalist political organization where local notables dominated the lower levels of the Republican People's party. The Kemalists made no effort to broaden the party's popular base

and to enlist the support of the peasants. Similarly, Kemalist ideology emphasized not the drastic restratification of society but rather harmony, national solidarity, and the prosperity of all segments of society.[21]

Another study by a leading Turkish political scientist concludes in this regard that "the Atatürk Revolution exploited the basic bifurcation between the educated elite and the uneducated masses, rather than deploring it or immediately attacking it." [22]

This failure to transform the national class structure has been one factor in the political problems that have plagued Turkey since Atatürk's death. Indeed, the creation of the Democratic party in 1946 and its stunning victory over the Republican People's Party in the general election of 1950 may have been major symptoms of the depth of the social and political problems inherited from the days of Atatürk. Since Atatürk's time, there has been a slowly broadening diffusion of power into the Turkish countryside, although the real inclusion of the provincial lower classes within the national decision-making structure remains to be seen.[23]

Questions concerning the depth of Atatürk's reforms are legitimate ones. His revolution did not transform the social, political, or economic conditions of the masses of Turkish peasants. Still, this failure should not be allowed to obscure the immensity of the social and political changes that Atatürk did implement successfully. At bottom, his revolution was a middle-class movement that destroyed a number of traditional symbols and built a new political system. In this sense, it was more radical than the American Revolution and in some re-

[21] Leder, "Collaboration Politics and the Turkish Revolution" (Paper delivered at the 1976 Annual Meeting of the Middle East Studies Association, Los Angeles, 11–13 November 1976), p. 29.

[22] Ergun Özbudun, *Social Change and Political Participation in Turkey* (Princeton, N.J.: Princeton University Press, 1976), p. 43. The writings of Frederick W. Frey also impressively document this position.

[23] See Frank Tachau, "Turkish Provincial Party Politics," in *Social Change and Politics in Turkey*, Kemal H. Karpat *et al.* (Leiden, The Netherlands: E. J. Brill, 1973), pp. 282–314; and Karpat's own article "Political Development in Turkey, 1950–1970," *Middle Eastern Studies* 8 (October 1972):349–375.

spects paralleled the French Revolution, also a middle-class affair. In the context of the time, and without the benefit of scholarly hindsight, it must stand as a revolution of modernization and a movement of substantial political development.

Politically, a 600-year-old national ruling institution and its attendant ruling class were destroyed and replaced by a middle-class elite that introduced new political ideas and institutions, including a political party of genuine consequence. These were structural transformations of lasting impact, which set the stage for subsequent political development, such as the birth of a political opposition (the Democratic party) that was permitted to win in elections. In this rare political event, in which an authoritarian regime voluntarily relinquished power, it was Atatürk's old lieutenant, the dedicated Kemalist Ismet Inönü, who made the decision to permit the opposition to win.[24]

In the section above, we have seen how Atatürk broke many of the traditional interpersonal patterns that had dominated patrimonial rule in the Ottoman Islamic culture. These and the broader political changes discussed above were successfully implemented despite the serious opposition of at least four groups. Of these groups, two were obvious forces of the *ancien régime* — the sultanate's political establishment and the omnipresent religious hierarchy. The two others, however, were groups of former liberal allies who were, ironically, more conservative than Kemal. These were the Young Turks on the one hand and the group of his earliest supporters and comrades on

[24] Inönü's decision was based on a number of personal, political, and ideological factors. First, he hoped at the time to demonstrate to the West the democratic nature of his regime. See Dankwart A. Rustow, "The Development of Parties in Turkey," in *Political Parties and Political Development,* ed. by J. La Palombara and M. Weiner (Princeton, N.J.: Princeton University Press, 1966), p. 122. Second, Inönü felt that the establishment of an opposition political party would help lower the level of discontent in the country. See Leslie L. Roos, Jr. and Noraloo P. Roos, *Managers of Modernization* (Cambridge, Mass.: Harvard University Press, 1971), p. 40. Third, Inönü and his advisors believed that the Republican People's Party was strong enough in the Turkish countryside to guarantee victory in any election. See Kemal Karpat, "Society, Economics, and Politics in Contemporary Turkey," *World Politics* 17 (October 1964):58. These positions are all drawn together and analyzed in the writings of Arnold Leder.

the other hand. In the case of the former, "... theirs was essentially a conservative revolution.... Imperialists in essence, blind to the new nationalist forces now at work in the modern world, the Young Turks aspired merely to conserve, if in a more liberal form, the Ottoman Empire of their forebears." [25] At the same time, old comrades such as Husayn Rauf, Ali Fuad, and Kâzim Karabekir were more liberal idealists and preferred democracy over revolutionary change. "Kemal was embarking on a social revolution. Rauf and his friends, at this stage, preferred social evolution." [26] Despite this encircling and committed opposition, Atatürk rammed through as much radical political change as was perhaps humanly possible.

A comparison of Atatürk and his long-time friend and trusted lieutenant, Ismet Inönü, also helps demonstrate the nature of Atatürk's revolution. Inönü had served Kemal loyally and was the one lieutenant who survived his leader's personality and inner-circle purges.[27] The two men complemented each other perfectly. Atatürk was direct, forceful, and mercurial, while Inönü was conservative, retiring, and unspectacular. When Atatürk died in 1938, Inönü was the natural choice to replace him as president. For the next 35 years, he played a

25 Kinross, *Atatürk*, p. 30.

26 *Ibid.*, p. 392. These associates were generally of well-to-do upper-class and upper-middle-class background and were therefore more closely tied to the old system than Kemal, who was obviously their social inferior. In 1924, this group resigned from the Republican People's Party and formed their own organization, called the Progressive Republican Party. Kemal used a Kurdish rebellion as the major excuse for disbanding the Progressive Party. For an analysis of the character of Atatürk's political elite, see Joseph S. Szyliowicz's study of leadership in modern Turkey in Frank Tachau, ed., *Political Elites and Political Development in the Middle East* (Cambridge, Mass.: Schenkman Publishing Co., 1975), pp. 23–68. Another good source is Frederick Frey's article in *Political Elites in the Middle East*, ed. by George Lenczowski (Washington, D.C.: American Enterprise Institute, 1975), pp. 41–82.

27 Toward the end, personal tensions that had been building up for many years between Atatürk and Inönü began to break into the open. Kinross reports one such exchange that took place in 1937. The pressured and normally unflappable Inönü lost his temper and blurted to Atatürk, "How much longer is this country going to be governed from a drunkard's table?" To this Atatürk coldly responded, "You seem to forget that it was a drunkard who appointed you to your post." Kinross, *Atatürk*, p. 486.

prominent role in directing Turkish political destiny. Inönü's most famous political decision was his call in 1945 for the formation of an opposition party (referred to above). This remarkable move transformed Turkey into a multiparty state and was an example of Inönü's great commitment to liberalization. In taking this action, Inönü not only broadened participatory politics in Turkey but also carved out a place for himself, independent of Atatürk, in the Turkish political pantheon.

Although many observers interpret Inönü's programs as moving far beyond the policies of Atatürk in the field of political development, there is another position that needs to be presented. The argument has been made that in promoting liberalization and introducing pluralist politics into Turkey, Inönü in fact hampered the system's capacity for development. By stepping aside and opening the arena to all comers, he introduced a period of tense and competitive factional politics that has ever since slowed the Turkish drive to develop. From the days of Menderes's prime ministry, beginning in 1950, to the debilitating political struggles in 1977 and 1978 between Suleyman Demirel of the Justice Party and Bülent Ecevit of the Republican People's Party, the political process in Turkey has been weakening.

The severity of the crisis is seen in the direct intervention of the military into the political arena in 1960, 1971, and, most recently, in September of 1980. Although the most recent military intervention has succeeded in bringing terrorism under control, there is considerable doubt whether this regime headed by General Kenan Evren will go back to its barracks anytime soon, although in early 1983 he permitted the limited formation of political parties. As unopposed candidate for the presidency in the November 1982 referendum, General Evren easily won a seven-year presidential term.

This position is supported strongly in an excellent and provocative study by a young Turkish social scientist and diplomat, who wrote that with Inönü's "democratization of political life, the principle of revolutionism was effectively shelved. ... The capacity of Turkish leaders to introduce orderly change from above, a capacity that was in evidence during

Atatürk's time, was lost for the sake and as a result of democracy. Atatürk had started a revolution; Inönü arrested it." [28]

There is certainly truth in both sides of this debate, which focuses directly upon the developmental dialectic discussed in Chapter I. Authoritarianism at the center endangers participation in the periphery (Atatürk's case). Liberalization, however, tends to create fragmentation, which in turn weakens capacity for development (Inönü's case). The parallel processes of modernization and political development must be continuing ones. Atatürk started a revolution. It was up to his successors to continue it, widen it, and deepen it.

MUHAMMAD REZA SHAH PAHLAVI:
THE TRADITIONALISM
OF A MODERNIZING MONARCH

In June of 1934, President Kemal Atatürk welcomed an important neighboring head of state to Turkey for a three-week official state visit. The visitor was Reza Shah, the founder of the Pahlavi dynasty of Iran. Like Atatürk, Reza Shah was a man of imposing presence. Standing well over six feet in height, he had the flashing eyes of an eagle and a personality that scorched friend and foe alike. The two leaders had much in common. Both were military men and avid nationalists who consolidated their nations and built strong central political control over their peoples. Both leaders also sought to modernize and reform their countries. Reza Shah, who was three years older than Atatürk, was greatly impressed by the latter's reform programs as well as by the level of modernity he witnessed in Turkey. Partly as a result of this visit, he lashed out at such symbols of tradition as the ulema, while at the same time sporadically modernizing the economic, educational, and mili-

---

[28] Osman Faruk Logoglu, "Ismet Inönü and the Political Modernization of Turkey, 1945–1965," Ph.D. diss. (Princeton University, 1970), p. 255. With regard to Atatürk's strategy of change, Logoglu writes: "There has been no rigorous exposition of the meaning of the well-established proposition that Atatürk tried to convert only the elite or the intelligentsia and did not really try to reach the peasant masses. The meaning of the corollary proposition that Atatürk had the insight to realize he could not change the masses without first transforming the elite needs to be restated as well." See pp. 255–256.

tary systems in his country. Yet Reza Shah's programs of reform never approached the depth or breadth of those instituted by his contemporary in Turkey.[29]

After participating in the military coup of 1921, Reza Khan crowned himself Shah of Iran in 1926. In so doing, he chose to continue patrimonial monarchy, a system of leadership that Atatürk had vigorously dismantled in Turkey. Patrimonial monarchism dominated Iranian politics until 1979, when Reza Shah's eldest son, Muhammad Reza, was overthrown by a massive revolutionary movement.

Although an impressive nation builder and leader who rose to power from a lowly and illiterate background, Reza Shah in the end only shuffled the old power relations in Iran. The major political change was the existence of a new royal family at the center of the system. By the time he abdicated in 1941, Reza Shah had acquired in his own name the largest landholdings in Iran and was drawing an annual income of well over $3 million a year.[30] Although he maintained parliamentary forms and procedures, he completely controlled the political process. His rule was absolute and oppressive; he disposed of whomever he considered to be a threat to himself or to his son.

It was within this repressive political climate that Reza Shah built a railway, founded a modern educational system, developed a national army, and supported such strong symbolic measures as the unveiling of women and the condemnation of the clerics. The old social structure and the traditional patrimonialism were strongly protected, however, by the new ruling Pahlavi family. One Persian source describes the patrimonial role of Reza Shah as follows: "The Shah expected that all government employees consider themselves completely subservient to his desires and that they not show any personality of their own. . . . Those favored by the Shah did their best to carry out his desires while at the same time trying to insure that these

---

[29] The major comparison of Atatürk and Reza Shah as modernizers is Richard H. Pfaff, "Disengagement from Traditionalism in Turkey and Iran," *Western Political Quarterly* 16 (March 1963):79–98.

[30] Great Britain, Public Record Office, F. O. 371/18992, from Mallet (Tehran), 28 November 1935.

efforts did not become too well known and thus draw fame upon themselves." [31] The last Shah of Iran, Muhammad Reza, once wrote that "all over the world, the father helps shape the character of the son. In my case, my father influenced me more by far than has anyone else." [32]

Muhammad Reza Shah Pahlavi was born on 26 October 1919. At the age of 13, he began his studies at Le Rosey School in Rolle, Switzerland. He returned to Iran four years later, and between 1936 and 1941 he received a military and political education that was directed primarily by his father. With the Allied invasion of Iran in 1941 and his father's humiliating abdication, Muhammad Reza became Shah of Iran. The next dozen years were very painful and insecure for the young Shah, as is well symbolized by the attempt on his life in 1949, which, face-to-face with an armed assassin, the Shah survived by "shadow-dancing and feinting." [33]

The Shah managed to dodge and weave his way through the 1940s, during which time he was the target of challenges emanating from many different directions. On the left, the Communist Tudeh Party threatened to capture the entire political system, while on the right, both knowledgeable statesmen and conservative clerics sought to control the Shah and to take power themselves. Foreign interference was intense, and the young king found himself sandwiched between nationalist fervor and imperialist power. It was during these early years that the Shah learned the art of political maneuver and perfected the traditional techniques of divide and rule. When such basic rationalizations of rule as charisma and religion are absent, the patrimonial leader is forced to rely entirely upon personal manipulative techniques. This was exactly the situation for the Shah of Iran in the 1940s; besieged and surrounded by opponents and critics, he managed to survive by constantly refining those methods of patrimonial rule that were at his disposal.

[31] *Sharq-i Tarik* [The Dark East] (Tehran: Taban Press, 1942), pp. 69–71. In Persian.

[32] Mohammad Reza Shah Pahlavi, *Mission for My Country* (New York: McGraw-Hill, 1961), p. 45.

[33] *Ibid.*, p. 57.

In the early 1950s, the Shah and the monarchy of Iran were faced with a challenge of the most serious proportions. A charismatic personality rose within Iran and, rallying the masses behind him, confronted the Shah and threatened to transform social and political patterns. Dr. Muhammad Musaddiq rose to influence primarily on the basis of his attack against foreign interests in Iran and his direct drive to nationalize the Anglo-Iranian Oil Company. Although the apologetic (as opposed to analytic) literature concerning Pahlavi politics has attempted to portray Musaddiq as somehow being in league with the British, the British had already, in their diplomatic reports in the 1930s, tagged him as "a demagogue and a windbag." [34]

Musaddiq was known in Iran as an impeccably honest personality who would refuse to accede to foreign interests. The dramatic proof of this was his successful campaign to nationalize the oil company. Musaddiq was prime minister from April 1951 to August 1953. During this time, he became internationally famous as he nationalized the oil company and slowly undermined the power and position of the Shah. He fell from office during the chaotic events of August 1953, which included the Shah's returning to Iran and the throne a few days after a hurried flight out of the country. Street fighting and military activity that month involved the Tudeh forces, pro-Shah elements, Musaddiqists, and Americans who directly intervened on behalf of the King. [35]

Much of Musaddiq's support came from the rising professional middle class, whose members tended to be highly nationalistic and critical of the corruption that pervaded the Iranian socioadministrative system. Musaddiq, who retained in his behavior vestiges of the old aristocracy from which he

[34] Great Britain, Public Record Office, F.O. 371/20837, Seymour to Eden, 12 April 1937. For the convoluted reasoning that implies Musaddiq's proximity to the British, see Ramesh Sanghvi, *Aryamehr: The Shah of Iran* (New York: Stein and Day, 1968), pp. 142–245, 213.

[35] For a reliable analysis of these controversial and complex events, see Richard W. Cottam, *Nationalism in Iran* (Pittsburgh: University of Pittsburgh Press, 1964), pp. 223–230. For a fascinating account by a leading American operative who helped plan and carry out the countercoup against Musaddiq, see Kermit Roosevelt, *Countercoup: The Struggle for the Control of Iran* (New York: McGraw-Hill Book Co., 1979).

had come, nonetheless entertained middle-class values and was able to gain strength and support across class lines. Although he may have been a poor politician in the Iranian context, Musaddiq was a charismatic leader who challenged the very roots of patrimonialism in Iran by directly threatening the Shah by disrupting the patterns of corruption that are often nourished in settings of informal personalism and omnipresent rivalry.[36]

The Musaddiq challenge represented an intolerable situation for the Shah, since it directly struck at the very foundation upon which all patrimonial leaders must base their power — their indisputable and central right to rule. The threat from Musaddiq was particularly serious because he donned a patrimonial mantle of his own that was heavily embroidered with charisma.[37]

Following the fall of Musaddiq, the Shah began a concerted program to solidify his position as leader of all Iranians. Between 1954 and 1961, he pursued a policy of consolidation through coercion and thus adopted political tactics reminiscent of those used by his father in the 1930s. Besides building up military resources such as the army and the gendarmerie, the Shah organized an extensive secret-police system (SAVAK) in 1957. This complex organization became a key element in Pahlavi politics from then on.

Beginning in 1963, the style of leadership of the Shah shifted to an emphasis upon the introduction of reform programs. Policies of coercion were balanced with programs of co-optation as the Shah initiated an impressive campaign to foster reform from above. In the mid-1960s, he spoke often about the need for revolutionary programs in Iran. By the end of the 1960s, he was quoting Lenin in his speeches, and more and more of his supporters were referring to opponents of the regime as reactionary, feudal, and right-wing. The Shah outlined the core of the reform program in January 1963, when he announced the six principles of the White Revolution. This

[36] Mussaddiq himself was not without patrimonial traits.

[37] E. A. Bayne writes that "the Shah's historic image was dimmed by the burning fire of Mossadegh's charisma." Bayne, *Persian Kingship in Transition* (New York: American Universities Field Staff, 1968), p. 160.

Revolution of the Shah and the People, as it was referred to in Persian, was expanded until it included 19 different points. The most important were the first 12: (1) land reform, (2) nationalization of forests and pastures, (3) public sale of state-owned factories to finance land reform, (4) profit sharing in industry, (5) reform of electoral law to include women, (6) literacy corps, (7) health corps, (8) reconstruction and development corps, (9) rural Courts of Justice, (10) nationalization of the waterways, (11) national reconstruction, and (12) educational and administrative revolution.[38] This program became the creed of the Shah and the Iranian political elite.

Despite these reforms, which were never completely and effectively implemented, political opposition, unrest, instability, and violence all increased in Iran during the last 15 years of the Shah's rule. By the mid-1970s, urban guerrillas dedicated to the overthrow of the Shah clashed constantly with security forces. Between 1972 and 1976, the Shah's long-time policy of blending programs of repression with those of reform was abandoned, and a period of stifling police rule was ushered in. People were arrested and harassed arbitrarily and often; censorship became unusually heavy-handed and indiscriminate; and for the first time during the Shah's rule, torture was systematically utilized in the prisons. A 1976 study prepared by the International Commission of Jurists reported that "there can be no doubt that torture has been systematically practiced over a number of years against recalcitrant suspects under interrogation by the SAVAK."[39] When questioned about tor-

---

[38] The last seven points were (13) the sale of stocks of all industrial plants to the public, (14) a national campaign against price gouging and inflation, (15) cost-free education for all, (16) the provision of food for the newborn up to the age of two, (17) the expansion of public insurance to include all classes of Iranians, particularly villagers and farmers, (18) the control of land price increases to the inflation rate or less, and (19) the requirement that government officials declare all private and family earnings.

[39] William J. Butler and Georges Levasseur, *Human Rights and the Legal System in Iran* (Geneva: International Commission of Jurists, 1976), p. 22. For various sources discussing the severity of secret police tactics in Iran, see Amnesty International, *Annual Report, 1974–75* (London, 1975); U.S. Congress, House Committee on International Relations, Subcommittee on International Organizations, *Human Rights in Iran* (Washington, D.C.: Government Printing Office, 1977); Philip Jacobson, "Torture in Iran," *Sunday Times* (London), 19 January 1975, p. 9.

LIFE OF MUHAMMAD REZA SHAH PAHLAVI:
MAJOR EVENTS

1919 Born in Tehran
1926 Reza Khan crowned Shah of Iran; Muhammad Reza declared Crown Prince
1932 Enters Le Rosey School in Switzerland
1936 Returns to Tehran; enrolls in military academy
1941 Reza Shah abdicates; Muhammad Reza takes oath as Shah of Iran; Tudeh party established in Tehran
1946 Russian army withdraws from Azerbaijan
1950 Shah announces intention to divide lands among peasants
1951 Dr. Muhammad Musaddiq becomes prime minister; nationalization of Anglo-Iranian Oil Company
1953 Fall of Dr. Musaddiq; Shah reassumes power
1957 Establishment of Security Organization (SAVAK)
1959 Shah marries Farah Diba
1960 Birth of Crown Prince Reza
1963 Announces White Revolution; countrywide riots and demonstrations put down with force
1967 Formal coronation of Muhammad Reza Shah and Empress Farah
1971 Celebration of 2,500 years of Iranian monarchy
1975 Establishes one-party system — the National Resurgence Party
1978 Masses of Iranian citizens riot and demonstrate against the Shah's rule; Shah institutes government by martial law
1979 Shah goes into exile; Ayatollah Ruhollah Khomeini returns to Iran after 15 years in exile
1980 Muhammad Reza Shah dies in Egypt

---

ture, the Shah said: "I am not bloodthirsty. I am working for my country and the coming generations. I can't waste my time on a few young idiots. I don't believe the tortures attributed to the SAVAK are as common as people say, but I can't run everything." [40]

---

[40] Gérard de Villiers, *The Imperial Shah: An Informal Biography* (Boston: Little, Brown and Co., 1976), p. 259.

This sharp shift in the direction of repressive rule sacrificed the more subtle and paternal dimensions of patrimonial rule to harsh police control. One result was a marked rise in opposition activity, which took the form of urban violence promoted by growing and dedicated guerrilla groups. Thousands of incidents occurred throughout Iran; new, superbly organized opposition groups even managed to infiltrate the Shah's highly touted security forces. The tighter the police turned the screws, the more fanatic the opposition became. Dozens of young women, along with the men, joined the guerrillas as a vicious circle of repression and reaction set in. Meanwhile, in the mosques throughout the country, religious leaders increased sharply their crucial social and political commentary.

Then, at the end of 1976 and in early 1977, and coinciding partly with the appearance of the Carter administration in Washington, the Shah began to cut back on the repression and tried to return to more flexible patrimonial tactics. A period of liberalization began and was accompanied by a marked decrease in guerrilla-sponsored violence. Letters, petitions, and communications of all kinds flooded the offices of the Shah and his political elite. When a leading Iranian newspaper raised a question in one of its columns concerning "what is wrong in Iran," it received over 40,000 letters. This kind of overwhelming response frightened the regime, and after an exchange of visits between the Shah and President Carter, the sporadic reversion to heavy-handed police tactics resulted in a wave of violence that shook the country to its roots in 1978. Drawing its inspiration from the charismatic, uncompromising leadership of Ayatollah Ruhollah Khomeini in exile in Iraq and then France, the popular opposition gathered momentum and strength as the year progressed. Rallying around the Shi'i religious leaders, individuals drawn from all social classes demonstrated violently against the Shah's rule in the city of Qom in January, in Tabriz in February, and in Tehran and other cities in March, April, and May. Then in August, September, and December of 1978, the opposition to the Shah exploded into mass marches and demonstrations involving hundreds of thousands of dissatisfied citizens.

Shaken and stunned in the face of massive national rebellion, the Shah tried a number of desperate measures of both concession and repression. Concessions were half-measures that only whetted the appetite of the popular opposition; repression gave the revolution over 10,000 martyrs and strengthened the resolve and commitment of the challenging forces. When the traditional twin tactics of alternating coercion and co-optation failed to stem the revolutionary tide, the Shah was left baffled and bewildered. Already somewhat weakened by a five-year struggle with cancer and psychologically unwilling to relinquish the mantle of absolute monarchy, he watched in disbelief as his people, always chanting "Marg bar Shah" ("Death to the Shah"), rose to overthrow him.

On January 3, 1979, the Iranian Majlis approved the Shah's reluctant appointment of Shahpur Bakhtiar, a liberal and former National Front member, as prime minister of Iran. On January 16, Muhammad Reza Shah left Iran for a "vacation" abroad — a vacation from which he was never to return. On January 31, Ayatollah Khomeini, the implacable foe of the Shah, returned to Iran in triumph after 15 years of exile abroad. The Shah spent the last 18 months of his life seeking a permanent residence in exile. After shuffling from Egypt to Morocco to the Bahamas to Mexico to the United States to Panama, the Shah returned to Egypt, where he died of cancer on July 27, 1980.

Patterns of Rule. Muhammad Reza Shah Pahlavi was a political leader who practiced to perfection the techniques and tactics of patrimonial rule for nearly four decades in Iran. As a king who ruled by emanation, he was presented to his people as the source of all ideas and the fount of all good. Each of the points in the White Revolution, therefore, was attributed to the Shah, and much has been written about how these ideas suddenly came to his mind.[41]

Individuals always competed with one another to have their ideas presented to the Shah, who they hoped would include

---

[41] See, for example, "Brilliant Idea was Born on a Murky Day," *Kayhan International* (Tehran), 22 November 1966, p. 4. This article explains how the idea of a literacy corps suddenly popped into the Shah's mind.

them in his personal program for national development. In his book published in 1978, the Shah patrimonially discussed his role as national mentor, teacher, and creator of revolutionary ideas: "I accept most willingly this mission for teaching and advice because of the knowledge I command on the most extensive scale of my country's national and international problems and because I am, myself, the architect and founder of the social revolution of which all Iranian developments of the day are the reflection." [42] The strength of this pattern of emanation is also seen in the words of one of the most powerful men in recent Iranian history, former prime minister, minister of court, tribal aristocrat, and lifelong friend and confidant of the Shah, Asadollah Alam: "I cannot say that he is faultless. Everyone, as you say, has faults. . . . [H]is fault to my mind is that he is really too great for his people — his ideas are too great for we people to realize it." [43] This kind of subservience, displayed even by the most important officials, is a central ingredient in patrimonial rule by emanation.

A special effort was made in Iran to portray the Shah to his people as an unquestioned patrimonial leader. Because he had to bargain for survival during the first twelve years of his rule and because he lacked charisma, the years following the fall of Musaddiq were years in which "a sophisticated apparatus would work assiduously to create the supreme patriarchal image, and a secret police would guard it." [44]

The source of emanation must be visible to everyone everywhere. Pictures of the Shah and his immediate family adorned government offices and public places throughout the country. Statues of the Shah stood in the middle of village squares, city parks, and even on the top of mountain peaks. Shrubbery in public gardens was cut in the form of Persian script spelling out the Shah's name. His likeness was woven into Persian carpets, and over 75 different sets of Iranian postage stamps carried the royal portrait. Millions of colored lights were lit

---

[42] Mohammed Reza Shah Pahlavi, *Towards the Great Civilization* (Tehran: n. p., 1978).

[43] Margaret Laing, *The Shah* (London: Sidgwick and Jackson, 1977), p. 231.

[44] Bayne, *Persian Kingship*, p. 167.

throughout the country on the Shah's birthday, and a huge party was held annually in his presence at Amjadieh Stadium in Tehran.

The Shah attempted to legitimize his rule in a number of other ways. He sought to develop systems of thought, for example, that stressed monarchical, religious, and reform considerations. The ideology of reform was developed to buttress the traditional rationalizations of monarchy and religion. The elite constantly argued that the Iranians had an inherent need for a monarchical political system. This was manifested in the continuous national celebrations and festivities that were organized for almost a decade to commemorate Iran's 2,500 years of monarchy. Nevertheless, it became increasingly difficult to reconcile philosophies of reform with philosophies of monarchy, since "the dialectic of king and modernizing polity has not been fully resolved." [45] High officials in the Military Academy in Tehran privately expressed the primary need for their study curriculum to rationalize (*ta'bir*) the institution of monarchy in view of the modern world.

The use of religion as a legitimating device was also difficult for the Shah, who had to compete in this regard with the mujtahids, who were the representatives of the Hidden Imam in society. The Shah attempted in various ways, therefore, to reveal his special relation with the divine. He argued that the peasants often referred to him as the Shadow of God, and he apparently believed that he was guided and guarded by some superhuman force. In his autobiography, the Shah credited his numerous escapes from personal and political disaster to "some unseen hand" and claimed that from childhood he "felt that perhaps there is a supreme being who is guiding me." [46] He stated that "my reign has saved the country, and it has done so because God was on my side," and that "God is my only friend." [47] In the end, however, the Shah decided to strengthen the rationalization of his rule by stressing an ideology of re-

[45] *Ibid.*, p. 97.
[46] Pahlavi, *Mission for My Country*, pp. 55. 58.
[47] See "An Oriana Fallaci Interview: The Shah of Iran," *The New Republic*, 1 December 1973, p. 17; and de Villiers, *Imperial Shah*, p. 273.

form, since this appeared more believable to growing forces within his society as well as to the twentieth-century world at large. This may have been one of his most critical errors.

The traditional characteristics of personalism, proximity, informality, and balanced conflict also permeated the rule of Muhammad Reza Shah. His was an "individual approach to kingship," [48] and he ruled at the center of a complex web of personal relations. It was especially in the early and middle years of his rule that the Shah had contact with as many officials and other personalities as possible. In this kind of political setting, the issue of physical proximity assumed reciprocal significance. Individuals held influence commensurate to their nearness to the patrimonial leader, while the leader felt it important to be in personal contact with advisors, friends, officials, and confidants. Just as the family patriarch deems it essential to his position as patriarch to maintain personal communication with all of his children, so also did the patrimonial leader consider it important to his position to be in touch with as many members of his society as possible. In Pahlavi Iran, there was tremendous pressure constantly exerted by individuals from all groups and classes to move towards the Shah, who was the locus of power. At the same time, the Shah stated that "one of the principal problems of government is to know the right people and in necessary numbers. Either these people must be presented to you — and you need time to become acquainted and to know them — or you must search for them." [49]

In this highly personal system of patrimonial rule, informality prevailed, and individuals were balanced against individuals. The Shah operated through informal meetings, personal cliques, and trusted groups of friends and family. Rivalry and tension were omnipresent; over the years, the Shah proved himself a master at playing key subordinates off against one another. As a result, for years no one became overly powerful and the leader remained far above any potential challenger. In the Shah's Iran, the network of balanced rivalry encompassed the royal family, courtiers, personal adjutants, minis-

48 Bayne, *Persian Kingship*, p. 239.
49 *Ibid.*, p. 193.

ters, military officers, and all economic and political figures of any important standing. This pattern was reflected most dramatically in the case of 12 different military and security organizations, all of which stood in rivalry with one another. This organizational tension was the direct result of the intense personal competition that marked the relations among the leaders of these agencies. It was the patrimonial leader who kept these lines of tension finely adjusted.[50]

Finally, the Shah of Iran always sought to maintain a special and direct control over the military. As Shah and Commander in Chief, he handpicked the military leaders, primarily on the basis of their loyalty to him. The downfall of several important politicians of the past occurred quickly after they challenged the Shah for control of the military. The Shah prided himself on his knowledge of military science and claimed that he understood the necessity of military power because of "my father's examples, *and* because I am a soldier." [51] His special emphasis on the military is seen in the huge expenditures that were funneled into military and security establishments. By the late 1970s, they absorbed approximately 40 percent of the Iranian budget. Between 1972 and 1977, U.S. military sales to Iran totalled $16.2 billion while the Pahlavi defense budget increased by nearly 700 percent over this six-year period.[52] The Shah of Iran once summarized his own view of his relation to the military in the peculiarly patrimonial phrase, "I am the army." [53]

The Patrimonial Path to Revolution. As long as Muhammad Reza Shah pursued proven programs of patrimonialism sea-

[50] For a detailed analysis of these kinds of patterns in Iran, see two articles by James A. Bill: "The Plasticity of Informal Politics: The Case of Iran," *Middle East Journal* 27 (Spring 1973):131–151; and "Patterns of Elite Politics in Iran," pp. 17–40 in *Political Elites in the Middle East* ed. by Lenczowski.

[51] Bayne, *Persian Kingship*, p. 139.

[52] U.S. Congress, Senate Committee on Foreign Relations, Subcommittee on Foreign Assistance, Staff Report, *U.S. Military Sales to Iran* (Washington, D.C.: Government Printing Office, 1976); and *The Christian Science Monitor*, 20 January 1978, p. 5.

[53] Bayne, *Persian Kingship*, p. 186.

soned with the flavor of serious reform, he was able to buy time and to maintain control. His land reform and literacy programs co-opted the ideas of the challenging professional middle class while proposing to improve the living standards of the masses of Iranian people. The Pahlavi game plan called for massive economic growth blended with moderate and controlled social reform all in the service of the preservation and perpetuation of the traditional patrimonial political status quo.[54]

The fact that the Shah's reform program was designed to protect rather than to transform traditional political patterns can be documented by analyzing the direction and the methodology of the reforms. The core of the "White Revolution" consisted of programs that could only buttress the patrimonial position of the ruler. Viewed from this perspective, the land reform program served to weaken precisely those forces that traditionally threatened the patrimonial leader, that is, the old aristocratic, landed families and the Shi'i religious establishment. By cutting back on the economic power of the ulema, the Shah hoped to improve his position relative to theirs. By replacing aristocratic officials at the national political level with workers and bureaucrats with no independent power base of their own, the Shah sought to strengthen the politics of emanation.

The actual administration of the reform program was implemented according to traditional patterns. Personalism, rivalry, insecurity, distrust, and uncoordinated ad hoc decision making prevailed. Political opportunists entered the arena and tainted and impeded the programs. The built-in rivalry that debilitated reform efforts was seen in the important task of land reform. At first, the ministries of agriculture, interior, and economy competed for control of the program. Later, a separate ministry of land reform and rural cooperatives was established, as well as a ministry of agricultural products and consumer goods and a ministry of natural resources. There

---

[54] For a detailed study of the Shah's strategy of patrimonialism and system preservation, see James A. Bill, *The Politics of Iran: Groups, Classes and Modernization* (Columbus, Ohio: Charles E. Merrill, 1972).

was also an agricultural bank and an agricultural development fund. All of these organizations, and others (e.g., the plan organization) were bound together in an interlocking network of competition that prevented any individual or any ministry from becoming too powerful — or too effective. It also prevented successful land reform from occurring.[55]

The Shah's reform programs suffered from other serious maladies. Patrimonial politics are susceptible to the abuses of corruption, favoritism, cronyism, and nepotism. In the Shah's Iran, these abuses bubbled outward from the very center of the system and became both more pronounced and more visible through the decade of the 1970s. When oil revenues increased from slightly more than $2 billion in 1972 to over $20 billion in 1974, the opportunities for graft, bribery, and general corruption also increased tenfold. In the process, the gap in income distribution increased significantly and the masses of Iranian people found themselves relatively worse off after the reform program than they were prior to 1963. By using and then abusing patrimonialism, the Shah in the end only alienated the very constituency whose support he was seeking to gain.

In 1971–1972, the Shah of Iran began a dramatic shift in his tactics of patrimonial rule. Coercion and repression took precedence over co-optation and reform. A major target of this new, hard-line policy was the leading members of the ulema. In a system of patrimonial rule by emanation, it is extremely difficult for the leader to tolerate competing centers of leadership. It is especially difficult when these individuals carry charismatic qualities derived from the ideology of Islam. Yet over the years, the Iranian shahs had managed to live in a state of uneasy coexistence with the Shi'i clerics and had allowed them to maintain their own sphere of influence. Between 1972 and 1976, however, the Shah's security apparatus attacked the religious leaders frontally; many were arrested and imprisoned, and some were executed. In the process, the Iranian govern-

[55] For documentation, see Eric J. Hooglund's excellent *Land and Revolution in Iran, 1960–1980* (Austin, Tex.: The University of Texas Press, 1982).

ment closed down religious publishing houses, disbanded religious student groups, and infiltrated mosque and endowment (*owqaf*) organizations. This policy alienated the entire religious establishment, and the mullahs rallied to the leadership of Ayatollah Khomeini, a leading mujtahid with unassailable opposition credentials.

The ineffectiveness and failure of many of the reform programs and the generally sad state of the lower-class masses provided a ready constituency for the harried religious leaders. Meanwhile, the Shah himself had lost his patrimonial touch and had committed the grave error of isolating himself from his people. The patrimonial leader at the center of the familial polity had cut himself off from his advisors and his people. With the deaths of shrewd old patrimonial cronies and advisors, such as Asadollah Alam and Manuchehr Eghbal, and with his own increasing megalomania, the Shah lost touch. Toward the end, he even refused to listen to the advice along his last line to reality, that of Empress Farah.[56] Instead, the Shah consulted seriously only with the American and British ambassadors, two outside diplomats whose own understandings of Iran were flawed and who were not really trusted by the monarch.

The very fact that the Pahlavi government was so deeply involved with the West (especially the United States) also only badly exacerbated the situation. Not only had the patrimonial leader lost touch with his own constituency, he had shifted his attention more and more to political, economic, and military alliance with outsiders. In the view of many of his former constituents, therefore, the Shah had forsaken the country, culture, and Shiʻi Islam for external friends. In the eyes of the Iranian people, the patrimonial leader had clearly deserted his family.

Ayatollah Ruhollah Khomeini, the immediate successor to the Shah and the hero of the revolution, has also led Iran

---

[56] As the Pahlavi monarchy collapsed, the Empress stated that the Shah refused even to listen to her advice and counsel. Among other things, she said, "The husband does not always listen to the wife." Personal interview (Bill) with Empress Farah Diba, 29 November 1978, Niavaran Palace, Tehran.

according to patrimonial principles. This is symbolized by the fact that when the Shah fell Iranians immediately replaced his pictures with those of Khomeini. Revolutionary Iran has been marked by mobs and masses of Iranian citizens behaving as the very embodiment of the Ayatollah. This is the politics of emanation par excellence. All the characteristics of patrimonial politics have prevailed during the post-Pahlavi period: personalism, proximity, informality, balanced conflict, and military activity. There has also been considerable violence and insecurity. Yet the Khomeini style of patrimonialism has differed significantly from that of the last Shah; it has carried several important advantages.

First, Khomeini is a genuinely charismatic personality. In this sense, he is much more similar to Dr. Musaddiq than to the Shah, who always had to labor under the disadvantage of an unimpressive and extremely dry personality. The Shah's person was deferred to largely because of the power that inhered in the office. Second, Khomeini holds legitimate religious credentials. The Shah had always had to stretch fact and imagination to portray a special Islamic legitimacy. Third, the Ayatollah has never been accused of personal corruption but rather has led a simple, spartan life. This has appealed to his popular constituency, which views him as a leader of, for, and from the people. It is also in direct contrast to the Shah, whose world included the splendor and opulence of palaces, banks, American movie stars, aircraft, modern art, and the Rockefellers. Fourth, the slogan "Neither East not West" indicates the Khomeinian preoccupation with a severe xenophobic stance dedicated to the destruction of all outside influence in Iran's social and political system. Since the West in general and the United States in particular were most closely associated with the former regime, they have been the major targets of attacks by the revolutionary regime. But the Soviet Union and Communism in general have also been criticized and condemned by the Ayatollah. This strain of patrimonial independence is much more appealing than the policy practiced by the Shah, who was widely viewed as a puppet and client of the United States.

These factors all combined to give Khomeini's revolutionary mode of patrimonialism its fifth and major strength: As patrimonial leader, Khomeini managed to build a mass base of support. Although he turned viciously on the old upper and middle classes, Khomeini has sought to improve the life of the masses of Iranian people. By stressing the needs of those he calls the *mostaza'fin* ("downtrodden," "dispossessed"), he has managed to build, sometimes brutally, a large and committed constituency. His government has not hesitated to take from the haves and to give to the have-nots. In this way, the Ayatollah has been able to remain a patrimonial leader with a mass constituency, unlike the Shah, whose patrimonialism rested on only the tiniest and flimsiest of support bases.[57]

Despite these considerations, the patrimonialism of Khomeini and his successors will someday have to come to grips with the related challenges of modernization and political development. A retreat into the past can at best be only a temporary solution. The support of the masses for a particular leader or political system will continue only so long as those who govern are able to meet the needs and demands of the population. If this support should evaporate, then the patrimonialism of Khomeini and his successors will share the same fate as that of Muhammad Reza Shah.

GAMAL ABDEL NASSER:
PATRIMONIALISM AND TRANSFORMATION

The man is at once feline and massive. His square build speaks of a peasant ancestry, the long remembrance of stubborn, fleshy gestures, the recompense of a heavy, miserable diet over many generations. But this son of the Middle Valley also carries Arab descent in his blood: a Bedouin strain had pursued for several centuries in Bani Murr District the synthesis of Ishmael and Pharaoh. Perhaps this gives his physique that deliberate alertness, his face that sharp breadth, his eyes that brooding nostalgia behind their hard, almost green, gaze. The Arab has risen ponderously, one might say, from his long submergence in the soil of Egypt.[58]

---

[57] For more detailed analysis of Khomeini's Iran, see chapter 9.

[58] Jacques Berque, *Cultural Expression in Arab Society Today*, trans. Robert W. Stookey (Austin, Tex.: The University of Texas Press, 1978), pp. 15–16.

Recent Middle Eastern political history is marked by the existence of a handful of leaders who have attempted to uproot many of the traditional social and political patterns that have prevailed in their societies. Besides Kemal Atatürk, discussed above, the other major case in point is Gamal Abdel Nasser of Egypt. Like Atatürk, Nasser adopted tactics of transformation that left some areas largely untouched, while in other areas fundamental efforts to change were made. The life and leadership of Gamal Abdel Nasser in particular deserves to be analyzed in this light, since Nasser introduced many revolutionary programs in a society that contains nearly one-third of the world's Arab population.

Gamal Abdel Nasser was born on 15 January 1918 in Alexandria. He was raised in the village of Beni Morr in Upper Egypt, the ancestral home of his family. Nasser's father was a postal clerk; his mother died when Gamal was eight years old. Since his father had remarried and was constantly being moved about in his work, Gamal spent long periods living with various relatives. As a secondary-school student, he developed a deep social and political consciousness. He harbored an early concern about the British presence in Egypt; at the same time, he grew to dislike the debility and dependence that marked the status of his country.

Nasser graduated from secondary school in Cairo in 1936 and afterwards entered the Egyptian Military Academy. Upon graduating from the academy in 1938 with the rank of second lieutenant, he was sent to serve with an infantry company in Upper Egypt. In 1943, Nasser was promoted to the rank of captain and was appointed an instructor at the military academy. In 1948, he distinguished himself in a losing cause in the Palestine campaign. As a patriotic officer, he was disgusted at the inefficiency and decrepitude of the Egyptian political regime. During the 1940s, moreover, Nasser began to blame imperialism and feudalism for the constantly deteriorating state of his country. He read widely and, as a history instructor, he refined his social and political ideas. It was during this period that he helped form the Free Officers movement and came into contact with the group of fellow officers who were to play the vital role in changing the course of Egyptian history over the next two decades.

On 23 July 1952, the Free Officers movement carried out a coup that overthrew King Farouk and his traditional regime. A Revolutionary Command Council of 12 officers, including Gen. Muhammad Naguib, took control of the government. At first Naguib was the titular political leader, but by the end of 1954 Gamal Abdel Nasser had ousted him and taken control. Nasser remained the internationally famous leader of Egypt until his heart attack and death on 28 September 1970. During these years, both Nasser and Egypt survived numerous vicissitudes, including crises ranging from an assassination attempt to an invasion by the combined forces of three foreign powers. During his 18 years of leadership in Egypt, Nasser's political activities were divided into three general and overlapping categories: (1) consolidation and maintenance of political power; (2) introduction and continuation of policies of social, economic, and political change within Egypt; and (3) development of an independent foreign policy.

During the first few years of his leadership, Nasser was preoccupied with the task of protecting the ascendant position he had acquired. This meant maintaining the cohesion of the military in general and the Free Officers group in particular, while at the same time repelling opposition forces mobilized by the Communists on the left and the Wafd Party and Muslim Brotherhood on the right. Nasser had strongly suppressed the Brotherhood by 1955; in the late 1950s and early 1960s, he moved sharply and successfully against Communism within Egypt; and by 1965, he had largely managed to destroy the influence of the wealthy bourgeoisie that had formed the backbone of the Wafd Party.

Although these were the most serious organized threats to his power, Nasser's government was faced with political challenges throughout its existence because his revolutionary programs were continually threatening vested interests. As his authoritarianism hardened in order to withstand these kinds of challenges, Nasser came to alienate substantial segments of former supporters within the intelligentsia, who chafed under a cloak of repression that tended to suffocate criticism and innovation from below. Democratization was deliberately sacrificed, since the consolidation and maintenance of power were considered essential to successful modernization.

Because Nasser was able to consolidate his forces, he was in turn able to institute change from above. This was in sharp contrast to societies such as Syria and Iraq, where military coups have bred only further military coups. Although certain individual freedoms were at times sacrificed, Nasser nonetheless instituted enough fundamental change to lay a new social, economic, and political foundation for Egyptian society.

Gamal Abdel Nasser once stated that he was a revolutionary and not a politician. He wrote, "Every people on earth goes through two revolutions: a political revolution by which it wrests the right to govern itself from the hand of tyranny, or from the army stationed upon its soil against its will; and a social revolution, involving the conflict of classes which settles down when justice is secured for the citizens of the united nation." [59] In analyzing the political history of post-1952 Egypt, Maxime Rodinson concludes that the two main goals of Nasserism were national independence and modernization.[60] Among the important sociopolitical achievements of Nasser's revolution are (1) the agrarian reform program, (2) the transformation and partial leveling of the class structure, (3) the elimination of corruption and nepotism in the personal household of the national political leader, (4) the continuing rise of achievement at the expense of ascription in the administrative system, (5) the expulsion of foreign influence, and (6) the strengthening of the pride and dignity of the Egyptian people. In his attempt to transform the traditional power structure, Nasser came to the conclusion that the process must be a continuing one. Land reform alone could not bring about this transformation, since it was neither deep enough nor fast enough to undercut the power of the entire traditional ruling class. It was in this context that Nasser instituted the extensive nationalization laws of the 1960–1963 period.

The successes and failures of Nasser's domestic programs rested to a great degree degree upon his ability to guide Egypt through the stormy seas of international politics. It was in this

---

[59] Gamal Abdel Nasser, *Egypt's Liberation: The Philosophy of the Revolution* (Washington, D.C.: Public Affairs Press, 1955), pp. 39–40.

[60] See Maxime Rodinson, "The Political System," in *Egypt Since the Revolution,* ed. by P. J. Vatikiotis (New York: Frederick A. Praeger, 1968), pp. 87–113.

broader area that the Egyptian president expended most of his political energy, and it was here that he witnessed his greatest triumphs and his greatest defeats. His tenure as leader of Egypt was clouded by deep problems directly associated with the Arab-Israeli confrontation, the American-Soviet cold war, the general drive for Arab unity, and the differing Arab stances concerning the entire issue of social and political change. In 1955, President Nasser attended the Bandung Conference, where he rubbed shoulders with Nehru, Sukarno, and Chou En-lai, and where he was considered a new leader of the Afro-Asian world. He returned home a hero for his role in a conference that condemned "neocolonialism" and supported "nonalignment." A few months later, Nasser accepted a Soviet arms offer and concluded a deal with Czechoslovakia that electrified the Arab world, since it indicated that Egypt was no longer dependent on the West and would pursue a course of positive neutralism.[61] That same year, Nasser refused to align Egypt with the Anglo-American-sponsored Baghdad Pact, and in 1956, John Foster Dulles withdrew the American offer to help Egypt finance the critically important Aswan High Dam. One week later, Nasser announced the nationalization of the Suez Canal Company, which in turn brought about the abortive invasion of Egypt by Great Britain, France, and Israel. The Soviet Union then took charge of the financing and construction of the High Dam. These events brought together the masses of Egyptians behind Nasser, who had proved to them that Egypt was an independent nation whose dignity could no longer be trampled upon. The significance of the Suez crisis "reached far beyond the event itself, causing a revolutionary transformation of the technocratic, reformist government."[62] It was a "charis-

[61] The arms deal took a great deal of personal and political courage on Nasser's part, since it was signed in the face of deep United States opposition. This was a time when American intelligence forces had helped rearrange political regimes in Iran (1953) and Guatemala (1954). When Egypt's panicky ambassador to the United States urged Nasser not to defy Washington in this way, he kept repeating the phrase: "Remember Guatemala, remember Guatemala." Nasser finally said, "To hell with Guatemala" and went ahead with the arms agreement. See Leonard Mosley, *Dulles* (New York: Dial Press, James Wade, 1978), p. 388.

[62] Jean Lacouture, *The Demigods: Charismatic Leadership in the Third World*, trans. by Patricia Wolf (New York: Alfred A. Knopf, 1970), p. 110.

LIFE OF GAMAL ABDEL NASSER: MAJOR EVENTS

1918	Born in Alexandria
1936	Graduates from Al-Nahda Secondary School in Cairo
1938	Graduates from Egyptian Military Academy
1948	Participates in Palestine campaign; distinguishes himself at Faluja
1952	Free Officers carry out coup against the government of King Farouk
1954	Becomes prime minister and then president of Egypt
1955	Attends Bandung Conference; concludes Soviet arms deal
1956	Nationalization of the Suez Canal Company and invasion of Egypt by Israel, France, and Great Britain
1958	Formation of the United Arab Republic; Nasser elected president
1961	Passage of wide-ranging nationalization laws; United Arab Republic dissolved
1962	Arab Socialist Union organization formed
1967	Arab-Israeli June War; Nasser resigns, but returns to power with massive popular support
1970	Dies in Cairo

matic situation" [63] that helped invest Nasser with extraordinary powers as a political leader.

These early successes were of sufficient magnitude to enable both Nasser and Egypt to ride out later disasters. The most serious of these was the June War of 1967, in which Israel (in an impressive and efficient military campaign) left Egypt battered and demoralized. Nasser, who must bear much of the blame for occasioning the conflict, resigned his position, to be called back only hours later by the Egyptian people, who seemingly genuinely wanted and demanded his leadership. The existence of Israel haunted Nasser's rule, and he was never able to confront this situation with the same style and success with which he addressed other thorny problems.

In the area of intra-Arab politics, the Egyptian president was only slightly more successful. The United Arab Republic, which was a political and economic union with Syria formed in 1958, was dissolved in 1961 when, among other things, the

[63] *Ibid.*

wealthy Syrian bourgeois families feared the impact of Nasser's revolutionary programs. Nasser sucessfully supported the Algerian rebels in Algeria, although in Yemen direct Egyptian military support failed to enable the revolutionaries to take control of the country. The latter adventure cost Egypt dearly in terms of domestic resources and international prestige. Despite this, however, President Nasser's revolutionary programs and ideas spread through the Middle East and acted as catalysts for change in the Arab world. If they did not lead to revolution from below, they inspired even the most traditional leaders to try to dissipate discontent by initiating developmental change. The land reform programs in Syria, Iraq, Tunisia, Iran, and Turkey, for example, all followed the Egyptian experiment in agrarian reform begun in 1952.

Patterns of Rule. Gamal Abdel Nasser's leadership broke with many of the patterns of traditional patrimonial rule. Although strongly authoritarian, Nasser's techniques did not include the promotion of self-deification. It is true that his image was protected and polished by his governmental and security forces, but he resisted pressures to invest huge resources in the glorification of his person. There were no statues of Nasser, for example, dotting the Egyptian landscape. Nor did his face adorn postage stamps and currency. The Egyptian President consciously sought to transcend the temptation to permit and promote personal exaltation and hero worship. One keen Western observer of Egyptian affairs wrote that "nothing irritates Nasser more than being treated like a modern pharaoh." [64]

A truly charismatic personality need not build monuments to himself and myths for his people; his charisma is based on his extraordinary actions. In Nasser's case, the leader also eschewed any special connection with the Divine, whether it be in terms of common ancestry or private visions. Although he never attacked the Islamic clerics in Egypt the way Atatürk did in Turkey, at the same time he did not attempt to build any particularly intimate political relations with them.[65] The fact

[64] Ibid., p. 119.

[65] For the finest investigation of Nasser's relationship to Islam, see Josef Muzikar, "Arab Nationalism and Islam," *Archiv Orientalni* 43 (1975):193–323.

that Nasser's charisma is traceable neither to manufactured mythology nor to religious connections indicates how divorced his leadership was from the traditional mold. It is precisely this kind of charisma that invested Nasser with the special strength necessary to maintain power and to promote deep change in the face of formidable problems, both internal and external.

The role of the military was crucial to Nasser's leadership. It was through a military coup that he first came to power, and it was through the support of the military that he could maintain power and institute reform. In the absence of a trained and efficient civil bureaucracy, the Egyptian President was able to call upon personnel from within the military organization to implement administrative and economic programs. As in traditional patrimonial systems, the military was an important prop in Nasser's political structure. There is, however, one important quality that separates the Nassers and the Atatürks from the more traditional leaders. The latter continue to present themselves in military guise and garb in order constantly to display their special and intimate relation with the military. They often explicitly state that they are an embodiment of the military. Nasser, on the contrary, retired from the army in 1955 and deliberately refrained from maintaining any military rank or title.

Personalism and informality are two related characteristics of patrimonial rule that persisted in the leadership of Gamal Abdel Nasser.[66] Nasser never succeeded in moving from rule by personalism to political institutionalization, and as a result there was a general lack of political participation and a general surplus of political insecurity in Nasser's Egypt. In the latter days of his presidency, heavy-handed maneuverers, such as presidential advisor Sami Sharaf and interior minister Sharawi Gomaa, were directing an increasingly disreputable intelligence system that reached into all corners of Egyptian society.

There is evidence, however, that Nasser was not insensitive to the need for wider political participation. He tried three

---

[66] The works of Robert Springborg impressively document Nasser as a patrimonial leader. See especially his "Patterns of Association in the Egyptian Political Elite," in *Political Elites in the Middle East*, ed. by Lenczowski, pp. 83–107.

times to construct a mass political party in order to insure a measure of popular participation. His last attempt, which was also his most successful, involved the formation of the Arab Socialist Union in 1962. Such structures were largely ineffectual in Egypt, since they existed as rather sterile appendages to Nasser's personal rule, which Nasser felt bound to strengthen in order to carry on the revolution. Despite the presence of personalism and informality, Nasser was able to break a number of the patterns that follow in the wake of patrimonialism.

The nepotism that stems from personalism and the corruption that often thrives in the net of informal politics were relatively absent in Nasser's style of leadership. Nasser himself was above reproach in this regard, and he led an austere life much in the style of Chou En-lai and Fidel Castro. Throughout the Middle East, Nasser was famous for his personal honesty and integrity. He spoke out constantly against opportunism, corruption, and favoritism. When he died in 1970, he was still living in the modest house that he had purchased as a young officer prior to the 1952 coup. He refused to use his power to further the causes of his family and relatives. Two of his uncles remained fellahin (peasants) in the village of Beni Morr, and his own daughters were unable to attend Cairo University because their entrance examination scores were not high enough.

Mohamed Heikal writes that Nasser "was never interested in women or money or elaborate food. After he had come to power the cynical old politicians tried to corrupt him but they failed miserably. His family life was impeccable." [67] Heikal goes on to point out that although Nasser received millions of pounds in donations, he died with only 610 Egyptian pounds in his personal account. The programmatic manifestations of this new style fostered by Nasser are evident in the Egyptian land reform policy, for, as one expert writes: "The even-handedness with which the distribution was carried out de-

[67] Mohamed Heikal, *The Cairo Documents* (Garden City, N.Y.: Doubleday and Co., 1973), p. 20. Some of Nasser's leading officials, including what Edward Sheehan calls "the Sharaf-Goma cabal," whose members "were nearly all corrupt," were less principled. Edward R. F. Sheehan, "The Real Sadat and the Demythologized Nasser," *New York Times Magazine,* 18 July 1971, pp. 6–7, 33, 35, 38, 42.

serves commendation; no suggestion of favoritism in either the taking of land from large owners or the distribution of it to recipients has arisen — a remarkable accomplishment in view of the inherent temptations to corruption." [68]

Although Gamal Abdel Nasser resorted to the traditional tactic of divide and rule, his collegues and confidants generally operated as a team in leading society. Admittedly, the team was a small and exclusive one. Lenczowski has pointed out that, with only three exceptions, Nasser managed to keep his group of young officers together through more than 12 years of the Revolution.[69] While he undoubtedly made the final decisions, the Egyptian President did consult seriously with his close advisors.

The patterns of patrimonial politics were partially uprooted by President Nasser as he endeavored to revolutionize his society. Although personalism continued to prevail, many of the other traditional traits were destroyed and replaced by new patterns. This represents a fundamental step in moving forward with the social and political dimensions of change.

Transforming Leadership. Despite some recent oil discoveries, Egypt remains one of the poorest and most densely populated societies in the world. Just before the 1952 military coup, a Rockefeller Foundation team reported that the situation of the peasants in Egypt was worse than that of the peasants in any other country in which they had carried out investigations — and this included China and India. According to this report, on a scale of 106.5 for perfect health, India rated 54 and Egypt 15. In one of the villages surveyed north of Cairo, nearly 100 percent of the population had bilarzia, a debilitating parasitical disease that attacks the kidneys and liver; 89 percent had trachoma; over 20 percent were typhoid or paratyphoid carriers. In a village with a population of 4,172, there was not

[68] Kenneth B. Platt, *Land Reform in the United Arab Republic*, A.I.D. Spring Review of Land Reform, 2nd ed., Vol. 8 (Washington, D.C.: Agency for International Development, 1970), p. 61.

[69] George Lenczowski, "The Objects and Methods of Nasserism," in *Modernization of the Arab World*, ed. by J. H. Thompson and R. D. Reischauer (Princeton, N.J.: D. Van Nostrand Co., 1966), p. 207.

one healthy person. Most of the villagers had from one to four major diseases.[70]

At the time of the report, the political system was a patrimonial monarchy in which all the negative characteristics of that kind of system were magnified. King Farouk often made national political decisions on the advice of his infamous "kitchen cabinet," composed of his valet, mechanic, butler, pilot, and doctor, among others. An Italian barber became Farouk's closest adviser, and Farouk named his brother-in-law (an honorary "colonel") minister of war. Nepotism prevailed in a demoralizing environment of political vice and personal corruption. Against this background, the changes wrought under Nasser's leadership were profound. Measured against the demands of the day and the progress of other non-Western societies, such as Israel, Japan, and China, Egyptian social and political change is perhaps less impressive.

Gamal Abdel Nasser was a transforming leader for three basic reasons: He consciously and determinedly sought to insure that his revolution be radical, political, and continuing in nature. In the 1962 Charter he wrote, "The needs of our country were such that it was not enough to patch up the old and decaying building, try to keep it from falling by means of supports and give the exterior a fresh coat of paint. What was needed was a new and strong building resting on firm foundations and towering high in the sky. . . ." [71] By distinguishing between reforming and transforming change in these kinds of terms, Nasser often indicated his sensitivity to the need to support fundamental social and political transformation. Because of this radical philosophy, Nasser "refused to endorse programs which were primarily political palliatives." [72]

Whereas the reforming leader tends to support economic and material development without altering the political system, the

[70] For a summary of the findings of the Rockefeller Foundation study from which these figures have been drawn, see Austin L. Moore, *Farewell Farouk* (Chicago: Scholars' Press, 1954), pp. 59–60.

[71] Nasser, The Charter, as quoted in J. C. Hurewitz, *Middle East Politics: The Military Dimension* (New York: Frederick A. Praeger, 1969), p. 133.

[72] Keith Wheelock, *Nasser's New Egypt* (London: Atlantic Books, 1960), p. 38.

revolutionary leader begins with and emphasizes the political dimension of change. Anouar Abdel-Malek writes that, in Nasser's case, "the principal blow was struck on the sociopolitical level"; Majid Khadduri asserts that "the Revolution's fundamental achievements were essentially political"; and Maxime Rodinson concludes that under Nasser the political structure was "completely reshaped." [73] The political change can be seen at two levels. The first level concerns the patterns of relations through which the political leader personally wields power. As is documented above, Nasser transformed these relations at several key points. The second level involves the more general and collective distribution of power, reflected primarily in the class structure. During Nasser's rule, the Egyptian class structure underwent radical change as the influence of the former ruling class, which was composed of both the landed and the industrial aristocracy, was destroyed. The gaps between the various classes were consequently greatly narrowed as a professional middle class composed of technocrats, managers, and professionals took control. It is on this basis that one observer has referred to the Egyptian revolution as "the first true revolution in the Middle East." [74]

Nasser carefully referred to the Egyptian revolution as *thawra* ("a persisting and lasting event") rather than as *inqilab* ("an overthrow"), since he recognized the need for the movement to press forward continually.[75] This forward movement, of course, was essential in order to prevent the old power structure from slowly and inexorably seeping back into prominence. The modernizing head of government is especially exposed to this danger since "the bourgeoisie attempts to minimize its losses by puffing up the leader. It cuts off some of its own flesh and feeds it to the hero to fatten him up, blow him up, lull him to sleep. Soon enough the deified leader will proclaim the revolu-

[73] For these quotations, see Anouar Abel-Malek, *Egypt: Military Society*, trans. by Charles Lam Markmann (New York: Vintage Books, 1968), p. 157; Majid Khadduri, *Political Trends in the Arab World* (Baltimore, Md.: Johns Hopkins Press, 1970), p. 162; and Rodinson, "The Political System," p. 111.

[74] Harry Hopkins, *Egypt: The Crucible* (Boston: Houghton Mifflin Co., 1969), p. 181.

[75] Lacouture, *The Demigods*, p. 94.

tion fulfilled in him and the class struggle resolved in him." [76]

In Nasser's Egypt, the old forces of patrimonialism made gallant efforts to infiltrate back into power, and in the late 1950s they were backed and provisioned by the wealthy bourgeoisie. Nasser confronted this challenge and overcame it with his nationalization programs of 1960–1963. This effectively tore the web of families who were the proponents of traditionalism. They had managed to survive the land reform program, since their control spanned industry and trade as well as land.

Although he successfully uprooted the traditional power structure in Egypt, Nasser never quite managed to establish a new sociopolitical system. Because of the resilience of the old system and the limited resources at hand, the Egyptian President felt it necessary to maintain an authoritanian technocracy, which alienated the intelligentsia and stifled creativity in the society. He was unable to broaden political participation, and therefore the revolutionary patterns he introduced at the center did not always take root in the countryside. The resources and energies fruitlessly expended in activities against Israel and in Yemen seriously injured his capacity to carry out social change in Egypt. Despite all of this, Nasser survived and, although badly scarred, continued to fight for the transformation of his country. His achievements in this regard, though sporadic, were nonetheless impressive enough to distinguish him sharply from most Middle Eastern leaders, both past and present. By the time he died in September 1970, Gamal Abdel Nasser was personally convinced that, with or without him, the revolution he had begun in Egypt would continue. In 1971, Nasser's longtime friend and colleague, Anwar Sadat, emerged as the new president of Egypt. Sadat proved to be an important leader in his own right, but his political programs contrasted significantly with those of his predecessor.

ANWAR SADAT: THE RETURN OF TRADITIONAL PATRIMONIALISM

Born in 1918, the same year as Nasser, Anwar Sadat spent much of his youth hating the British and contemplating politi-

[76] *Ibid.,* p. 293.

cal questions. Like Nasser, he came from the lower echelons of the professional middle class. His father, a hospital clerk, was a great admirer of Atatürk, and a picture of the Turkish hero hung in the Sadat house. Sadat entered the Egyptian Military Academy with Nasser in 1936 and graduated with him in 1938. From this time until the successful coup in 1952, he dedicated himself to secret political opposition. During these years, he plotted constantly against both the British and King Farouk and intrigued his way into and out of prison. At one point, he even sought Nasser's permission to blow up the British Embassy. When released from his second imprisonment in 1948, Sadat eked out an existence as a journalist, truck driver, porter, and used-tire salesman. With his military commission restored, Sadat was the one who announced the news of the successful coup of July 1952 to the Egyptian people.

During the 18 years of Nasser's presidency, Anwar Sadat hovered constantly in the shadow of his leader. Although the hotheadedness of his youth occasionally broke to the surface, Sadat did a remarkable job of cloaking his explosive ambition and peasant shrewdness beneath a patient and plodding subservience to Nasser. He refused to join political cliques and power circles, preferring instead to live a life of material pleasure and leisure. Few took him seriously. Meanwhile, he watched and waited, learning all the time. When Nasser died in 1970, Sadat was one of the few members of the original Revolutionary Command Council still around. In 1969, Nasser had shopped around for a new vice-president; he chose Anwar Sadat.

When Sadat succeeded Nasser as president, everyone looked past him to the political heavyweights who would undoubtedly direct Egyptian affairs in the future — menacing figures such as Minister of Presidential Affairs Sami Sharaf, Minister of Interior Sharawi Gomaa, and powerful leftist and Arab Socialist Union figure Ali Sabry. Meanwhile, the patient and poker-faced Sadat went about his business quietly, easily, and disarmingly. He made appearances throughout the country, building popularity as he went along; he silently sprinkled a few loyal spies here and there; and, most important, he came to an agreement with the key army officers.

Then, in May 1971, when he had carefully gathered evidence that Sabry and the others had been plotting a coup, Sadat suddenly struck. He forced Ali Sabry to resign on 2 May. Ten days later in another lightning move, he fired secret police head Gomaa and happily accepted the resignation of five other ministers, including that of Sami Sharaf. That autumn over 90 persons were tried. Sabry, Sharaf, and Gomaa, among others, were jailed.[77] Anwar Sadat had succeeded in consolidating his power.

Once he became president of Egypt, Sadat found himself under great domestic and international pressure. Despite this, he managed to maintain himself in power for over a decade. One of the most important tactics that he used throughout his career was to deny repeatedly that he ever sought political power. In his autobiography he strongly denied that he ever had any interest in political office. Yet the reader of his book cannot help observing that Sadat never refused a political post offered him. Nor, deep down, was he ever pleased that he was an outsider to the Revolutionary Command Council. In his own words; "Why did they attack and ridicule me, as though I was an outsider who wanted to usurp their rights or a stranger who spoke a different language? I was sad. . . ." [78]

Sadat was able to make up for his absence of Nasser-like charisma through a brilliant ability to make the right political moves at precisely the right times. While floating somewhere above political factions and ideological positions, he often darted down to center stage to announce and personally implement dramatic and unprecedented political decisions — deci-

[77] Sharawi Gomaa and several less prominent members of the Sabry group were released from prison when President Sadat granted them amnesty in January 1977. Former minister of war Lt. Gen. Muhammad Fawzi had already been pardoned by Sadat in January 1974.

[78] Anwar el-Sadat, *In Search of Identity: An Autobiography* (New York: Harper and Row, 1978), p. 122. For examples of Sadat's insistent denials that he was ever interested in power, see pp. 83–84, 90, 126, 136, 138, 150, 196, 204, and 314. This autobiography, although fascinating and important reading, is rather flagrantly self-serving. This is particularly true of Sadat's personal evaluation of Nasser. For a more positive assessment of Nasser's statesmanship, written by a different member of Nasser's entourage, see Heikal's *The Cairo Documents*.

sions that left the world gasping. The most noteworthy of these moves included the expulsion of Soviet advisers from Egyptian soil in July 1972, the initiation of the fourth Arab-Israeli war in October 1973, the historic trip to Israel in November 1977, and the announcement of a framework for peace with Israel at Camp David in September 1978. Whenever domestic political discontent threatened his government, President Sadat responded by announcing a major new policy with a flair and flamboyance seldom seen in Middle Eastern political history.

Anwar Sadat's dramatic sense of timing was developed within the patrimonial context. He was a traditional patrimonial leader par excellence. As we have seen, President Nasser retained much of the patrimonial style in his rule, while at the same time instituting revolutionary changes at many points in the Egyptian system. Sadat spent much of his presidency busily repairing these tears in the body politic. The traditional power structure so severely disrupted during the two decades of Nasserist rule was reinstated by President Sadat. In this sense, he sought to roll back Nasser's revolution.

Upon taking the reins of power in Egypt, Anwar Sadat immediately began to liberalize and democratize Egyptian society. Economically, this meant an opening (*infitah*) of the system to foreign investment and capital. Politically, the liberalization expressed itself in terms of a cautiously guarded return to more political participation. In the words of one informed scholar of Egyptian politics, the early years of Sadat's rule represented an "inclusionist" patrimonialism, while Nasser's style was "exclusionist." [79] Sadat permitted a wider network of individuals to participate in political decision making, in contrast to Nasser, who had relied upon a smaller core of trusted assistants. One result of this was that although Nasser had had to involve himself directly in many matters, Sadat adopted a more Olympian approach to matters that were not only time-consuming but also political briar patches.

Nor was the Egyptian president always consistent in this regard. "He has invoked democracy and the rule of law, then — without too delicate a regard for either — swept all his sus-

---

[79] See Springborg, "Patrimonialism and Policy Making in Egypt."

pected rivals off to jail. He has promised real power to the people, and gathered most of the Government into his own hands." [80] Sadat was interested not in converting Egypt into a liberal democracy but rather in lengthening and strengthening the patrimonial strands in a way that would recapture the traditional power structure of Egypt, with him as unquestioned leader. The evidence for this tendency is impressive.

In his first book, published in 1957, Anwar Sadat penned a line that could serve as a classic lead sentence in any manual on patrimonial rule: "In Egypt, personalities have always been more important than political programs." [81] Sadat himself acted accordingly by drawing his family and friends into the center of the political system. His brother-in-law, Mahmoud Abu Wafia, was for a time secretary-general of the most important forum within the Arab Socialist Union. Two of his daughters married members of the most important and wealthy aristocratic families in the country, the families of Sayyid Marei and Osman Ahmad Osman. The former (already discussed in Chapter III) was Sadat's Speaker of the People's Assembly and a personal advisor to the president, while the latter was the most powerful contractor in the country.

Sadat was visibly susceptible to the pomp and circumstance so important to traditional patrimonial leaders. Although he did not live quite the life style of the Shah of Iran, he was easily more self-indulgent than was Nasser. He had a dozen presidential villas and wore field marshal's uniforms designed by Pierre Cardin. He spent more time perhaps with the international jet set than with his own people. The enormous gap here was clearly visible in September 1979 when Frank Sinatra performed a concert before the Sphinx and the pyramids for one of Mrs. Jihan Sadat's favorite charities. The spectacle was attended by "over 400 partygoers from the United States and Europe who enjoyed what was probably the most extravagant social affair Egypt had seen since before the 1952 revolution that overthrew King Farouk." Before dedicating a song to Mrs.

---

[80] Sheehan, "The Real Sadat," p. 42.

[81] Anwar el-Sadat, *Revolt on the Nile* (New York: John Day Co., 1957), p. 27.

Sadat, Sinatra ventured an opinion about President Sadat: "He really is a great cat. I just adore him." Along with the concert was an international fashion show in which Pierre Balmain introduced his seasonal collection from Paris. His mannequins marched around "in white overcoats and matching jackboots, then in soft dresses and pajamas, and finally in gold fig-leaf bikinis. The models, who had been flown in from Paris, wore Pharaonic jewelry designed by Bulgari, with a total value put at $10 million." Before the show, the wealthy international guests dined on cold lobster, veal, and crepes. "Outside the enclosure's flapping cloth walls, a cordon of white-uniformed policemen, some with automatic rifles, shoved away curious Egyptians from a nearby village." [82]

The major difference between Nasser's and Sadat's style of rule was the service to which Sadat's patrimonialism was put. Class lines deepened and class divisions became wider in Egypt during the period of Sadat's presidency. This was seen in the political unrest that broke periodically to the surface in Egypt between 1971 and 1981.

In 1972 and 1973, student demonstrations rocked Egypt, and in 1974 an insurrection at the military academy in Cairo was put down with force. Riots in Cairo on New Year's Day 1975 and in April of that year at the major textile center at Mahalla al-Kubra were sparked by social protest and class disaffection. Then, in January 1977, thousands of Egyptians drawn from several social classes demonstrated in violent protest against the government's decision to cut back its subsidies on food costs. The army was called in to suppress the rioters in the worst civil upheaval in Egypt in 25 years. These demonstrations (especially those in 1975 and 1977) carried heavy overtones of outright class conflict. In 1975, the cry was "We do not need a Pasha but we need a President," and in 1977, one of the slogans was "Where is our breakfast you dweller of palaces?" [83] In the 1977 incidents, the patrimonial leader's wife, Jihan, was herself one

[82] The quotations in this paragraph are taken from *The New York Times*, September 28, 1979.

[83] See R. Michael Burrell and Abbas R. Kelidar, *Egypt: The Dilemmas of a Nation, 1970–1977*, The Washington Papers, no. 48 (Beverly Hills, Calif.: Sage Publications, 1977), p. 72.

of the targets of criticism and was given such labels as "the uncrowned queen" and "tomorrow's Cleopatra." [84]

Then, in June 1981, serious riots between Muslims and Copts flared again in the working-class districts of Cairo. By the fall of that year, Sadat was hard-pressed at home as signs of widespread disaffection and alienation bubbled ominously to the surface. Muslim associations and organizations multiplied in number and size and an estimated 40,000 private mosques served as centers for critical discussion of the deep social and political problems that plagued Egypt. In August 1981, over 200,000 people gathered at Abdin Square in Cairo for a prayer rally. In the first week of September, President Sadat suddenly responded by orchestrating a major crackdown on all sources of potential opposition. His police arrested more than 1,500 people, closed down seven publications, transferred over 100 writers, journalists, and teachers from their jobs, deposed the Coptic Patriarch from his position, and moved to place the 40,000 "free" mosques under direct governmental control. Sadat angrily justified this uncharacteristically severe crackdown by stating that it represented an attack against "indiscipline" that had come to dominate Egyptian society. This was the very word that the Shah of Iran had often used to justify the repressive policies of his regime in the years just prior to the revolution there.

On 6 October 1981, one month after he had carried out his political crackdown, President Anwar Sadat was reviewing a military parade held to commemorate Egyptian successes in the October 1973 war. At approximately 12:40 P.M., four Egyptian soldiers leaped from a truck in an artillery unit and charged the presidential reviewing stand in a grenade and automatic weapon attack. In this surprise attack, the soldiers assassinated Anwar Sadat as he stood to greet them on a public stage before the eyes of the world in Cairo. The consummate actor and colorful, courageous political leader died at a time when he had clearly lost touch with reality in his own country. "Even after the show was over, he had gotten the role and he went on playing. It was catastrophic." [85]

---

[84] *Events,* 11 March 1977, p. 18.
[85] The words of Mohamed Hassanein Heikal as reported in *The Christian Science Monitor,* 2 December 1981.

In the end, Anwar Sadat was a patrimonial leader who became a pseudomonarch and who governed Egypt according to his interpretation of modern, Western pomp and circumstance. According to one informed Egyptian scholar, "Sadat lost control of the internal situation and was, in response perhaps, turning into a neurotic despot slashing right and left." [86] He shifted from being "the paternalistic pious head of the Egyptian family to the single-minded, threatened, vindictive dictator who eliminates any criticism of him and any opposition to his programs.... Two processes were at work in the meantime: a Sadatization of Egypt on the one hand, and a deification of Sadat on the other — the rebirth of the Egptian pharaoh." [87]

Anwar Sadat's patrimonial rule in the service of tradition brought back class animosity to Egypt. His open-door policy only served to widen the gap between the very rich and the teeming masses of the poor. According to Burrell and Kelidar, "Perhaps the most dangerous aspect of this is that the average Egyptian has been becoming more impoverished at a time when the affluence of a small number of Egyptians has been made ever more apparent. The availability of Western imports — imports widely regarded as nonessential luxuries under Nasser's rule — have heightened the sense of impoverishment and deprivation." [88] The fact that rich Arab oil magnates from the Gulf shaykhdoms vacationed in Egyptian resorts and mansions in Alexandria while thousands of Egyptians worked as skilled laborers in the shaykhdoms was an irony not lost on the Egyptian public.

Ever after the 1977 riots, President Sadat emphasized his patrimonial prerogative of control by coercion. Students and other university dwellers were assured from then on that participation in demonstrations and illegal political party membership were punishable by life imprisonment. Sadat redefined

---

[86] Fadwa El Guindi, "The Killing of Sadat and After," *Middle East Insight* 2 (January/February 1983):23.

[87] *Ibid.*

[88] Burrell and Kelidar, *Egypt*, p. 32. This excellent little book convincingly demonstrates that widening class divisions in Sadat's Egypt led to great political discontent and discord.

his views on liberalization when he told Egyptian students that "politics have no place in our universities" and that "democracy too can have teeth and fangs." [89] After the September 1981 crackdown, he explained to the Egyptian people that they had "to understand that democracy has its own teeth. The next time it is going to be ten times as ruthless." [90]

Anwar Sadat was in some ways a more accomplished patrimonial leader than was his predecessor, Gamal Abdel Nasser. He had more experience, greater flair, the political support of the United States, and considerable economic assistance from the oil-rich conservative Arab countries. Yet Sadat's personal and patrimonial style was enlisted more than Nasser's in the defense of the status quo, thereby defying inexorable social forces in Egypt, which grew more explosive with time. As we have seen, Nasser himself was not averse to patrimonial tactics. But he was at the same time dedicated to a continuing program of social change and to the transformation of the class structure of Egypt. He tried to generate and absorb change. As a result, he ruled Egypt for nearly two decades, despite accepting full responsibility for political and national catastrophes such as the June war of 1967.

Sadat became entangled in his own rhetoric and tried to convert international fame into domestic credibility and support. He slowed political development at home while accelerating modernization through a policy of *infitah*. This mode of patrimonial rule ran in the face of the needs and aspirations of the masses of Egyptian citizens who were turning increasingly to Islamic movements for support and sustenance. Sadat's assassins were members of an Islamic fundamentalist group, and although they were tried and executed, they represented only one tiny part of the overall movement in the country.

Sadat's successor, Hosni Mubarak, faces an almost impossible political task. Egypt's social, economic, and political problems remain as intractible as ever. An air force officer for 25 years and the loyal vice-president of Sadat for six years, Mubarak is closely associated with Sadat and his policies. Once he took

---

[89] *Ibid.*, pp. 41–42.
[90] *The New York Times*, 27 September 1981.

over the presidency of Egypt on 14 October 1981, however, Mubarak immediately tried to distance himself from Sadat's method of rule. He had no intention of repeating the mistakes of his predecessor. Unostentatious and low-key, Mubarak has consciously avoided the opulent and visible patrimonial style of President Sadat. He has attempted to attack corruption, to compromise with the opposition, and to seek to come to grips with Egypt's domestic problems immediately and directly.

In his speech to the Egyptian parliament shortly after he became president, Mubarak described the new course of national action as one of "seriousness, purification, no hypocrisy, no corruption, no playing around with the minds of the people, and no discrimination between the ruler and the ruled." [91] Despite his good intentions, President Mubarak has yet to deliver politically and economically. And pressure continues to build in the Egyptian polity. Muslim fundamentalist forces persistently press in upon Mubarak's government, leading to new arrests and promising future confrontation and violence. In October 1982, President Mubarak extended the state of emergency for another 12 months, indicating that the situation remained tense in Egypt. Mubarak points out that "what counts is achievements, not statements." [92] He must somehow produce such achievements or he may well go the way of Anwar Sadat.

LEADERS AND CHANGE: A CONCLUDING PERSPECTIVE

Our case studies of selected Middle Eastern leaders indicate the extraordinary persistence of patrimonial politics in the area. Even revolutionary and charismatic leaders such as Atatürk and Nasser retained characteristics of the patrimonial style. This is one reason why it is supremely difficult to transform national power structures and to introduce political development in Middle Eastern countries: Can one build new political systems using old tools?

Kemal Atatürk and Gamal Abdel Nasser did indeed introduce significant change at various points in their social and political systems. Although it has become common to question

91 *The Middle East*, December 1981, p. 19.
92 *Ibid.*, p. 18.

the depths of the changes they wrought, there can be little doubt that they were in many ways revolutionaries. But they had unusual advantages. Both gathered great personal and political momentum because of their impeccable credentials as nationalists. They had successfully defied and defeated great European colonialist powers. And both men had an impressive charisma that is seldom seen in the Middle East.

In succeeding their illustrious predecessors, Ismet Inönü and Anwar Sadat were faced with the need to continue and deepen ongoing programs of revolutionary change. Both men chose initially to liberalize and to expand political participation in their societies. Lacking the charisma of Atatürk and Nasser, they sought to build a broader platform of legitimacy and support. Ironically, in the process of doing so they oversaw the gradual decline of revolutionary programs in their societies. The traditional power groups and classes that had been defeated and dismantled by Atatürk and Nasser regrouped and returned to influence. In the case of Egypt especially, the negative dimensions of patrimonial politics seeped back into the nooks and crannies of the system.

The challenges of the day are such that patrimonial modes of rule alone will not enable Middle Eastern leaders to satisfy the demands of new social groups and classes. Although this style of rule is so strong that it will perhaps be always present in the Middle East in one form or another, it must be exercised in the context of a strengthened capacity to generate and absorb transforming change. Traditional patrimonial monarchs (such as the former Shah of Iran), who promote limited change, provide only a limited answer to the challenge. Modern patrimonial moderates (such as the late Anwar Sadat of Egypt), who stifle political development while promoting a certain level of modernization, are also unable to confront the mounting social problems of their societies successfully. In this context, it is not accidental that both the Shah and Sadat met grim personal and political fates. Even newer and bigger versions of the Atatürks and Nassers would have a difficult time in the contemporary world of the Middle East. The problems are many, and strong but sensitive leaders are few.

CHAPTER VI

Violence and the Military

THE TRADITION OF VIOLENCE

Are the traditions of violence in the Middle East unusual in any way? Historically, there were many violent encounters among groups: tribal raids, colonizing expeditions, wars. Prowess in battle and success in raiding have historically been virtues in the Middle East, especially among the many nomads of the area. Individual lives have not always been very highly valued by rulers; the beautiful folktale *The Thousand Nights and a Night* is full of examples of this. Even in more recent times, roads were built with the corvée, taxes were collected with the bastinado, and army conscripts were obtained through coercive means. Blood revenge and the concomitant blood feud were well known. Assassination of rulers was not unknown and not unapproved. Rulers themselves, notably the Ottoman sultans, went about neutralizing their ambitious relatives or retainers with draconian severity.

Does this indicate that there was an especially strong tradition of violence in the Middle East? It is essential to compare the Middle East with other areas during the same periods. Selim I was hardly more bloodthirsty than Henry VIII. Salah al-Din was no less generous and chivalrous than his famous adversary Richard *Coeur de Lion* (and was surely more generous than Richard's brother John). The Old Man of the Mountain, the religious leader of the Assassins, was assuredly no worse than Pope Alexander VI and his son Cesare Borgia. During the period of the Crusades, the European Christians were as violent as their Muslim adversaries. If anything, the Middle Easterners were less bloodthirsty, less cruel, less violent. Of wars the world has had many; the Middle East has had no more than its share.

The contemporary patterns of urban violence in the Middle East are somewhat different from those in Western Europe and the United States. Student riots and demonstrations have long been a part of the Middle Eastern culture; in recent years, such riots and demonstrations have become a part of European culture as well. But there is much less individual criminal violence in Cairo or Tehran than in New York or Paris. Even in areas such as the Northwest Frontier Province in Pakistan or Afghanistan where men have traditionally gone armed, there is considerably less violence than might be expected. (In Afghanistan today, of course, any tendencies toward violence can be absorbed by the continuing civil war, in which the Soviet Union is a partner. As of January 1983, with 110,000 troops in Afghanistan, the Russians have been unable to pacify the country.) Although Arabs have fought Israelis as Israelis, they have seldom fought them as Jews; whatever else he was, Hitler was a Western European, living in the twentieth century. The wave of kidnappings and political murders in Europe in the late 1970s (exemplified by the Moro murder in Italy in 1978) shows that few areas are immune to terrorist violence. The evidence simply does not support the contention that the tradition of violence is significantly greater in the Middle East than in other areas.

TERRORISM AND ANTICOLONIALISM

At the end of the First World War, the Middle East remained firmly colonialistic. France and Italy controlled all of North Africa except Egypt, which was still to suffer a British occupation for more than a generation. Palestine (including today's Jordan), Iraq, Kuwait, and Aden were in British hands, as was Cyprus in the Mediterranean. Syria and Lebanon were French. By the 1960s all of this had changed, and the process of throwing off these colonial bonds produced much violence.

The Rif rebellion in Spanish Morocco in 1921 was one of the earliest of the struggles against colonialism.[1] Under the leadership of Muhammad Bin Abdul Krim, it splashed over into French Morocco, and it was French military might that finally destroyed the Rif force. But this was essentially a war of independence and must be considered under that category.

Much of the anti-French and anti-British activity in Egypt, Palestine, and Syria took place in the 1920s. There was certainly opposition to the British in Iraq, but timely concessions and the presence of King Faisal (until 1933) did much to re duce violent outbreaks there. There was also tribal upheaval in the shaykhdoms east of Aden throughout the twenties and thirties, but this stemmed less from anticolonialism than from general tribal unrest. Although the tribes of the Middle East were an anachronism by the 1920s, their leaders stubbornly resisted central authority and forced settlement. This was true in Iran, Afghanistan, India (the western Muslim provinces), Sudan, and Libya. It was also true in Iraq, Jordan, and Saudi Arabia; along the borders of these countries "frontier forces" were established to deal specifically with tribal raiding parties and other groups of this kind. This is where the famous Peake Pasha and Glubb Pasha began their careers. There is still warlike tribal unrest in the Middle East, but it has very much diminished as the tribes themselves have become less powerful and less independent. But even today in the Israeli Negev there are about 40,000 "nomads" whose settlement is a problem for any Israeli government.

In Egypt, a sullen and unhappy population endured a British occupation throughout the twenties and thirties with only periodic outbreaks of violence. There was, however, serious rioting on a number of occasions.[2] This was directed not only against the British, but also against Egyptian governments and the political institutions of the time. There were also assassinations. However, the real waves of violence occurred after the

---

[1] See David S. Woolman, *Rebels in the Rif: Abd el Krim and the Rif Rebellion* (Stanford, Calif.: Stanford University Press, 1968).
[2] See John Marlowe, *A History of Modern Egypt and Anglo-Egyptian Relations 1800–1956*, 2d ed. (Hamden, Conn.: Archon Books, 1965).

Second World War. The war had solved little for the Egyptians; accumulated frustrations produced a paroxysm of violence against whatever convenient targets could be found. The most destructive of these outbreaks took place in January 1952, on a day that came to be called Black Saturday. The day before, British troops in the Suez Canal Zone had attacked (with some provocation, of course) a group of Egyptian policemen, killing about 50. In response, the Egyptian populace went on a rampage. Led by extremist elements, including the Muslim Brotherhood, mobs set fire to much of modern Cairo, concentrating on the luxury hotels and foreign-owned stores and establishments. Altogether at least a dozen Europeans were killed, and damages to the city ran more than $50 million. Order was restored only late in the day, when the army was finally permitted to intervene.[3] The 1952 Revolution was now only months away.

There is hardly space to chronicle the many episodes of terrorist violence in the Middle East before and after the Second World War. There is, however, one prominent example of terrorist violence that needs to be examined in some detail. It is, of course, the example of Palestine (Israel).

The Palestine problem that has plagued the Middle East throughout the twentieth century might be said to have had its beginnings in 1897 at the meeting of the First Zionist Congress in Basle, Switzerland.[4] At that meeting, a resolution was passed favoring a national home for the Jews in Palestine. The British gave their imprimatur to this notion in 1917 in the Balfour Declaration, and in effect the Palestine problem was born. The idea of a national home in Palestine was nurtured by continued persecution of Jews in Eastern Europe and finally by genocide during the Hitlerian period, which resulted in large-scale immigration of Jews into Palestine. Not all of the Jews

[3] See Chapter 12, "The Burning of Cairo," in Jean and Simone Lacouture, *Egypt in Transition* (London: Methuen and Co., 1958).

[4] There is a wealth of literature on Zionism and the Arab-Israeli question. For a full treatment of Zionism, see Ben Halpern, *The Idea of the Jewish State*, 2d ed. (Cambridge, Mass.: Harvard University Press, 1969). For another perspective, see Fred J. Khouri, *The Arab-Israeli Dilemma*, 2nd ed. (Syracuse, N.Y.: Syracuse University Press, 1976).

who left Europe went to Palestine, but the influx was great enough in the twenties to alarm the Arab inhabitants. By the end of the Second World War, the number of immigrants was so large that it had become impossible to secure Arab approval for their settlement in Palestine.

Great Britain held a League of Nations mandate for Palestine and was thus responsible for regulating the entry of Jews into Palestine, for maintaining public order, and for preparing the country for eventual independence. These tasks were ultimately too difficult; in May 1948, the British simply disengaged themselves from the situation. War between the Jews and the Arabs was the result of this disengagement.

It is difficult to pinpoint the moment when Palestinian Arabs first resorted to violence. An important early example of Palestinian violence, however, was the riots in Jaffa in 1936, during which a number of Jews and Arabs were killed. One result of these riots was an organized effort (led by Haj Amin al-Husseini, the Mufti of Jerusalem), to oppose Jewish immigration and the British mandate. This organized opposition led to further unrest, riots, demonstrations, raids, and retaliatory police actions. At first, the Arabs directed their energies against the Jews. Arab mobs attacked Jewish merchants. They also attacked Jewish farming settlements, sometimes damaging fields and sometimes injuring individuals. But inevitably Arab terrorists began to make systematic attacks on the British, who, as the occupying power, were facilitating Jewish settlement in Palestine. The Jews began to form their own terrorist and defense organizations, first to challenge the Arabs and finally to confront the British. The British also began to fight terror with terror, and thus terrorism in Palestine ultimately became three-sided. It is well to remember that before (and for a time after) the establishment of Israel in 1948, there was no central authority in the area that all Jews respected. Thus, there were several extremist terrorist groups that many Jews (and later Israelis) abhorred but that others supported. Best known among these were the so-called Stern gang and the Irgun Zvai Leumi. The Irgun was well organized; one of its early leaders was Menachem Begin, who was to become prime minister of Israel in 1977. Several spectacular incidents of violence emanated from these extremist terrorist groups. In 1944, Lord Moyne (British minister of state for the Middle East) was assassinated in Cairo; July 1946 saw the bombing of the King David Hotel in Jerusalem (with 91 dead). In September 1948, Count Folke Bernadotte, United Nations mediator in Palestine, was assassinated in Jerusalem. Such acts of course had their political effects, including benefits, not only with Palestine (or Israel) but in the international community as well.[5]

These events in Palestine demonstrated the appropriateness of terrorism as a weapon against a colonial power. It was Jewish, not Arab, terrorism that won the early rounds in Palestine; but the lesson was not lost on the Arabs, who in the sixties began to resort to terrorism of their own against the Israelis; the activities of the al-Fatah guerrilla forces are an example of such Arab terrorism. A determined terrorist campaign is difficult to cope with; it is not a matter that armies or police deal with very effectively.[6]

Terrorism is universally condemned but just as universally employed. It is the natural weapon of the weak, but even governments use it as an effective substitute for more difficult or expensive operations. Terrorism, with random and unexpected targets, often leads to anguish and despair among the population. Responses to terrorist acts are often emotional and are usually out of proportion to the real effects of the acts themselves. It is not necessary to describe in detail the many examples of terrorism against the Israelis in the 1970s or the various terrorist acts (termed retaliation) carried out by the Israelis against the Arabs. Such terrorist acts have been numerous and,

---

[5] Howard M. Sachar's *A History of Israel from the Rise of Zionism to Our Time* (New York: Alfred A. Knopf, 1976) is an excellent and detailed account of all the events in modern Israeli history. Acts of terrorism are well covered and explained.

[6] King Hussein mounted military efforts against the guerrilla forces in Jordan with some success; this success was largely due to the fact that many guerrillas had ceased to be strictly guerrillas and had formed fairly large-scale military groupings concentrated in areas accessible to military attack. The civil war in Lebanon demonstrated how difficult it is to deal with such groups when they have become well entrenched and enjoy some international support.

until some accommodation between the Arab and the Israeli governments comes about, are almost certain to continue.

The points to note here are that terrorism often pays off; that it is a cheap and easily used weapon; and that few countries or peoples refuse to use it. (Some even approve of their own brand; in December 1982 Israel issued a series of 20 postage stamps commemorating 20 "martyrs" in the Israeli struggle for independence. Some were simply terrorists. In terrorism as in all things, it makes a difference whose ox is being gored.)

Another interesting example of the uses of violence in the anticolonial struggle occurred in Aden and the adjacent territories of the hinterland. Again Great Britain was the colonial power involved. By the sixties, Britain was well launched on its plan to disengage from the Middle East. It hoped to leave in Aden the semblance of an independent and friendly Arab government to which power could be transferred. This government was to be called the South Arabian Federation and was to be a conglomerate of minor shaykhdoms. All of these plans came to naught.

One problem was that there was no viable political system that could easily be constructed from the hodgepodge of fragmented systems that were to be found in Aden and the adjacent territories. Just as important, from the early sixties to the middle sixties, Nasserist influence was ascendant in the Arab world; in addition, there was civil war in Yemen. Nationalist organizations quickly came into being in Aden City. Terrorists began to strike against the British and their client shaykhs and against each other. A virtual battle between Arab troops and British forces was fought in June 1967. Two nationalist organizations, the National Liberation Front (NFL) and the Front for the Liberation of Occupied South Yemen (FLOSY), vied with each other for power. Both frightened some of the pro-British shaykhs away from participating in a British-sponsored government. Assassination and the threat of assassination were used with skill and success. The British were squeezed out. The NLF proved victorious over FLOSY. When the British left in late 1967, the NLF organized the government of the People's Republic of Southern Yemen.

The goals of British exodus and the termination of British

influence had been successfully achieved through indiscriminate violence and terror. Independence did not, however, mean an end to internal terror.

A government that survives a period of terror is hardly likely to be very generous or understanding of the rights of politically despised minorities. Internal Israeli politics, for example, especially with respect to the Arab minorities, quickly became calloused and unresponsive. Terror and violence throughout the Arab world have produced an atmosphere in which freedom of expression, legitimate opposition, broad political participation, and a climate of moderation have often had to give way to more extremist forms of politics.[7]

WARS OF INDEPENDENCE

What distinguishes a war of independence from the violent terrorist campaigns that are mounted against a government or a colonial regime? Sometimes the distinction is shadowy. Where insurgents have established a sizable and regular military force and are able to maintain it in the field for some length of time, there is manifestly an internal war of some sort. But what exists may be so ineffective and so poorly organized that it hardly merits the label of internal war. In fact, a war of independence may have gone through several such preliminary phases.

The conflict that broke out in May 1948 between the Israelis and primarily the armies of Egypt and Jordan was more properly an international than an internal war, since the adversaries involved were distinct national entities. The Israelis naturally look upon it as a war of independence. But it was primarily a war not against other Palestinians (Arabs), but rather against outsiders.

There are, however, several quite legitimate examples of wars of independence in the Middle East. The Rif rebellion against the Spanish and French in Morocco was certainly a war

[7] An eloquent account of current Israeli policies towards the Arabs under its control can be found in Raja Shehadeh, *The Third Way. A Journal of Life in the West Bank* (London: Quartet Books, 1982); see also the excellent study by Ian Lustick entitled *Arabs in the Jewish State: Israel's Control of a National Minority* (Austin, Tex.: The University of Texas Press, 1980).

of independence. Muhammad Bin Abdul Krim formed an effective and viable government for a time. It maintained internal order, held sway over considerable territory, and effectively put together a fighting machine that was defeated only with difficulty by the French and the Spanish.[8] Unfortunately, Abdul Krim was never able to secure international recognition of the legitimacy of his regime. With military defeat, his government collapsed and he went into exile.

A more recent example of a Middle Eastern war of independence is the war fought by the Algerians against the French. Indeed, it may be described as a classic case. France had annexed Algeria in the 1830s and over the years had increasingly insisted that Algeria was essentially and irretrievably French. Although perhaps nationalism in the modern sense did not develop until the 1920s, rebellion, demonstrations, and disturbances were common in nineteenth-century Algeria. They were generally local in nature and were not self-consciously nationalistic. But the French were never to know peace, although they poured money and settlers into the country and consciously thought of the area as part of France.

By the end of the Second World War (in which French North Africa was involved), a century of the French presence had not offered native Algerians much in the way of economic opportunity or political participation. What had been tolerated by the "colonies" in earlier years had now become intolerable. A decade after the Second World War, the collapse of the French colonial empire was well under way. Successive French governments hoped that Algeria could be saved. Although many Algerians were apathetic, terrorist efforts by

[8] General Manuel Silvestre was defeated and killed in battle (22 July 1921); General Navarro was captured (9 August 1921); and in 1922 General Damaso Berenguer, high commissioner of Spanish Morocco, resigned under fire. Berenguer was replaced by General Ricardo Burgueti, who lasted less than a year. General Miguel Primo de Rivera, the Spanish dictator after 1923, was forced to a policy of *abandonismo* in the summer of 1924. The famous Marshal Lyautey was dismissed as French commander in 1925 when the Rifians successfully attacked in French Morocco. Marshal Petain journeyed to Morocco to give his support. It was during all this fighting that Colonel Francisco Franco was promoted to brigadier at the age of 33. What a galaxy of Spanish and French generals to have met their match in Muhammad Bin Abdul Krim! See Woolman, *Rebels in the Rif*, passim.

Algerian leaders and the intransigence of the French (including the use of extreme terrorist tactics by the French themselves) gradually produced an Algerian community that was fairly united against the French. The early moderate Algerian leader, Ferhat Abbas, was replaced by the more radical Ahmad Ben Bella. Between 1954 and 1960, a major, although unusual, war was fought between the French army and increasingly effective Algerian guerrillas. The French could not win and abandoned their position in 1962. In the course of the conflict there was a coup d'etat in France (and a short-lived army takeover in Algiers). Ben Bella was himself forced out in 1965 in a coup led by Col. Houari Boumedienne.

The struggle against the French had been long and painful. The key to Algerian success, however, had been the half-dozen years beginning in 1954. Starting in November of that year, the National Liberation Army (NLA) gradually increased the territory it controlled throughout the country. By 1956, it controlled small but nevertheless significant areas in eastern Algeria, in the mountains close to Tunisia. By 1957, the NLA had enlarged its scene of operations to cover the entire Algerian coast, and the territories it controlled had correspondingly increased. By November 1958, all of populated Algeria was honeycombed with areas of NLA control and influence.

The French army — already demoralized from more than a century of defeats and embarrassments — could not win strategic victories over its guerrilla opponents, who later organized themselves into sizable military units. It did win tactical victories, but these were not enough. The French army therefore began a brutal, terrorist campaign against its opponents and those it thought were its opponents. This campaign of counter-terror, carried on haphazardly at best, was no more successful than the army's military campaigns had been. The cost of the struggle was immense for both Algeria and France, but the struggle showed the inability of a modern and well-equipped army to liquidate a war of liberation that had captured the support of the masses.[9]

[9] See Alistair Horne, *A Savage War of Peace: Algeria 1954–1962* (New York: Viking, 1978) for a very readable account of the war. Most of the Algerian successes were guerrilla in nature; the NLA did not begin its formal existence until 1958.

The Kurdish rebellion in Iraq is interesting in that it was a struggle not against a European colonial power but rather against a "native" Arab government. The Kurds are not Arabs, although they are Muslims. Their ancestral lands have become divided by the present-day borders of Turkey, Iraq, and Iran. The Kurds are an intractable mountain people who have caused difficulties for every government under which they have lived. Before 1918, Iraq (including Iraqi Kurdistan) was part of the Ottoman Empire. After the First World War, Great Britain secured a mandate to Iraq, but its control was never strong. Certainly, the government in Baghdad held weak authority over outlying areas, including those of the Kurds in the north.

The Kurdish rebellion can be laid at the door of one man as much as any: Shaykh Mulla Mustafa al-Barzani. Majid Khadduri suggests that the merging of the Kurds with the Arabs into a group with a single national consciousness was impossible because of Shi'i concern about the enhanced position of the Sunnis in any such amalgamation, as well as because of the growth of Arab nationalism in recent years. (The Kurds are neither Shi'ite nor Arab.) At the end of the Second World War, al-Barzani led an attempt to establish an autonomous Kurdistan. With the collapse of his attempt, he left for the Soviet Union, to return only after the Kassem revolution in 1958. The military government of Iraq at that time was unable to solve its Kurdish problem. Fighting between Kurdish and government forces assumed major proportions, particularly in the first half of the 1960s. During the military campaigning season, government troops made inroads into the Kurdish-controlled territory; with bad weather they retired. Throughout this time, great efforts were made to negotiate some settlement.

Although neither side eschewed negotiation in theory, it is difficult to see what could have been negotiated. To the central government, national prestige and security as well as petroleum resources were involved; to the Kurds, nothing less than their independence was at issue, although they demanded such things as Kurdish ministers in Baghdad. But the fact was that no national Iraqi army was strong enough to penetrate the Kurdish territories and destroy their fighting forces. Every year or so the central government (often a new one) would announce the end of fighting and a rapprochement with the Kurds. Just as regularly the fighting would break out once more. The most serious claim that a settlement had been made occurred in 1970. But when, in the late spring of 1972, the Iraq Petroleum Company was nationalized and production of oil in the northern fields fell, the Kurds once more expressed their dissatisfaction.

There seems to be little hope today for real Kurdish autonomy. The Kurds are under too many jurisdictions; their territory is landlocked and they have few resources; the world does not care about them. This became clearly evident when Iran abruptly withdrew its support of the Kurdish rebels in 1975. Kurdish ability to withstand Iraqi military incursions was seriously weakened, and once again the central government announced the end of the rebellion. The old warrior, al-Barzani, was forced to flee to Iran. He lived in Washington, D.C., in exile until his death. Meanwhile, with the fall of the Shah in 1979, Iranian Kurds decided that they would rebel against *their* central government in Tehran. Although the fighting that ensued resulted in many casualties among both Kurds and government forces, neither side has been able to completely prevail. Although it seems highly unlikely that Kurds in either Iraq or Iran will ever win independence, Kurdish irredentism certainly continues to survive.

There are other examples of struggles against "native" governments in the Middle East. In 1972, the Sudanese government announced the end of the fighting between southern blacks and northern Arabs that had gone on (with little publicity) for years. Casualties had been heavy. The blacks had been unable to secure their independence, but they had created serious difficulties for the central Sudanese government for a considerable period of time.

The Yemeni civil war in the 1960s was hardly a war of independence, yet it was a bloody and major conflict. In the early 1970s, the Dhofar province in western Oman was the scene of an abortive effort to break up Omani authority and control. The rebels were aided by Southern Yemen and the People's Republic of China; Oman itself accepted the aid of Iranian troops in the struggle in Dhofar.

Conflicts of this kind tend to occur in transition, both because internal political systems are themselves changing and because old colonial relationships are breaking down or atrophying. The Middle East is, of course, not the only area in which conflicts of this nature have occurred, but it is an area in which the conditions encourage these conflicts.

What are these conditions in the Middle East?

1. *A weakened central authority.* Where the central authority is colonial in character, successive efforts to undermine that authority by nationalist forces will ultimately be successful. Should a transfer of power occur, the new regime itself is often weak. A nationalist successor regime is thus often susceptible to coups or renewed conflict.

2. *Transitional systems.* Middle Eastern political systems are everywhere challenged by the forces of change. As we noted in Chapter I, the imbalances, inequalities, and frustrations that accompany transitional politics often give rise to organized and unorganized violence.

3. *Ideological confrontation.* Although lip service is paid by many to such goals as Arab socialism or Arab nationalism, there is in fact considerable ideological conflict in the Middle East. This conflict tends to support large-scale violent movements, which may be generated by other factors.

4. *The presence of unassimilable minorities.* The Middle East is, of course, not alone in this: Witness the South Tyroleans in Italy, the Roman Catholics in Ulster, the French Canadians. But in conjunction with other conditions, this has led and will lead in the future to violent movements against central authorities. These minorities may be described sometimes in religious terms, on other occasions in racial, tribal, or ethnic terms. We have spoken of the blacks of southern Sudan and the Kurds of Iraq. But Iran is riddled with minorities, so much so that some authorities on Iran claim that an *Iranian* nationalism is impossible. Pakistan is another case; it seems constantly on the brink of falling apart, with Baluchis, Sindis, Punjabis, and Pathans going their separate ways. The Baluchis are especially interesting since their territory is in both Iran and Pakistan; some Baluchi leaders claim an independence from both countries. Israel has its Arabs, a group so large and

disaffected that it is difficult to see how the Israelis can deal with them in the future.

5. *A tradition of external interference.* Although their role is diminishing, the French and British are still involved in Middle Eastern affairs. The United States is involved too, as is the Soviet Union. And the Middle Eastern countries themselves are not loath to interfere in one another's affairs. Egypt was noteworthy in this respect under Nasser, and Libya and Iran also have reputations for interference.

6. *International Wars and Conflicts.* The perennial conflicts between Israel and its Arab neighbors, Syria, Jordan, and Egypt, are discussed elsewhere in this volume. But Israel widened the scope of these encounters by bombing an Iraqi nuclear reactor in 1981. Israel's justification for this act was that the reactor *might* be used to make nuclear weapons and these weapons *might* be used against Israel. Indeed the Israeli government declared that it would not permit Arab states to possess the means to produce nuclear weapons. But whatever the rationalization the act was clearly an armed attack on another Middle Eastern state.

In the summer of 1982 Israel attacked Lebanon — ostensibly, it later argued, to destroy the PLO military units there. But actually the Lebanese took many of the casualties and much, perhaps most, of the fighting was with Syrian forces in Lebanon. Again, whatever the motives, this act — labeled "Operation Peace for Galilee" in Israel — was also an attack on another Middle Eastern state.

We also have witnessed another major conflict between the Middle Eastern countries with the Iraqi attack on Iran in 1980. Iraq's strong man, Saddam Hussein, worried over the possibility of Iran's revolution splashing over into Iraq (where a majority of the Arabs are Shi'ites), attacked Iran with the thought of destroying the revolution or at least pulling Ayatollah Khomeini down. It was a grave miscalculation. The Iranian military forces, with all their problems, proved not to be the pushover Saddam expected; his own army proved not to be so able. With heavy casualties on both sides, immense destruction of oil and other facilities, the war continued to drag on in early 1983. Other Arab states, notably Saudi Arabia, aided Iraq but some did not, Syria being prime among them. The United States extended token assistance to Iraq; its ally Israel sent some help to Iran. This conflict is discussed in the chapter on the Persian Gulf.

Sometimes attacks come from outside the Middle East. The only example that we have (at least since the Suez attack by Great Britain and France in 1956) of an attack on a Middle Eastern country by another country outside the Middle East is the December 1979 Russian movement into Afghanistan to shore up the leftist government there. The Russians have been there ever since, with troops numbering over 100,000 in "occupation." Controlling the cities, they have not been able to pacify the countryside. We have in effect a civil war with the added presence of an outside force. It resembles both the Vietnam War and the Yemen War, where Egypt was the outside force. It is interesting that in both the latter cases the outside force was ultimately compelled to leave. Perhaps it is easier for the Soviet Union in Afghanistan, but the occupation has turned out to be expensive, and Russian casualties have been well over 10,000. Casualties among the Afghans, of course, are much larger.

THE MIDDLE EASTERN MILITARY

Many forms of violence in the Middle East are directly attributable to the role that the military institutions of the area seek to play. (It is well to distinguish between armed forces and police forces in the modern state. The latter are primarily responsible for enforcing the criminal law, for administering a variety of regulations, and for facilitating the proper functioning of certain activities, such as those of the traffic police. The police may also contain a *secret* cadre, such as SAVAK in Iran, which during the Shah's regime conducted surveillance over the populace, undertook counterespionage, and carried out whatever extralegal activities seemed desirable (official assassinations, for example). Quite obviously, police, both open and covert, may engage in violence and may encourage or retard various legitimate forms of political change. Yet the police in the Middle East never act on their own. They are relatively weak and often are poorly equipped. They are the tools of political henchmen, and their own officers are rarely powerful enough to carry out independent policies. They are often corrupt. Certainly they possess little popularity among the population at large. They are vulnerable and often expendable, regardless of the institutional power they sometimes have. In short, they are not armies.)

What are the functions of an army in the Middle East? The prime function of any army (or air force or navy) is the external defense of the state. In the Middle East, however, the army has many other functions: to maintain internal control and stability, to serve as a symbol of independence, to perform certain modernizing functions, and to uphold the honor of the state. Few Middle Eastern states need armies to defend themselves against external foes. This is either because they have few enemies in the military sense or because the enemies they do have are so powerful that no armies they might assemble could perform their defense mission successfully. No Lebanese army could defend itself against any of its neighbors. Nor could any Iranian army or Afghan army defend itself against the Soviet Union.[10] Manifestly, Israel has needed its army, which so far has been successful in defending Israeli territory.

Most Middle Eastern states spend more resources on their armed forces than is strictly necessary to maximize the chances for successful defense. In one sense, these expenditures can be viewed as a payoff to the military for performing other functions and duties. The military, it is assumed, desires late-model jet aircraft, heavy tanks, rapid promotion, and pleasant officers' clubs. But in another sense, it is important to many countries to exhibit their status by investing in gaudy and expensive military equipment. If conspicuous consumption is important to the individual, conspicuous military consumption is vitally important to the typical political system in the developing world.

Military systems, however, do perform other functions that justify their existence. Perhaps the most important of these

---

[10] We speak here of organized military forces, not guerrilla forces such as those the Soviet Union is currently fighting in Afghanistan.

functions in the Middle East is that of maintaining a regime in power. In this role, the army defends the government from its potential or actual internal foes. Martial law is often instrumental not only in putting down disturbances but in rooting out the opposition and forcing unpopular decisions upon the people. The army has certainly played these roles in societies such as Turkey, Iran, Pakistan, Egypt, Jordan, Iraq, Sudan, Libya, Syria, Algeria, and Morocco. Jordan's King Hussein, for example, has owed his throne repeatedly to the loyalty of the army. Without that army he would not be king. The same might be said for Muhammad Reza Shah Pahlavi of Iran up to 1978–1979.

Sometimes a supporting army will operate so disastrously (as one did in East Pakistan in March 1971) that the regime it maintains collapses because of its ineptitude. The Lebanese army was unwilling or unable to control domestic turbulence, which led to civil war in 1958 and again in 1975. And a supporting army sometimes spawns enough dissidence within its own ranks to endanger the regime very directly. The several attempts on King Hassan's life in Morocco originated at the highest command levels of the military forces.

Armed forces — the Egyptian army and the Shah's Iranian army come particularly to mind — sometimes have played educational and practical roles. Large numbers of recruits, often of village origin, will pass through the army, becoming socialized politically, as well as in other ways, in the process. They may be taught a trade as well as to read and write. In this way an army can serve as a modernizing device. It may also participate in road building or other construction work. In Iran under the Shah, young recruits served in large numbers as literacy and development corpsmen throughout the countryside.

Middle Eastern armies in many ways resemble armies elsewhere. Some are large, while others are quite small. Some are really professional; others are as unprofessional as it is possible to be. The amount and kind of equipment they have vary widely from country to country. The relation between officers and men and the methods of recruitment are other aspects of Middle Eastern armies that have varied.

Of all Middle Eastern armies, that of the Israelis[11] has perhaps achieved the most spectacular victories over foreign foes. It has proved victorious in three wars: in 1948, 1956, and 1967.[12] Although in 1973 the outcome was less favorable for the Israelis, their armed forces nevertheless prevailed.

The Israeli army is of necessity a citizen army; virtually all Israelis, men and women, have an obligation to serve.[13] It has had, in mobilization particularly, a high élan. Its higher-ranking officers, whether they are as brilliant as they are often claimed to be, are very capable.

The Israeli skill in mobilizing their armed forces quickly is particularly impressive. Their Arab adversaries are much less efficient in this. But the conflict in 1973 showed that both the Syrians and the Egyptians had mastered to a surprisingly large degree the problems involved in utilizing sophisticated weapons. They were unusually successful in the employment of surface-to-air missiles, and the Israeli air losses were most severe. Israeli casualties in this war were also higher than Israeli casualties in any other conflict since 1948. Although the Israelis were tactically surprised, they did succeed ultimately in penetrating into Syria beyond the Golan Heights and into Egypt beyond the Suez Canal.

In 1982 in Lebanon the Israelis engaged the Syrians. The Syrian air force's disastrous encounters with the Israelis were

[11] By far the best book on the Israeli army is Edward Luttwak and Dan Horowitz's *The Israeli Army* (New York: Harper and Row, 1975). See also Chaim Herzog *The Arab-Israeli Wars: War and Peace in the Middle East* (New York: Random House, 1982).

[12] There seems to be little doubt that Israel found the so-called War of Attrition with Egypt (1969–1970) frustrating and unrewarding. It led to dependence on the thinly held Bar-Lev Line, which crumpled in the 1973 fighting.

[13] There are a number of exemptions open to women that are not available to men; moreover, women are not expected to assume combat roles. As to the "citizens" army, retired General Mattityahu Peled, in an article on the op-ed page of the *New York Times* (30 December 1982), argues that the old citizen army has largely gone by the board, and that what the Israelis now have is a standing army. He attributes this change to the immense military aid from the United States — about $2.5 billion in fiscal 1983 but including economic aid. Peled argues that "more than 75 percent of it can be expected to go beefing up Israel's defense expenditure."

well publicized. To a very great degree, the Syrian problems were a product of American planes (especially F-15s and F-16s), including a type of AWACS, and poor Russian equipment, particularly their surface-to-air missiles.

On the ground the Syrians did not do so badly. The Syrian army is a very powerful one indeed. Although the Israelis still possess superior armed forces with respect to the Arabs, the gap between them is certainly lessening.

The Turkish army allegedly is a powerful one, well equipped and well trained. It is not a citizen army like the Israeli army, but its base (population and other resources) is much broader and greater than that of the Israeli army. This army has not been tested in war recently, unless one counts its occupation of portions of Cyprus. Its record in the Korean War was excellent; in an earlier day, it had a very fine record in the First World War and in the ensuing struggle with the Greeks.

On the contemporary scene, it is difficult to envision the Turks engaged in military hostilities with any of their Arab neighbors. Their major potential foe is the Soviet Union — Turkey is a member of the North Atlantic Treaty Organization (NATO) because of this — but it is difficult to see how the Turks could defend themselves against the Soviet Union in any but the most conventional of conflicts. The Turks themselves view the Greeks as enemies, too. Against such a foe they would acquit themselves very well.

Turkey was until recently the recipient of massive American military aid and was an American military client. But since the Turkish invasion of Cyprus on behalf of the Turkish minority, political relations between the United States and Turkey deteriorated, with sharp curtailment of military assistance. This deterioration was, to a large degree, the result of the effective lobbying of large numbers of Greek-Americans. The Turks began to reassess their membership in NATO and their relations with the Soviet Union. By 1978 the United States began a reassessment of its own and has once again resumed economic and military assistance to Turkey.

Iran under the Shah was also a military client state of the United States, although its substantial petroleum wealth as well as the proud, independent policy of the Shah made American influence there something less than predictable. Iran's military force was among the top half-dozen in the world in terms of equipment and size. Most of its equipment had been purchased from the United States, and an American military mission for training purposes was a large and well-established fixture of the Iranian scene for many years. The Shah wanted the very latest and most sophisticated of American weapons, usually in large numbers. The continuing need for this equipment was not always apparent. The result of the purchase of the equipment was that great military and political ambitions were attributed to the Shah. Despite the incredible buildup of the Iranian forces, they remained under the Shah basically untested. Whatever his ambitions, his armed forces played only a small role in Middle Eastern affairs; as much as anything they were used to bolster the Shah's regime.

With the coming of the revolution, many of the Shah's generals fled abroad; many others were killed or imprisoned. The army suffered serious damage in the chaotic conditions of 1979–1981. But as an institution it gave its loyalty to the new government. It soon was embroiled in fighting the Kurds and then in defending Iran against a major attack by Iraq. It has, along with the Revolutionary Guards, acquitted itself well against the Iraqis. Would it do as well against the Turks? It could hardly contend with the Soviet Union. But as the war winds down with Iraq, it will remain the major armed force of the Persian Gulf, and all the more impressive because it has fought, and done so successfully.

In the spring of 1983 the Afghan army, with the massive aid of Soviet troops, was fighting Afghan "rebels," those who dislike the leftist government and its sponsor, the Soviet Union. The Soviet Union seems content to fight a low-grade struggle against the Afghan guerrillas. In the long run the Russians are likely to succeed but at a very heavy price.

The Pakistani army was tested against the Indians and was found wanting. Although strongly aided for years by the United States, the Pakistani army appears, at present certainly, to be of little threat to its neighbors. But General Zia, Pakistan's president, continues to clamor for more American military aid.

As a category, these armies of the non-Arab Middle East include the strongest as well as some of the weakest in the area. In contrast with Arab armies, these armed forces have been relatively reluctant to interfere in the political arena. In Iran, the army did not intervene to bolster the Shah in 1979; in Turkey, it has moved, apparently reluctantly, to support the "principles of Kemalism." In any event, army rule in Turkey has been quite unlike army rule in most places.[14]

Only in Pakistan has the army interfered broadly in political life for an extended period of time. And in Pakistan, in the wake of the disastrous war with India in 1971, the armed forces were so discredited that they permitted their most vocal critic, Zulfikar Ali Bhutto, to simply take over the government. By 1977, the armed forces had intervened once again, this time to jail Bhutto. The bloody coup in Afghanistan in the spring of 1978 was led by the army.

Armies in the Arab world also differ widely. Those of the very small Arab states — Kuwait, Lebanon, Yemen, Tunisia, and so on — are, of course, of no international consequence, and are perhaps of little consequence altogether. In the 1958 civil war in Lebanon, the army refused to intervene; its commander was subsequently elected president. In the second Lebanese civil war (1975 to date), the army was incapable even of preserving its entity as an independent force and collapsed.

In 1948, the finest of the Arab armies was the British-officered Arab Legion of Jordan.[15] This army fought in the first Arab-Israeli war and, within the limits of its supplies and its size, fought very well. It fought again in the 1967 war. The overall result was defeat, but the Israelis were and continue to be very impressed with the fighting qualities of the Jordanian army.[16]

14 See Metin Tamkoç, *The Warrior Diplomats* (Salt Lake City: University of Utah Press, 1976), for an extended discussion of the role of the armed forces in Turkish politics.

15 See John B. Glubb, *The Story of the Arab Legion* (London: Hodder and Stoughton, 1948). For another account of the Legion, see P. J. Vatikiotis, *Politics and the Military in Jordan* (New York: Frederick A. Praeger, 1967).

16 Luttwak and Horowitz (*The Israeli Army*, p. 267) have this to say: "[The 6 June Jordanian attack near Jenin in the West Bank] was the most effective counter-attack launched by any Arab army during the

In 1970, the Jordanians were strong enough not only to defeat the Palestinian guerrillas in Jordan but to stand off briefly an intervening Syrian force. The Jordanian army is small and poorly supplied, but retains a high degree of professionalism.

Until 1973, the Syrian army was of little military consequence against the Israeli army. Its record in the October War, however, was substantially different. Its soldiers fought not only bravely but with remarkable skill and coordination. Over the years, the Syrian army has spawned many coups; its ranks are severely divided along communal and family lines. The Syrian army reflects the permanent instability of the Syrian political system. Yet since 1970, Gen. Hafez al-Assad, president of Syria and himself an Alawite, has given the Syrians a remarkable degree of stability.

The Syrians feel militarily threatened not only by the Israelis but by the Iraqis as well. In spite of these threats, Syria intervened in the Lebanese civil war and brought some of the fighting to a halt, leaving behind an occupation force of some 30,000 men. For the size of its country, the Syrian army is an experienced, well-led, and increasingly well-equipped force. In a future engagement the Israelis might find the Syrians difficult to handle.

It is difficult to speak with much assurance of the contemporary Iraqi army. Units have fought on occasion on the Israeli borders, but never with any great success. The Kurdish revolt in Iraq prospered as long as Iran was willing to supply the Kurds with weapons; the Iraqi army achieved no noteworthy supremacy over the Kurds. Yet it was well equipped with Soviet weapons and was taken seriously. After its ill-starred war with Iran, however, it is likely to be viewed with less concern. It is a threat to Kuwait of course, and probably Saudi Arabia, but not Syria.

The Saudi armed forces, like all things Saudi, are changing rapidly. Saudi Arabia is a military client state of the United States. The armed forces are small and are not yet thoroughly

---

war . . . [and the commander of the Jordanian Fortieth Armored Brigade in this struggle, Shaker Ben Zaid, was] the outstanding soldier on the Arab side. . . ."

professional. Indeed, the regime would be very suspicious of high-ranking professional soldiers who might be tempted into political intervention. The Israelis fear the Saudis less than they do the advanced military equipment that the Saudis receive from the United States; the Israelis contend that in a crisis Saudi aircraft, for example, could be lent or given to other more belligerent Arab states and that, if necessary, Saudi air bases close to the Israeli border could be utilized by enemies of Israel. In 1978, this was the backdrop to congressional debates over the sale of jet fighters (F-15s) to Saudi Arabia and still later to those over the sale of AWACS to Saudi Arabia. But it does not seem that Saudi Arabia poses a direct military threat to any of its major neighbors.

A counterpart in some ways to the Saudi army was the army of King Idris's Libya before the coup of 1969. The coup officers in Libya were young and of relatively low rank. In any event, the Libyan army, even with the material resources it now commands, is not a strong or well-organized force. Libya and Egypt fought a short engagement near Tobruk in the summer of 1977. The Libyans were no match for the Egyptians. Although Libya has intervened in Black Africa and has threatened Sudan, it is Libyan money, as distributed by Colonel Qaddafi, that is feared in the Middle East, not Libya's armed forces.

Tunisia, caught between Libya and Algeria, is hardly likely to engage in military adventures. Its army's role must be defined within that general context. Morocco is more powerful than Tunisia, and its regime more aggressive. There have been armed conflicts along its borders with several of its neighbors. And in 1971 and 1972, attempted coups showed that within the armed forces' ranks there was enough dissension to endanger the regime. Yet when the march into old Spanish Sahara was essayed, it was done peacefully and without the display of weapons.

The Algerian armed forces seem most likely to be able to dominate western North Africa in the future. The power base of Algeria is greater than those of its neighbors, and its politics may encourage military adventure. For the present, however, in the midst of rapid economic modernization, the military's role has been a muted one.

The Egyptian army, with all its shortcomings, remains the most interesting of the Middle Eastern armies. It has had more combat experience than most Middle Eastern armies, although this has not always been reflected in superior performance. It has now fought in four Palestinian wars (1948, 1956, 1967, 1973) and has also fought a long, debilitating war in Yemen. Originally equipped with miscellaneous weapons acquired from the West, it received its first influx of Soviet arms in 1955; today it still possesses much Soviet equipment. It was partially trained in the late 1940s and early 1950s by a number of former German officers who had sought asylum in Egypt. In 1952, the army mounted a coup against the old monarchical regime; one result was the reequipping and reorganizing of the armed forces. After the 1967 war, Soviet advisors concentrated on the retraining of middle-rank field officers and on building up a network of sophisticated surface-to-air missiles. The results of this aid program were evident in the October War in 1973. By the late 1970s, Egypt was attempting to reequip its armed forces with American weapons. Egyptian and American forces have engaged in joint maneuvers.

The Egyptian military ought to be able to dominate the area. Egypt has a large, fast-growing population and also sufficient experience to build armed forces of high quality. Its major enemy is, of course, Israel, but its national interests involve at least Sudan (with its control over the Nile River flow) and possibly eastern Libya.

The missions of the Egyptian armed forces have generally exceeded their abilities. Before the October War in 1973, the Egyptian military forces were held in low esteem. It was assumed that their ranks were filled by men who were so technologically backward that modern sophisticated weapons could not be used. Many of the officers clearly lacked leadership skills, and the cleavage between these officers and their men was marked. Altogether these factors produced a military organization that had to be characterized as inept.

Either this analysis was wrong or very substantial changes had occurred between 1967 and 1973 — or so the results of the 1973 fighting seem to indicate. Perhaps a little of both! Indeed, the army might never have been as bad as it was made out to be. The destruction of the airfields and planes by the Israeli air force in the early hours of the June War (1967) made the Egyptian army's mission in Sinai then an impossible one. The fact that, in the very peculiar environment of Sinai, Israeli tactical surprise swiftly won several encounters should not necessarily have meant that the Egyptian army was badly organized or officered at all levels. Perhaps the very highest echelons were incompetent in the past. Field Marshal Amer was the main example of incompetence in 1967; since then, many high-ranking officers have been cashiered, including several in late 1973. Perhaps army morale and the psychology of defeat did undermine the past chances for success. And perhaps the educational skills of soldiers do make a difference. The 1973 fighting, however, did break the myth of Israeli invincibility and demonstrated that the Egyptian army was still an army to be reckoned with.

Sudan is of much less importance than Egypt. It has several enemies. Its black southern population has had contacts with Ethiopia. It is not inconceivable that Sudan could become militarily involved with one of its Black African neighbors. But Egypt, precisely because Sudan sits athwart the Nile, is its major concern. Although relatively warm today, relations between the two have not always been good. The Sudanese army is weak and suffers most of the defects common to other Arab armies.

Before 1955, the only arms suppliers to the Middle Eastern countries were the Western powers. This dependence was radically altered by the Soviet-Egyptian arms agreement of 1955. A year later, the Egyptian army and much of its equipment were seriously damaged by the Israelis. The Soviet Union replaced the equipment lost and provided increased facilities for the training of Egyptian military personnel. By 1961, East German and Soviet military missions in Egypt had begun to reorganize the military forces there. During the months that followed, substantial Soviet military aid (along, of course, with other kinds of aid) was provided on a continuing basis. This aid included bombers of all types, tanks, MIG-21 supersonic jet interceptors, and SAM-2 ground-to-air missiles.

Much of this equipment was lost in the June War (1967),

and once again the Soviet Union provided replacements. By 1970, several Soviet squadrons of fighter planes were actually stationed in Egypt. These included the very latest jet fighters. Tanks, heavy howitzers, ground-to-ground missiles, and other miscellaneous equipment, as well as approximately 15,000 Soviet military personnel, were among the largess offered to the Egyptians.

The future of the Soviet military presence in Egypt was compromised in July 1972, however, when President Sadat ordered all Soviet military personnel to leave Egypt. At the time, there was considerable speculation concerning why the Soviet technicians were summarily expelled. There had been dissatisfaction with the inevitable interference that these technicians and other military advisers generated. President Sadat himself said that the Russians had been too cautious; apparently, they had been unwilling to give the Egyptians certain offensive weapons. The Soviet expulsion pleased the United States, and, in effect, Sadat was appealing to the United States to offer a quid pro quo by exerting pressure on Israel to withdraw from the Arab lands seized in 1967. The United States either would not or could not do this. The result was that Sadat returned to the military solution and won surprising political and military rewards. In early 1974, Egypt had an army with restored morale, and with the cooperation of Arab oil-producing states had forced the Israelis to reconsider their occupation of Sinai. Sadat thus achieved an important victory, one that later made it possible for him to visit Jerusalem and offer an accommodation to the Israelis, and later still, to negotiate his separate peace at Camp David.

Egypt was not, of course, the only Middle Eastern nation to receive military aid from the Soviet Union, although it was the chief recipient of such aid. Major shipments were made to Syria and Iraq, and lesser amounts were given to Sudan, Libya, Algeria, Yemen, and South Yemen. By American standards, these were mostly radical regimes, and it is not surprising that the Soviet Union has found it useful to supply them. Soviet aid has not always meant that the regime receiving it has proved very grateful or has demonstrated this gratitude.

The case of Egypt (and, by 1978, Iraq as well) should make that apparent.

We can sum up Middle Eastern armies with the following observations:

1. Middle Eastern armies vary widely in terms of size, equipment, training, and élan.

2. Few are well equipped to carry on the primary mission of defending their nation's borders, and even fewer are capable of initiating offensive military action externally.

3. For many, the most basic mission is maintaining a particular regime in power.

4. With certain non-Arab exceptions, Middle Eastern armies are likely to be heavily involved in politics.

5. Middle Eastern armies tend to be relatively small with respect to the population of their states, and their defense budgets are not unusually high as a percentage of gross national product (GNP).[17] But there are important exceptions — obviously Syria, Israel, and Saudi Arabia, and, to a lesser extent, Egypt.

6. Middle Eastern armies are seldom homogeneous, but rather are often "continually rent by internal cleavage and conflict."[18] This has been particularly true of the Syrian, Lebanese, and Iraqi armies.

7. The officer class in modernizing armies tends to display characteristics different from those of the officer class in traditional armies. Even more marked are the characteristics of those portions of the officer corps that are prone to coups. These modernizing officers are likely to be young and of

---

[17] See J. C. Hurewitz, *Middle East Politics: The Military Dimension* (New York: Frederick A. Praeger, 1969). Although the figures in this study are considerably out of date, they illustrate the points made. Another somewhat dated study supports these general hypotheses and indicates that the particular societies in Jordan, Iraq, Israel, and Iran are among the world leaders in both categories. See Bruce M. Russett, "Measures of Military Effort," *American Behavioral Scientist* 7 (February 1964):26–29.

[18] James A. Bill, "The Military and Modernization in the Middle East," *Comparative Politics* 2 (October 1969):54.

middle-class origin, often have experience abroad, and usually are extremely nationalistic.[19]

THE COUP D'ETAT

The coup is by now a well-established part of the Middle Eastern political process.[20] It need not be particularly violent, although the threat of violence is always present. Generally, few lives are lost in the coup itself, but recriminatory trials may eliminate numbers of individuals in the post-coup period.

To examine the Middle East during just the last thirty years, only Morocco, Tunisia, Israel, Saudi Arabia,[21] Lebanon, and Jordan have not undergone coups.[22] The potential for coups in most Middle Eastern countries (including Israel) remains high.

Sometimes a coup leads to revolution: Egypt is an example, and so is Iran. But often it does not: Syria offers an instance. Almost always the coup is carried out, although not always inspired, by military officers of field-grade rank. Generally, these officers have been radically oriented, and the coups they have mounted have been put together in the name of innovation and modernization.

Usually such coups produce governments that are weak. The first task of such governments is to consolidate power, and, while doing so, they inevitably neglect the goals that rationalized their coup. Gradually conditions worsen, often leading to a subsequent coup. The chain is broken when the leaders of a particular coup are competent or lucky enough to be able to alter political conditions and legitimate their own supremacy. Coup leaders not surprisingly are interested primarily in

[19] *Ibid.*, pp. 54–57.

[20] See Carl Leiden and Karl M. Schmitt, *The Politics of Violence: Revolution in the Modern World* (Englewood Cliffs, N.J.: Prentice-Hall, 1968), for a theoretical discussion of the coup d'etat and revolution.

[21] This depends upon the exact definition of *coup*. In 1964, Prince Faisal was able to legally and legitimately depose his brother Saud as king.

[22] In Morocco, Lebanon, and Jordan, attempts at coups have been made, and in Lebanon over the past several years chaos has sometimes made it difficult to point to a legitimate government. Note the ambiguous status of Major Haddad's rump government in southern Lebanon.

short-term political payoffs; long-term solutions to political problems are usually neglected. Let us examine two cases of the Middle Eastern coup d'etat.

The Egyptian Coup. In the spring of 1952, the conditions in Egypt made a coup likely.[23] Much depended upon the response of the British, who continued to occupy the Suez Canal Zone. King Farouk and his government were thoroughly discredited. The regime's claims to Sudan and to Palestine had ended ignominiously. The Egyptian army had been defeated and humiliated and was resentful. The Israeli presence was a running sore. It was difficult, if not impossible, to maintain order in Egypt — Cairo had been ravaged by mobs in January.

Eliezer Be'eri has this to say about the prelude to the 1952 coup:

> In the Egypt of 1952 there was revolutionary ferment. The mass outburst of Black Saturday in January, the violent struggle for the evacuation of the British bases and the frequent government crises were clear evidence of this; and the movement of the Free Officers was also one of its expressions. Moreover, the class struggle in town and country was becoming more and more acute. In 1951 there were 49 workers' strikes. In the second half of 1951 there were several uprisings of peasants who demanded ownership of the large estates they were cultivating, and in a number of instances the rebellions were quelled only by bloodshed. The forces which controlled the communications media and public opinion maintained a conspiracy of silence about the struggles of the workers and peasants, and only fragmentary accounts came to the knowledge of the public and to history. But whoever wanted to listen could hear subterranean rumblings in 1952 that announced an approaching volcanic eruption.[24]

A clandestine group of young army officers, led by a lieutenant colonel named Gamal Abdel Nasser, had for some years planned an eventual political intervention if the government

[23] See Leiden and Schmitt, *The Politics of Violence*, for a detailed discussion of the Egyptian coup of 1952.

[24] Eliezer Be'eri, *Army Officers in Arab Politics and Society*, (New York: Frederick A. Praeger, 1970):102–103.

did not in some way meet its demands and needs. This group was forced to crystallize its plans in the early summer of 1952, when it became apparent that the government had learned much about its existence and was about to move against it. At the same time, the internal situation in Egypt had completely deteriorated, and it seemed that almost no effort would be needed to topple the regime.

The coup, in spite of all the coffeehouse planning over the years, was a patchwork of last-minute decisions. Nevertheless, everything worked beautifully. The king and his ministers had already left the heat of Cairo for Alexandria by 22 July. Late that night, a small body of troops took over the command headquarters in Cairo and then arrested as many leading politicians and possible opponents as could be found in the very early hours of the morning. The British, who had military forces in the Suez Canal Zone, sat on their hands. The king found no support in the army or from the British and went into exile. Egyptians of all classes greeted the coup with enthusiasm. An old and respected general, Muhammad Naguib, accepted the nominal role — he later was tempted to make more of it — as head of the junta, the Revolutionary Command Council. The coup was a success. The junta survived relatively intact to lead Egypt into revolution and into an assortment of international and domestic adventures.

This coup can be characterized as one evolving from a conspiracy of young army officers against a very weakened and discredited old regime. There was no foreign intervention. Enthusiasm for the coup was so widespread and lasted so long that it permitted a genuine revolutionary consolidation of power to occur. The coup's leader, Nasser, was unusual in his political skills and in the inordinate popular appeal that he engendered.

Most other Middle Eastern coups, however, have been far different from the Egyptian case. Those in Syria from 1949 to 1970 were noteworthy for the brevity of the regimes they inaugurated. The difference, though, lies not so much in the actual mechanics of the takeover as in the subsequent history of the succeeding regime. When that regime is unable to command loyalty or to legitimate its existence, it is hardly likely to be able to move seriously in the direction of modernization and political development. In Syria, General Hafez al-Assad has been in power since 1970; it is the longest period of stability possessed by any modern, independent, Syrian government. The history of Iraq has been similar to that of Syria in this respect; it may be useful to examine it for a moment.

The Iraqi Coup. Iraq has had a history of coups. The Bakr Sidqi coup of October 1936 was, for the Arab world at least, the first of a long chain of military coups. "The Iraqi coup of 1936 was the first of its type . . . [and] was typical of many that followed, both in their organization and in the course they took. The way in which the military dictatorship met its end was also typical — it was overthrown by a coup of other military officers." [25] On 10 August 1937, Bakr Sidqi was assassinated in Mosul, and the conspirators themselves mounted a successful revolt. They permitted the existence of a semi-independent government, however, and in December 1938 they were forced to intervene. When the king died in April 1939, the military officers were successful in demanding that Abd al-Ilah be named regent. In 1941, the army intervened once again, this time to back Rashid Ali in his clash with the British over their presence in Iraq. The Rashid Ali revolt, as it was known, was of course put down by the British, with the aid of Glubb Pasha and the Arab Legion. It eventually ushered in, under the control of Nuri al-Said, a period of reasonable stability in Iraqi politics.

In the summer of 1958, Nuri was prime minister and Abd al-Ilah was still the power behind the young king, Faisal II. Abd al-Ilah was widely hated in the country. The debacle of the Palestine war of 1948 had seriously undermined the position of Nuri and the regent. Nuri had consistently clung to his British friendship in good times and bad, and had incurred considerable distrust from many of his own officers as a result. After all, the Western defense alliance, in which Iraq alone of all the Arab states participated, was called the *Baghdad* Pact:

---

25 *Ibid.*, p. 19.

Radio Cairo spoke for many Arabs in denouncing the Iraqi government's attachment to what it called Western "imperialism." In the summer of 1958, then, there was much dissatisfaction with Nuri and his government, and much uncertainty over the role that Iraq would play in the Arab world. This was reflected in the feelings of the officer class. Any Arab army, but particularly any Syrian or Iraqi army characterized by family, religious, and political cleavages, would have produced conspiratorial groups, and in Iraq the precedents for army intervention were well known. (Kassem himself had been a minor figure in the Bakr Sidqi group.) Abdul Karim Kassem was involved in conspiracy at least as early as 1956; by 1957, he headed — it is said, merely because he had seniority over his colleagues — a sizable collection of officers who were determined to strike against the government at the first appropriate opportunity.

That opportunity came in July 1958. The Iraqi government decided to transfer an army brigade to Jordan — it may be recalled that Lebanon was in turmoil at the time — and the brigade chosen was the twentieth (including a battalion commander, Abd al-Salam Arif, later president of Iraq), whose temporary divisional commander was Kassem. The brigade was issued ammunition and ordered to go through Baghdad on 13 July on its way to Jordan.

Instead, Kassem overthrew the regime, murdering in the process the young king Faisal, his uncle and heir, Abd al-Ilah, and Nuri al-Said, the prime minister. After only five years of the Kassem regime, Kassem himself was murdered and his government overthrown, with Arif the successful survivor. Those five years were turbulent ones for Iraq, with army revolts and assassination attempts. Had Kassem's personality been different and his power base wider, and if some of the political problems of the area had been resolved, he might have established a government that had greater permanence. In short, he failed at legitimation and found it impossible to embark on long-range political development. The same generally was true of his immediate successors. It is only in 1968, with the rise of General Ahmad Hasan al-Bakr that an Iraqi regime has been able to move ahead with the business of modernization and political development.[26] The current (1983) strongman in Iraq, Saddam Hussein, is not a military officer, but he had obviously had military backing. It is unlikely that he can survive long a peace with Iran amid the inevitable humiliation of the Iraqi army.

Non-Military Coups. Some coups occur without military intervention. In Sudan, a military dictatorship was established in November 1958 by Lt. Gen. Ibrahim Abbud. Six years were to follow before Abbud was finally ousted, but in the interim there were several attempted coups, continued difficulties in the south, and unending political discord. "What is unique in Abbud's overthrow is the fact that this regime was not destroyed by a military coup but by a popular uprising, and he was compelled to yield his position to civilian authority." [27] Students in Khartoum demonstrated against the regime in October 1964, quickly winning adherents from the mass of citizenry. A more or less general strike occurred. Abbud began dismantling the military structure that he had erected, an act that aroused so much popular enthusiasm that he himself was forced to resign on 15 November.

In this example, it is clear that the army had been unable to solve any of the major problems, particularly the disastrous racial struggle in the south. Those army leaders who had assumed power had also lost much of the support of the army as a whole, and if Abbud's regime had not collapsed of its own weight in late 1964, it would surely have fallen to a military putsch. In any event, in 1969 a successful coup was staged, and Sudan returned to the more normal role of Arab military politics.

The December 1971 war between India and Pakistan, beginning with the insurrection in East Pakistan in March and ending with the creation of Bangladesh, resulted in another military regime's collapsing of its own weight. In the brief life

---

[26] Be'eri (*ibid.*, p. 178) argues that in some ways the Iraqi coup was revolutionary. The masses seemed to be involved politically, and significant institutional alterations did occur (that is, the monarchy was destroyed and the Iraqi connection with the Baghdad Pact was nullified).

[27] *Ibid.*, p. 218.

of Pakistan, the army had always been influential, but its most important assumption of responsibility came with the rise of Gen. Muhammad Ayub Khan in 1958. Ayub was a figure of considerable charm, charisma, and ability, and indeed Pakistan under his control underwent some modernization and a modicum of political development. But East Pakistan, separated from Western Pakistan by 1,000 miles of Indian territory, harbored many seeds of resentment against its Western partner, and the quarrels with India, particularly with respect to Kashmir, remained unsolved. In 1969, Gen. Agha Yahya Khan, the army commander in chief, replaced Ayub, but he too was unable to advance viable political solutions. Leaning ever more heavily on military force to keep the East Pakistanis in line, he permitted that situation to deteriorate into civil war, which was to lead to war with India. The Indians beat the Pakistanis decisively: the result was that the military was so discredited that an opposition civilian political figure, Zulfikar Ali Bhutto, could, with the acquiescence of the military, virtually name himself president. One of Bhutto's first acts was to retire or otherwise rid himself of large numbers of officers. By 1973, however, Bhutto had begun to rely increasingly on senior officers such as Gen. Tikka Khan for support. By 1977, Bhutto's influence with the military had fallen, along with his control of the domestic political situation. The result was another coup, this time led by army general Zia al-Haq. One of Zia's first acts was to have Bhutto tried and sentenced to death. The fact remains that demoralization of the military in the absence of alternative military leadership can result in the rise of a civilian government, but it is rare.

As Muhammad Reza Shah's political system fell apart in 1978 he tried desperate measures to retain power and authority. With the failure of a government composed of senior military officers, he turned to an old opposition leader, Shapour Bakhtiar. It was Bakhtiar who persuaded the Shah to leave Iran in early 1979 for a vacation; it was also Bakhtiar who was the legitimate prime minister when, shortly after the Shah's departure, Ayatollah Ruhollah Khomeini arrived in Iran from France. Khomeini's influence in Iran was such that he was able to destroy Bakhtiar's government by ignoring it, appointing his own prime minister and in effect taking over the position that the Shah had occupied. Whatever titles, positions, and mechanisms emanated from all this confusion here was another example of a popular coup in which the military were bystanders.

One last quasi-example. When the disastrous June War (1967) struck Egypt, even Nasser offered his resignation. The armed forces were so insecure and bloodied that they could offer no resistance to wholesale sackings of their leading officers. Nasser remained in power, backed up by a newly made army. Many of the old leaders, including Nasser's friend Abd al-Hakim Amer, were swept into disgrace. And even after the October 1973 War, Sadat found it convenient (and was able) to shake up the top echelon of the army.

Coups, although common in the Middle East, are not unique to the area. The conditions that give rise to them exist elsewhere as well. The coup is a very specific type of violent action. It is almost completely restricted to military forces, for these forces have a monopoly on the weapons that permit them to enforce their will. Popular agitation can dissolve the legitimacy of a regime and facilitate its dissolution. But the coup, sudden and forceful, is not a thing that masses of people, whether they be professors, students, shopkeepers, or even policemen, can easily (if at all) put together. In the Turkish revolt of 1960, general agitation led to an uprising of the cadets at the military academy, but the essential part of the entire action was the intervention of the army. Because the coup has essentially a military nature, it brings to political power a class of individuals who are not completely representative of the political wellsprings of the masses of people:

1. They tend to be imbued with notions of honor and prestige and seem easily tempted to venture into foreign embroilments and adventures.

2. They are generally narrowly educated. This is, of course, not true when they are compared to the great masses of people in the Middle East, nor is it strictly true with respect to technology. But a major who is quite competent in supervising the repair of a tank may botch things up as the newly appointed minister of finance, and indeed he often does.

3. They emphasize discipline and order above all else. Al-

though they themselves were disloyal to their military oaths in overthrowing a previous regime, they now demand unquestioned obedience, and sometimes enthusiasm, from the population along any path of modernization they choose to follow.

4. They are very willing to use repressive force to gain their ends domestically and military force to achieve success in international affairs.

One coup, because it fractures the myth of legitimation, encourages future coups, although in fact none may follow immediately. (Thus the 1973 coup in Afghanistan set the stage for the far bloodier one in May 1978.) Since the army can spawn the coup so easily, one continuing task of the junta leaders is to keep their fellow officers, and especially their younger cohorts, under control. Benefits are usually ladled out generously. Officers' clubs with subsidized prices and pleasant facilities are conspicuous. Rapid promotion, generous pay and leaves, fancy uniforms, new military equipment — all of these become necessary to keep the army under control. The Saudi military in the 1980s is an excellent case in point.

But they are not sufficient. Inevitably, new cadres of officers come into being whose members desire power rather than perquisites and are willing to be critical of their superiors and their superiors' decisions. This discontent is exacerbated when the army has been forced into an enterprise that adds little honor or luster to its men — a Yemen military expedition, for example. Indeed, the junta members must draw a narrow line. The army must be humored and honored, yet controlled, but not enough to encourage its men to rebellion. Sometimes a Middle Eastern army is split along so many sectarian and political lines that there is almost no way to eliminate constant conspiracy. No army has illustrated this better than that of Syria, which often has seemed to be in a state of constant revolt. Yet, by 1983, Syrian President (and former air force general) Assad had given the Syrians the longest period of stable government in their modern history.

THE REVOLUTION

We must distinguish between the coup and the revolution. By the former we mean nothing more complicated than the sudden overturning of a regime, usually by the army. Such an overturning may result in nothing but superficial personnel changes. Revolution is a lengthier process and involves more permanent and deep-seated changes in the social, political, and economic structures. A revolution may be preceded by one or more coups, and in the course of its development, include still further coups and political rearrangements. It may include elements of counterrevolution.

Revolutionary changes may occur without coups or even without changes in regimes; even violence is not an absolutely necessary ingredient. But it is difficult to deliberately carry out deep-seated revolutionary change without extraordinary effort, and this effort often involves violence or the threat of it; it certainly involves the destruction of old habits and institutions. Of course, many rulers call themselves revolutionaries when at best they are reformers. The late Shah's White Revolution was more reform and modernization than it was revolution. Saudi kings who talk about deep-seated changes do so without much enthusiasm. The same is true of King Hassan in Morocco or for that matter King Hussein of Jordan. Kings are in a precarious position in the last quarter of the twentieth century; revolution will inevitably sweep them aside; yet to forestall revolution, they think that they must reform. By instituting piecemeal reforms and modifying programs, such leaders only heighten expectations and sharpen aspirations for more radical change. The failure to institute revolutionary programs of transformation in the end costs them their power and, in some cases, their lives. History teaches us that reforming monarchs have often been the last monarchs.

The entire Middle East shares, to some extent, the elements of revolutionary change. In certain countries we can, however, more properly affix the label "revolution" to the changes that are occurring. Changes here are more deep-seated, less evolutionary, perhaps more destructive, probably more violent. In July 1952, the Egyptian *ancien régime* was toppled by a coup; half a dozen years later there was no doubt that Egypt was in revolution. The old political parties had been outlawed, a land reform scheme inaugurated, the public economic sector enlarged, and, in general, the old bases of political power destroyed.

We can also fairly firmly label revolutionary the cases of Algeria and Turkey, at least in this century. Marginal cases are Syria and Iraq. Although much change has occurred in Tunisia, it is largely evolutionary in character. Whatever is the outcome in Afghanistan no one will recognize in it the old country and its institutions. Some sort of revolution is inevitable there. Indeed most Middle Eastern countries have undergone some revolutionary change that is often a reflection of the revolutionary environment of the entire Middle Eastern area.

Currently the most revolutionary country in the Middle East is Iran, and much of the concern in neighboring states lies in the revolutionary ferment of Iran rather than in its military powers. The Iranian revolution is not typical of twentieth-century revolutions, which tend to be modernizing and secularizing. In Iran many Muslim clerics have wanted to reestablish an Islamic environment, on the assumption that what the Shah had was not Islamic, and in attempting this essentially uncertain network of change they have introduced much unhappiness, anomie, and resentment. The *image* of Islam that some clerics have is simply immiscible with the twentieth-century world, and continuing unrest and violence will almost certainly characterize Iran until some pluralistic compromise is reached on revolutionary goals.

Of course, the continuing revolution in Iran is not entirely directed by clerics, and its priorities have not been sorted out. In this it resembles revolutionary France in the eighteenth century, which went through kaleidoscopic changes in religion, science, government, and many other areas until it fell into some sort of stability with the rise of Napoleon. But that Iran is in revolution there can be no doubt, and it is revolution that has ripples throughout the Middle East.

In Iran there was no military coup ending the Shah's rule and ushering in something else. But generally speaking, revolutions are initiated by coups. What seem to be the conditions that can transform the military coup into revolutionary action?

In the Middle East, one of the conditions for this transformation has been, after the initial coup, the presence of radically oriented leaders with sufficient resources and popularity to struggle for the long haul rather than for mere momentary perpetuation in power. Mustafa Kemal (later Atatürk) or Gamal Abdel Nasser are prime examples of such leaders. Time is an essential ingredient — time to perform and time to transform. Nasser had at least 16 years, Kassem less than a half-dozen. Ayub had a decade; Abbud fumbled six years away. Some Arab military leaders have had only months.

Another essential condition is the possession of resources, mainly political resources, that can permit the diversion of energies from "system maintenance" to "system transformation." How popular are the coup leaders? How detested were their predecessors? How well known are they in the armed forces, and what connecting links do they have with other political, religious, and economic power centers? Also, of course, how radical are they? They must have been radical enough to mount a coup, assuming that they want something more than mere power. Mere power is always hard to maintain for those who want to transform. But before revolution can proceed, it must be led by those who desire revolutionary transformation (or at least can be led into desiring it by reading the public will).[28]

Khomeini has so far had four years to set Iran on a revolutionary path. But Khomeini is an old man; he personally does not have the time to carry out all his changes. To the degree that he turns out to be *essential* to revolutionary change in Iran, the final product may not have changed very much. Certainly Khomeini in 1979 was enormously popular throughout Iran. He or his chief supporters have squandered much of that popularity over the past four years. Yet, he has managed to maintain the support of the lower-class masses throughout. It remains to be seen what will occur when he passes from the scene.

One revolutionary can catalyze another. The example of an

[28] For an analysis of the relationship between political violence and political change, see James A. Bill, "Political Violence and Political Change: A Conceptual Commentary," in *Violence as Politics: A Series of Original Essays,* ed. by Herbert Hirsch and David C. Perry (New York: Harper and Row, 1973), pp. 220–231.

Atatürk could inspire a Nasser (and even Husni al-Za'im in Syria quoted Atatürk approvingly in 1949). A Nasser in turn can galvanize an Arif in Iraq or a Sallal (if not very well) in Yemen.

Nor should the presence of Israel as a revolutionary catalyst be discounted. In spite of the enmity with which the Arab Middle East, at least, views it, Israel has been a model for development for many Middle Eastern governments. Israeli military successes naturally emphasize the value of the changes within Israel, but even had this not been the case, any system as modern as that of Israel would inevitably have had repercussions among its neighbors.[29]

We have said little about the "revolutions" in Lebanon since 1958. This is because there has been relatively little revolution per se there, although there has been enormous violence and internal war. Christian family gangs — that of the Gemayel family well represents the rest — have fought each other; they have also fought the Muslims. The Palestinians have been another target (the by now well known massacre in September 1982 was by Christian weapons, however complicitous the Israelis were in the event). Shi'ite Muslims have fought Sunnis. Lebanese whatever their complexion have fought Syrians. All this fighting is for power rather than for revolutionary change. It can be asserted that so much violence over so long a period must result in some change that is revolutionary; this may turn out to be true in Lebanon, but so far it is not a good example of revolution.

ASSASSINATION IN THE MIDDLE EAST

Considerable research on assassination has been done in recent years[30] in the wake of the deaths in the United States of

[29] For a tightly knit argument demonstrating the various ways in which Israel has acted as a stimulant to radical and revolutionary change in the Middle East, see George Lenczowski, "Arab Radicalism: Problems and Prospects," *Current History* 60 (January 1971):32–37, 52.

[30] See Murray C. Havens, Carl Leiden, and Karl M. Schmitt, *The Politics of Assassination* (Englewood Cliffs, N.J.: Prentice-Hall, 1970), for a general discussion of the systemic impact of assassination. See also James F. Kirkham, Sheldon Levy, and William J. Crotty, *Assassination and Political Violence* (Washington, D.C.: Government Printing Office, 1969),

such figures as the Kennedy brothers and Martin Luther King. Assassination itself has been part of the political scene throughout all of history.

Is there a climate for assassination in the Middle East? Assassination seems to have some complex relationship with political turbulence. Such turbulence has, of course, characterized the Middle East. Assassination may occur at all levels; in the United States it has largely been restricted to the highest political levels, whereas in the Middle East it has pervaded the entire political spectrum. Table VI.1 lists the assassination attempts on chiefs of state and heads of government in the Middle East over the last 65 years.

Table VI.1 does not include the alleged 17 unsuccessful attempts on the life of King Hussein of Jordan. In addition, other prominent individuals have been assassinated. These have included Sir Lee Stack, sirdar of the Egyptian army (1924); Lord Moyne, British minister of state in the Middle East (1944); Count Folke Bernadotte, United Nations mediator in Palestine (1948); Ja'far al-Askari, minister of defense in Iraq (1936); Abdullah al-Hajri, president of the Yemeni supreme court and former prime minister (1977); Kemal Jumblatt, leader of the Druze community and former head of the Progressive Socialist party in Lebanon (1977); and president-elect Bashir Gemayel in Lebanon (1982).

The last half-century in the Middle East has been a transitional one, characterized by continued big-power exploitation, the frenzied growth of nationalism, the expansion and confrontation of ideology, and the consequent uncertain struggles for power. These seem to be conditions in which assassination is nurtured. Potential assassins are produced by the chaotic and anomic transitional period; they are encouraged by ideological rationales. They direct their efforts against power holders with varying degrees of success and impact.

An assassination can have a high impact when (1) the system is highly centralized, (2) the political support of the victim is

---

particularly Supplement F (pp. 545–552), "Assassination in the Middle East." See also Carl Leiden, "Assassination in the Middle East," *Transaction* 6 (May, 1969):20-23.

TABLE VI.1 *Assassination in the Middle East: Attempts on*
Chiefs of State and Heads of Governments 1918–1982

Year	Political figure	Country	Successful	Unsuccessful
1919	Habibullah Khan	Afghanistan	x	
1919	Muhammad Sa'id	Egypt		x
1920	Drubi Pasha	Syria	x	
1924	Zaghlul Pasha	Egypt		x
1930	Isma'il Sidqi Pasha	Egypt		x
1932	Isma'il Sidqi Pasha	Egypt		x
1933	Isma'il Sidqi Pasha	Egypt		x
1933	Nader Shah	Afghanistan	x	
1935	Abdul Aziz Ibn Saud	Saudi Arabia		x
1937	Bakr Sidqi	Iraq	x	
1937	Mustafa Nahhas Pasha	Egypt		x
1945	Mustafa Nahhas Pasha	Egypt		x
1945	Ahmad Mahir Pasha	Egypt	x	
1948	Nuqrashi Pasha	Egypt	x	
1948	Imam Yahya	Yemen	x	
1949	Muhsin al-Barazi	Syria	x	
1949	Husni al-Zaim	Syria	x	
1949	Muhammad Reza Shah Pahlavi	Iran		x
1950	Riad al-Sulh	Lebanon		x
1950	Sami al-Hinnawi	Lebanon	x	
1951	Riad al-Sulh	Jordan	x	
1951	King Abdullah	Jordan	x	
1951	Liaqat Ali Khan	Pakistan	x	
1951	Ali Razmara	Iran	x	
1954	Gamal Abdel Nasser	Egypt		x
1955	Adnan al-Malki	Syria	x	
1958	Abd al-Ilah	Iraq	x	
1958	Nuri al-Said	Iraq	x	
1958	King Faisal II	Iraq	x	
1958	Sami al-Sulh	Lebanon		x
1959	Abdul Karim Kassem	Iraq		x

Note: Country indicates where event took place.

highly personal, (3) the "replaceability" of the victim is low,
(4) the system is in crisis and/or in a period of rapid political
and social change, and (5) if the death of the victim involves
the system in confrontation with other powers.[31]

[31] Kirkham, Levy, and Crotty. *Assassination*, p. 551.

TABLE VI.1   (continued)

Year	Political figure	Country	Successful	Unsuccessful
1962	Imam Muhammad al-Badr	Yemen		x
1964	Ahmad Ben Bella	Algeria		x
1964	Adib al-Shishakli	Brazil (Syrian)	x	
1965	Muhammad Reza Shah Pahlavi	Iran		x
1965	Hassan Ali Mansur	Iran	x	
1967	Levi Eshkol	Israel		x
1968	Muhammad Ayub Khan	Pakistan		x
1971	King Hassan	Morocco		x
1971	Wasfi al-Tall	Egypt	x	
1972	King Hassan	Morocco		x
1973	Shaykh Muhammad Ali Uthman	Yemen Arab Republic	x	
1975	King Faisal	Saudi Arabia	x	
1977	Ibrahim al-Hamdi	Yemen Arab Republic	x	
1978	Mu'ammar Qaddafi	Libya		x
1978	Ahmad al-Ghashimi	Yemen Arab Republic	x	
1978	Salim Rubay Ali	People's Democratic Republic of Yemen	x	
1978	Sardar Muhammad Daoud Khan	Afghanistan	x	
1979	Nur Muhammad Taraki	Afghanistan	x	
1979	Hafizullah Amin	Afghanistan	x	
1980	Hafez al-Assad	Syria		x
1981	Muhammad Javad Bahonar	Iran	x	
1981	Muhammad Ali Raja'i	Iran	x	
1981	Anwar Sadat	Egypt	x	
1981	Saddam Hussein	Iraq		x

Surely it would be rare if all these conditions obtained. But they do characterize many Middle Eastern political systems.

The Saudi system is certainly a highly centralized one (that is, one with a high bureaucratic dependence upon the central authority in the most trivial decision-making situation), but it is also inefficient, and inefficiency produces practical decentralization. Political support, in Egypt for Nasser, for example, or in Jordan for Hussein, was indeed a highly personal thing. Often a movement or an organization does not survive the death of its leader. (Certainly the death of Hassan al-Banna in February 1949 had profound repercussions on the fortunes of the Muslim Brotherhood.) Because of the personal quality of this leadership, it is difficult to replace a suddenly assassinated leader, that is, to replace him with someone who can continue unabated the program already in being. Moreover, the Middle East is in political and social change and parts of it are often in crisis. Now and then, outside powers are tempted to intervene with an assassination.

These conditions do not, however, inevitably produce assassinations. Somehow, too, when they occur, the system seems to survive. Leaders are replaced, if sometimes poorly. Peoples' memories are short, the shock passes, and the system continues to live. Moreover, the Middle East, for all that the different countries have in common, is not a strictly homogeneous area. Syria in the 1940s and 1950s was replete with assassination, but until that of Sadat in 1981 there had been no important assassinations in Egypt since the Revolution (1952);[32] there were, of course, attempts against Nasser's life. So far as we know, Saudi Arabia was devoid of assassination until the murder of King Faisal in 1975, yet its neighbor Yemen has had several in recent history.

It is difficult to generalize about the Middle East. As an area, it has had a large number of high-level assassinations; however, it is difficult to assert that, as a phenomenon, assassination is endemic there. In spite of a certain vulnerability to assassination, there is little evidence that assassination has been very effective for its practitioners.[33] An assassination of a public figure in the Middle East is noteworthy for the shock it causes. Rioting often occurs, with varied public displays of

[32] Except for the assassination of the Jordanian prime minister when he was visiting Egypt in 1971. The assassins were almost certainly Palestinians.

[33] This has been true everywhere in the world. See Havens, Leiden, and Schmitt, *Politics of Assassination,* passim.

official and unofficial grief. The lamentations over, it is surprising how quickly the system adjusts to the loss of a leader.[34]

CONCLUSION

The Middle East has its modicum of violence. Street violence — the riot, the demonstration — is indeed endemic and occurs over trivial provocations. Middle Eastern students have been politically volatile and active for much longer than their Western counterparts. Middle Eastern governments have been more repressive against potentially violent movements than have Western governments. The Arab armies have been politically involved quite often. Most Middle Eastern countries have undergone coups; a few, major and prolonged revolution. Assassinations of public figures have occurred not infrequently.

What does this mean in terms of a regime's viability and stability, and how does it affect the course of political change in the area? The answer needs to be drafted in several parts: student demonstrations and street riots probably do not influence political change more than they do in most other places in the world, including the more developed areas. Yet, to mention just a few examples in the last decade, such riots and demonstrations have had a definite impact upon the political processes in Sudan, Afghanistan, Egypt, Turkey, Iran, and Jordan — and in Israel, too.

Perhaps assassinations have been more frequent in the Middle East than in other parts of the world. It is difficult to compare world areas in this regard. The very multiplicity of political systems multiplies the targets for assassins. It seems fair to say that, although the systemic effects of assassinations in the

34 When Nasser died in September 1970, Egypt was plunged into a paroxysm of grief. Without much enthusiasm, the leadership rallied around Anwar Sadat, one of the original members of the RCC. Yet a year later Sadat was firmly in power. Although Nasser was not forgotten, he was now viewed without tears and was the subject of increasing criticism and nostalgic disenchantment. Of course, it is true that Nasser was not assassinated but died a natural death. Yet he had died without warning, and his death had much the same impact as it would have had had he been assassinated. When Sadat was killed there was even less *Egyptian* grief, although that of the international community was significant. Few Egyptians mourn Sadat today.

Middle East have generally not been great, they have exceeded those in the West. What were the real effects of the deaths in 1951 of King Abdullah of Jordan and Liaqat Ali Khan of Pakistan, for example? There is no way of knowing. But in any event it seems highly unlikely that assassination seriously affected the ongoing sociopolitical patterns. On the other hand, there is no doubt that such action has occasionally reoriented change, sometimes speeding it up, and sometimes radicalizing it. Probably at most such actions add just one more element to the turbulent adventure called politics in the Middle East.

The most obviously important element of political violence in the Middle East is the phenomenon of military intervention resulting in the coup d'etat. One version of the Egyptian constitution contained the admonition to the army to strike should the nation's honor be threatened; such constitutional authorization seems to be needed rarely by those "young" officers who are impatient for change and see themselves as the vehicle for dramatic improvement of the lot of their countrymen.

Colonel Qaddafi of Libya seems in many ways untypical (certainly if contrasted with, say, a Gen. Muhammad Ayub Khan), yet there is much about him that is characteristic of those who make coups. He appears to be impetuous and impatient. He has quite obviously fed upon ideology and found it palatable. He is eager to remake not only Libya, a task that might be feasible, but the Arab world. Yet however confident he is of his competence to perform the tasks of political and economic rejuvenation, he is not altogether prepared to assume them. (This is generally but not wholly true of coup officers. Some Egyptian officers involved in the 1952 coup proved to be highly competent in civilian bureaucratic matters.) He is puritanical and may mistake the symbols of things for their substance. It is possible that he will survive long enough to learn how to survive even longer (probably he has already done so), although occasionally, when there have been ripples of discord in his cabinet, the world has expected him to be toppled. In the spring of 1978, he was the target of an assassination attempt that resulted in the death of several visiting East German officials, and again in 1982 he broke up another coup attempt.

Whether Qaddafi is typical or not, enormous amounts of national resources in one country or another are wasted in the process of permitting young army officers to experiment with their nation's destinies. Quite obviously, political change, although not always political development, is modified, stymied, given tangential thrusts, perhaps on occasion even enhanced by the accidental nature of the junta in power. This kind of change is an expensive, inefficient, haphazard process. Little can be said for it except that sometimes it works. Sometimes army intervention is the only way that a country like Yemen can get into the twentieth century; yet in many ways the Sallal coup in Yemen failed. Whatever Faisal's, Khalid's, or Fahd's virtues as a modernizer, would Saudi Arabia have been further along the road to modernization, and especially to political development, under some young Saudi colonel? [35]

Revolution is a unique phenomenon, and thorough revolution is rare in the Middle East. It requires time; a sympathetic, yet patient, population; and radically oriented political leaders who can maintain themselves in power with modest investments of energy, reserving their greatest resources for the revolutionary changes they desire to bring about. These leaders must be properly inspired and must have the vision to see beyond immediate political demands and benefits. Revolution often, although not invariably, occurs in areas where there are no foreign involvements. Whatever else he was, Atatürk in Turkey was an isolationist; he was also the greatest Middle Eastern revolutionary in the twentieth century. With regard to Nasser, it is difficult to claim that his unending confrontations with the Israelis, as well as his adventures in Yemen and elsewhere, were very conducive to revolutionary change at home. Nevertheless, he was a revolutionary, and fundamental

[35] In a private interview in 1970, the prime minister of Iran bitterly stated that if all the reforms being implemented in that society were introduced by some colonel, then Iran would be praised the world over. Since Iran was a monarchy, however, observers were being unfairly critical. The prime minister's comments indicate that monarchical elites are quite conscious of their eroding positions at a time when larger and larger numbers of people clamor for both modernization and political development. Personal interview with one of the authors (Bill), Tehran, 5 December 1970.

changes in the fabric of Egyptian life were wrought under his inspiration.

The Middle East is in a state of ferment. The political process has not yet been tamed, and violence is often a part of its ways of seeking change. One must view all of Middle Eastern politics from this perspective.

Effects of the International Community. One of the notions held most strongly by the leaders of the Islamic Government of Iran has been that the United States constantly interfered in the Iran of the Shah, conned him into exhorbitant arms purchases and a foreign policy that was more in the interest of the United States than it was in that of Iran. American readers may object to so bald a statement, but there is nevertheless considerable truth in it. The United States has interfered; so does the Soviet Union and so did Britain and France. So do other Middle Eastern powers, including Israel, which has made Lebanon its private stamping ground over the last decade.

Nevertheless, the great powers have a unique responsibility. They are the ones most likely to possess a military-industrial complex and thus most likely to become arms merchants. Over the years they have dumped an enormous amount of military hardware in the Middle East. This is what an official American report had to say about conventional arms transfer (1972–1981):

Near East and South Asia. By far the greatest Third World regional arms market is the Near East and South Asia. In recent years, this region has accounted for nearly three-quarters of the dollar value of arms agreements made with the major world suppliers. The Near East and South Asian states purchase the largest quantities; the most sophisticated kinds; and the widest variety of air, naval, and ground force arms. Over the last decade, the region has received about 85% of the surface-to-air missiles and some 70% of the heavy and light armor and the supersonic fighters exported. About half the artillery, missile-equipped patrol boats, and military helicopters have been shipped to the region, as well as about 40% of the subsonic, combat aircraft and roughly 30% of the major and minor surface warships and other military aircraft. The Near East and

South Asia acquired just under one-fourth of the submarines provided during the decade. That the region does not acquire a share of each of these types of arms proportional to the money expended suggests the high level of sophistication (and hence the high cost) of the armaments purchased.

Although almost all states in the region have a rudimentary arms-making capability, Israel, Egypt, and India are developing, with foreign licensing and technical assistance, major weapons or arms industries of their own. Only Israel, however, is emerging as an important supplier, although many of its major arms transfers have been used or refurbished weapons originally produced elsewhere.[36]

Where a region is awash with weapons there often is a temptation to use them. By indiscriminate sales or gifts of weapons to Middle Eastern States, the United States and the Soviet Union have increased the probability of warlike acts. And to return to Gen. Peled's comments on American aid and modern Israel, let us quote from his article in the *New York Times* a bit more extensively. He begins by quoting approvingly David Ben Gurion's statement that "The army shall not determine its own organization . . . and it shall certainly not decide on matters of war and peace." He then says,

These principles were carefully observed until the Six-Day War. But as the army became more powerful and prestigious in the wake of its 1967 victory, the unwritten precedent began to give way. The army's prestige was somewhat shaken after the Yom Kippur War, but the high command shrewdly blamed the Government and its parsimony for what went wrong. Successive governments have accepted this explanation and have refused to limit defense spending, enabling the military to enlarge the standing army beyond all realistic needs. The logic the military establishment uses to justify the increase defies all reason: Even the peace with Egypt, which relieved the army

[36] *Conventional Arms Transfers in the Third World, 1972–81,* Special Report No. 102, United States Department of State, 1982. Note that "Near East and South Asia" does not precisely coincide with our definition of the Middle East. The obvious inclusion of India should be noted. Still, the conclusions remain valid for the Middle East as well. Currently the three largest recipients of American military and economic assistance are Israel, Egypt, and Turkey.

of the heavy task of holding the Sinai, was given as justification for a 50 percent increase of the defense budget. *The Government could not accede to such preposterous demands without the help of billions of dollars in American aid.*

More than anything else, the invasion of Lebanon last summer showed that David Ben-Gurion's worst fears have become a reality: The military establishment imposed the war on a skeptical, bewildered nation and a Government trapped by its desire for spectacular achievements. From the beginning, the Government found it was unable to control the army or Defense Minister Ariel Sharon. Moreover, the army was able to field a force larger than the one that fought in the Sinai in 1967 without calling up the reserves — making it much easier for the Government to submit to the army's demands.

In the year before the invasion — a year of unprecedented quiet on the Lebanese border due largely to the cease-fire between Israel and the Palestine Liberation Organization that the American envoy, Philip Habib, arranged in July 1981 — the Israeli Chief of Staff, Gen. Rafael Eitan, was asked why he advocated an invasion of Lebanon. He answered: "What do you suppose I have built a large modern army for?"

We Israelis must answer to ourselves for that and for our disregard of David Ben-Gurion's warning. *But I, for one, would also like to ask the American taxpayer: "Why are you giving us the rope with which to hang ourselves?"* [37]

The above quotations deal with conventional arms. What about nuclear weapons? It is foolish to think that the weapons catalogs of international arms merchants will not someday include nuclear arms or the "kits" with which to build them. In the Middle East it seems certain that the Israelis possess such weapons now. Pakistan, despite recent disclaimers by General Zia on his year-end (1982) trip to the United States, could build nuclear weapons. Within ten years, "according to U.S. intelligence sources," [38] Libya, Egypt, and Iraq could construct these weapons. By the year 2000 there will likely be a good many such weapons of destruction in the Middle East.

[37] 30 December 1982. Original source of quotation from David Ben Gurion unknown. Italics are authors'.
[38] See *New York Times,* 14 July 1981, p. A6.

The area is vulnerable to nuclear warfare. Passions run high in the Middle East. Since the United States is the only nation actually to have used such weapons, we should understand well the temptation for other countries to use them too. With their use, the Middle East as we know it will have been destroyed.

CHAPTER VII

The Imprint of Ideology

THE NEED FOR LEGITIMATION

The process of legitimation is very complex.[1] The need for legitimation of whatever authority that has been established in a political system is, however, readily apparent to the most ordinary middle-grade army officer who engineers a coup. Most of the decisions promulgated in any political system are accepted not because of the application of naked force but because they seem to be made by legitimate authority and are enveloped in an aura of legitimacy. Governments that have little actual force at their disposal often linger long after their

---

[1] The modern analysis of the process of legitimation really begins with Max Weber. In any system there are those in authority, whatever the method they have used to secure that authority. The stability of their authority position is facilitated to the degree that they are able to convince those whom they rule that they rule because they ought to rule, should rule, must rule, would be failing in their responsibility if they did not rule, and justly rule. In short, they rule because their position is a legitimate one. Coup leaders rule because they have been successful in seizing power; they seek legitimacy by doffing their uniforms and abandoning their military rank, by submitting their rule to referenda (usually carefully controlled), by seeking the approbation of other centers of legitimate authority (religious leaders, kings, or parliaments), by emphasizing their attachment to traditional or cherished symbols, and, of course, in a myriad of other ways. See "legitimacy" in Julius Gould and William L. Kolb, eds., *A Dictionary of the Social Sciences* (New York: Free Press, 1964). See also Michael C. Hudson, *Arab Politics, The Search for Legitimacy* (New Haven, Ct.: Yale University Press, 1977).

ability to coerce has vanished. Thus, the regime of King Farouk in Egypt was moribund long before it fell in 1952, but it had considerably greater legitimacy than power, and it was, until its demise, a functioning system. A similar statement could be made about the regime of King Idris in Libya (overthrown in 1969), although that regime was less colored by corruption than Farouk's had been. And of course the Shah's legitimacy had long fled before his fall in 1979.

All political elites attempt to maintain their legitimacy and, if possible, to increase it. Every revolutionary government immediately seeks to establish legitimacy; where it is unsuccessful in doing this, its life is usually short, and some more successful claimant takes its place.

Every government attempts to increase the sense of its legitimacy on the part of its population. There are a variety of methods of doing this, including the steady application of power, the recourse to symbols, and the constant verbal reiteration of the government's position. We are particularly interested in this chapter with this verbal umbrella of political solidification. Often facilitated by a controlled or at least a docile press, the government leaders unleash a barrage of arguments, exhortations, appeals, promises, statements of principles, and so on. Wherever possible, these ideas are related by their proponents to already *accepted* notions or *cherished* ideas or *popular* individuals. Gradually this mishmash of argument may assume some semiorganized and rational form; it is then called ideology. Ideology is the most important manifestation of the legitimizing process.

What is the role of ideology in the Middle East, and how is it connected with the processes of modernization and political development?

THE NATURE OF IDEOLOGY

Ideology is a widely used term[2] that connotes those congeries

[2] The literature on ideology is not voluminous. For interesting commentary on the historical development of the term, see the leading essay in George Lichtheim, *The Concept of Ideology and Other Essays* (New York: Random House, 1967). See also Karl Mannheim, *Ideology and Utopia* (London: Routledge and Kegan Paul, 1936); David Apter, ed.,

of beliefs and assertions that rationalize behavior patterns.[3] It seems to be necessary to justify all of one's acts. These rationalizing explanations constitute ideology; the beliefs themselves, of course, need not be true, nor need they be consistent or logical. But the beliefs ought to be persuasive, particularly to the populace.

Ideology has always been crucial to politics. It exists in an infinite variety of forms. One puts together a personal ideology as a hodgepodge of what one has heard and read. But one may also accept large chunks of preformed ideology from the sources of propaganda: the government of the day (in both its official and unofficial organs), the religious spokesmen, and, in general, the spokesmen for various interest groups.

The absorption of ideology is facilitated by the growth of communications media. Even the call to prayer in the Middle

---

Ideology and Discontent (New York: Free Press, 1964); Gustav Bergmann, "Ideology," *Ethics* 61 (1951):205–218; and the articles by Edward Shils and Harry M. Johnson in the *International Encyclopedia of the Social Sciences*, new ed. (New York: Free Press, 1968); Max Mark, *Modern Ideologies* (New York: St. Martin's Press, 1973); and Lewis S. Feuer, *Ideology and the Ideologists* (New York: Harper and Row, 1975).

[3] Julius Gould says, "Ideology is a pattern of beliefs and concepts (both factual and normative) which purport to explain complex social phenomena with a view to directing and simplifying socio-political choices facing individuals and groups." Gould and Kolb, *A Dictionary*, p. 315. Chalmers Johnson makes similar points very well when he says, "No revolution ever occured without ideology. It is one thing for a citizen to think he knows *why* a revolution is needed; it is quite another to know *how* to go about making a revolution and to know what to put in place of the institutions that revolutionary violence destroys. Some people have argued that the revolutionary is like Hercules: having cleaned the Augean Stables, he is under no obligation to fill them up again [Nasser believed this at first]. As a matter of fact, he always does so, obliged or not [as indeed Nasser quickly learned]. Revolutionary ideology supplies answers to the questions why, how and what — that is to say, it offers a critique of present conditions, a strategy for the use of political violence in order to change those conditions, and a vision of an improved society. It is of course true that leaders and adherents of revolutionary movements are influenced by a variety of motives, and that for an observer to rely solely on an understanding of their shared ideology in trying to explain their behavior would be folly. The problem obviously is not either to ignore or to fixate on the role of ideology in politics but to conceptualize it properly and to study it as one input into the overall processes of political cognition and motivation." *Autopsy on People's War* (Berkeley, Calif.: University of California Press, 1973), p. 114.

East is today in many places electronic. The raucous radio in the coffee shops; the newer television sets in the big cities; the gaudy collection of newspapers, magazines, and placards; the amplified speech — all of these today permit Middle Eastern governments to communicate more readily with their people, to propagandize, to ideologize. The dissemination of ideology is one of the main forces of legitimation and as such is one of the chief functions of any government, whether it be stable or revolutionary, democratic or autocratic.

Much of the energy of Middle Eastern governments is spent in the dissemination of ideology and in the denunciation of alien ideologies. Because at any one time a fair share of the Middle Eastern political systems are run by military adventurers, Middle Eastern ideologies tend at times to be piecemeal and makeshift. And since the Middle East is in the midst of modernization and change, ideologies there tend to reflect the rapid alteration of values. Finally, because of the turmoil (much coming from the unending Arab-Israeli confrontation) that characterizes so much of the area, Middle Eastern ideologies are often extremist and violent in tone. The current (1983) massive struggle between Iraq and Iran, whatever other reasons there may be for its existence, is ideological. Indeed, modern clerical Iran is a sort of ideological pulsar, periodically spewing out huge amounts of ideological energy, enough at least to frighten Pakistan, Saudi Arabia, and other parts of the Gulf, and, of course, Iraq.

Ideology plays an important role in the formation of political culture, the process of political integration, and the development of "public opinion." Dankwart Rustow refers to ideologies as the "foundations of politics" in his brief comparative study of Middle Eastern political systems.[4] He develops as the main themes of Middle Eastern ideology (1) nationalism, Communism, and the issues of monarchies against republics; (2) traditionalism against persistent change; (3) "monism" against pluralism; and (4) religion against secularism. On the other

---

[4] *Middle Eastern Political Systems* (Englewood Cliffs, N.J.: Prentice-Hall, 1971).

hand, Robert Springborg suggests in a perceptive article[5] that the old ideologies are dead. He suggests:

> [The] center of gravity of newly emerging isms may be labeled, depending in part on the observer's normative evaluation, as conservatism, liberalism, pragmatism, realism, or, what to some may not have an entirely pejorative connotation, opportunism. That which might fit equally well is the opprobrious title of *wasatiya* (middlism) given to Nasserism by the leftist theorist, Sadek al-Azm. Middlism implies, among other things, falling between the two stools of secularism and religion and, at least in the case of Nasserism, might more accurately have been termed obscurantism.[6]

We shall return to these themes below.

IDEOLOGY IN THE MIDDLE EAST

Even in the most quiescent and stable system, there are sources of new ideology. In the Middle East, the turbulence of continued revolution, the frenetic and emotional struggles with modernity, the impacts of alien resources and demands, and the continuing uncertainty of political settlements all make the area alive with ideological fermentation. But what is the general nature of this ideology?

Middle Eastern ideology reflects both the concerns of the area as a whole and the very particular concerns of its political subdivisions. There are considerable overtones of religion in the

---

[5] "On the Rise and Fall of Arab Isms," *Australian Outlook* 31 (1977): 92–109. Of the old ideologies, he says, "Arab nationalism, Arab socialism, Nasserism, and positive neutralism now evoke thoughts of dust covered anthologies on library shelves, whereas less than a decade ago they were provocative Arab battle cries" (p. 92).

[6] *Ibid.*, p. 92. The quotation concludes, "Certainly Nasserism and the present strand of political thought I am trying to identify share the schizophrenic tendency made necessary by a dual society of addressing secular appeals to the secular and religious appeals to the faithful, but then it is only those who are content to be permanently on the sidelines of Arab politics who opt entirely for one or the other. The middlism of Nasserism, however, to the extent that it rested on anything and did not entirely fall between two stools, was based on the success of emotive Arab nationalism and Arab unity, which were in the final analysis both strategies and tactics for confronting imperialists and neo-imperialists and their lackeys in the area."

ideologies of the Middle East. Surprisingly, since the country
had in a sense a religious birth, this is less true in Israel than
in some of the other countries. But even in Turkey the religious
themes are never wholly absent. It is believed that men are
better because they are Muslims and that governments are better because their behavior accords with Islamic morality. Islam
offers the best path to modernization and its achievements, or,
for others, the best return to an earlier, better day. All that
men can aspire to can be found in Islam; thus Jamal al-Din
al-Afghani found in Sura 42 (line 36) of the Quran the justification for a democratic consultative assembly.[7] Man should want
things because they are countenanced by God and should move
to action to achieve them. There is a tremendous reservoir
of religious will among the peasantry and the urban poor.
The newer middle and managerial classes are less overtly religious, but they still couch ideological aspirations in religious
terms.

The last half-dozen years have increased to a very marked degree the religious aspects of political quarrels and national
goals and aspirations. Lebanon began coming apart in 1975,
an event often blamed upon the Palestinian presence, and by
1983 the violent struggle between Christian and Muslim, Sunni
and Shi'ite, Christian and Druze made almost hopeless any
sort of national consensus. The year 1982 witnessed a religious
internal war in Syria by the government against its religious
enemies; in the process a large part of Hamah in northern
Syria was destroyed. Egypt continued to spawn extremist religious organizations, one of which assassinated Sadat in late
1981. Shi'ite uprisings, whether in Saudi Arabia, Bahrain, or
Iraq, underline how delicate the political hold of some Middle
Eastern governments is. The Middle East is going through a
religious revivalism; how long it will last is problematical, but
while it lasts it colors all ideological characterizations of the
national will. General Zia in Pakistan comes to mind. Pious

---

[7] Majid Khadduri develops this point at length in his *Political Trends
in the Arab World: The Role of Ideas and Ideals in Politics* (Baltimore,
Md.: Johns Hopkins Press, 1970), pp. 28–32. This valuable book deals
very directly with the question of ideology.

and sanctimonious today, eager to return to the *Sharia,* constantly mouthing Muslim clichés, General Zia was hardly that as he rose in a hard-drinking, westernized army to be appointed its commander by Zulficar Ali Bhutto. But, opportunist or otherwise, he finds it today politically very expedient to emphasize the religious nature of his mission.

Ideology often carries overtones of what might be termed "identity resolution." The Arabs constantly ask themselves, "Who am I?" and "What is an Arab?" Their constant questioning suggests a modern uncertainty concerning identity. Do Arabs really exist? If those so labeled keep conjuring up reassurances for themselves, apparently they do, but what are they, and what connections do they have with Arabs in times past? The answer, of course, is ideological. The Arabs imagine that they are as they would like to be and emphasize historical associations that they find currently comfortable. They are by no means alone in this. The Shah celebrated (1971) the twenty-five hundredth anniversary of monarchical rule in Iran, although what he really had in common with the ancient Medes and Persians is somewhat uncertain. Some Turks, too, (since Kemal Atatürk's time, at least) have tried to identify themselves with the Qaramanids, the Ottomans, and other distinguished forebears.

Most uncertain of all Middle Eastern peoples in this regard, however, have been the Israelis. Their connection with their ancient counterparts in Palestine is tenuous at best, and yet it is the necessary raison d'être for the modern Israeli state. Israel was founded as a haven for Jews; it is scarcely surprising that who and what Jews are continues to be disputed. But this concern for identity goes far beyond normal discussion. Are we really Jews? If so, what makes us Jews? What are our characteristics? How should we act because we are Jews? Israeli ideology is heavily laden with questions such as these.

Middle Eastern ideology is also highly nationalistic. Nationalism is a product of collective resentment and the sharing of discontent. There are few people in the Middle East who cannot concoct some sort of justification for being resentful against others, usually foreigners, for the malaise of the times, for the chronic underdevelopment of the area, and for their legacy of political and social problems. Nationalistic energy is itself a pseudo-resolution of the problems facing a people, for blaming others[8] makes the unsolved difficulties more palatable.

It is manifestly easier to share discontent when people share other things — a living space or a language, for example. One might, without doing too much harm to Ibn Khaldun's original concept, refer to nationalism on the village and tribal levels as *asabiyya,* that sense of togetherness of family and clan that solidified a people against its external environment.

The Middle East is notorious for its artificial spatial boundaries, often originally drawn at the whim of colonial powers. But whatever their origin, these boundaries sometimes enclose a nationalism of their own, a *wataniyya* nationalism — an Egyptian or a Jordanian nationalism. The strength of these nationalisms rises and falls with the viability of programs and leaders. Egyptian (qua Egyptian) nationalism reached a peak before Nasser, fell as his popularity among Arabs (qua Arabs) increased, and rose with Nasser's death and the installation of Anwar Sadat as president of Egypt. Certainly in the late 1970s, in the wake of Sadat's visit to Jerusalem and his later adventures at Camp David, it was very strong indeed. But since his death Hosni Mubarak has played a cautious *Arab* role, and the Egyptians may be reversing the field again. Jordanian nationalism has often been weak in the face of Arab nationalism and the appeals of various Palestinian guerrilla groups.

The boundaries of a state may also contain minority groups generating nationalisms of their own. The ideological message they broadcast proclaims the injustice of their lack of independence and demands boundaries coterminous with the areas occupied by their populations. The Kurds in Iraq are an excellent example; so at one time were the Armenians in Turkey. The Palestinian Arabs, wherever they are to be found, are a similar group. But not all minorities produce identifiable nationalistic ideology, even when discriminated against. For example, the Christian Copts of Egypt have little nationalism of their own, although they may embrace Arab nationalism less

[8] The Iranian cry that Carter was Satan and that the United States was evil is an example of this aspect of nationalism.

than enthusiastically. And today's Armenians, although they have no significant national movement, continue to assassinate Turkish officials in revenge for Armenian massacres 60 years ago.

Sometimes a nationalism splashes over boundaries to form a larger movement. The most noteworthy example of this is, of course, Arab nationalism — *qawmiyya*. Its strength and appeal wax and wane with the vitality of such issues as the Israeli "menace," the cooperativeness of the oil cartels, and the pervasiveness of some cold war.

Nationalistic ideology, then, contains a mixture of these elements but always contains beliefs about the rightness of the cause, the inevitability of its victory, and the catastrophe to those who impede it. Certainly much of what is interesting in current Middle Eastern ideology flows from its nationalist content.

The Middle East is in the midst of social revolution. Revolution is one of the most potent of the producers[9] of ideology. Even the most modest of coup leaders finds it necessary to justify an illegal and treasonable activity in the palatable terms of defending the constitution, attachment to the people, honor, dignity, or morality. Ideology in this case is merely the rationalization for an action that is expected to increase support for the coup. However naïve a coup leader may be, he must offer a program for the future and must lubricate it with appropriate propaganda to insure its acceptance.

The first stage in building an ideology is usually nationalistic. Even in his earliest statements (1969), Qaddafi emphasized his rejection of European colonial exploitation of Libya. One immediate result was the destruction of all non-Arabic public signs in such cities as Tripoli and Benghazi, an act of tremendous symbolic impact, but of little if any practical value. Nevertheless, ideologically, this act emphasized the regime's rejection of nonindigenous values. Qaddafi also trumpeted his support for the Palestinian refugees and the Arab struggle

---

[9] See Carl Leiden and Karl Schmitt, *The Politics of Violence: Revolution in the Modern World* (Englewood Cliffs, N.J.: Prentice-Hall, 1968), for a discussion of revolutionary ideology.

against Israel. This is a safe ideological stance throughout the Arab world, and it usually costs nothing.

Ideological declarations such as Qaddafi's may not reflect any real goal at all but rather serve to divert attention from other acts. However, assuming that revolutionary leaders do have ideological goals, these must be packaged for public consumption. In the Middle East, a social revolution is in progress. Its ideology proclaims the need for land reform, the enlargement of the public sector, the liberation of women, the introduction of democracy (of necessity, vague in detail), and, in general, the establishment of some form of "Arab" socialism. At the same time this revolutionary movement has been confronted by another popular one, a revolutionary religious movement in which the Quran is the template for progress, modernization (Westernization) is eschewed, women are expected to seek more traditional modes of achievement and democracy, however vague it may be, becomes vaguer yet. This movement is very potent indeed, and we witness today the massive clash of ideological revolutionary currents. It should be added that where Marxism has blossomed, modernization has also; thus in Afghanistan probably the chief underlying cause of the "rebellion" against a central Kabul leftist government (and ultimately its Soviet protectors) was rural unhappiness with too-rapid modernization and the apparent destruction of Muslim values.

How is ideology disseminated in the Middle East, and to whom is it directed? The national leader always sets the tone and articulates the main themes of what might be called the official ideology. What people already believe is, of course, also largely ideological. But the government's ideology prevails in newspapers, on television, and in other easily controlled channels of communication. When the leader speaks, his remarks may be printed and endlessly rebroadcast. These remarks may be elaborated upon by newspaper editors, official spokesmen, and ministers of "national guidance" for years. In the process of its dissemination, the message often becomes internally inconsistent and many of its parts outdated.

In the United States, much ideology emanates from government sources, but there is also much that comes from the United Auto Workers, the American Medical Association, the

American Legion, and a host of other groups, each with its own interests. In contrast, in the Middle East, the major source of ideology is the government of the day and its propaganda organs. Smaller organizations are not always permitted to exist, and when they do exist, they are seldom permitted to pursue ideological ends different from those of the government. Usually they ape the government's views, sometimes endorsing views that may, in fact, be inimical to their own interests. Thus, newspaper editors and publishers have been known to applaud the nationalization of their own newspapers.[10] Moreover, in most Middle Eastern countries, if the press is not owned outright, it is rigidly censored and controlled. Even in Israel, proud of its democracy, there is the ubiquitous military censorship of newspapers and books. The same is true of radio and television broadcasting and of the importation of books and periodicals. What governments do not own, they control, although often inefficiently.

Individuals may reject, alter, or simply ignore an official government ideology. They may even be ignorant of it. In some Middle Eastern countries, lip service only is given to some of the ideological disseminations of the government, not only among the educated but among the peasantry as well. This should hardly be surprising.

Middle Eastern ideologies vary greatly. This might be expected in an area where governments themselves often change. But the policies of a relatively stable regime can also change, sometimes rapidly, and such changes must be justified. Nasser, for example, oscillated between warm friendship and enmity for Jordan's King Hussein. Egyptian newspapers dutifully explained and reiterated Nasser's latest views. Current views may change before earlier ones have been fully disseminated among the rank and file; not unnaturally, this sometimes leads to confusion.

In spite of the many contradictory changes that an official ideology may undergo, it usually has a veneer of plausibility. In some respects it is addressed to an audience that never exists: a

---

[10] This occurred, for example, when the Egyptian press was nationalized in the early 1960s.

collection of perfectly loyal and passive automatons. But rarely do the existing audiences talk back. What they accept, with whatever degree of pretense, is a rationale for the status quo in both domestic and foreign political programs. Superficially, the ideology often makes sense. It often includes the following notions: (1) A true way, perhaps Jordanian or Turkish or Egyptian, exists. (2) Those who have ruled in the past and those who interfere from without have subverted the true way. (3) Those who now rule or who are about to rule represent a return to the true way and will interpret its provisions in modern times. Of necessity, a glossary of exhortations and explanations is offered. The ideology may draw upon long-accepted traditional values, or it may be radical in its orientation and makeshift in its manufacture.

Ideology tends to be vague and ambiguous; after all, it must appeal to large numbers of divergent peoples. Middle Eastern ideology is no exception to this. Goals may be phrased as the "better life," "justice for all," "genuine equality," and the "Islamic spirit." Even in Israel, present policies are justified in terms of eventual "true peace."

Let us examine in some detail several types of Middle Eastern ideology: religion, nationalism, and "revolutionary socialism."

THE PATINA OF RELIGION

Religion is itself essentially ideological. In the Middle East, other ideologies have always had to adjust to the religious proclivities of the people. An Arab socialism must be grounded in Islamic history and thought, even if expounded by an Arab Christian. The nationalist propaganda of a country such as Syria or Iraq must conform to the Islamic background. Even the Turkish nationalism of Kemal, essentially secularist, was not as negative toward religion as is sometimes thought. And it is instructive that, with the advent of the Turkish Democrats in 1950, government propaganda took a very religious turn that garnered considerable support from peasantry and others alike.

It is interesting that the presence of Islam is sometimes adduced as evidence for the historical lack of success of ideological Communism. The argument made is that Communism is godless and therefore of no appeal in Muslim countries. The question of whether this is true is simpler to ask than to answer. The difficulty in answering hinges partly on the difficulty of measuring the success of an ideological message. Communism has rarely been the official ideology of any Middle Eastern state, with the recent exceptions of Afghanistan and Southern Yemen. It has not had the advantages in dissemination that other ideologies have had. Its lack of success, then, may be because of a number of factors, of which the lack of religious emphasis is only one. The "successful" ideologies may or may not be successful because of their religious hue. But if the religious argument is true, the lack of appeal of Communism can only underline the latest religious aspects of ideology in the Middle East.

An added word on Afghanistan: It may well be that the Afghans who rebelled against a leftist government did not do so over abstract ideological slogans, however godless their content might be, but rather over the practical, down-to-earth interference by that government with such things as marriage, divorce, waqfs, inheritance, and education. It is a reminder too of what Bernard Lewis observed about Kemalist Turkey, that the greatest popular resentment among the people to the Kemalist reforms was directed at the least important (other than symbolically), the so-called Hat Law, which required men to wear headgear with brims.

We have already discussed the role of Islam in Chapter II. H. A. R. Gibb has said,

> The history of Islam in the nineteenth and twentieth centuries is a history of revival and efforts at readjustment under the double stimulus of challenge from within and pressing dangers from without. Slowly at first, and not without setbacks but with increasing momentum, the Muslim community has gathered itself together and begun to look to its defenses; reawakened and alert, it is searching for the programme with which to advance united into an unknown and unpredictable future.[11]

[11] *Mohammedanism* (London: Oxford University Press, 1950), pp. 165–166.

Majid Khadduri, in a chapter entitled "Revival of Islam," quotes Muhammad: "At the turn of each century there will arise in my nation a man who will call for religious revival." [12] In the twentieth century, several individuals in various parts of the Muslim Middle East have seen themselves in this role. Islam was decadent; the Muslim lands were overrun and exploited by foreign powers; the old piety was eroding in the face of contacts with the West. Ayatollah Khomeini in Iran is merely the latest.

One of the more interesting of the reformers was Hasan al-Banna of the Muslim Brotherhood (see Chapter II). Al-Banna's original messages, of course, were designed to gain followers and to rally them with enthusiasm. Here we are interested in al-Banna and the Brotherhood as contributors to ideology. The times were bad and decadent, he claimed, but not so bad that dedicated attachment to the Quran, catalyzed by his own guidance, would necessarily fail to save the Islamic world. By the time of his death in 1949, he had gained the support of many thousands; by then, however, his own goals had altered. He was now intrigued with his possible role as the political leader of Egypt. His words had changed over the years; the religious motif in Egyptian ideology now emphasized the imminence of the Muslim victory. In the succeeding years, this, of course, has vanished. The Muslim Brotherhood now plays a less significant role in the Middle East.

Nonetheless, the Brotherhood left a permanent mark on Middle Eastern ideology. The mass nature of the movement, the popularity of its program, and its longevity even in adversity demonstrated to all the popular doctrinal nerve that it had probed. Contemporary Middle Eastern ideology, official or otherwise, reflects this basic attachment to religion and concern with its values. This is manifestly not due to the existence of the Brotherhood alone; in Egypt, the experience of the Brotherhood merely pointed up a basic ideological bent that already existed. So much that is political becomes embedded in the Middle East in religious themes. Every Muslim movement finds a response, and one like the Muslim Brotherhood generates an enthusiasm that is wholly unexpected by a Westerner. Even in nationalism one finds religious overtones; they were certainly not absent in the Turkish nationalist Ziya Gökalp or in the Arab nationalist Sati al-Husri, noted below.

NATIONALISM

Some of the terminology that we will use in discussing Middle Eastern nationalism has already been introduced.[13] Nationalism refers to a particular type of political behavior; as such, it colors the current strains of ideology in the Middle East. What nationalists preach is, of course, ideology. Nationalism, like religion, also inspires a prodigious amount of ideology.

The core of any nationalistic ideology is what might be termed lococentricity;[14] the insiders have special qualities and values that set them apart from their neighbors, particularly those considered outsiders. Those insiders who share special qualities have not always been able to solve their problems — an understatement for most of the Middle East — and the reason, in ideological terms, can only be that they have been prevented from doing so by malignant outside forces. But now that they are free or about to be free — one special quality of nationalistic ideology is that the special people are never really free; they are always combating their enemies — their true skills will come to the fore, and problems, hitherto unsolvable, will rapidly dissipate.

Whatever features differentiate the insiders from their neighbors must reflect an innate value that must be preserved at all

[13] There is, of course, a considerable literature on nationalism, some of it specifically on the Middle East. One of the earliest of the latter is Hans Kohn, *Nationalism and Imperialism in the Hither East* (New York: Harcourt, Brace and Co., 1932). See also Walter Z. Laquer, *Communism and Nationalism in the Middle East*, 3d ed. (London: Routledge and Kegan Paul, 1961); and Kemal H. Karpat, ed., *Political and Social Thought in the Contemporary Middle East* (New York: Frederick A. Praeger, 1968). For Iran, see Richard W. Cottam, *Nationalism in Iran* (Pittsburgh: University of Pittsburgh Press, 1964). See also Part 6, "Radical Arab Nationalism," in *The Political Awakening of the Middle East*, ed. by George Lenczowski (Englewood Cliffs, N.J.: Prentice-Hall, 1970).

[14] The portion *loco* refers not only to the Latin *locus* ("place") but also to the well-established American connotation of eccentricity and madness!

costs. Language is an obvious example of such a value. In the nationalistic Turkey of Atatürk, it was thought necessary to junk the Ottoman Turkish, filled with words borrowed from other languages and expressed in the Arabic alphabet, and produce a pure Turkish. Success in this endeavor was not really possible. It was one thing to rid the language of a cumbersome Arabic alphabet, and this the Turks did, but it was quite another to sell nationalistic neologisms in place of old-fashioned loan words. In the Arab world today there is a frantic effort to elevate Arabic to a modern technical language. Great efforts have been made to put together an Arabic technical literature and to emphasize the worth of the language above all others. Likewise, the Israelis have insisted on resurrecting the equally unwieldy Hebrew language. Any explanation of this other than one grounded in nationalism is inadequate.

A great deal, too, is made of the long and rich history that each people possesses. The Turks hark back to their golden ages as do the Persians and Afghans. Even the Israelis, modern and tough as they are, spend an inordinate amount of attention on extolling their historical connection with the Biblical lands. Until recently, the Egyptians were in their Arab phase of nationalism, and so they stressed things Arab. Their history, however, is far older than that of the Arabs and far richer. So lately they have returned to an "Egyptian" phase.

Qawmiyya nationalism did not arise until after the First World War, but there was ample evidence of local, or *wataniyya,* nationalism. The case of Egypt is particularly important as well as interesting. By the late 1870s, Egypt was under the weight of foreign financial and political control. In 1881, an officer named Arabi led a military revolt against the Khedive, Tawfiq, for surrendering his government to foreign influence. The Arabi revolt was put down only by British military intervention, which began an occupation of Egypt that was not to end until 1956. Arabi Pasha was not so much an ideologue as he was a man of action, but his abortive act was to spur a popular indignation and resentment that were to last for many years. Egyptian (*wataniyya*) nationalism had become a major force.

The most important of the early Egyptian nationalist ideo-

logues were Mustafa Kamil and Muhammad Farid.[15] Theirs
was the first major Egyptian nationalist party (al-Hizb al-
Watani), and theirs also were the most articulate and popular
of the nationalist newspapers, pamphlets, and books that galvanized Egyptian opinion against the British occupation. Kamil
was particularly forceful. Had he lived — he died in 1908 at the
age of 34 — he might well have acquired sufficient strength to
achieve some modicum of Egyptian independence.

By the time of the First World War, the various nationalist
groups were beginning to experiment with violence. In 1910,
the prime minister, Butrus Ghali Pasha, was assassinated by a
nationalist because he had supported a proposal to extend the
Suez Canal concession. With the end of the war, new nationalist
figures and movements arose. Egypt demanded the right to send
a delegation to the peace conference in France. The British
strongly resisted this demand; the birth of the Wafd ("delegation") party was the result. Its leader was the incredibly popular Sa'd Zaghlul, but his early death, like that of Kamil, sapped
the nationalist movement of the leadership needed for expelling
the British. Egypt was a hotbed of nationalism until the advent
of Nasser, but it was a wataniyya nationalism rather than a
broader Arab nationalism that characterized its politics.

In the Middle East prior to the First World War, the Ottomans were the outsiders. An Armenian national movement
against the Ottoman Turks existed for a time. Although the
Kurds were troublesome, they had no national movement of
any consequence at that time. In Syria, the Arabs (or a few of
them anyway) formed secret societies that were ultimately considered the beginnings of Arab nationalism. In Turkey itself,
dissatisfaction with the regime resulted in the Young Turk
movement (culminating eventually in a coup d'etat), but at first
this nationalism was Ottoman, and adherents were expected
to be recruited from various minority groups.

The most fervent and interesting nationalisms, however,

---

[15] An excellent article on the early Nationalist party in Egypt is
Arthur Goldschmidt, Jr., "The Egyptian Nationalist Party: 1892–1919,"
in Political and Social Change in Modern Egypt, ed. by P. M. Holt (London: Oxford University Press, 1968), pp. 308–333.

were the product of the First World War. In Afghanistan, the Afghans fought their third war with the British in a century; with it they achieved their independence. But they quickly sank into quiescence, and there was no articulated (or nationalist) ideology for years.[16] In Iran, a coup in 1921 put a newspaperman and a soldier in power; the soldier, Reza Khan (later Reza Shah), survived. There were many minorities in Iran — Kurds, Azerbaijanis, Bakhtiyaris, Qashqa'is, Baluchis, Arabs, Turkomen, for example — and all were now urged to follow the *Iranian* nationalism. This early nationalism of Reza Shah was intended, insofar as it was created at all, to facilitate the building of a modern nation. In passing it must be said that, given the foreign exploitation of Iranian petroleum resources, the periodic aggressive incursions of Soviet policy into Iranian politics, and the overt military ocupation of Iran during the Second World War, there were plenty of targets for nationalist ire.

Nationalism and its ideology reached a peak in Iran during the Musaddiq period. Muhammad Musaddiq was a longtime nationalist leader in Iran, who reached the apogee of his success and influence in the nationalization of the Anglo-Iranian Oil Company in 1951 and then finally fell in a contest with the Shah in 1953. "It is no exaggeration," Cottam remarks, "to say that for the first time in Iran's very long history a national leader had appeared who enjoyed the respect, devotion, and loyalty of the vast majority of politically aware Iranians." The Americans viewed Musaddiq as a highly dangerous and irresponsible radical. The Shah viewed him as scarcely less dangerous; his own position was seriously undermined by the popular reform measures advocated by Musaddiq. But Musaddiq (in Cottam's words) was "obsessed with his struggle against foreign imperialism," [17] and he was not able to put together a

---

[16] This is essentially true notwithstanding the issue of Pushtunistan, which troubled Afghan-Pakistani relations for years. Pushtunistan (the land of the Pushtus) was in any event not congruent with Afghanistan. The movement failed. Yet ironically enough, with the huge mass of refugees from Eastern Afghanistan in Pakistan in the wake of fighting in Afghanistan, a sort of ghost Pushtunistan may be emerging in the NWFP (Northwest Frontier Province).

[17] Cottam, *Nationalism in Iran*, p. 22.

viable domestic program. He was overthrown in 1953. Ideologically, he had strong liberal tendencies within the Iranian context and sought to alter the traditional power base that supported the Shah and the current political institutions. In foreign policy, he was adamant that Iran's resources be developed for its needs, purposes, and goals rather than for the benefit of foreign concessionaries (as indeed had been the case for a very long time).

The collapse of the Shah in 1979 and the establishment of new systems under clerical guidance are not precisely a nationalist movement. The emphasis was on Islam, yet any system would have to maintain a viable national character for Iran. Such things as the seizure of American hostages and the war with Iraq lent nationalist energy to the system's leaders. Nevertheless currently Iran is an anomaly with respect to nationalism.

In Turkey, the nationalist movement is inextricably connected with the name of Kemal Atatürk, the founding hero of the modern Turkish nation. Kemal was an authentic military hero of the First World War, who rallied the Turks in the period after the war to oust the occupying Greeks and neutralize the French, the British, and the Italians, who sought to exploit a defeated Turkey. He abolished first the sultanate, then the caliphate, and instituted major social and religious reforms; he also abolished polygamy and the use of Arabic script in writing Turkish; in general, he forged a new *Turkish* (not Ottoman) nation. He led Turkey until his death in 1938. Of course, there was a Kemalism, of which nationalism was only a part, and Kemal himself had a hand in formulating its principles. Kemalism purported to be composed of six ingredients: nationalism, populism, secularism, statism, socialism, and revolutionism. The ideological nature of this statement needs no elaboration. It is interesting that in 1960 when the Turkish army intervened and overthrew the government of Adnan Menderes, they did so on the grounds that the principles of Kemalism were in danger.

Moroccan nationalism was given a boost by the struggle of Abdul Krim for independence in the early 1920s. But it was only with the religious (as well as political) leadership of Muhammad V in later years that Moroccan nationalism developed into a formidable movement with an appropriate accompanying ideology. There was little if any Algerian national movement until the end of the Second World War; much the same could be said of Tunisia.

Still less was there either nationalism or its ideology in Libya. Libya was underdeveloped and underpopulated. It fought no war of independence. It was a loosely formed confederation under a Senussi monarch, King Idris. The coup of September 1969 was a surprise; much ideology was generated by it. Revolutionary Libya, under the leadership of Qaddafi, has assumed new responsibilities in the Arab world and is developing a nationalist ideology.

From the point of view of nationalist ideology, Syria offers an interesting case. It had been in Syria before the First World War that early patriotic Arab societies had been formed,[18] and Faisal's Arab contingents had been in the vanguard of Allenby's troops as Damascus had been freed from Turkish rule. Indeed, Faisal attempted to establish himself as king of an Arab Syria, but was militarily ousted by France in 1920, in the battle of Maysalun. France was merely asserting its claims under wartime agreements with the British. Although France remained in Syria and Lebanon for more than 20 years, it was beset with tremendous nationalist agitation there. Syrian nationalists had some difficulty in distinguishing between adherence to a strictly Syrian nationalism and adherence to an Arab one.

The most interesting of the Syrian nationalist ideologues was Antun Sa'ada, founder of the Syrian Social Nationalist party.[19] The party was formed in 1932 when the French still controlled Syria; Sa'ada was executed by the Lebanese in 1949. By that time, he had been compelled to widen the horizons of his nationalism to emphasize its Arab qualities. But at first, he was essentially a Syrian nationalist. "The Syrian nation," he said, "represents the unity of the Syrian people with a long historical past stretching back to prehistoric times ... [and

[18] For details, see George Antonius, *The Arab Awakening* (Beirut: Khayat's, 1961).
[19] See Labib Zuwiyya Yamak, *The Syrian Social Nationalist Party: An Ideological Analysis* (Cambridge, Mass.: Harvard University Press, 1966).

there is a] psychological superiority of the Syrians, which is not the result of unconstrained mixture [of peoples] but of the superb quality of homogeneous mixing, perfectly in harmony with the type of environment. . . ." [20] The ambivalence in Sa'ada's thinking is reflected in what he wrote:

> The aim of the Syrian Social Nationalist Party is to effect a Syrian national social renaissance capable of achieving its ideals and restoring to the Syrian nation its vitality and power. The party also aims to organize a movement that would lead to the complete independence of the Syrian nation, the consolidation of its sovereignty, the creation of a new system to safeguard its interests and raise its standard of life, and the formation of an Arab front. . . . Syria is one of the nations of the Arab world and is fitted for the leadership thereof. . . . Syrian nationalism is the only practical method and the basic prerequisite for Syrian regeneration and the consequent participation of Syria in Arab affairs.[21]

Syrian society demanded reformation. Not unnaturally, given his Christian heritage, Sa'ada insisted in his program of reformation upon a separation of church and state, the lessening of the religious role, the abolition of feudalism with a concomitant economic reorganization, and the creation of a strong army.[22]

What is apparent is that Antun Sa'ada began his career as a student deeply concerned about the fate of Syria. As his commitment grew and popularity of his movement became more apparent, his need was to integrate a purely Syrian movement with the Arab nationalist movement, itself in its infancy. His solution was to speak of Greater Syria, which was to encompass substantially more of the Arab world than the Syrian borders did at that time, and then to the naturalness of Arab leadership being Syrian. Probably Sa'ada's movement would have gone into eclipse in any case, but his death deprived it of effective leadership. Arabs progressively interested them-

---

[20] This English translation is taken from Karpat, *Political and Social Thought*, pp. 95–96.

[21] *Ibid.*, pp. 96–97. Majid Khadduri (*Political Trends*, p. 192) sums up all this very well in eight principles of Syrian national superiority.

[22] Karpat, *Political and Social Thought*, pp. 87–94.

selves more in Arab nationalism than in Syrian, or Egyptian, or Sudanese, nationalism.

Before discussing Arab nationalism, it is well to note one other local nationalism in the Middle East — Zionism. Ideologically, modern Zionism stems from the late-nineteenth-century efforts of such men as Theodor Herzl, who believed that the solution of the "Jewish question" could exist only in the establishment of a "national home" for the Jewish people. Quite early, twentieth-century Zionists decided that their national home was in Palestine. Here, Jews might at last be in a majority and be able to create their own political future. Men like Herzl, and later Weizmann and Ben Gurion, faced the need to persuade Jews to follow their cause and also to persuade the world and its leaders to permit the experiment to occur. Thus, Zionism was the nationalism of a people widely dispersed and lacking a territory. By 1917, Weizmann had persuaded the British to issue the Balfour Declaration,[23] which stated that the British government "viewed with favour" the establishment in Palestine of a national home for the Jews.

It was not until the rise of Hitler and his pogroms against the Jews that immigration of Jews into Palestine in sufficient numbers could make possible the dream of a *politically autonomous* national home. But these large numbers provoked dissatisfaction among Palestinian Arabs and concomitant uncooperativeness among the British. Ultimately, of course, a Jewish population in Palestine proclaimed the independence of its state, Israel, and then defended it in four wars (1948, 1956, 1967, 1973) against the Arabs. Zionism, in its original sense, is, of course, passé today: the national home has been established and its viability achieved. In its place is Israeli nationalism. Its ideology calls attention to an ancient history, reminds the world of injustices to Jews, denounces Arab accusations of imperialism, sounds a continual tocsin of dangers to Israel and world Jewry, and in general proclaims the superiority of Israeli ideas and programs. In short, it is a typical nationalism. But if Sa'ada could dream of Syrian leadership of a united Arab

[23] The major work on this declaration is Leonard Stein, *The Balfour Declaration* (London: Vallentine-Mitchell, 1961).

world, there can be no comparable Israeli dream. The Israelis cannot lead other minorities or their Arab neighbors in a supernationalism.

The most interesting contemporary Middle Eastern nationalism is that of the Arabs, not as Egyptians or Saudis or Libyans, but as Arabs. Although this nationalism still appears today to be deep-seated and significant, it is almost entirely a twentieth-century phenomenon and, indeed, is really a product of the post-Second World War period. Before that war, many young Arabs — those, for example, at the American University in Beirut — identified themselves as Muslims when asked what they were. When pressed further, they might reply that they were Iraqi or Lebanese. In Egypt, before the rise of Nasser as an *Arab* leader, most Egyptians thought of themselves as simply Egyptians and felt little attachment to the Arabs qua Arabs in Jordan or Tunisia. Thus, although the roots of Arab nationalism undoubtedly go back another 20 years and more, this nationalism was not a powerful and driving force until later.

The catalyst for the rise of Arab nationalism, *qawmiyya Arabiyya,* was undoubtedly the growth of the Zionist movement in Palestine, culminating in the establishment of Israel in 1948. Nationalism requires a target for its spleen, and although the British, the French, and others filled this role for individual Arab states, no one of these powers could serve satisfactorily for all Arabs. But the Jewish penetration of Arab Palestine could and did serve as just such a target. Israeli success in the war of 1948, fought primarily against Jordan and Egypt, made each of these two societies more aware of its Arabness. In the recriminations after the war, the dissensions and divisions among the Arabs seemed to have been the primary cause of the military defeat. The cry for Arab unity — that is, unity against the invader, the Israelis — began to grow in earnest.

Early Arab nationalism lacked a leader — King Abdullah of Jordan, General Nuri of Iraq, Shukri al-Quwatli of Syria, King Farouk of Egypt, King Abdul Aziz Ibn Saud of Saudi Arabia, none of these would do — until the Egyptian revolution in 1952. The titular leader of the coup, Gen. Muhammad Naguib, turned out not to be that leader either. It was not until the rise of the tremendously popular Nasser, whose charisma and success against the British pushed him permanently into a position of prominence and adoration, that Arab nationalism and the drive for Arab unity became the rallying cry of nearly all Arabs.

The uneven drive for Arab unity can be seen in a number of recent attempts at cross-national political integration. Syria and Egypt formed the United Arab Republic in February 1958 (to be dissolved in 1961); a few days later, the Arab Federation (of Jordan and Iraq) was formed (to last until July 1958). The United Arab Republic plus Yemen became for a time the United Arab States. In 1971, Libya, Egypt, and Syria formed the Federation of Arab Republics. In 1973 Libya and Egypt were to "merge." Most of the attempts at integration stemmed largely from the disgrace of defeat at Israeli hands — by 1958, twice — and the realization that only a united Arab front could defeat Israel; all collapsed because the forces of disunity were still paramount in the 1950s and 1960s. The existence of Israel was not in itself sufficient to create a durable and effective unity.

But regardless of the practical inability of the Arabs to unite or to defeat the Israelis, Arab nationalism became the political force of the Arab world and an ideology quickly blossomed to give it élan. No Arab leader was immune to its lure or to the dangers of disregarding it. Let us briefly examine some of this nationalist ideology and note its main themes.[24]

Abd al-Rahman al-Kawakibi was one of the precursors of *Arab* nationalism. Writing at the turn of the century about the Arabs and their qualities, he said, among other things, that the Arabian peninsula was favored by God, that "of all countries it is the most free of racial, religious, or sectarian intermixture ... [the] most worthy to be a land of free men. ..." These Arabs, he claimed, "are the most ancient of nations in having a polished civilization, as is shown by the proliferation and the excellence of their wisdom and their literature." The Arabic

---

[24] For introductory commentary, see Hans E. Tütsch, *Facets of Arab Nationalism* (Detroit, Mich.: Wayne State University Press, 1965).

language, he asserted, "takes greatest care of knowledge." The Arabs have practiced "equality of rights" from the earliest of times and have always believed in the "principle of consultation in public matters." Needless to say, he claimed (in a very modern utterance) that the "Arabs know best, of all people, the principles of Socialist living." [25] Al-Kawakibi wrote in a popular religious newspaper, and his audience was in some ways a peculiar one; moreover, in the same period one could find similar statements in the American press about the Americans. Nevertheless, it is the ideological stuff of nationalism. Arabs are the best, with the best history, the greatest potentialities for all that is itself best. The theme was often repeated in later years, although usually in more sophisticated forms.

Who are the Arabs? Are they merely those who speak Arabic or who identify themselves as such? According to the first Arab Students' Congress in 1938 in Brussels, the Arabs are those "who are Arab in their language, culture, and loyalty." Who else? The Arab homeland is a "sacred heritage." Arabs feel "the necessity of independence and unity"; hence, Arab nationalism. [26] The new Arabs have awakened and press on to the glorious future, meanwhile proscribing any lesser fanaticisms than Arab nationalism itself.

"Arab nationalism," said Abdullah al-Ala'ili,

> is the consciousness of the Arabs of their complete social existence, a consciousness which is internal and not merely external objective knowledge, so that the image of the Arab community as a spiritual and living complex, is everpresent to their conscience. Every Arab must feel with an instinctive compulsion the strong existing connections and ties, in such a way that the community is transferred for him from the externality of life to the internality of the soul.[27]

An interesting figure in the history of Arab nationalism was Sati al-Husri. Born in 1880, he long contributed to nationalist ideology, but probably experienced his most influential period with the rise of Nasser. He argued that nationalism was noth-

[25] Quotations from Sylvia G. Haim, ed., *Arab Nationalism: An Anthology* (Berkeley, Calif.: University of California Press, 1962), pp. 78–80.
[26] Quotations, *ibid.*, pp. 100–101.
[27] Quotation, *ibid.*, p. 120.

ing more complicated than the merger of the self with the movement that transcends all selves; that is, in the words of Karpat, "he increasingly advocated the fusion of the individual into the nation, even if this meant sacrificing the individual's freedom." [28] He undertook the rationalization of this fusion, or self-identification, in terms of religious mysticism. It is surprising — or is it? — how many propagandists of Arab nationalism, even Christian Arabs, find it useful to extol the distinctive virtues of Islam. Islam is something the Arabs really claim for themselves, however many other peoples may be Muslim as well; after all, Muhammad, whatever else he was, was an Arab. Al-Husri has been popular and influential in the modern Arab world as the fortunes of its struggle for unity have waned.

Those who are Arab nationalists often suggest that foreign powers are to blame for all that is bad and unfortunate in the Arab world. Charles Malik, a distinguished Lebanese scholar, was not above saying, "The Western world is responsible for the situation in the Near East on every level of that situation." [29] He goes on to accuse the West of a lack of unity, responsibility, sincerity, understanding, and love.[30] Although this accusation is probably not untrue with respect to the West's attitude toward the Middle East, it does not explain, as the nationalist insists it does, all of the defects of the area.

Still, the Arab nationalist also argues that whatever the problems, Arab nationalism will solve them. Moral fervor and attachment to the eternal ideals of the Arab nation will somehow lessen the contemporary agony of political crisis and economic stagnation. This is the way of all nationalism.

To whom are these ideological pleas addressed? To some degree, they are addressed to audiences that do not exist. In no political community is there a sharp division between the makers of ideology, whose attachment to the details of their ideology is questionable, and the absorbers of ideology, the masses

---

[28] Karpat, *Political and Social Thought*, p. 55. Karpat includes a selection from al-Husri's writings, as does Sylvia G. Haim in her *Arab Nationalism*. For an excellent study of the life and thought of al-Husri, see William L. Cleveland, *The Making of an Arab Nationalist* (Princeton, N.J.: Princeton University Press, 1971).

[29] Quotation, Karpat, *Political and Social Thought*, p. 220.

[30] *Ibid.*, pp. 221–222.

of people waiting for a message and the opportunity to demonstrate in its favor. Ideology is produced by the interactions of persons, of elites and masses, of intellectuals and nonintellectuals. It is the hypostatization of emotional ideals, the natural idealistic exaggeration of beliefs. No one quite believes his own ideology! But it is useful to him perhaps in his search for identity to lose himself in the immensity of a faith that he does not quite believe. The matter is far too complicated to go into fully here, but the faithlike qualities of ideology are well known: the psychology of its true believers is yet to be fully investigated. Moreover, exaggeration as a polemical device is often effective. Men will applaud and follow those who do not equivocate, even where equivocation would be rational. Political leaders, the wielders of ideology, must generally go where applause leads them. Elite and masses, then, invariably find themselves together out on the ideological limb.

An important point remains to be made:

> As Richard Pfaff astutely observed . . . the ultimate function of Arab nationalism would not be to unite the Arab states, but to serve as an ideological bridge in the nation building process between independence and the rise of state-based nationalisms. Seemingly it has performed that function and is now receding as Egyptian, Syrian, Iraqi, and other Arab nationalisms continue to capture the political imaginations of ever larger numbers of citizens. This change in identification from the Arab *ummah* (total Arab community) to individual Arab states has as its most important consequence the increasing imperviousness of the citizens of the various Arab states to appeals from beyond the borders. Nasserism is a waning pan-Arab force not only because its founder died, but also because it increasingly is foundering on the rocks of Syrian, Iraqi, and other nationalisms. In turn, the political elites of these countires now need worry less about their popular support being undercut by charismatic foreigners; hence it can be expected that the defensiveness formerly so manifest in the Syrian, Iraqi and other Arab elites will gradually give way to self-confidence based on the successful completion of the state and nation building processes.[31]

[31] Springborg, "On the Rise and Fall," p. 101. Springborg refers to Pfaff's observations in "The Function of Arab Nationalism," *Comparative Politics* 2 (1970):158–159.

Even in collapse, if the persuasive Pfaff-Springborg thesis is to be believed, Arab nationalism has facilitated the local development of *wataniyya*. Should the Arab-Israeli dispute diminish in force, this development would emerge even more strongly. It might be added that, in 1983 at least, Iran's Ayatollah Khomeini represents for many Muslims — largely Shi'ite of course but Sunni as well — a Nasserite individual.

ARAB SOCIALISM

This volume points up the vast political change occurring in the contemporary Middle East. Some of this change, such as that resulting from many of the successive coups in Syria and Iraq, is superficial, but much of it is increasingly deep-seated and substantial. Social revolutions of one sort or another have occurred in Egypt and Turkey, and one is occurring in Iran. Moreover, in most of the rest of the Middle East, revolution in the form of violent exchanges of personnel and policy has been a common occurrence.

Twentieth-century social revolution is largely *socialistic;* little wonder that socialism has had a profound ideological impact upon the Middle East. But everywhere in the world, socialism has acquired an adjective: Russian socialism, Chinese socialism, African socialism, Arab socialism.[32] In the Middle East and Black Africa at least, the reason for this appears to be the need to find ideological roots in the past.

It would seem to many that Arab socialism was the personal creation of President Nasser in Egypt, but this is mistaken. The genius of Nasser was that he was generally attuned to what was in the air, and his greatest successes were the articulation of already half-formed and popular doctrines.[33] Yet there

---

[32] An invaluable source has been Sami A. Hanna and George H. Gardner, *Arab Socialism: A Documentary Survey* (Leiden, The Netherlands: E. J. Brill, 1969).

[33] Hanna and Gardner (*ibid.*, p. 23) quote Fayez Sayegh most appropriately in this regard: "In whatever direction [Nasser] has pursued his policies — be it agrarian reform or socialism, Arab unity or neutralism — he has merely put into effect what many other Arabs before him had longed for. Corresponding to every element of 'Nasserism' there had been prior Arab ideas, longings, dreams. But dreams they had remained, for the most part until Nasser succeeded in transforming them into tangible reality.... This is especially true of socialism as an essential element of

is no doubt that he contributed to the popularity of Arab socialism and spread its name and features far more widely among the Arabs than would otherwise have been possible.

The Arabic word for "socialism" is *ishtirakiyya*.[34] Socialist doctrine was disseminated and socialist movements existed in the Middle East prior to the Second World War.[35] Socialist and Communist movements were in early stages of maturation in Palestine by 1919, Egypt by 1920, Syria and Lebanon by 1930, Iraq by 1932, and Jordan by 1935.[36] But the links between Arab socialism and these early traditional socialist movements are not strong.

Arab socialism has its roots in (1) the educational experiences of the Arab intellectuals in the 1920s and 1930s and their imbibing of traditional socialist doctrine; (2) the ideological creations of such movements as the Ba'th, and such writers as Michel Aflaq and Salama Musa; (3) Nasser's early experiences at Bandung (1955) and with such figures as Tito, Nehru, Chou En-lai, and Nkrumah; and (4) the need for reform and the natural tendency to reject traditional political and economic values. In any event, socialism was in the wind throughout the developing world, and it was hardly surprising that Nasser would give it his ideological blessing. At the same time the traditional organizations were often outlawed and pushed underground — as in Egypt, where all party opposition was prohibited. And, years later, in 1971, Anwar Sadat, as Egypt's president, continued to argue that Egyptians did not want class struggle; rather, he said, they wanted unity.

Nasser said: "Democracy is political liberty; socialism is so-

---

the revolutionary Arab Nationalism which prevails in the Arab world today." (Original citation: "The Theoretical Structure of Nasser's Socialism," *St. Antony's Papers*, pp. 9–10.)

[34] This Arabic term actually means something more than socialism. Literally, it means "to share," "to become a partner with others." And it carries moral overtones.

[35] Rather indispensable for the early period is Laqueur, *Communism and Nationalism*. See also Ervand Abrahamian, *Iran Between Two Revolutions* (Princeton, N.J.: Princeton University Press, 1982); and George S. Harris, *The Origins of Communism in Turkey* (Stanford, Calif.: The Hoover Institution on War, Revolution and Peace, 1967).

[36] Laqueur, *Communism and Nationalism*, passim.

cial liberty; the two cannot be separated. They are the two wings of true freedom, without which, or without either of which, freedom cannot soar up to the horizons of the anticipated tomorrow." [37] Socialism is, according to Nasser, the pursuit of sufficiency, justice, and freedom.[38] Sufficiency is nothing more complicated than acquiring enough of the world's goods to give substance to life. As Sayegh says, "Only the vigorous, methodical pursuit of sufficiency, ... can make possible the establishment of social justice and meaningful equality of opportunity." [39] Not only Egypt, but the entire Arab world, was underdeveloped, notwithstanding the huge petroleum deposits in some of the Arab states. And even where petroleum was extracted, few Arab states (at least until the 1970s) had derived either a very fair share of its value or much benefit from the use of royalties from its sale. In Egypt, Nasser struck first at the Suez Canal Company in 1956, whose revenues had been but little shared with Egypt. The acquisition of the canal and the use of its revenues to help build the High Dam at Aswan did help build sufficiency. But nationalization and sequestration of properties proceeded in other areas of Egypt and ultimately in other parts of the Arab world. These corrected not insufficiency, but maldistribution. This is surely evident in the much vaunted land reform in Egypt and later in Iran. Land reform in itself solves no problems in sufficiency; indeed the gross agricultural product may be lower because of the breakup of natural agricultural producing units.[40] But this, too, had become a part of socialism.

By justice, Nasser meant "freedom from exploitation and the enjoyment of an equal opportunity to develop one's abil-

[37] Actually in *The Charter for National Action,* Chapter 5 (1961). Quotation noted in Fayez Sayagh, reprinted in Hanna and Gardner, *Arab Socialism,* p. 108.

[38] Hanna and Gardner, *ibid.,* p. 108.

[39] Quoted in *ibid.,* p. 109.

[40] For a general discussion of land reform, see Doreen Warriner, *Land Reform in Principle and Practice* (Oxford: Clarendon Press, 1969). See also Doreen Warriner, *Land Reform and Development in the Middle East* (London: Oxford University Press, 1962); and Gabriel S. Saab, *The Egyptian Agrarian Reform, 1952–1962* (London: Oxford University Press, 1967).

ities and to receive a fair share of the national wealth";[41] this philosophy is attractive, especially to those who will never have that fair share. But one should not criticize blindly. What does justice mean but the attempt to reach for ideals such as these? To Nasser they were an inescapable part of Arab socialism.

Freedom, to Nasser, meant "participation in the shaping of the nation's destiny." [42] Again an ideal? Perhaps, but not quite. Although the Fabian Socialists in England had many years before conceived, as their socialist goal, the enfranchisement of more people and the creation of a more representative parliament, Nasser's views on *participation* were perhaps somewhat more parochial. Participation eventually meant symbolic participation; it meant participating in mass rallies and demonstrations (and often meant being trucked into the big cities for this purpose); it meant holding membership in whatever national political organizations were formed (that is, the Arab Socialist Union); it meant voting enthusiastically for the policies of the regime. Even Nasser's successor, Anwar Sadat, found it necessary to build illusory majorities, such as the 98 percent support claimed for the *new* constitution in the fall of 1971 or later the referendum of support in 1978.

Arab socialism in Egypt has at least been the rubric under which much social and economic reform has been planned. The position of women has improved — Iraq and Egypt were the first Arab states to have female cabinet ministers — limitations on incomes have been instituted, and workers have been given membership on governing boards of industry. Controlled rents, attempts at controlled prices, the introduction of agricultural cooperatives, the beginnings of health services in remote villages — all of these and many more reforms have been introduced under the aegis of socialism. Some of the early socialist measures were undercut by Sadat; at the time of his death Egypt was in many ways once again a happy-go-lucky entrepreneurial mecca.

But, however many genuine steps toward reform were under-

[41] Hanna and Gardner, *Arab Socialism,* p. 108.
[42] *Ibid.,* p. 108.

taken, ideology remained the vanguard. All problems were to be solved by the combination of Arab socialism and Arab nationalism; at times, the ideological line between these two grew vague. And the emphasis was always Arab; it was not merely socialism that was being adopted but a very special variant — Arab socialism.

The limitations of space prevent us from discussing this movement to the degree that it deserves. But before leaving the subject of Arab socialism, a word must be added about the Syrian party, the Arab Ba'th.[43] The Ba'th is a remarkable party, one of the few genuine indigenous parties in the Middle East. It was founded by Michel Aflaq and Salal al-Din al-Bitar in 1943. In later years, Aflaq became a leading theoretician of Arab socialism, although it was always labeled Ba'th socialism. To Aflaq, Arab socialism is a product of Arab, not European, history,[44] and is "an alternative method of attack on the problems of modern society, a middle way between capitalism and communism." [45] Ba'thist ideology is nationalistic and is "a means by which Arab glory can be regained." [46] At the same time, Aflaq argues that socialism can come to all Arabs only when their dreams for unity have been realized. As for Marxists, Aflaq explicitly rejects the class struggle and most other doctrinal positions. The Ba'thists believe that their "socialism will come about as a result of the conviction of the majority of the people, that socialism answers the need for a moral and just order in society." [47]

An examination of the Ba'thist Constitution reveals some of the multifarious concerns of its members over the years. The

[43] In English, sometimes called the Arab Ba'th Socialist party, sometimes the Arab Resurrection Socialist party. Its constitution, discussed in the text, can be found in Haim, *Arab Nationalism*, pp. 233–241 (translated from the French). This translation is reproduced in Kamel S. Abu Jaber, *The Arab Ba'th Socialist Party: History, Ideology, and Organization* (Syracuse, N.Y.: Syracuse University Press, 1966), pp. 167–174. In Hanna and Gardner, *Arab Socialism*, pp. 305–312, is to be found another version, translated by Leonard Binder and originally published in *The Middle East Journal 13* (1959):195–200.

[44] Abu Jaber, *The Arab Ba'th*, p. 99.

[45] *Ibid.*, p. 100.

[46] *Ibid.*, p. 101.

[47] *Ibid.*, p. 105.

first paragraphs are utter nationalism and reveal, if anything, the desire to move away from all things that were associated with colonial practices. It is only with Article 26 that Arab socialism is revealed. Land reform (or redistribution) is called for (Article 27); exploitation of labor is denounced (Article 28). "Public utilities, enterprises based on great natural resources, large-scale industries, and means of transport are the property of the nation to be administered directly by the State. All (relevant) foreign companies and concessions are to be abolished" (Article 29).[48] The owners of small industries are to be regulated, although their property is not necessarily to be confiscated (Article 31). Article 32 is important: "The workers will be associated with the administration of [their] factory, and the sum of their wages will be determined by the state in proportion, also to be determined by the state, to the value of their work." [49] Anyone can own buildings, but not anyone can rent them to others (Article 33); not surprisingly in a Muslim community, inheritance rights are protected (Article 34). No one can lend at interest any longer (except, it is implied, state banks) (Article 35).[50] In the section labeled Social Policy, the party establishes its claims in maintaining the sanctity of the family and in encouraging the propagation of children; it intends to raise the standards of public health and other aspects of the welfare state. It also supports the maintenance of the freedoms of speech and the press (within limits!) and the development of education.

The Ba'th was the vanguard of socialism in the Arab world before the rise of Nasser, and its constitution is the manifesto of the socialist revolution there. (But one should compare the Egyptian National Charter [1962], the Statute of the Arab Socialist Union of Egypt [1961], and the Egyptian Constitution [1964] with the Ba'thist Constitution and other modern Arab constitutions.)[51] It might be added that today both Iraq and Syria claim to have Ba'thist governments (although Aflaq is

---

[48] Binder's translation, Hanna and Gardner, *Arab Socialism*, p. 309.

[49] *Ibid.*, p. 309. This is certainly unlike the socialism of the West.

[50] By 1978, the Saudis had established an interest-free bank that would share in the profits made from the money lent.

[51] The Egyptian documents are in Hanna and Gardner, *Arab Socialism*.

loyal to Iraq); not unnaturally, given current Arab politics, these two Ba'thist regimes are often at loggerheads.

It is difficult to overstate the importance of socialism (of which Arab socialism is but one variety) in the ideological coloration of the Middle East. Much is done in its name; much more is promised as its inevitable results. But several important points stand out. Most Middle Eastern socialism is pragmatic rather than doctrinal. It is usually connected with nationalism. Its origins are always given in local terms, and its character is inevitably derived from local history and customs.

COMMUNISM

Communism in some ways has not been a major ideological force in the Middle East. The People's Democratic Republic of Yemen (South Yemen) is Marxist and the socialism in its constitution is more accurately labeled Communism.[52] The current Afghan government (supported by the Soviet Union) is socialist on a Soviet pattern. The situation in Afghanistan is fluid, but in South Yemen there has been stability for some years. Neither of these states has had much ideological influence on its neighbors. Currently in the area, with the exception of the states just mentioned, there are no major Communist parties (the Tudeh party in Iran is unlikely to be of significance while Khomeini lives). In general Communist leadership has been less than noteworthy. The Soviet presence comes and goes in Egypt, Syria, Iraq, and even Libya, but this presence leaves no viable political residues of Communist ideology. Indeed indigenous Communists have often been harassed, imprisoned, and executed.

There has been continuing discussion of the possible reasons for the poor acceptance of Communist ideology in the Middle East, at least of that emanating from the Soviet Union.[53] There

[52] Robert W. Stookey describes the constitution in detail in his *South Yemen: A Marxist Republic in Arabia* (Boulder, Colo.: Westview Press, 1982).

[53] Manfred Halpern sums up the various arguments quite well in his *The Politics of Social Change in the Middle East and North Africa* (Princeton, N.J.: Princeton University Press, 1963), passim (and particularly pp. 156–162).

are those who believe that Communism, because it is atheistic, could never be compatible with Islam; there are also those who believe that this is largely irrelevant to the question of its acceptance. Halpern pointed out in 1963 that "to the degree that tradition survives, the Middle East is unready to receive modern ideas, including Communism." [54] This is really more persuasive than the "Islamic bulwark," hypothesis, even if it needs to be qualified. Land reform, neutralism, Arab socialism, and many other things accepted in the Middle East are also "modern," but the difference is that they have been espoused by popular indigenous leaders. There seems to be no compelling reason to assume that Communism, ideologically, will never appeal to Middle Easterners or eventually become important in the Middle East. Human beings, despite their cultural differences, are much the same after all and seem equally susceptible to the ideological viruses they encounter.

It is important to note that although there is no strong current Communist movement in the Middle East, there have been three occasions, in addition to the two mentioned above, since the Second World War when the Communists have come within an eyelash of real control. These were in Syria in the late 1950s, in Iran in the early 1950s, and in Iraq during Kassem's regime. Although in the last case one can argue that the Communists were as much exploited by Kassem as they were able to exploit in return, it is foolish to minimize the possible results of their success. And it was precisely on these three occasions that covert American intervention was mooted.

Do these instances underline the strength of Communist ideological appeal? Only partly. In the Middle East, as elsewhere, a Communist movement may evolve out of all proportion to its popular appeal, because of the organizational and political skills of its leaders. But almost any ideology that promises change has some appeal in the Middle East. A Communist ideology promises, among other things, a better life through rapid development. The Soviet model is only one of the various Communist models of development that has appeal. In Egypt, the Yugoslav model was particularly attractive;

[54] *Ibid.,* p. 159.

today the Chinese model is making inroads in the ideological thinking of many Middle Easterners. Whether or not any particular model is followed by the political elite of any particular country, there is no doubt that all Communist models point to rapid change, and that is precisely what is so appealing about Communism in the Middle East.

Nevertheless, Springborg is not convinced of the viability of the Communist alternative.

> . improbable is the secular leftist alternative, for while the clock cannot be turned back, neither can it be turned ahead. Given the presence of dual economies, religiously committed peasant bases, patrimonial political systems, and fragmented, unincorporated social systems, communist or socialist vanguards are facing insurmountable tasks. Like the religious fanatics on the right, the Marxists on the left do pose a threat to incumbent political elites in that they could overthrow regimes, but it seems inconceivable that they could then go on to remake society to conform to their religious or socialist model. Like their semisecular predecessors, Moslem Brothers or Marxists, if they were to seize the reins of power, would only retain them by relying on patrimonial bureaucratic authority and by tailoring their political appeals to the preferences and prejudices of the various constituent parts of their citizenry, some of which would be secular, some religious, and some at points in between. Presumably it would be the elite that would change in either composition or outlook, not the society.[55]

Communist ideology indeed appeals most to the educated middle classes. There is some appeal to the industrial working class, but not that much, despite the fact that the Communist message has been directed more specifically to the workers than to others. To the rural peasantry, the appeal is less discernible. What has hurt the Communist appeal most has been its contradictions with another ideology, that of nationalism.

The situation is an interesting one. Here are two clashing ideologies. The strength of one has hurt the success of the other. The Soviets have always been injured in the Middle East because of their Moscow-oriented campaigns. Communist

[55] Springborg, "On the Rise and Fall," p. 107.

cadres have been wiped out in Iraq, Iran, and Syria, and the Soviets have only stood by and watched. In Egypt, in spite of open friendship with the Soviet Union and enormous Soviet aid, Nasser and his successor, Sadat, strongly suppressed the Communist movement. This has invoked only weak protests from Moscow. In Israel, Communists have had a difficult ideological time adjusting the exigencies of domestic Israeli politics to the international stance of their mentors. In addition, ironically, it is modernization itself that is a stumbling block for acceptance of Communist ideology.[56] Communism is too modern for many Muslims!

Halpern has argued that Communism has failed as an ideology in the Middle East.[57] In a very direct sense, this may be true, but Communism has nonetheless had a tremendous impact in that it has formed many traditional elites to modernize out of self-defense. These elites have perceived the proximity of viable Soviet and other Communist models, have daily listened to the mesmeric propaganda from Soviet radio stations, and have not failed to note the restlessness of their own populations. This restlessness is present largely in the middle classes and certainly not among the rural poor. But it has spurred these elites to save what they can, while they can, in effect to create their "white revolutions."

SUMMARY

The world and man have always been ideological; there has always been a need to rationalize an existence, a program, a

[56] Stookey in his *South Yemen*, says this, "The most obvious opposition to the restructuring of South Yemen [traditional] society has occurred in the field of female participation in public activities. The GUYW [General Union of Yemeni Women] is a 15,000-member organization under firm party guidance. It has been given the task of establishing training schools to educate girls in various clerical, mechanical, and industrial skills, and in 1975, 1,500 women were enrolled in such centers as resident students. *Protest by conservative parents, however, forced the closure of the centers in the Fourth and Sixth Governorates in 1978.*" Emphasis supplied. Stookey's reference to this paragraph is Maxine D. Molyneux, "State Policy and the Position of Women in South Yemen," *Peuples Méditerranéens*, no. 12 (July-September 1980):33–49.

[57] See Halpern's chapter "Middle East and North Africa" in *Communism and Revolution: The Strategic Uses of Political Violence*, ed. by Cyril E. Black and Thomas P. Thornton (Princeton, N.J.: Princeton University Press, 1964).

goal. But the late-twentieth-century world is one of intense communicative activity. Disparate views are circulated rapidly and find crannies and crevices in human minds in which to lodge, perhaps to multiply, certainly to affect political life. The Middle East is no exception.

Before the Second World War, a volume in comparative government (say, of the Middle East, although in fact none had been written at that time) could have been written about constitutions, legal frameworks, institutional structures and patterns, parliamentary rules, and conventions, with no mention of the political forces that give life to a system. It is no longer possible to do this.

It is impossible to understand the Middle East today without trying to comprehend the hold that religion has on its people (the hold that finally forced Bourguiba in the fall of 1971 to abandon his efforts to control Ramadan), the pervasive and corrosive influence of nationalism, and the attempts at modernization through attachment to socialism. These are, of course, ideological, and the Middle East can be properly understood only through an attempt to understand the bases of its ideologies.

And, in the last quarter of this century, as Asia, Africa, and now Europe seem awash in the seas of terrorism, it is important to reexamine the ideological dimensions of dissent and to reevaluate the traditional notions of political legitimacy. Perhaps in the Middle East it is imperative to do so.

CHAPTER VIII

The Arab-Israeli Connection

THE MIDDLE EAST is a gigantic culture area surrounded by other culture areas markedly different from it: Black Africa, Europe, and Asia. The Arab World is part of the Middle East, but by no means all of it. Imbedded in, and near the center of, the Arab world is the small state of Israel, whose activities and conflicts with neighboring states sometimes absorb all the attention we give the Middle East. Such was the case in the summer and fall of 1982. The fact remains that in the long run Israel is but a small part of the Middle East, and its problems are of the same dimensions. The reason why the conflict termed Arab-Israeli has lasted as long as it has and has remained intractable is big-power interference. Henry Kissinger admits as much in a colorful description of his behavior during the 1973 war,[1] although he does so mellifluously, somewhat piously, a bit defensively, but also proudly. The 1973 war was indeed fought between Israelis and Arabs, but they were surrogates for Americans and Russians, flexing their muscles and testing their weapons. Gen. Ariel Sharon, Minister of Agriculture in the first Begin government and for a time Minister of Defense in the second, was Israel's finest tactical general. Able and very tough, ambitious and willing to take chances, he did not look much like a pawn, but that is what he was, in the sense that

---

[1] Henry Kissinger, *Years of Upheaval* (Boston: Little, Brown and Co., 1982), Chapters 11 and 12.

neither the 1973 war nor the 1982 invasion of Lebanon could have been fought successfully without American weapons, ammunition, and supplies. The case is equally if not more true of the Arabs. Syria did very well against Israeli weapons in the early stages of the 1973 war because the Russian weapons had a technological edge. In 1982, Syria's operations against the Israelis, at least in the air, were disastrous because the edge was gone; American weapons in Israeli hands easily outmatched Russian ones in Syrian hands. Thus weapons are tested. In short, when the moment comes that both the Soviet Union and the United States agree to contain their respective friends in and around Israel, the conflict will move to a back burner. The conflagration continues for several reasons, but among them are the flammables that the United States and the Soviet Union continue to toss into its midst. Someone like President Reagan (or any past American president, with the possible exception of Eisenhower) or Henry Kissinger will naturally blame the Russians and their ambitions. The fact is that the United States and the Soviet Union are equally active in deploying a policy that keeps this conflict alive.

What is meant by "Arab-Israeli conflict"? It might seem simple to define who the Israelis are, but there are problems here. Jewish Israelis predominate in Israel, and it is these who are most sensitive to a conflict and participate in its continuing construction and coloration. There are Arabs living in Israel, too. Some are not very loyal to Israel; others give little trouble and much lip-service to the Israeli authorities. Most of these are equally interested in the conflict but do not support an Israeli success. The Druze in Israel [2] are somewhat different. Some of them are indeed loyal to Israel and serve in the Israel Defense Forces, which other Arabs are not permitted to do. Whatever the attitudes of the Druze, they contribute little to the conflict. Israel itself has a diaspora of supporters worldwide. Most, but not all — Jerry Falwell considers himself such

---

[2] The Druze are adherents of a heretical offshoot of Shi'i Islam based on various mystical and concealed non-Islamic beliefs. They are concentrated in northern Israel and adjacent areas of Lebanon and Syria and are Arabs.

a supporter — are members of Jewish communities here and there in the world. These communities support Israel with money and sometimes people (a large number volunteered in 1973 to fight for Israel; a much smaller number in 1982). Naturally, they want the Israelis, with whom they have a very special bond, to be successful in their conflict with the Arabs.

Now who are the Arabs engaged in the conflict? Most Israelis can't resist telling a gullible visitor that all Arabs without exception, from Morocco on the west to Oman on the east, are the active and deadly enemies of Israel, and waiting to pounce. The unlikelihood of this should be apparent to most who think about what it means. But the statement makes excellent propaganda. (It is not unlike Mr. Reagan's oft-expressed conviction that there is a Russian behind every tree.)

Let us explore this a little further. King Hussein of Jordan is certainly an Arab and by this hypothesis is certainly an enemy (indeed he is an enemy but a cautious one). In 1970, when Hussein was in trouble fighting the Palestinians and Syrians, he asked the United States to ask Israel in turn for an air strike against the Syrians. The Israelis were not unwilling in principle, but the bargaining took too long, and the strike was never made. In the midst of the 1973 war between Syria and Israel, Hussein felt compelled to send a small force to aid the Syrians. He again asked the United States, through Great Britain, to ask Israel if it minded his putting in this symbolic force. These stories both come from Kissinger's memoirs, the first from *White House Years*[3] and the second from *Years of Upheaval*.[4] Kissinger's comment in the latter sums it all up:

> Only in the Middle East is it conceivable that a belligerent would ask its adversary's approval for engaging in an act of war against it. This, quipped Dinitz when I later submitted the proposition to him, was how "to fight with all of the con-

[3] Henry Kissinger, *White House Years* (Boston: Little, Brown and Co., 1979), Chapter 15, passim. It is only fair to say that the story must be inferred in Kissinger's account. The story of Hussein's request is even more specifically stated in William B. Quandt, *Decade of Decisions: American Policy Toward the Arab-Israeli Conflict 1967–1976* (Berkeley, Calif.: University of California Press, 1977), Chapter 4.

[4] Kissinger, *Years of Upheaval*, p. 506.

veniences." Predictably, the Israeli response a day later was to say no. One could not expect a nation fighting for survival formally to agree to the reinforcement of its enemies; *but the Israeli reply made no threat of retaliation or of expanding the war.*[5]

Strange enemies indeed!

Actually, the only serious military enemies the Israelis have had are Egypt, Jordan, and Syria.[6] The rest have either stayed out of the war, sent symbolic forces, or contributed money. No Arab state has been a friend over the years, but most have not acted out their animosities against Israel. If we referred to the Egyptian-Syrian-Jordanian-Palestinian–Israeli conflict instead of the Arab-Israeli conflict, there would still be ambiguity in the term.

What is the conflict itself? It is a confrontation whose nature has been continually changing. The conflict of 1948 is not at all the same as that of 1983. The Israelis, Egyptians, Syrians, Jordanians, and Palestinians of 1948 were not the same as they are in 1983. Both the participants and the quarrel have been transformed.

First, it is necessary to detail a concept that may already be familiar to many readers: Zionism. Israel is one of the very few states that can claim a religious raison d'être, but it is unique in that it was founded as a *national home* for those of one religion, in this case the Jews. The movement to create this national home was called Zionism. It came into existence largely because of the upsurge of anti-Semitism in late-nineteenth-century Europe. But anti-Semitism was less a religious movement than a racist one. Anti-Semites found their targets not merely in Jews per se, but in people they did not like or whom they feared or envied. They often identified these people as Jews and offered as evidence such flimsy things as names, physical appearance, associations, and ancestral religious practices. It would not be necessary to point this out here except that a national home for Jews would in practice have to be a

---

5 *Ibid*. Emphasis the authors'.

6 The Palestinians are, of course, enemies, but they are not a sovereign country.

national home for *all those oppressed by anti-Semites as Jews.*
As a result, Israel's population has always contained many who
are not very attached to Judaism as a religion; they may be
cultural Jews (in the same sense that there are cultural Christians or Muslims who may in fact be atheists) but nevertheless
fall into some category to which anti-Semites are hostile.

Anti-Semitism, an extremely complex concept and phenomenon, has been around for a long time. So has the Zionist idea
that the Jews should have a home (= state?) of their own
where they need not fear the discriminations, persecutions, and
pogroms that stud the long history of the Jewish people. It
came into focus in the 1890s with the Dreyfus case in France,
at least in the sense that it galvanized an Austrian journalist,
Theodor Herzl, into founding and leading the modern Zionist
movement. Herzl was a remarkable leader, and he succeeded in
persuading many of the justice of his cause. But those who increasingly called themselves Zionists were a varied lot; many
did not — nor do they today — agree as to what should constitute Zionism and what sort of home should be formed. Zionism was for the most part the creation of European and American Jews (the Ashkenazim) not of Oriental Jews (the Sephardim). The latter (60 percent of the Jewish population), ironically, outnumber them in Israel today, although the elite
remains the Ashkenazim.

Early Zionist meetings were often scenes of great discord and
argumentation. One of the first problems to be debated was
where the national home was to be. Several places were suggested — Uganda, Brazil, Sinai — but the Zionists soon agreed
that the national home should be in Palestine, the ancient
home of the Jews. Surely this is hardly surprising; moreover, it
was reasonable on all levels, and to many people other than
Jews. In the Balfour Declaration of November 1917, the British
government formally agreed to the idea of a national home for
the Jews in Palestine. The Declaration stipulated, however,
that the rights of neither Jews elsewhere nor of non-Jews in
Palestine were to be jeopardized by the establishment of a
national home in Palestine.

There were problems. "Palestine" was simply a vague geographical term. Moreover, it was not empty, although the early

Zionists adopted the slogan "The land without people — for the people without land." [7] The vast majority of its people were Arabized descendants of the ancient Canaanites and of the Philistines from whom the region takes its name. When Herzl began his crusade the Jews were a small minority. From the first to the nineteenth century A.D., they had often numbered no more than one or two thousand; in 1845 there were 11,000; in 1918 the Jewish community was 56,000, less than a tenth of the total population of about 600,000. Before the First World War Palestine was a part of the Ottoman Empire. After that conflict it was divided in two parts: Palestine, to the west of the River Jordan; and Trans-Jordan to the east. Great Britain administered both areas as League of Nations mandates.

The non-Jewish Palestinian residents at the end of the war were the kernel of the evolving population called the Palestinians today. They were almost entirely Arab, largely Muslim, and mainly farmers. Thus Zionists who came to Palestine to settle had to cope with a population that was already there. In the earliest days they had money to buy land; there was still enough to go around, and there was little friction between Arabs and Jews. Within a few years this began to change.

The conflict originally was nothing more than the friction that grew between two communities as one enlarged and expanded while the other found itself increasingly exploited and pressed for concessions. Arabs came to look upon the arriving Jews as "outsiders" and were frightened by them and the prospect of more of them. What did a national home mean? Arabs asked. How could Arabs compete with the financial resources, even if relatively modest, that came from abroad to help the Jewish community? How could they maintain their lands, their jobs, their sense of security in a land that had been theirs for centuries in the face of this peaceful invasion of outsiders?

Here was the first dimension of the conflict: the tensions between two communities, Jewish and Arab, one very small at the beginning, the other very large. The Zionists who came were mostly from Europe. Many were educated and had a wider

---

[7] Israel Zangwill, "The Return to Palestine," *New Liberal Review,* December 1901, p. 627.

variety of skills than did most of the Arabs. They were supported, too, from Jewish communities abroad. They were imbued with a drive to establish their dream with energy and determination. The example of Golda Meir is unusual only in the sense that she rose individually to far higher positions than have the great bulk of human beings. Born in Russia, she came as a small child to Milwaukee as an immigrant (her father was a carpenter). She was educated in Wisconsin, lived for a time in Colorado, became enamored with both Zionism and a young man named Meyerson, moved to New York, and in the early 1920s persuaded her husband to emigrate with her to Palestine. Her autobiography[8] describes the difficult life they led, the sacrifices they made, the pioneering spirit they possessed. Golda Meir had perhaps more drive than most Zionists and certainly most Arabs in Palestine. It was hard to compete with people like her.

This intercommunal conflict, because at first it was no more than that, was exacerbated by the emerging Arab nationalism that was alive not only in Palestine but in Lebanon, Syria, and Iraq, and indeed to one degree or another throughout the Arab world. Many Arabs had fought against the Turks in the First World War for what they thought was to be their independence. Great Britain played them false, and when the war ended Arabs found themselves almost everywhere under the control of either France or Great Britain. The first Arab national movement[9] was directed against the Turks; after the war it was redirected against the French and British. It is hardly surprising that later it found a target in the growing and threatening colony of Jews in Palestine.

Arab nationalism (*qawmiyya*) suggests that the Arabs are one people, not Syrians, Iraqis, Egyptians, or Palestinians. Like all nationalisms it extols the virtues of the insiders — the Arabs. As most Arabs are Muslims, it was easy to connect up the greatness of Islam with the nation of Arabs. Nationalists must have targets to prosper, and as suggested above they were easy to find.

---

[8] Golda Meir, *My Life* (New York: G. P. Putnam's Sons, 1975).
[9] See George Antonius, *The Arab Awakening: The Story of the Arab National Movement* (Beirut: Khayat's, 1938; reprinted 1955).

What is not as well recognized is that Zionism was in effect a Jewish nationalism, with the usual characteristics of other nationalisms. The Jews considered themselves a chosen people, whose language was Hebrew (which many had to learn). They too, like the Arabs, had many virtues. They had made distinguished contributions to Western arts and science. They had in Judaism one of the oldest religions in the world, a religion great enough to spawn two other great religions, Christianity and Islam. Jews historically had been a target; Hitler was only the latest, and perhaps the worst, in a long list of individuals and peoples who had discriminated against and persecuted the Jews.

Nationalism is a cementing ideology. It gave Zionism the energy to survive and to achieve. Today for Jews living in Israel, and for many who do not, there is no question of whether or not an Israeli nationalism exists. What Israeli nationalism has done has been to turn all of the many historical enemies of Jews into Arabs. The Arabs have become *the* enemy of Jews, the target that all nationalisms need.[10]

The Arabs, of course, find it a very remarkable transmogrification that they have been made, like the ancient Israelitic scapegoat, to bear the accumulation of emotional and ideological baggage of Jewish discrimination and persecution. Why the Arabs? The answer is simple. They were there, and the Germans, Russians, and others were not.

Thus by the 1920s the conflict was one of interests and nationalisms. The British recognized that there was a problem and made efforts to get the Palestinian communities to work together. It must be said that from the earliest days Jewish Palestinian organization and leadership were very much superior to those of the Arab Palestinians. Whatever else is said of Yasser Arafat, the leader of the Palestine Liberation Organization (PLO), he has been the most effective leader the Palestinian Arabs ever had.

Had Hitler not come to power in 1933 it is entirely possible

10 The Israelis have more or less made up with Germany. And in 1982, admittedly with difficulties, Zubin Mehta and the Israeli Philharmonic Orchestra played Wagner!

that there would never have been an Israel. By the late 1920s Jewish immigration into Palestine had fallen to a trickle. As Americans we are all the "sons and daughters of immigrants," as Franklin Roosevelt once told a DAR convention. Our ancestors left their homelands because of persecution, or famine, or the threat of war, or the lack of opportunities. But Palestine in 1920 was not a land of opportunity as America has been to many. It was a land of sacrifice and difficulty. It would be unnatural to expect Jews in America or Europe or wherever, in the absence of conditions of harassment and discrimination, to leave for Palestine *unless* their dedication to Zionist ideals was so very great as to make sacrifice and hard work literally an attraction. Most Jews are not that dedicated to Zionism; in 1982 there were nearly twice as many Jews living in the United States as in Israel. There are large numbers of Sabras (Israelis born in Israel) who now make America their national home. According to reliable estimates at least 300,000 and possibly as many as a half-million Israelis have chosen to emigrate.[11]

Without the rise of Nazism in Germany, the great exodus of European Jews would not have occurred, nor would the Holocaust have taken place. In the decade before Hitler came to power in 1933, Jewish immigration to Palestine totaled 95,300. During the five years after 1933 no less than a quarter million entered (66,000 of them illegally).[12] The flow slowed drastically in 1939 with the implementing of the British White Paper restricting Jewish immigration to no more than 15,000 annually. The conflict had already produced violence, bitterness, and an intractable problem for the British in Palestine.

There was a great deal of ugliness in this situation, and both sides were guilty of excesses. Terrorism accompanied the political disputes; lives were lost and property was destroyed. By the end of the Second World War, Great Britain found itself unable any longer to bear the heavy responsibilities of empire.

[11] Clifford E. Gladstein, "Israeli Emigration: A Study in Fact, Fiction, and Consequence," master's thesis, The University of Texas, Austin, Texas, 1982; Chapter II. According to Israeli's Central Bureau of Statistics, the rate of emigration declined from 31,800 in 1980 to 7,400 in 1982.

[12] These data are from Edwin (Viscount) Samuel, *A Lifetime in Jerusalem* (London: Vallentine, Mitchell, 1970), pp. 153–154.

These responsibilities were especially heavy in Palestine, where the British had not succeeded in establishing rapport with either of the communities and were forced to station 100,000 troops in an effort to maintain order. In May 1948 the British withdrew and left the Jews and Arabs to fight it out among themselves.[13] Arab villages and Jewish kibbutzim were both targets of armed squads, and many of them became victims of the violence that swept the country. Because the Jews (now the Israelis) won, they were able to reestablish their own communities. For the Arab Palestinians, the consequences of the fighting were more complicated. Some remained in Israel. Some were already in Jordanian-controlled (the West Bank) or Egyptian-controlled (Gaza) territory. Others became refugees in one or another of the surrounding Arab countries by being driven from their homes or by fleeing to some sanctuary. Israel was established as a state, and many Palestinians who had lived in Israeli territory were now homeless.

There was now another dimension to the Arab-Israeli conflict. Until 1948 the conflict had its roots in the Arabs' unhappiness and fear over the flooding of their land with Zionist settlers, coupled with the spin-off energies of the clash between two cultures and two nationalisms. With the 1948 war, the conflict had to be defined in terms of the creation of a new group of refugees, the Palestinians, many of whom had lost their homes and their property. Others had lost their lives.

What the Israelis call their war of independence in 1948–1949 created about 700,000 homeless Arabs. In subsequent years the number of Palestinian refugees has naturally increased.[14] Some refugees fled to neighboring Arab countries, but they were

---

[13] William Roger Louis, *The British Empire and the Middle East, 1945–1951* (London: Oxford University Press, 1983) contains the definitive account based on the archives.

[14] No census has ever been taken of the Palestinians. The volume *A Compassionate Peace*, published for the American Friends Service Committee (New York: Hill and Wang, 1982) gives the following figures: Israel, .5 million; West Bank and Gaza, 1.25 million; Jordan, 1.1 million; Lebanon, 300,000; Syria, 180,000; Kuwait, 170,000; Egypt, 40,000; Saudi Arabia and Persian Gulf states, 45,000; Iraq, 16,000; Libya, 7,000; Europe and the Americas, 50,000. Other informed estimates show substantially higher figures, totaling about 4 million.

not particularly welcomed or well treated there. The main political argument used by Arab countries in not absorbing Palestinian refugees was that to do so would in effect serve Israel's cause by lessening the pressure on it to permit the Palestinians to return to their homes and to compensate them for their losses. In fact the refugees were political pawns, and life for many of them and for their descendants was harsh. Those left behind in Israeli territory were reduced to the status of second-class citizens.

The Palestinian issue was clear in 1949 and has since changed in only minor details. In essence, the Arabs say of the Palestinians that (1) they were driven from their homes; (2) they should have the right to return; (3) they should be compensated for the loss of their property; (4) they should have the right to establish a Palestinian state, or "entity," on Palestinian soil; and (5) no final settlement of the Arab-Israeli dispute can be had until these rights are recognized.

The Israelis, on the other hand, argue that (1) the original Palestinian refugees left voluntarily and in effect abandoned their homes and property; (2) it would be politically impossible for Israel to take them back and economically impossible to pay the inflated Arab claims for property lost; and (3) the establishment in or contiguous to Israel of an independent Palestinian state, possibly bent on the subversion or destruction of Israel, is impossible to contemplate. As of 1983, the Israeli government refuses to negotiate or deliberate with the PLO at all, ostensibly on the grounds that it is a terrorist organization but actually in order to prevent any sort of Palestinian state from emerging. The Israelis do not want a Palestinian state under any circumstances; what they wanted for themselves they deny to another people.[15]

---

[15] With reference to the earlier (1973) Geneva Conference, in which Arabs and Israelis (and others) together would forge peace, Kissinger has this delightful quote: "The enthusiasm of the Israelis, who had long demanded such a meeting, diminished directly in proportion to its imminence." *Years of Upheaval*, p. 747. Needless to say, nothing came of the Geneva Conference. In early 1983 another conference, involving Israel, the United States, and Lebanon, and convened for the purpose of ridding Lebanon of foreign troops, dragged on inconclusively; the Begin government was hardly unhappy about this.

The above delineation was the core of the problem. But the 1948–1949 war produced other issues that became a part of the expanded conflict. Although unconcerned with Palestinian rights, the Israelis fully expected, since they had won the war against the Arab states, to be an accepted part of the Middle East. Israel wanted, and continues to want, its legitimate right to exist to be recognized at least by its principal Arab neighbors. Egypt in 1979 actually did this (there has been an exchange of ambassadors), but no other Arab state has done so. Still, 1983 is far removed from 1949. It is possible to imagine, after some *quids* and *quos,* the Arab world finally accepting an Israel, but not without some basic concessions from the Israelis.[16]

At various times and to varying degrees, the Israelis and the Arabs have been afraid of each other. The early Israel had every reason to be concerned about continuing hostilities. Although it certainly won its war, it did so barely; there was no compelling reason to believe that it would be able to defeat future attacks easily. Arab rhetoric about what the Arabs intended to do helped create a kind of Masada complex. In 1949 the Israelis probably did quite sincerely believe in *shalom* (peace). The Arabs were also afraid of the Israelis and had strong notions about Israeli expansionism and warlike activity. After the 1956 and 1967 wars, in which Arab arms were bested so effortlessly by Israel, many Arabs developed a fear that would not go away. Yet, as Ezer Weizman has said,[17] probably the "war of attrition" in 1969–1970 resulted in defeat for the Israelis, although Egypt paid a frightful price in destruction and carnage for its "victory." The 1973 war, also, was not easily classified as an Israeli victory. The Israelis have known this if no one else has. The following quotation from Kissinger is of interest:[18]

[16] Israel bought off its chief enemy, Egypt, by returning the Sinai, but the price of similarly accommodating Jordan and Syria (to say nothing of the Palestinians) by returning the West Bank and the Golan Heights seems to the Israelis to be too high.

[17] See also Yaacov Bar-Siman-Tov, *The Israeli-Egyptian War of Attrition, 1969–1970* (New York: Columbia University Press, 1980) for a full account.

[18] Kissinger, *Years of Upheaval,* p. 560.

I have often been asked to describe the most moving moment of my government service. It is difficult to compare memorable events in such a variety of cultural and political settings. Yet surely my arrival in Israel on Monday, October 22, 1973 ranks high on the list.

We reached Lod (now Ben-Gurion) Airport in Tel Aviv at 1:00 p.m. local time. Much was written afterward about how eager Israel was to continue the war and how painful it found the cease-fire. No one would have guessed that from our reception. Soldiers and civilians greeted the approaching peace as the highest blessing. Israel was heroic but its endurance was reaching the breaking point. Those who had come to welcome us seemed to feel viscerally how close to the abyss they had come and how two weeks of war had drained them. Small groups of servicemen and civilians were applauding with tears in their eyes. Their expression showed a weariness that almost tangibly conveyed the limits of human endurance. Israel was exhausted no matter what the military maps showed. Its people were yearning for peace as can only those who have never known it.

The 1973 war led, of course, to Camp David and ultimately to the return of Sinai to Egypt.

With the advent of the Begin government in 1977, Arab fears increased because Begin's terrorist background with the Irgun and his long-time leadership of the right-wing Herut party were a discomforting combination with what had become a first-class fighting machine. His government has not disabused them. He has made threats in all directions, attacked Lebanon (the PLO there being targeted) repeatedly, bombed gratuitously an Iraqi nuclear facility, and in the early summer of 1982 launched a full-scale attack into Lebanon, destroying West Beirut in the process. It should be remembered that today Israel has the finest army in the region (and the fourth most powerful in the world), supplied with the most sophisticated arms from an American arsenal. There is every reason for current Arab fears.

All of this adds another element to the conflict. If most Israelis want *shalom,* most Arabs want *salaam:* peace. Successive wars, now six of them over some 35 years, are growing old for all.

After 1967 several similar issues emerged. In the 1967 war

Israel conquered Sinai and Gaza from Egypt, the West Bank from Jordan, and the Golan from Syria. Leaving aside the West Bank and Gaza, as part of original Palestine, this conquest resulted in the Israelis' holding Egyptian and Syrian territory for the first time. They didn't want to give it back, or could not. The Sinai has now been returned; but the Israelis first extended their own law to the area of Golan they held and later annexed it. This act makes Syria a permanent enemy. When the West Bank was taken in 1967 Old Jerusalem fell into Israeli hands.

Jerusalem is a special case. Unfortunately, it has deep religious meaning to Jews, Christians, and Muslims alike. It is easily forgotten that all three of these religions believe in the same deity; Muhammad, indeed, conceived of his seventh-century mission as bringing together Christians and Jews as believers in their God's later messages (the Quran). In this he was unsuccessful. Many Jews, Christians, and Muslims see their particular dogmas as ultimate truths, and there is no prospect of reconciliation of their differences. In the meantime, most awkwardly, they all cherish the Old City of Jerusalem. Logically, the Muslims should control it since they accept many of the historical Jewish and Christian leaders and beliefs as their own; Jesus is a major prophet in Islam. But whoever controls the Old City, all should be free to enter it, to worship there, and to leave without hindrance or harassment. It is easy to construct a reasonable solution of this problem: a joint Jewish-Christian-Muslim control comes instantly to mind, or perhaps an international administration. Among Muslim Arabs — the Saudis, notably — the status of Jerusalem is a very important issue indeed, and it surely is an issue of some significance to all Muslims, Arab or otherwise, wherever they are to be found. A solution will have to be found for it in the ultimate accommodation.

There was still another political dimension to the conflict and its settlement. Israel is open to the Mediterranean, but its outlet to the Indian Ocean and beyond is contingent upon two passages being free and open. The Straits of Tiran, off Sharm al-Shaykh, where the Gulf of Aqaba joins the Gulf of Suez to form the Red Sea, is the first major narrows through which

Israeli shipping from the port of Elath must pass. The second
lies off Yemen at the southern exit of the Red Sea and is called
the Bab al-Mandab. The Egyptians have from time to time
blocked the Gulf of Aqaba, and this has led to war with the
Israelis. The Israelis argue that international waterways should
be open to all flags. This argument applies also to the Suez
Canal (under Egyptian control since 1956). As far as Egypt is
concerned, this issue was settled by the 1979 peace treaty with
Israel. The canal is open to Israeli flags and cargoes; the Egyptians have agreed not to close the Straits of Tiran again. But
those straits could be closed by Saudi Arabia, although it is
highly unlikely, and the Bab al-Mandab could conceivably be
closed by some other Arab state, such as South Yemen. Thus
the issue, though dormant at the moment, awaits a final settlement.

In 1981 and 1982, actions of the Israeli government raised
several new issues that complicate any final accommodation of
the conflict. An Iraqi nuclear facility was bombed and destroyed by Israeli planes on 7 June 1981. The justification of
this act by Prime Minister Begin was that this facility *might*
make nuclear weapons, which in turn *might* be used against
Israel. Israel, itself a nuclear power possessing nuclear weapons,
has persistently refused to sign the Nuclear Non-Proliferation
Treaty (Iraq is a signatory) or to permit inspection of its nuclear installations by the UN Atomic Energy Agency. The attack on Iraq was unanimously condemned on June 19 by the
UN Security Council. Israel, nevertheless, stated in the days
that followed that no Arab state would be permitted to possess
such weapons or the means to produce them. This grandiose
talk can hardly mean much in the long run, but obviously in
any settlement of the conflict such a policy would have to be
specifically renounced by the Israelis.

There seems little doubt that the Israelis would like to re-
draw the map of Lebanon a bit. For the past several years they
have maintained the Lebanese territory south of the Litani
River as a buffer area run by a Lebanese Christian puppet (the
word does not seem too strong), Major Saad Haddad. On 6
June 1982 Israel launched a major attack into Lebanon, which
carried it to Beirut and the Bekaa Valley. It fought relatively

few Lebanese, but many Palestinians and Syrians. Israel would like to reconstruct Lebanon, if possible, as a Christian state, with the Muslims scattered and well under control. The prospects of this are dim at best. Indeed the situation is so fluid that it would be absurd to make precise predictions at this time (early 1983). Yet this issue of Lebanon is also part of the contemporary conflict.

Let us recapitulate. The Arabs require:

1. The right of Palestinians to have a home (= state) of their own.

2. The right of Palestinians to return to their original homes and/or to be compensated for property losses.

3. The freeing of Jerusalem (the Old City is meant here) from Israeli control.

4. The return to Syria of the Golan and to Arab hegemony the Palestinian territories of Gaza and the West Bank (in other words, a return to the 1967 borders).

5. The assurance that Israel will not attempt to interfere in the internal affairs of contiguous and near-contiguous Arab states.

6. The guarantee that Israeli military adventurism will cease.

The Israelis, on the other hand, require:

1. That the Palestinians not have a separate state of their own.

2. That Judea and Samaria (that is, the West Bank) as well as Gaza will remain under Israeli military control.

3. The end of PLO or any other kind of Arab terrorism against Israel.

4. That the Arab world accept the legitimate existence of Israel.

5. That the threat of war against Israel by Arab states cease.

6. That some sort of defendable border between Israel and its Arab neighbors be maintained.

7. That Israeli shipping in international waterways not be hindered.

8. That Old Jerusalem remain under Israeli control.

It is readily apparent that these two sets of requirements are irreconcilable without major concessions on all sides. It is also clear that Arabs and Israelis alone will be unable to come to any concessionary meeting of minds, at least in this generation. In another 50 years the environmental situation may well have changed so much that a solution will not be so difficult to negotiate. Meanwhile only the superpowers — primarily the United States and to a lesser but real extent the Soviet Union — can force a settlement between the Israelis and the Arabs.

THE ARAB-ISRAELI WARS

War is a violent, armed conflict of major dimensions that usually lasts for a considerable period of time. Without questioning von Clausewitz' famous dictum that war is but "the continuation of political intercourse with the admixture of other means," the distinct differences between military conflict and what may be called political war, economic war, or ideological war should be recognized.

A battle is normally thought to be a clash at arms of relatively short duration and usually, but not always, a part of a larger conflict (war). The question then arises whether there have been a half-dozen Arab-Israeli wars, or one war with a half-dozen major battles. If the latter is true, one historical parallel instantly comes to mind: the so-called Thirty Years' War, from 1618 to 1648, which involved much of northwestern Europe, in which many battles were fought. And the negotiations that ended it (culminating in the Peace of Westphalia) dragged on for four years. Armed conflicts have punctuated the Arab-Israeli imbroglio over a period of approximately 35 years. The flash-points of violence — in 1948–1949, in 1956, in 1967, in 1969–1970, in 1973, and in 1982 — are customarily referred to as separate wars rather than battles, but the point is debatable.

In discussing these wars, the significance of the terms "tactical" and "strategic" should be kept clear. After every war there is usually some discussion as to exactly who won, and what was won. It is not always simple to come to a clear, unambiguous judgment. If, for example, one looks today at Japan and the Federal Republic of Germany, one may well wonder to what degree they in fact lost the Second World War! The concepts of "tactical and strategic victories and losses" are important to a full understanding of the many conflicts which the Israelis have now had with some Arabs. A "strategic victory" with respect to some event or series of events means that, seen from the perspective of some country, its long-range interests and goals have been enhanced, made more viable and more likely of achievement. Conversely, something that does not enhance these long-range interests cannot be held to be a strategic victory; it may indeed be a serious strategic loss. The term "tactical" refers to short-run objects that are gained, in this case by military means. Every Israeli colonel — for that matter any officer in any army — would say that the first aim of a commander is to win a battle. If done, it is called a tactical success; if not, a tactical failure. It is sometimes said that Bobby Lee won every battle but lost the war; this is not quite true and a bit unfair to the Union generals involved, but there is enough truth to illustrate the point here. A brilliant tactical military victory may be (or become) a major strategic loss. The most brilliant war that Israel has won was the 1967 June War; yet it unquestionably was a strategic loss of major dimensions. Some Israelis haven't realized it yet.

In considering these "wars," one should resist the impulse to blame one side or another — to try to identify the white and the black hats — in terms of who started the particular conflict or what was done in it. Political science is primarily concerned with what happened and why. In Dean Acheson's words, the important thing in thinking about international affairs "is not to make moral judgments or apportion the blame, but to understand the forces which are at work as a basis for determining what, if anything, can be done."

The following is a list of who initiated each of the six conflicts:

1. The Israeli 1948–1949 war of independence began as an internal war between Palestinians and Jews, with no identifiable beginning date and no obvious aggressor. The new state of Israel was attacked from outside by Egypt and Jordan in a major war; other Arab states were involved in minor ways.

2. The Weekend War of 1956 was a clear case of Israeli aggression against Egypt.

3. The June War of 1967 found the Israelis making a pre-emptive air strike that destroyed the Egyptian air force. But they were certainly provoked by Nasser and his rhetoric, and one can only say that each side seems equally to blame. (Begin himself, however, has termed the war simply as an attack on Egypt.)

4. The War of Attrition (centering around the Suez Canal), 1969–1970 was an Egyptian idea.

5. In 1973 it was an Egyptian and Syrian attack on Israel that achieved tactical surprise against the Israelis. The Israelis often call this the Yom Kippur War; to the Arabs it is the Ramadan War.

6. The Israelis plainly were the aggressors in the 1982 incursion into Lebanon.

Some of these specific conclusions may be challenged, but most reasonable observers would accept the fact that both sides have resorted to conflict when it suited their purposes. War occurs when other methods of achieving goals fail, or seem to fail, and no nation has a monopoly on virtue here.

A common observation about the various wars is that Arabs could never finally lose one and the Israelis could never finally win one. That merely means that it is conceivable that Israel could be destroyed (here we are not talking about *nuclear* options), which would be the final (?) victory for Arab arms, but no one can imagine the Israelis destroying the Arabs — all those stretching from Morocco to the Persian Gulf — claimed by Israel to be its enemies. Thus, no matter how militarily successful Israeli arms may seem to be in any specific encounter, there is always some new dark cloud of conflict forming on the horizon. Israel can never achieve final peace with its Arab neighbors by arms alone.

Looking at the wars that Israelis and Arabs have fought with one another, one is struck by how good the Israeli Defense Forces really are. It is today the finest army (in Israel the army includes navy and air force) in the Middle East, and in terms of modern sophisticated equipment the fourth strongest army in the world (after the United States, the Soviet Union, and China). This was not always so. It has grown to be an effective army from very humble beginnings.

With the exception of the Jordanian Arab Legion, the quality of Arab armies was mediocre around 1948. They are considerably better today, but it is difficult to measure how strong an army is until it fights, and then all sorts of factors come into play. Conclusions about effectiveness continue to be elusive.

There remains the plain fact that Israelis usually, but not always, win military conflicts they become involved in. (We refer here to tactical victories.) The question naturally arises why this is so. Several explanations have been suggested. One is that an Israeli qua Israeli is simply innately a better soldier than an Arab qua Arab. Another explanation is that there has been a general gap technologically between Israelis and Arabs. A case can be made for this but not a really strong one. In 1948 the Syrian army was new to independence, not well equipped, and dependent upon somewhat outmoded French military ideas. The Jordanian army in 1948 was basically officered by the British, but by the time of the second Jordanian-Israeli conflict, in 1967, the British were gone and in their place were Jordanian officers of relatively little experience. Yet the Israelis say that the Jordanians have been their most professional opponents.

The Egyptian army in 1948 wasn't yet independent; its officer ranks were riddled with old cronies of the king. It was mediocre at best. One of the young officers of the 1952 coup in Egypt, Major Abdal-Hakim Amer, later rose quickly to the rank of Field Marshal, a rank for which he was unqualified.

The Israeli high command in 1948 had its deficiencies, although Yigael Allon was highly competent. The army suffered from interference from David Ben-Gurion, the prime minister, and from adventurers of whom Moshe Dayan was merely the most flamboyant and successful. It was only after the 1948–1949 war that Israel found a top-notch chief of staff in Yigael Yadin, who rebuilt the armed forces along professional lines, ultimately to be followed by Dayan, who gave the army panache, élan, and perhaps some *chutzpah*. The 1967 war was led by the very competent Yitzhak Rabin, with an air force built by Ezer Weizman, and in all the wars from the 1950s on the Israelis have had the services of the talented tactical general, Ariel Sharon. All of these officers — 100 percent of the higher ranks — were Ashkenazim. They were indeed better educated than the Sephardim and more aware of the implications of being modern.

Certainly, having their backs to the wall in 1948–1949 was also an advantage to the Israelis. But the most important factor, it would seem, is that Israel was a state in becoming. There were no traditional rules to follow; young men with energy and imagination had opportunities to gain experience and could come up with non-textbook solutions to military problems. One is reminded, although such parallels are never fully trustworthy, of the American army in the Revolutionary War and, nearly 100 years later, the Union generals — Grant, Sherman, and Sheridan — who changed the nature of war; and also of the young Red Army of the 1920s, the Japanese armed forces both before the First World War and in the beginning months of the Second. There are many examples of Israeli spontaneity, on-the-spot brilliance, willingness to take chances, but most important, the ability to change methods and tactics in the midst of battle. Nothing better illustrates this than the Israelis' change in armored tactics in the middle of the 1973 war. The fact that the United States, with its resupply of Israeli materiel, in a sense permitted this, does not negate the fact that they did it.

Is this a technological gap? The Arab armies and their leadership had many old ideas to overcome. Victory in war is sometimes a matter of confidence, and the Arabs have rarely had it since 1948.

In an extension of this idea, the Egyptians are a case in point. In 1948 the Egyptian army was equipped with arms, trucks, and other materiel cast off by the Americans and British after the Second World War. Their officers had no combat experience; such ideas about military science as they had came from the British. After Nasser came to power, he recruited German ex-officers to design a defense system in Sinai and to give tactical advice in the retraining of the Egyptian army. This was shown to be wanting in 1956, and Nasser turned to the Russians. The Russians thought they had won the war against the Germans in 1945 by the sacrifice of hundreds of thousands of foot soldiers who advanced in wave after wave. Should the Egyptians not do this? After all, they had plenty of people as compared with the Israelis, in addition to equipment. This thinking collapsed in 1973. Today Egypt, under Hosni Mubarak, is at least flirting with American arms and military principles. Meanwhile, the Israelis have devised their own principles.

In any event, there has been a gap in achievement in many fields. The Israelis lead the world in water-desalination technology, in laser-induced isotope separation, and in certain minor phases of computer technology. They have built their own fighter aircraft, albeit with American engines, and their own tanks, trucks, and small arms. Admittedly, they prefer to have F-15s and F-16s, AWACS, and so on from the United States; nevertheless, no other Middle Eastern state has done so much on its own. The skills learned have paid off.

Some technical observations:

1. The Israeli armed forces are "citizen" in nature. Literally everyone, including women, belong, and are all expected to do their duty. Arab armies tend to be made up of full-time professional soldiers. One might expect the latter to be superior, but they are not. Noncommissioned ranks are usually conscripts, often (but not always) peasants and illiterate. The Israelis, by drawing upon the contributions of the great mass of their civilian population in times of emergency, have waged war that is supported because "everyone" is in it. (In 1982 there was much dissension in and out of the army over the war, but there was never full mobilization; in any case this dissension is unusual.) Arab armies fight without the same sense of commitment and psychological sense of participation back home. There is no doubt that the quality of the armies is a function of all this.

2. Israel has won because it has usually had superiority in the quality of its arms. This was not true in 1948–1949, but in all the subsequent wars, with the possible exception of the early days of the 1973 war, they have had better aircraft, bet-

ter tanks, and more troops than their adversaries have had. This was particularly true in 1982.

3. Although Israel is a small state with a small population (4,055,000 at the end of 1982, of whom 3,300,000 were Jews), so also are Lebanon, Syria, and Jordan (even Saudi Arabia, its close neighbor, is small in population). The exception is Egypt. Although the arable portions of Egypt are only about 5 percent of its total area, its population today is approximately 44 million. The proportion of GNP spent by Israel on defense is staggering: nearly one fourth. The most important point here is that in their battles over the years with Egyptians, Syrians, and Jordanians, the Israelis have been able to concentrate locally a superiority of men, tanks, and guns. This has often given them victory.

4. The air weapon played no significant role in 1948–1949. The Egyptians had almost no air cover in 1956 and none whatever in 1967. In 1973 the Israelis lost their air superiority, at least for a time. In 1982 the Palestinians had no air force, and the Syrians were quickly routed. Air superiority has often been a key factor.

Let us now comment briefly on the individual wars and their objectives.

Israel proclaimed itself a state in May 1948 upon the departure of the British. International diplomacy had attempted to partition Palestine into a state for Palestinian Jews and one for Palestinian Arabs. Some sort of internal or civil conflict between Arab and Israeli factions was to be expected, ending in victory for the Israelis, who were far better organized than the Palestinians, who even let the opportunity slip by to form a state of their own. The situation was altered, however, by the entry into the conflict of Egypt and Jordan (Syria and Iraq were involved in a minor way; Lebanon pretended to be; no other Arab state did anything). The motives of Egypt and Jordan were not purely altruistic, in the sense of seeking to liberate the Palestinians. Both wanted to grab as much Palestinian territory as they could. The Arab Legion was successful in acquiring the West Bank and the Old City of Jerusalem. Egypt ended up with only the Gaza Strip, next to Sinai along the Mediterranean. It was a relatively short war interrupted by several truces. The Israelis won their war of independence, although they were not strong enough to push the Jordanians back or to expel the Egyptians. It was an immense strategic victory for them.

By 1956 the Israelis had a much better army than in 1948–1949, while the Arab armies had not improved much. Arab nationalism was now very alive, and the Nasserite period had begun in Egypt. Palestinians had mounted small-scale but annoying raids into Israeli territory. The Egyptian-Czech arms deal of 1955 disturbed the Israelis, and their worry increased when the Russians also agreed to supply modern weapons to Egypt. These events, in the Israelis' view, begged for some forceful response.

Israel's inclination received powerful encouragement from the British and French, who were determined to recover by force the Suez Canal, which had been nationalized by Nasser, quite legally, in July 1956. They devised an overly-clever plan that ended in confusion. They proposed an Israeli attack on Sinai, ostensibly threatening the canal, while they themselves would make an air and naval assault on the canal from their staging point in Cyprus. Concealing from the world their collusion with the Israelis, they would gruffly order the Israelis *and* the Egyptians to approach the canal no closer than ten miles. The Israelis agreed to the strategy on condition that a French air squadron be stationed at Lod airfield to protect Tel Aviv from air attack. (It was never used.)

In October, the Israelis attacked, followed with some delay by the French and British. The Egyptians were no match for this coalition. The Egyptians have always claimed that they deliberately abandoned the Sinai to oppose the Anglo-French attack; the Israelis argue that they drove the Egyptians out. The British and French incurred the opprobrium of much of the world, and were deserted politically by the United States. Dwight D. Eisenhower was furious that, uninformed, he found a war beginning at the height of his campaign for reelection as president.

The British and French troops were evacuated under UN pressure. The Israelis were forced, largely by Eisenhower, to give up Sinai in early 1957. Israel gained from the war formal guarantees that the Gulf of Aqaba would be open to Israeli shipping, and also a sense of military superiority over the Egyptians.

Eleven years of uneasy "peace" followed, punctuated by belligerent rhetoric, raids, and reprisals. Nasser meanwhile became the charismatic leader of Arab nationalism, campaigning for Arab unity and promising the Arabs fulfillment of their aspirations through their attachment to his cause. By 1967 he was well armed by the Russians and, presumably, prepared for combat with the Israelis. There is much evidence that he did not want war with Israel at this time. In retrospect, however, it is clear that he made four serious mistakes:

1. He had become involved in a civil war in Yemen, and some 70,000 of his best troops were there, as well as much military equipment.

2. He was carried away by his own rhetoric. Words are sometimes used as a substitute for combat, and Nasser's words in the late spring of 1967 were provocative to the point of foolish bravado.

3. He demanded that the UN Emergency Force troops, stationed along the eastern and southern reaches of Sinai since 1957, should leave. Probably he expected that the UN would refuse, or temporize; instead, the force promptly withdrew, removing the buffer between the Egyptian and Israeli armies.

4. Notwithstanding his now dangerously exposed position, Nasser closed the Straits of Tiran, blocking the exit of Israeli shipping from the Gulf of Aqaba. Israel had made publicly clear that it would consider this move an act of war.

Plans for the Israeli air attack on 5 June were astutely based on efficient military intelligence. It was timed for the exact moment when Egyptian pilots had just landed from their routine morning reconnaissance flights and were relaxing over coffee or tea, while their generals had not yet made their way through Cairo's congested streets to their headquarters. The Israeli air force hit the Egyptian airfields so effectively that within several hours the entire Egyptian air force had been destroyed. This made the land war in Sinai child's play for the

Israelis. Without air cover the Egyptian forces in Sinai were doomed, and the Israeli army was on the banks of the Suez Canal within three days. King Hussein had, on 30 May, signed a defense pact with Nasser and placed the Arab Legion under Egyptian command. Upon the outbreak of hostilities, Jordanian artillery shelled the New City of Jerusalem. Israel retaliated with an invasion that placed the entire West Bank, including the Arab quarter of Jerusalem, under Israeli control. After some debate, the Israeli high command regrouped its forces and attacked the Syrians on the Golan heights, from where the Syrians could bombard Israeli towns and farms on the plains below. Thought virtually impregnable by some military analysts, the Golan was conquered by the Israelis in 24 hours. All in all, it was the Israelis' most brilliant tactical victory. They had a considerable body of world opinion behind them, but it was the last war in which a friendly world community welcomed their victory.

They had captured, by military force, portions of the national territory of Egypt and Syria, in clear violation of a basic principle of the UN Charter. The implacable enmity of these neighbors was thereby assured so long as this territory remained in Israeli hands. Israel's refusal to relinquish it, in defiance of insistent demands of the UN Security Council and General Assembly, contributed to destroying the broad and profitable network of international relations Israel had patiently built up over two decades; by 1983 the only reliable friend of any consequence Israel had left was the United States.

The West Bank and Gaza Strip had ostensibly been held by Jordan and Egypt in trust for the Palestinians. The seizure of these lands by Israel obliged the Palestinians to abandon trust in the Arab states as champions of their cause. Under dynamic new leadership, the Palestine Liberation Organization asserted control of the Palestinians' own struggle to regain their homeland. There was no longer any possible question that they comprised a distinct nation with its own national interests. Palestinian interests, it soon became clear, clashed with those of Jordan, Syria, and Lebanon, and military confrontations between Palestinian guerrillas and forces of these three countries (on a larger scale than the pin-prick encounters between Palestinians and Israelis) extinguished any realistic expectation that the Palestinians could eventually be absorbed in the Arab states surrounding Israel. The hostile population of the occupied territories[19] could be controlled only by naked force, and the repressive administration further damaged Israel's international image.

More seriously, Israel adopted a policy of settling its own citizens in these territories, preventing economic and agricultural enterprise by the indigenous residents, and integrating the infrastructure into Israel's own. By late 1982, 103 settlements had been established in the West Bank alone, with an Israeli population of approximately 25,000. It was calculated that if the number were brought to 100,000 no future Israeli government would be able to give up the territory.[20]

The Old City of Jerusalem, on the West Bank, is a unique case. The city is sacred to Islam, and the Muslim world will never be satisfied to see it completely in the hands of non-Muslims. It will poison the relations of Israel with Muslim states and will almost certainly remain a potentially explosive issue for many years to come.

The war thus placed new and grave obstacles in the way of attaining Israel's true long-term national goals of being accepted by its neighbors and living at peace with them. In the fall of 1967 King Hussein toured the world's capitals and, speaking for Nasser as well as himself, asserted forcefully that Israel could have land or peace, but never both. The assertion appears as valid today as in 1967. Concrete confirmation was to come in 1979 with the signing of a peace treaty between Egypt and Israel by which the Sinai Peninsula was returned to Egypt. The evacuation, conducted in phases, was completed in April 1982. Peace and the restoration of Egyptian territory however, came only at the price of two intervening wars.

The 1967 war produced short-term gains for Israel. In addition to the euphoria provided by its brilliant military success, Israel was able to exploit the Sinai's oil resources; the expense and uncertainty of its fuel supply were substantially eased. The

---

[19] About 800,000 in the West Bank and a half-million in the Gaza Strip.
[20] *The Christian Science Monitor,* 10 November 1982.

Straits of Tiran were reopened, probably for good. Nasser's stature as a viable leader of the Arab world slumped dramatically. Nevertheless, Israel's largest hostile neighbor, though checked, was not checkmated.

This became evident in 1969, when Egypt initiated low-grade hostilities across the Suez Canal. Artillery shelling, rocket fire, and commando raids continued well into 1970, on such a scale on both sides that the conflict became known as the War of Attrition. Egypt sustained terrible losses in the destruction of its towns and cities along the canal (notably Suez and Ismailia). Israel's losses were also considerable. Israel's static defense lines along the canal were so broken up that they were abandoned and a flexible system of response, the Bar-Lev Line, was created. Above all, Israeli casualties exceeded those in any previous armed confrontation, except that in 1948–1949.

Nasser died in September 1970. His vice-president and successor, Anwar Sadat, had long been Nasser's associate, but had not occupied the most important positions. His early months were absorbed in consolidating his authority; in May 1971 he narrowly suppressed a left-wing coup. His character and policies have been variously interpreted. Henry Kissinger, who first met Sadat in late 1973, was prepared to find in him "one of the many volatile leaders in the Arab world whose posturing, internecine quarrels, and flowery eloquence were as fascinating to contemplate as they were difficult to fathom. *But from that meeting onward, I knew I was dealing with a great man.*" [21] By the time Kissinger finished his panegyric Sadat was being compared to the colossal statues of the Pharaoh Ramses: "The figures are larger than life; yet their faces are infinitely human and their gaze leads us to distant horizons. Such a man was Anwar Sadat.... Anwar Sadat has already earned the immortality of which his Egyptian ancestors dreamed — as an inspiration if we succeed, as a shaming example if we fail. One way or another, the cause of peace will be his pyramid." [22]

---

[21] Kissinger, *Years of Upheaval*, p. 646. Emphasis the authors'.
[22] *Ibid.*, p. 651.

Not all Egyptians thought so highly of him, nor all observers. One recent analysis explains the end (the Camp David approach) in less conventional terms:

> [Sadat] found himself throwing away the Arabs' assets one by one. The position of relative strength which, in spite of the counter-crossing [of the canal], he had enjoyed on the morrow of the war, was reduced, as time passed, to one of abject weakness and desperation. He took the easy road, the only one his temperament allowed. The Israelis did have something to offer Egypt: they did not hold that Sinai, unlike the West Bank, was an inalienable, God-given part of the Jewish homeland; they did not consider it vital to their security as they did the Golan Heights. In order to recover Sinai for Egypt, Sadat embarked on a stealthy, go-it-alone diplomacy, the effect of which was to make it even harder for everyone else, Syrians, Jordanians and Palestinians to recover *their* territories.[23]

In other words, Sadat sold out the Arabs, particularly the Syrians and Palestinians, in order to get Sinai.

Sadat became a master of the unexpected, of psychological warfare, of risk taking. Whatever people may think of him, he was a master politician with a gift for the bold and flamboyant gesture. In 1972 he evicted Egypt's Russian military advisers but preserved enough Soviet friendship that the supply of arms was not entirely suspended.

He did not hide his intention of going to war with Israel; on the contrary he announced it from the rooftops, giving timetables and specifics. He did this so often that when, in October 1973, the Egyptians crossed the canal and put the Israelis into disarray it came as a shock to everyone, including Israelis, Americans, and the Egyptians! Accident, luck, design? It didn't matter because it worked.

The Egyptian crossing took place as what the military like to call a "set-piece battle." In such a battle everything is planned. Each man knows his specific task and carries it out. Nothing is left to chance, however impossible that really is. Contingencies have been provided for with spelled-out re-

[23] David Hirst and Irene Beeson, *Sadat* (London: Faber and Faber, 1981), p. 170.

sponses. Goals are specified. Sadat's goals in 1973 were more modest than he claimed them to be publicly. He sought to cross the canal and break the Bar-Lev line of defense. He wanted to inflict sufficient punishment on the Israelis to bring the stalled dispute over Sinai back into the political arena, this time with the Americans and perhaps the Russians playing too. If everything went well he would have a new deal with plenty of face cards. The same could be said of Assad and Syria, who attacked Israel along the Golan front at the same time as Sadat crossed the canal. Ultimately Sadat's great tactical error was that he failed to recognize that he could not easily exploit the early success in achieving his initial goals. Facing possibly the best army in the world — man for man — he foolishly decided to go for broke.

At the outset the Egyptians and Syrians achieved tactical surprise. Their SAM missiles destroyed an estimated 75 Israeli planes. On the ground, using wire-guided missiles, they were equally successful against Israeli tanks. Both the United States and the Soviet Union resupplied their surrogates. American assistance proved more successful and made possible the advantageous military posture of the Israelis at the war's end. Without resupply of any side it is likely that the Israelis would have been able to stabilize the two fronts, but they did not have their accustomed instant success. They had been scared; the best measure of it was the near hysteria of the Israeli government in the early days of the war, when they pleaded for American support for an in-place cease-fire. Regardless of the postures at the end of the war, the Israelis knew that they had lost it, in military ways and certainly in political ways. It was the beginning of fallbacks in Golan and Sinai. Although these were quite limited, they were the first territories of those captured in 1967 to be given up by the Israelis, and the only ones until Camp David, itself an extension of the victory won by the Arabs in 1973.

The last Kissinger disengagement agreement was in 1975. In 1976 Americans elected Jimmy Carter president. In the spring of 1977 the Israelis elected a new Knesset, which formed a government of the Likud Bloc, led by Menachem Begin, the old Irgun terrorist, and his Herut party. By November Sadat was in Jerusalem. Camp David came in 1978, and the peace treaty between Egypt and Israel in 1979.

Despite Sadat's trip to Jerusalem, the Israelis continued their military activity. In the spring of 1978 they mounted a heavy raid into southern Lebanon and encountered unexpected trouble with the Palestinians, who did not turn and flee but fought effectively. In June 1981 the Israelis bombed and destroyed a nearly finished Iraqi nuclear reactor on the grounds that the Iraqis *might* build bombs there to drop on Israel. There was an outcry over this rather incredible act, but the United States, Israel's only major supporter, registered no more than a pro forma protest (Iraq, after all, was a Soviet client). Israel repeatedly retaliated for Palestinian terrorist attacks by bombing raids on Lebanon. In July 1981 about 500 Lebanese were killed in a raid on Beirut apartment buildings.

On 6 June 1982 the Israelis launched the sixth in the long series of military conflicts. After intensive bombardment of Beirut and PLO positions in southern Lebanon, they entered Lebanon in a major thrust, swept aside the Palestinians and, less easily, the Syrians in the South, entered Beirut, and then proceeded to destroy West Beirut, where the PLO was installed. Ultimately, the PLO forces in West Beirut were evacuated, with American, French, and Italian supervision.

It is interesting to explore the motive for this invasion of Lebanon, which cost the Israelis several billions of dollars, a minimum by mid-1983 of 500 Israeli soldiers killed, and the opprobrium of much of the world, including supporters of Israel in the United States and even many Israelis themselves. In the first instance Israel claimed its action was in retaliation for the wounding of an Israeli diplomat in London on 3 June. After careful investigation by the British police, however, Prime Minister Thatcher stated that there was no evidence of PLO involvement and that PLO representatives themselves were on a "hit list" in possession of those arrested for the crime.[24] Next, the Israeli government declared that its objective was to clear southern Lebanon of PLO guerrillas who had

[24] *The New York Times,* 7 June 1982.

bombarded northern Israel. However, as there had been very few such incidents since July 1981, when a PLO-Israel cease-fire had been arranged by U.S. diplomat Philip Habib, the Israeli explanations began looking more and more like a stuffed non sequitur. By August the Israelis argued that they were there to free Lebanon (by which they meant the Christian right-wing Lebanese) of both the PLO guerrilla units and the Syrian peace-keeping force. A more plausible explanation, although one not officially avowed, may have been to nip in the bud any effort to negotiate a settlement of the dispute over the West Bank and Gaza, and thus to thwart any attempt to force the Israelis to give up the remaining portions of old Palestine to the Palestinians. Egypt, an essential participant in the autonomy negotiations called for by the Camp David agreements, in fact withdrew from the talks upon the Israeli invasion of Lebanon.

These are some features of this war, which has not completely ended as this is written (early 1983):

1. It turned out not to be a major military undertaking for the Israelis. The Palestinians retreated — they had no air cover — and were eventually trapped in West Beirut. In general the Syrians did engage on the ground, but their air force and missile sites were damaged grievously. The Israelis mobilized only a quarter of their reservists.

2. Although there was little opposition to the Israelis' march to Beirut, neither the PLO as the fighting force nor the Syrian army was defeated. The Israelis could doubtless have defeated either or both, but in the event they did not. With the evacuation, the bulk of the PLO escaped to sanctuary, weakened but not destroyed. The Syrians more or less remained where they had been. They too lost something, but their armed forces were essentially still intact.

3. At the time of writing there are no reliable casualty figures. The Israelis have admitted to nearly 500 dead. There are currently no official figures for the PLO or the Syrians. The latter probably lost fewer than 100 men. The Lebanese police estimated that about 5,000 civilians were killed in the attack on Beirut. This figure seems low, just as the figure of several

hundreds of thousands is certainly exaggerated. Much damage to cities and towns in Lebanon occurred. By contrast, the Israelis lost around 2,000 men in 1973 and fewer than 200 in 1967. The Phalangist attack on Palestinian refugee camps near Beirut, with the apparent connivance of Israeli officers, added another 500 or more casualties to the war.

4. The great powers did not intervene as they had in 1973. The Soviet Union, although it must have been embarrassed by the failure of its weapons in Syrian hands, did little ultimately beyond replacing them. The United States, while exhibiting a certain official sympathy for announced Israeli objectives, from the very first requested a cease-fire and an Israeli withdrawal. It was the persistent efforts of veteran diplomat Philip Habib, backed by a new secretary of state, George Shultz, that were ultimately successful in arranging a cease-fire and a PLO evacuation. (Nations agree to cease-fire when other options seem disadvantageous to them.) American military resupply to the Israelis was less than normal during this period. The Arab world was in no position to intervene. If Syria faced defeat with an escalation of the conflict, no other Arab state was in a position to take military action.

5. There was very little support in the world for the Israeli action. The aggression was too naked, the reasons for it too unconvincing, the human tragedies resulting from it too apparent. Israeli support in the United States reached a low.

It is too early to speculate here about the eventual results of this war. They seemed clear enough by the middle of August 1982, however, to former Israeli foreign minister Abba Eban:

> Israel would be stronger, prouder, less anxious, less mournful and more secure today if the war had ended in the first week without the unhappy episode of the encounter with Beirut. The balance sheet would have shown a clear surplus of advantage. The northern parts of Israel had been removed from the range of PLO weaponry, a "mortal blow" (in Mr. Arik Sharon's words) had been struck at the PLO, the Syrian missiles had been eliminated, and Israel's deterrent capacity had been immensely strengthened by the inspired performance of the Israeli forces, especially in the air. The Palestinian illusions about Syrian and Soviet solidarity had been exploded by

the apathy of Damascus and Moscow. If the Israeli government had been true to Mr. Begin's promise to the nation and the world on June 8 and had "ceased fighting" after creating the 40 kilometre buffer zone there could have been no shadow on our success. Moreover, these objectives had all been achieved in an atmosphere of domestic consensus and international understanding.[25]

Of course the Begin government did not stop there. Eban insists that even militarily there may well have been a loss:

As it is, we are in a position for the first time to strike the balance between gain and loss in the Beirut operation, and it shows a tragic deficit. The gain lies in the transfer of a few thousand PLO terrorists from a place where they were unable to do Israel harm to a place where they *may or may not* be immobilized from militant action. This is a gain principally in comparison with the contingency of the "military option"; in larger terms we have no basis on which to reach a positive judgment. It may even be the case that the bulk of the PLO activists will be geographically nearer to Israel than they were in Beirut! [26]

For this "marginal" gain in Beirut, Eban says, the Israelis have paid a cost. He lists the casualties in the armed forces for an objective of questionable value as a cost. He adds the Lebanese deaths and injuries. Furthermore,

In the meantime our relations with Egypt make a mockery of the peace treaty idea.... Relations with France and with Europe as a whole are seriously lacking in mutual confidence. The United States will accept the abandonment of the "military option" with relief, but there is a lack of trust in the recent dialogue, and there is a certainty of American "Palestinian" initiatives which will bring no joy at all to the Likud government, and perhaps little to the rest of us.

But the chief casualty for Israel, beyond the battlefield itself, lies in the transformation of what the word "Israel" conveys to many of its friends as it flashes across their consciousness. The immediate association in recent weeks has been the

25 *The Jerusalem Post International Edition* no. 1137 (August 15–21, 1982).
26 *Ibid.*

crash of steel against buildings, the screams of bereaved and wounded, the children lining up for water denied by an Israeli "blockade," the rat-infested garbage heaps, the collapse of those thin layers of civility which shelter human beings against their own human vulnerability. It is little short of idiotic to believe that this movement of opinion could have been arrested by technical means such as a transfer of responsibility for "hasbara" from one Cabinet desk to another, or the enlistment of people abroad skilled in the propagation of exaggeratedly favourable publicity for tooth-paste or automobiles. The erosion has occurred among the well-informed, not the ill-informed. . . .[27]

The significance of President Reagan's initiative that Eban refers to lies in the fact that no American president since Eisenhower has said so much publicly, or demanded so much of the Israelis. In Israel too — as was the case of the United States during the Vietnam war — the rise of an internal opposition, small still but determined, indicates the depth of emotions and feelings over this action. Not just politicians but people from many backgrounds have joined in vocal protests, including Avraham Burg, who fought in the war and who is the son of Dr. Yosef Burg, head of the National Religious Party and a member of the Begin Cabinet.

The Israelis have mounted a tiger and have found no easy way to dismount. An occupation of Lebanon will continue to drain Israel of resources, and more lives will be lost. It is difficult to see, in any cost-benefit analysis, just what the Israelis have gained that is as precious as what they have lost.

NEGOTIATION AND SETTLEMENT

The world is somewhat weary of the Arab-Israeli dispute. Many wonder why it cannot be settled. Why can't reasonable people sit down together and work out solutions to the issues that divide them? Camp David is often pointed to as an example of what can be done if there is enough will, determination and, of course, reasonable people. The answer is that people in general are not reasonable and it is itself unreasonable to expect them to be. Or, phrased differently, we differ

27 *Ibid.*

among ourselves as to what constitutes fairness, justice, and reason. Where ambitious political leaders perceive their interests to be at stake they can be, at least to outside observers, very unreasonable indeed.

It is naïve to expect that some day Arabs and Israelis will suddenly sit down together and over innumerable cups of coffee and tea work out a solution to their problems. It is also naïve to believe that if the right plan were presented, clever and detailed enough, all would embrace it. There are problems in international politics that have no solutions. "Solutions" sometimes come about when the problems themselves have changed, where the environments have altered, or where not solving something is more costly than coming to accommodation.

One of Camp David's major elements was the return of Sinai to Egypt, and this was completed in the spring of 1982. From 1967 to 1982 (or at least to 1973) the Israelis had ample opportunities to negotiate the return of Sinai. They did not, partly because internal Israeli politics made it difficult (as it was difficult for the United States to return the Panama Canal to Panama) and partly because the Israeli governments over those years simply did not want to and felt no need to. It was the 1973 war that provided the encouragement to negotiate, and it was Sadat's willingness to desert his Arab brothers to sign a separate peace with Israel that made it worthwhile. Trading Sinai for Egyptian neutrality finally didn't seem so bad a deal to the Begin government. Knowing that Egypt would sit on the sidelines made the 1982 invasion of Lebanon possible. (It was also lubricated with American money and theatrics.) When it was over, Begin and Sadat were made Nobel peace laureates, debasing that coinage a bit more.

Negotiations to accommodate Arabs and Israelis began long before there was even a state of Israel. The first Lord Samuel, British High Commissioner in Palestine in the early 1920s, made genuine efforts to bring the two communities together in some sort of advisory council. Then vastly outnmbering the Palestinian Jews, the Palestinian Arabs thought it unfair that the Jews should have comparable representation to their own, so they boycotted everything. Neither side would cooperate with the other or with the British unless some very clear-cut advantage was apparent.

Meanwhile the Jewish population in Palestine was rising, making Arab fears more acute and thus less likely that the Arabs would turn to cooperation. By the end of the Second World War a weary Britain was thinking seriously of abandoning its mandate in Palestine, and did so in 1948.[28] The United Nations then entered the negotiating process and adopted its partition plan in 1947. Under this proposal Palestine would be divided into two portions. Although Jews constituted at the time 650,000 out of a total population of slightly less than two million, they were to receive 56.4 percent of the land. Moreover, the land they were to receive contained many Arab inhabitants, although very few Jews were in the area allocated to the Arabs. The Arabs naturally objected to the plan (the United States supported it), but it all became irrelevant with the 1948–1949 war, in which the new Israel got all of Palestine with the exception of the West Bank and Gaza. Even if implemented, the UN partition plan was an unlikely survivor. The war at least made Israel partially viable, even if it did little for the Palestinians.

After that war, Israel and the Arab states involved (except Iraq) initiated armistice agreements. The ceremonies took place on the island of Rhodes and were facilitated by Ralph Bunche on behalf of the United Nations. (His predecessor, Count Folke Bernadotte, had been murdered in September 1948 by members of the Stern Gang, a Jewish terrorist organization.) At this point many Israelis thought that they had won their right to exist as a nation, and, aside from eventual peace treaties and freedom of navigation for Israeli ships, there was little to negotiate. Minor border rectifications were indeed ironed out with Jordan and Egypt. On the other hand, the absence of control over Jerusalem was a serious question mark for the future.

There were to be no serious negotiations for a very long time to come. Some obvious reasons stand out. The Arab world

---

[28] See William Roger Louis, *The British Empire and the Middle East, 1945–1951* (London: Oxford University Press, 1983).

was in turmoil. In March 1949 the Syrians went through their first military coup. In 1951 King Abdullah was assassinated in Jerusalem (by a Palestinian). In 1952 King Farouk was thrown out of Egypt, and a young army colonel, Gamal Abdel Nasser began his climb to fame. Although the Arab defeat in Palestine could hardly be behind all of these disparate events, certainly it was an important element in them. There was no sympathy in Israel for permitting the repatriation of Palestinians or compensating them for property lost. Large numbers settled permanently in refugee camps in Gaza, Jordan, Syria, and Lebanon. Many of them or their descendants are still there.

There was a time in the mid-1950s when Nasser, the most prominent Arab of his generation, might have made some sort of accommodation with the Israelis. Had he done so other Arabs might have done so too. We shall never know. What we do know is that the Eisenhower administration, coming to office in 1953, was less committed to Israel than its predecessor, that of Truman. And Nasser was a fresh face. Egypt was yet to suffer the humiliating defeats of 1956 and 1967. In 1954, however, came the Lavon affair in Israel, which almost tore the country apart. Without going into all the murky details,[29] the essential features are these. An Israeli intelligence effort in Egypt to sabotage, among other things, American installations there (e.g., information libraries) was uncovered by the Egyptians, who meted out heavy penalties to the Israeli agents captured (including two death sentences). It turned out that the Israeli defense minister, Pinchas Lavon, knew nothing of the operation but was forced to take responsibility in Israel, not so much for the purposes of the operation as for its failure. But if its purpose was to prevent an American-Egyptian rapprochement as well as accommodation between Israel and Egypt, it could hardly be said to have failed!

Notwithstanding the Lavon affair, hostile public rhetoric on both sides, and the massive Israeli raid on Egyptian-held Gaza in February 1955, Nasser took the initiative in exploring the

---

[29] It is well and briefly described in Richard H. Curtiss, *A Changing Image: American Perceptions of the Arab-Israeli Dispute* (Washington, D.C.: American Educational Trust, 1982) Chapter 6.

prospect of a political settlement with Israel focusing on final border demarcation and Palestinian refugees. An American Quaker intermediary, Elmore Jackson, held unpublicized discussions with both Nasser and Ben Gurion (then Israeli defense minister) during which even a personal meeting between the two leaders was considered. The negotiating environment, however, was rapidly deteriorating, with the impending British evacuation of Suez (alarming to the Israelis), the mounting scale of raids on both sides, and the Egyptian-Russian arms deal in the summer. By the end of 1955 the diplomatic exchange was terminated.[30]

The 1956 war came and went, and although Israel was forced to disgorge Sinai and Gaza, which it had captured, this did not come about because of Arab-Israeli negotiations. It was simply American overt pressure plus background Russian threats that obliged the Israelis to retreat. This war could hardly be said to have advanced the cause of peace.

Nor could the 1967 war a decade later even remotely be said to have made peace more likely. This time no one forced the Israelis to relinquish their territorial gains, and they were left with ticking time bombs for the future. Neither Syria nor Egypt, at least, could afford to abandon the Golan and Sinai permanently.

The only negotiations following the 1967 war took place in the United Nations. After intensive consultations, the UN Security Council approved its Resolution 242 [31] on 22 Novem-

[30] *The New York Times*, 28 November 1982.

[31] The operative provisions of Resolution 242 are as follows:

1. Withdrawal of Israeli armed forces from territories occupied in the recent conflict

2. Termination of all claims or states of belligerency and respect for and acknowledgment of the sovereignty, territorial integrity, and political independence of every state in the area and their right to live in peace within secure and recognized boundaries free from threats or acts of force

3. The necessity of:

a. guaranteeing freedom of navigation through international waterways in the area

b. achieving a just settlement of the refugee problem

c. guaranteeing the territorial inviolability and political independence of every state in the area, through measures including the establishment of demilitarized zones.

ber 1967. Its language is ambiguous in some important respects: it had to be, in order to be acceptable to both Israel and the Arab states. It is now furthermore anachronistic, since it leaves out of account the subsequent emergence of the Palestinians as an independent and influential political force. Nevertheless, Resolution 242 has been a major element in all later plans and discussions of an Arab-Israeli settlement, including Camp David.

When Nasser died in 1970, there was a chance for the Israelis to negotiate something with Sadat if they had been in the mood to move toward a settlement. They made no effort. The 1973 war, however, made it necessary for them to seek some accommodation.

At this point, Henry Kissinger enters the scene. He managed the remarkable feat of resupplying the Israelis militarily (thus making it possible for them to continue the war) while convincing Anwar Sadat of his fair intentions by "saving" the Egyptian Third army from destruction. Russian threats and a momentary American military alert were parts of the final script. Some say that Kissinger staved off a third World War. Kissinger claimed that he wanted to see that the Egyptians won enough to negotiate, and that the Israelis lost enough to be forced to negotiate and to make concessions. It turned out that way indeed — this is why the 1973 war is so important — but perhaps it was not all due to the master technician of Foggy Bottom.

So at last, in 1973, 1974, and 1975, with the catalyzing energies of shuttle diplomacy accompanying the process, the Israelis surrendered a portion of western Sinai and a small part of the Golan. But they were not prepared to do more. The government of Yitzhak Rabin, following that of Golda Meir, was ineffective, weak, and riddled with scandal. Only with the election of Menachem Begin and the Likud bloc (under Herut party leadership) in 1977 did new life come to the Israeli government.

It was then that Sadat offered to go to the Knesset itself in Jerusalem to argue his case, acknowledging not only the legitimacy and sovereignty of Israel in the process but also that modern Jerusalem was its capital. This trip was not altogether spontaneous. Begin and Sadat had felt each other out through intermediaries in Morocco and Rumania. But it broke on the world as an incredible surprise and it led to Camp David.

The trip to Jerusalem and the subsequent Camp David accords could come about because (1) Egypt's leader, Sadat, was willing to abandon his position in the Arab world in order to get Sinai back; and (2) Israel under Begin was willing to surrender Sinai for the neutralization of Egypt and for the postponement of dealing with the Palestinian problem. Each side deemed certain benefits sufficient in exchange for certain payments. There is no reason to believe that this came about because of any general willingess to solve the overall problem. It is naïve to believe that the "principles" of Camp David can be applied to the Palestinians, or the Golan, or Jerusalem. If and when these issues are settled, the results will come from different pressures, advantages, and trade-offs.

It gradually became apparent that Egypt and Israel would probably not reach agreement, in the negotiations called for by the Camp David accords, on the sort of autonomy to be given the Arab population of the West Bank and Gaza, and that if they did, the Palestinians, in all likelihood, would not cooperate in it. In the effort to renew movement toward a negotiated peace, other formulas were advanced from various quarters. In October 1981 Crown Prince (now King) Fahd of Saudi Arabia proposed a plan, firmly based on UN resolutions, calling for Israeli evacuation of all territory seized in 1967, dismantling of Israeli settlements there, the establishment of a Palestinian state with East Jerusalem as capital, and affirming the right of all countries in the region to live in peace. The clear implication that Israel has the right to exist was a dramatic departure in Saudi policy, and it drew sharp criticism from less conservative Arab states. Nevertheless, the substance of Fahd's program was adopted unanimously by an Arab summit meeting at Fez on 9 September 1982 as the basis for a negotiated resolution of the Israeli-Arab dispute. PLO Chairman Arafat was a participant. Of the 22 Arab League members only Egypt (whose membership remained suspended) and intransigent Libya were absent. On 1 September, President Reagan had already set forth proposals calling for full autonomy for the West Bank and Gaza in association with Jordan; a freeze on construction of Jewish settlements in the territories; and negotiations of an "undivided" Jerusalem.

All these plans were met with fevered rejection by the Begin government. The latter's behavior since the Camp David talks has, indeed, been anything but reassuring. The conclusion is inescapable that the Begin government does not desire any agreement that does not constitute an abject surrender by the Palestinians and other Arabs of all they have fought for over a generation. Yet it was apparent in 1982 that not all Israelis, nor all their sympathizers in the United States, supported the Israeli government. The mindless Phalangist butchery of refugees in the middle of September, abetted by the top Israeli officers, and the unconvincing excuses offered by the government for these acts churned up a massive protest within Israel itself. In late September a demonstration of nearly 400,000 people in Tel Aviv demanded the resignations of Begin and Sharon. Two Israeli newspapers, including *The Jerusalem Post,* editorially called for the resignations of Begin, Sharon, and General Eitan, the chief of staff. Particularly significant was the disaffection within the army itself. A number of senior officers expressed their indignation, and several resigned in protest.

Israel will not always be led by Menachem Begin, or embarrassed by Ariel Sharon, or compromised by Rafael Eitan. Others will take their places, other policies will be pursued, new vistas of statesmanship will emerge. Such things will be necessary if a final settlement is to be found.

THE AMERICAN-ISRAELI CONNECTION

Relying solely on its own resources, Israel could not preserve its military preponderance over its neighbors. Lavish economic and military support from the United States, coupled with consistent American political and diplomatic backing, has given Israel the option of avoiding the measures required for peace with the Arab states.

Until the mid-1950s, Israel, with private financial help from its friends abroad, was almost self-sufficient economically. Official aid from the United States was at quite a modest level. In 1956, for example, less than 1 percent of the American foreign aid appropriation went to Israel. The picture changed dramatically after the 1973 war. Total military and economic aid reached $2.5 billion in 1974. For FY 1983 the figure was the same, representing nearly one fourth of the total U.S. foreign aid appropriation. Israel also asked for a very substantial increase for FY 1984.

Budgeted aid, however, is only the tip of the iceberg. A very wide variety of devices have been introduced into American law, making the effective annual transfer of assets from the United States to Israel much more than twice the formal appropriation figure. Only a few examples can be mentioned here. Nominally, all American arms transfers to Israel are sales; in practice, however, up to half the price is immediately forgiven as a grant, and the rest is subject to concessionary financing, that is, loans with long grace and amortization periods, at interest rates 2 to 5 percent below those available to ordinary borrowers. Since 1979 Israel has borrowed heavily from the Export-Import Bank at concessionary terms. Israel is exempt from the American Department of Defense "buy American" policy, and its military sales in the United States, even where they compete with domestic producers, are exempt from customs duties. (95 percent of Israeli exports to the United States, in fact, enter duty free.) The concessionary terms of United States weapons sales to Israel are a one-way street; the United States pays the full price — in cash — for Israeli military hardware. Private contributions to Israel are tax-deductible — a unique privilege — and any institution considered under Israeli law as charitable is ipso facto so qualified in the United States. The United States has adopted self-denying policies with respect to arms sales to such countries as South Africa, Nicaragua, and Argentina, to facilitate Israeli supply of these markets. Under memoranda of understanding negotiated by Henry Kissinger, in any future crisis situation in world oil supply, such as the 1973–1974 Arab embargo, the United States is obligated to provide Israel 150,000 barrels a day to Israel from its *domestic* production; the loss to America's GNP could amount to between one and one-and-a-half billion dollars a month for the duration of the emergency. All in all, the United States furnishes at least 75 percent and probably as much as 80 percent of all aid Israel receives from abroad.

Despite this lavish support, Israel's economy is in a parlous state. It runs an annual trade deficit of over $5 billions. Foreign aid generates half of its GNP of around $20 billion. Its known government debt obligations abroad stand at the same figure, $20 billion, and those of private Israeli banks may come to $3 billion more. In January 1983 its foreign exchange net reserves were probably nil. To service its debts and remain solvent, it was estimated that Israel would have to raise at least $9 billion and possibly as much as $12 billion during 1983.

Israel's critical dependence upon American economic support gives the United States an enormous potential leverage over Israeli policy. The Arab states are well aware of this, and have great difficulty in understanding why the United States refuses to restrain Israel from actions that the United States government publicly disapproves of and that obviously endanger American interests in the region. The reason, of course, is rooted in American domestic politics. Israel has a very large and uncritical constituency in the United States, not confined to the American Jewish community. Zionist organizations have the best-organized and most influential lobby in the country, and it is almost completely responsive to the suggestions of the Israeli government. Sympathy for Israel, however, extends to a large number of Christians who believe that the establishment of Israel is a fulfillment of biblical prophecies. Many other Americans draw an analogy between the Israelis and the frontiersmen of our own history, and consider it proper that Palestine (and more?) should be possessed by those who will develop and modernize it, at whatever cost to the less advanced original people.

A balanced American policy, and the prospect of peace, depend crucially on an informed, discriminating electorate supporting national policies consonant with America's true interests as well as with equity for all parties to the Arab-Israeli conflict.

THE FUTURE

Many of the issues of the dispute between Israel and the Arabs have passed into history. Most Arabs would probably be content to accept Israel as a permanent part of the Middle East. Navigation rights have been gained by the Israelis. Peace with

Egypt, if fragile, has been achieved, and the Sinai, legally at least, is once more a part of Egyptian territory. These issues at least have undergone change.

But some have not. The core of what are left is the Palestinian question. At no time since 1948 has worldwide support for a Palestinian homeland (= state) been as great as it is today. This homeland inevitably must include Gaza and the West Bank. The Begin government has adamantly refused to entertain any concessions.

But almost certainly some concessions will have to be made by both Israelis and Palestinians. The latter may get most of the West Bank, for example, but not all of it. They may be compelled to maintain the West Bank free of offensive weapons. They may find few alternatives to some sort of connection with Jordan, at least for a time. But some kind of Palestinian state seems inevitable, and the necessary concessions from Israel to make this possible will come about. Both sides will compromise, however, only when other options are not open to them. All of this will take time.

Some adjustment will ultimately have to be made with respect to Golan, although the time needed for this may be long indeed. The Israelis will have to leave Lebanon and abandon their notions of Lebanese Christian puppets, be they Haddads or Gemayels. In a broader sense, the Israelis will have to jettison their military posturing and adventurism if true peace is to come. In the current world the Israelis are militarily threatened by no one, yet their armed forces are a constant danger to Lebanon, Syria, Iraq, and Jordan, and to Saudi Arabia and Egypt as well.

It is likely that Israel possesses nuclear weapons, although it has not admitted that it does. Nuclear scenarios in the Middle East are frightening because most countries there are very vulnerable to the use of nuclear weapons. Israel itself is and could literally be destroyed by a determined nuclear attack. But so are Egypt, Lebanon, Syria, and Jordan. Given enough time, any state that wants such weapons will presumably be able to acquire them, but this is not true at the moment. Assuming Israeli possession of a nuclear capacity without corresponding capabilities on the part of its Arab neighbors, is it likely that Israel would use such a capability? It behooves all Americans to remember that of all the states in the world only the United States has actually used nuclear bombs in war, against the Japanese in 1945. It should not stretch one's imagination to conceive that all other states might use such weapons too, given the right provocative circumstances. There is nothing in Israeli behavior to suggest that Israel would be different. If Israel's survival required the use of these weapons, they would be used. This realization is a part of the backdrop to the future, its negotiations, and any settlement that may evolve.

But the backdrop contains other factors that ought not to be overlooked:

1. The proportion of Jewish Israelis in the population at large is probably now slightly declining and in absolute numbers is leveling off. Yet these are the Israelis who are loyal to the concept of Israel, and it is they who would have to defend it in future conflicts. At the same time, the population of the surrounding Arab world continues to grow.

2. The proportion of immigrant Israelis is falling, and that of the native born (the Sabras) is rising. More important, the proportion of the Sephardim (or Middle Eastern Jews) is now more than half, although the Sephardim have only a small proportion of high government and army positions, in contrast to the Ashkenazim, or European Jews. This change in proportions is likely to have a major influence on future politics and policies in Israel.

3. The gap between the military technology in Israel and that in the Arab world (primarily in Egypt) has probably passed its peak, although of course it is still there. But no longer can one say that it is the struggle of one age with another.

4. Israel is locked into a most unfortunate economy, with enormous inflation (130 percent) and a defense budget that is impossibly large for its population. Seriously lacking in natural resources, Israel is today hostage to the outside world (primarily the United States) for economic assistance.

5. Israel has almost no support in the world community. That from the United States has possibly peaked; at least in

late 1982 it was much less than it had been a few years before. Although Russian support for its Arab clients perhaps has lessened, it is not likely to disappear. The Arab world in general has picked up much recent political support in Europe and Asia. The chances are good that this support will not quickly evaporate; it is hardly beneficial to the Israelis.

6. Although the United States energy crisis eased somewhat with the recession, our dependence upon Arab (largely Saudi) oil is still there. To the degree that this is so, we are open to Arab political influence. This can be uncomfortable. It is not unreasonable to assume that some Arab oil leverage is being, and will be, applied to the United States to lessen its historically uncritical support of Israel.

7. Camp David produced euphoria for a time. But even the formal peace treaty between Egypt and Israel cannot guarantee that some future Egyptian government will not find the pressures for renewed conflict with the Israelis irresistible. Moreover, Egyptian and Israeli governments come and go; there is no predicting what aberrant and conflicting policy paths they may pursue in the future.

8. The essential factor for peace in this troubled area is the Palestinians. Their 4 millions must be consulted and in some manner must be accommodated. The bulk of the Palestinians consider the PLO their legitimate representative. The Israelis may not want to deal with the PLO, but without doing so there can be no peace.

The Israelis have often said that Arabs do not want peace and that the Palestinians are still determined to destroy Israel. Whatever the degree of truth in this view, the fact is that various Arab leaders have made overtures to the Israelis that go a long way to meeting the legitimate needs of Israel.

It does not seem likely that a government headed by a Begin or a Sharon will ever negotiate seriously with the Arabs. Ultimately, however, it is very likely indeed that some Israeli government will be prepared to make the necessary concessions with respect to Golan, Gaza, and the West Bank, as well as some new adjustments in the status of Jerusalem.

The Arabs, too, may have to concede something. The new

Palestinian state, if indeed it comes into being, may have to be neutralized or at least demilitarized. Yasir Arafat may have to step aside in favor of other Palestinian leaders. Borders may have to be adjusted.

The time is right in the mid-1980s for some resolution of this 35-year-old conflict. If the chances are missed, almost certainly there will be continued warfare.

CHAPTER IX

The Challenge of Revolution and the Persian Gulf

THE ECONOMIC AND a good share of the political heartland of the Middle East is situated around the Persian Gulf, a shallow body of water that separates the Arabian Peninsula from Iran. Clustered around the Gulf are eight countries: Iraq, Iran, Oman, the United Arab Emirates, Qatar, Bahrain, Saudi Arabia, and Kuwait. Taken together, these countries account for 60 percent of the world's proven reserves of petroleum. On any given day, seven to eleven million barrels of oil pass through the famous Strait of Hormuz, the narrow 25-mile-wide passage at the lower Gulf, which leads into the Gulf of Oman and the Arabian Sea. Throughout 1982 and into 1983, approximately 50 ships per day passed through the Strait, most of them oil tankers. Before the Iran-Iraq war, the numbers were even higher, averaging approximately 70-80 ships per day.[1] This body of water, however is more than a "Petroleum Gulf." It is the center of regional and international political rivalry because of its enormous geo-strategic significance. One superpower, the Soviet Union, exists physically in very close prox-

[1] In 1981, the average number of daily transits through the Strait was exactly 50; based on statistics for the first seven months of 1982, the 1982 average was 55 transits per day. These data were provided the authors by the Department of Navy of the Sultanate of Oman, Muscat, Oman, 8 August 1982.

imity to the Gulf, while the other superpower, the United States, has defense and security arrangements with certain local countries that border on the Gulf. Above and beyond these considerations, the countries of the Persian Gulf are in themselves inherently unstable, contentious, and insecure. This latter consideration is in the end the central and basic problem of the area. And it is this internal, regional, political dimension that we shall emphasize in this chapter.

Of the eight political units that coexist around the Persian Gulf, only two have thus far experienced major political revolution, Iraq in 1958 and Iran in 1978–1979. The other six countries continue to be governed in the traditional patrimonial mode, with political power concentrated in the hands of ruling families. With the partial exceptions of Oman and Bahrain, these traditional governments have large natural and financial resources at their disposal. The ruling elites of these societies utilize these resources to enable them to confront the deepening challenge of revolution that has emanated from the Iraq and Iran experiences. With the Iranian revolution in particular, this challenge has intensified, and the traditional governments in the Gulf now find themselves desperately attempting to develop programs and policies that will enable them to weather the growing threat. The fact that these systems have been able to survive, and even to flourish, in a region through which the winds of revolution blow so strongly is worthy of analysis.

There are two major reasons why the traditional monarchies and mini-monarchies of the Gulf have successfully protected their systems into the 1980s. First, petroleum reserves and prices have been such that the ruling families have had at their disposal the resources needed to placate their populations by meeting the growing social and economic demands of this constituency. Since the actual size of the indigenous populations of these six countries is very small, it has been easy to upgrade the lifestyles of citizens enormously as a result of policies of distribution and redistribution of the wealth. Saudi Arabia, for example, with an estimated population of six million native Saudis, has been in recent years receiving $100 billion annually in oil revenues. In Abu Dhabi, the major unit in the

United Arab Emirates, only 20 to 25 percent of the total population of 235,000 is native; in Kuwait's population of 1.3 million, no more than 40 percent are native Kuwaitis. Yet the oil revenues of these two mini-states has been in the neighborhood of $15 to 18 billion annually. In such situations, it is therefore not surprising that the rulers have been able to provide their people with free housing, education, and medical care, along with many other perquisites and opportunities. The existence of huge financial wealth along with very small native populations makes it possible for governing elites to buy off much social and political discontent. This consideration is, however, a necessary but not sufficient cause for the continued stability of these traditional regimes in the area. The existence of great wealth is itself no guarantee that revolution will not occur; the political will and capacity to distribute that wealth is also essential.

The traditional governments of the Persian Gulf have been characterized by several key examples of astute political leadership in the 1970s and early 1980s. These leaders have been especially sensitive to the needs and demands of their people and have recognized the importance of staying in touch with all strata and tribes in their societies. One of the greatest of all of these traditional leaders was the figure of Faisal ibn Abdul Aziz, ruler of Saudi Arabia from 1964 to 1975. Faisal boasted over half a century of political experience, for already at the age of 13, he was leading diplomatic delegations to London. In Abu Dhabi and Dubai, Shaykhs Zayid and Rashid have been two of the shrewdest and most experienced leaders in the entire Middle East. They have led their countries since 1966 and 1958, respectively, and have proven again and again their skills as political mediators and negotiators. It was primarily because of their support that the United Arab Emirates was formed as a political unit in December 1971. In Bahrain, Shaykh Isa is an extremely shrewd politician who is consistently underrated by outside observers. Oman's Sultan Qabus stands as an enormous improvement over his father, Said, whom he replaced in a coup in 1970. With the exception of Qabus, all of these leaders have relied very heavily upon the informal institution of the *majlis* where they have been regularly available to hear personally the requests and complaints of their people. Until very recently when his health deteriorated, Shaykh Rashid of Dubai held four majlises daily. The first began at 6:00 a.m.; the second met at 10:00 a.m. At 7:00 in the evening another open meeting was held, and Rashid conducted his final majlis beginning at 9:30 p.m. Sometimes this late session would continue until the early hours of the morning. Today, Shaykh Isa of Bahrain holds his majlises regularly every Friday, Sunday, and Tuesday morning, as well as one on Saturday night. Such open meetings are encouraged by the rulers themselves who set the style for other members of the ruling families and political elites who also hold their own majlises.[2]

Through the continued implementation of this direct, personalistic democracy of the desert, along with the resources available to enable them to meet the demands heard in such settings, these traditional leaders have been able to hang on to power in an age of violent rebellion and revolutionary change. In other words, they have been able to promote rapid modernization with the traditional social and political instruments upon which they rest their very rule. Despite this impressive record, each and every one of these traditional systems in the Gulf possesses significant weaknesses and problem areas. The revolution of modernization itself heightens expectations and sharpens aspirations, all of which must be confronted and met on a continuing basis. In this turbulent environment, these weaknesses take on special significance.

The traditional countries of the Persian Gulf face the following seven problems: (1) the shortage of indigenous manpower; (2) the dramatic growth of professional middle classes; (3) the challenge of Islamic fundamentalism; (4) the existence of an unacceptable degree of corruption in ruling circles; (5) an extremely close association with the Western great powers by the ruling elites; (6) a huge and increasing gap between economic modernization on the one hand and political devel-

---

[2] The information in this paragraph was gathered in a research trip to Oman, the United Arab Emirates, and Bahrain in August of 1982.

opment on the other hand; and (7) the major issue of succession and political rulership for the future.[3]

The manpower problem has become more pronounced with time as each of these countries has chosen to institute major programs of industrialization and economic growth. In Saudi Arabia, for example, the Third Five-Year Plan (1980–1985) was budgeted at $260 billion, but Saudi planners privately had estimated that the figure would be closer to $400 billion. Saudi government expenditures went from 5 billion Saudi riyals in 1970 to 245 billion riyals in 1981. The two industrial cities of Jubail and Yenbo are mushrooming out of the desert and are expected to have populations of 300,000 and 150,000 respectively by the year 2000. In Jubail, a construction force of 35,000 is building a city whose industrial area is expected to be as large as that of Riyadh and Jiddah put together. This new city will have 14 major industrial plants, 250 ancillary industries, and 170 schools. Between 1975 and 1980, everything seems to have tripled in the Kingdom. Bank branches increased from 80 to 175, and hotel rooms expanded from 6,000 to 17,500. In this "billionic era" of modernization in Saudi Arabia, all these projects must be carried out with an effective indigenous labor force of approximately one million people. Even with the large influx of two and a half million expatriate workers, labor remains a serious problem in Saudi Arabia. Besides the economic and technical problems, there is the additional sensitive social and political issue of native populations being flooded by the immigrating waves of external laborers.[4]

The dramatic growth of modern educational facilities also carries serious political implications as larger and larger numbers of young people from the Gulf acquire higher modern educations, both at home and abroad. They then enter the job market with high expectations, many now sensitized to new ways of doing things and with a newly-developed political consciousness. As they return from abroad in increasing numbers,

[3] Another somewhat less urgent problem that confronts these countries is the issue of political competition among the various ruling governments of the Gulf. Much of this problem derives from rivalry over boundaries and border determinations.

[4] The data in this paragraph are the result of a research trip to Saudi Arabia in January 1982.

they are no longer as easily absorbed into the high-level political and administrative positions that they have come to expect. Although many enter the private sector, where they often are able to make private fortunes, not all succeed here either. The professionals and technocrats that are either not absorbed or absorbable into the traditional system become disgruntled and decry the personal favoritism, professional incompetence, and political repression that they allege is endemic to the systems in which they now live. Universities are the breeding grounds of this new class, and as the countries build such institutions of higher learning, the ruling elites have come to understand the political risks involved. Saudi Arabia now has five universities; the United Arab Emirates opened the new University of Al-Ain in 1981; even Oman is now developing its own national university, Sultan Qabus University, scheduled to open in 1985. Besides these schools, the six traditional countries of the Gulf have an estimated 40,000 students studying in institutions of higher learning in the United States and Western Europe. These students will form the questioning, challenging future professional middle classes in the Gulf.

The huge revenues that have followed in the wake of increased oil prices and that have fueled the modernization programs referred to above have also multiplied the opportunities for corruption. The sums involved have been enormous as individuals have used their personal political or familial positions to pile up huge fortunes. Corruption, of course, exists in all societies, but the hundreds of billions of dollars that have accrued to the Gulf countries in recent years have only intensified the phenomenon. Since wealth begets wealth and wealth follows power, many of the leading political actors or those closely associated with them are among the most avid practitioners of corruption. The ruling families usually have a handful of members who carry well-earned reputations for their financial greed and insatiable appetites for material wealth. Since 1974, this corruption has become especially visible and blatant, and certain public figures seem to flaunt their opulent lifestyles. This, in turn, has begun to give way to increasing criticism among the populations of these countries, who resent the levels of corruption that they perceive as morally unacceptable and nationally demeaning.

Between 30 November and 3 December 1979, the Kingdom of Saudi Arabia was shaken by a rebellion of several hundred Muslim extremists, who occupied the Great Mosque in Mecca. Hundreds on both sides were killed in the fighting in which Saudi security forces faced completely dedicated and committed insurgents in a religious setting. During this time, Shi'ites in the Eastern Province also rose against the regime, and they too had to be put down with force.[5] Other incidents have occurred in the Eastern Province in the Spring of 1980 and again in the Spring of 1982. In December of 1981, a coup attempt in Bahrain involving over 70 young Muslims whose inspiration came from Iran was uncovered and defeated by Bahraini authorities. There is no doubt that the resurgence of Islam is being felt throughout the Gulf area and that this revival has the deepest kind of political ramifications. The complaints heard most often from those who have chosen to embrace Islam with this special fervor concern the rapid westernization and modernization of their societies, the personal corruption of their political leaders, and the political repression that they see accompanying this moral decay. The drive is to first purify themselves and then to purify their own countries. One of the major criticisms of Juhayman ibn Sayf al-Otaybi, the military leader of the insurgents who laid siege to the Great Mosque, was the corruption that he claimed dominated the actions of the Saudi leadership. Although the ruling families of these Gulf countries are staunchly Muslim themselves, their commitment to and practice of Islam is considered highly suspect to much of the population in their countries. In the words of one leading observer and scholar of Islam, theirs is the "Islam from Above" as opposed to "Islam from Below." [6] It is the Islam from Below that is a major challenging force around the Gulf.

In this context, the very close linkages that many of the rul-

[5] For excellent, more detailed accounts of the Great Mosque incident, see Robert Lacey, *The Kingdom* (New York: Harcourt Brace Jovanovich, 1981), pp. 478–491; and David Holden and Richard Johns, *The House of Saud* (New York: Holt, Rinehart and Winston, 1981), pp. 511–538.

[6] This distinction has been pointed out to us by Mohammed Ayoob in personal discussion. See also Mohammed Ayoob, ed., *The Politics of Islamic Reassertion* (London: Croom Helm, 1981).

ing families have with the West in general and with the United States in particular increasingly work against their legitimacy at home. The breakneck pace of modernization with its heavily Western component runs against the drive to return to Islamic roots. Also, the continued strong support of the United States for the state of Israel has damaged both America's image and the image of Arab political leaders who work closely with the United States. This became especially clear in the summer and fall of 1982 with the Israeli invasion and occupation of Lebanon. In this military mismatch, which saw Israel utilize American-made aircraft to bomb hospitals, schools, mosques, homes, and refugee camps, Arabs throughout the Gulf watched in horror as other Arabs suffered and died before their very eyes on television. One of the results of the Israeli aggression of the summer of 1982 was to drive a small wedge between the United States and its traditional allies in the Gulf. Another less known effect was the fact that the Israeli action helped widen the gap of confidence between the peoples of the Gulf countries and their political leaders whose very association with the United States indirectly implicated them in the Israeli bloody adventure. The fact that the governments of these Arab countries were powerless in the face of Israeli military superiority only made the matter worse. In the words of one Gulf minister with whom we spoke in August of 1982, "What is the American government trying to do, destroy us?" [7]

A major problem area, and one that has been alluded to in the discussions above, is the tension between the extraordinary economic growth on the one hand and the absence of political development on the other hand. In no other area of the world is the division between industrialization and political development so pronounced as is the case of the Persian Gulf. Rapid modernization carries with it the problems of manpower shortage, growing middle classes, deepening corruption, and closer ties with the West. These in turn all contribute to growing popular dissatisfaction and an ultimate reaction, seen today in the form of the resurgence of Islamic fundamentalism. In the face of such serious challenges, the traditional countries of the

[7] Personal interview, Gulf shaykhdom, 19 August 1982.

Persian Gulf require especially sensitive and prescient leadership. What does the future hold in this regard?

The next generation of political leaders in the Gulf generally appears at this point generally not to be of the same quality of the present generation. Table IX.1 presents the names and birthdates of the rulers and their designated successors in the six traditional countries of the Gulf. In the case of Abu Dhabi and Dubai, the sons of Zayid and Rashid seem clearly inferior to their fathers both in personal charisma and in political acumen. In Oman, succession to Sultan Qabus could also prove to be a major difficulty as the Sultan has no son who would normally succeed to power. In Bahrain, Crown Prince Hamad is more enlightened and carries great promise as a political leader. In Qatar, Kuwait, and Saudi Arabia, the future is less certain. Although there are relatively competent successors in the wings of the royal families, it will be difficult for them to improve upon their current rulers, Khalifah (Al Thani), Jaber Ahmad (Al Sabah), and Fahd (Al Saud). The social and political challenges to the traditional regimes in the Gulf will surely magnify with time. The ability of the Gulf leaders to meet these challenges remains to be seen. If this ability should be lacking, then we may expect a great deal of political upheaval and revolutionary violence in the Gulf in the late 1980s.

The internal social and political problems that plague the traditional patrimonial Gulf countries do not exist in a political vacuum but rather continue to fester in an explosive regional context where the seeds of revolution blow in the winds from the Iranian north. Since the impact of the Iranian revolution has had a great and continuing influence upon the entire Middle East and has been especially forceful in the Gulf region, it is essential to attempt to analyze the realities of this revolution in more detail.

IRAN AND THE CHALLENGE OF REVOLUTION

The Shah's regime in Iran crumbled in 1978–1979 when the people of that country rose en masse to overthrow the Pahlavi government. Muhammad Reza Shah Pahlavi's style of patri-

TABLE IX.1 *Traditional Patrimonial Leaders and Designated Successors in the Gulf, 1983*

Country	Ruler (Birthdate)	Successor (Birthdate)
Saudi Arabia	Fahd bin Abdal Aziz Al Saud (b.1921)	Abdullah bin Abdul Aziz Al Saud (b.1923)
Kuwait	Jaber Ahmad Al Sabah (b.1926)	Sa'd Abdullah Al Sabah (b.1930)
Qatar	Khalifah ibn Hamad Al Thani (b.1934)	Hamad ibn Khalifah Al Thani (b.1950)
Bahrain	Isa bin Salman Al Khalifah (b.1933)	Hamad bin Isa Al Khalifah (b.1950)
Oman	Qabus bin Said Al Bu Said (b.1940)	(None Designated)
United Arab Emirates		
Abu Dhabi	Zayid ibn Sultan Al Nuhayyan (b.1908)	Khalifah ibn Zayid Al Nuhayyan (b.1949)
Dubai	Rashid ibn Said Al Maktum (b.1912)	Maktum ibn Rashid Al Maktum (b.1941)

monial rule had been rotting from within for some time as repression and corruption became two of the major characteristics of the regime. Meanwhile, the Shah cut himself off from his own people, and the channels of access to the government and to the political elite had withered into nothingness. The gap between the rich and the poor became a chasm in the 1970s, and the Shah gathered all power into his own hands while turning his secret police (SAVAK) loose on the people. In the end, the Iranian revolution is best described as a multiclass uprising in which the lower-class masses along with the major part of the burgeoning middle classes joined hands against the Pahlavi ruling family surrounded and supported only by a military and secret police apparatus. During the revolution, the Shi'i religious establishment became the organizing nodes of the movement and after the overthrow it was the ulema who gradually took control of the government of revolutionary Iran.

In 1983, the Iranian revolution commemorated its fourth anniversary. The first four years of post-Pahlavi Iran were not pleasant years, as the Islamic Republic of Iran found itself mired in social chaos, economic hardship, political repression, and a costly war with neighboring Iraq. In 1981 and 1982 particularly, violence and an undeclared internal war stalked the cities and the countryside as an inexperienced, harsh regime of religious extremists remained locked in mortal combat with a series of committed terrorist groups dominated by the radical Islamic Mujahedin-i Khalq. The violence and turbulence that occurred in Iran after the revolutionary overthow of the Shah should not have come as a complete surprise to students of Iran and of comparative revolutions. There are two major sets of reasons for the predictability of the continuing chaos in Iran. The first series is found in the particular characteristics of Iran itself, while the second resides in the more general phenomenon of revolution.

Any successor to the Pahlavi regime would inevitably have had to face a number of formidable if not impossible conditions for governance. Some of these difficulties were caused by the former style of rule, while others are endemic to the social and cultural composition of Iran. The new revolutionary government inherited the following eleven deep-seated and inter-related problems: (1) the total lack of any effective political institutions that could promote popular participation; (2) an absence of an experienced, committed, and charismatic cadre of political and administrative leaders; (3) a deep and persistent class conflict that had been intensifying through time; (4) the widespread atmosphere of personal distrust and cynicism; (5) the fragility of an economic system characterized by an extremely primitive infrastructure; (6) a multitude of serious ethnic and tribal cleavages; (7) a demoralized military in disar-ray; (8) the unique role of Shi'i Islam, whose leaders had little constructive experience; (9) the crushing violence of the revolu-tion itself, in which over 10,000 people lost their lives in the year between January of 1978 and February of 1979; (10) a host of regional enemies both in the Gulf and in the Middle East generally; and (11) the continued inopportune policies of great powers such as the United States, whose intervention only magnified many of the aforementioned difficulties.[8]

The ongoing political upheaval in Iran is also explained by the dynamics of major revolutionary movements, which histori-cally have reflected a number of similar patterns and uniformi-ties. A close examination of classic revolutions such as those that occurred in England in the 1640s, France in the 1790s, and Russia in the years following 1917 reveal several stages through which all these movements pass. Although his model does not fit the Iran case exactly, Crane Brinton's *The Anatomy of Revolution* is most suggestive in helping us better understand the stormy events in Iran.[9]

According to Brinton, the roots of revolution are located in the programs and policies of the *ancien régime*. After a dra-matic takeover, when the old system is overthrown, the early

---

[8] Much of the analysis of revolutionary Iran has been presented in dif-ferent form in the following published articles: James A. Bill, "The Un-finished Revolution in Iran," *International Insight* 2 (November/December 1981):6–9; James A. Bill, "Power and Religion in Revolutionary Iran," *The Middle East Journal* 36 (Winter 1982):22–47; James A. Bill, "The Arab World and the Challenge of Iran," *Journal of Arab Affairs* 2 (October 1982):29–46.

[9] Crane Brinton, *The Anatomy of Revolution* rev. ed. (New York: Vin-tage Books, 1965).

revolutionary government is controlled by liberals and moderates. This rule is usually short-lived and is inexorably replaced by a government of extremists whose single-minded fanaticism and lack of concern for liberal democratic values enables them to defeat the moderates rather easily. As they face continued resistance from political opponents, including both sympathizers of the old system and the now-alienated moderates, the rule of the extremists hardens into what Brinton terms The Reign of Terror and Virtue. This is the low point and crisis of the revolution as violence and repression reign supreme. Ultimately, a national reaction to this period of brutality sets in, and the time of the extremists gives way to a period of Thermidor, or convalescence, which witnesses a swing back to political and social moderation. The cycle is completed with the accession of an authoritarian leader or dictator who puts an end to the threatening anarchy.

In Iran, the period of moderate power began with the premiership of Shapour Bakhtiar (five weeks), passed through the prime ministership of Mehdi Bazargan (nine months), and ended with the presidency of Abol Hassan Bani-Sadr (17 months). In the 27 months of moderate influence, each of the moderate governments became progressively more radical as it fought for survival in an atmosphere of extremism. The fact that Bani-Sadr was in many ways more radical than moderate helped him to survive as long as he did. He was one of those moderates who "often behave quite immoderately." [10] The recruiting ground of the Iranian moderates was the professional middle class, that is, the secular intelligentsia represented politically by organizations such as the National Front — a grouping not wholly unlike the Girondins of the French Revolution or the Menshiviks of Russia.

According to Brinton, "The moderates are not great haters, are not endowed with the effective blindness which keeps men like Robespierre and Lenin [or Khomeini] undistracted in their rise to power. In normal times, ordinary men are not capable of feeling for groups of their fellow men hatred as intense, continuous, and uncomfortable as that preached by the extremists

[10] Brinton, *Anatomy*, p. 123.

in revolution. Such hatred is a heroic emotion, and heroic emotions are exhausting." [11] In this atmosphere, even the Bani-Sadrs are doomed. The supreme irony in the case of Bani-Sadr is his own thorough familiarity with Brinton's model of revolution — a model he referred to in a public speech in Tehran in February 1980 before a large crowd of his revolutionary constituents.

In the case of the Iranian revolution, the period of extremism overlapped with the last months of moderate political influence. With the dismissal of Bani-Sadr on 22 June 1981, the extremists found themselves with the field to themselves. Without the intervening buffer of moderation and Bani-Sadr's presidential legitimacy, the extremist right, represented by the Islamic Republican Party (IRP), and the radical left, represented primarily by the Mujahedin-i Khalq, entered into direct and violent confrontation. Motivated partially by fear and partially by ideological conviction, groups on the radical left attacked the extremist religious right. As moderate thinkers among both the ulema and secular population retreated for cover, the two wings of extremist ideologies entered a period of brutal repression and violent reprisal.

One week after Bani-Sadr's dismissal, a bomb exploded in the face of hard-line mullah Seyyid Ali Hussein Khamene'i, wounding him seriously. The next day (28 June 1981) a 60-pound bomb exploded at IRP headquarters, killing 74 members of the Iranian political elite, including the founder of the Islamic Republican Party, Ayatollah Muhammad Hussein Beheshti. The extremist right responded in kind as tens of thousands of suspected "leftists" and "counterrevolutionaries" were arrested and imprisoned. Daily gun battles and periodic bombings took place in the streets of Tehran in 1981 and 1982. On 30 August 1981, the Head of Government and the Head of State were assassinated together. President Muhammad Ali Raja'i and Prime Minister Muhammad Javad Bahonar died in a bombing of the heavily guarded Prime Ministry. The period of the Terror had come to Iran with a vengeance.

In describing the rule of extremists and the reign of terror,

[11] *Ibid.*, p. 146.

Crane Brinton lists 13 different characteristics of this violent period.[12] All but one of these characteristics are clearly evident in the Iranian case. A half dozen merit brief discussion. Two principles that are closely interrelated are the extremists' fanatic devotion to their cause and their willingness to act ruthlessly to protect and further this case. Brinton could have been speaking about the leaders of the Islamic Republican Party when he wrote that "our orthodox and successful extremists, then, are crusaders, fanatics, ascetics, men who seek to bring heaven to earth." [13] There is little doubt that men like Muhammad Ali Raja'i was just such a person. Raja'i concluded a long speech to the nation on 15 August 1981 with the following words: "I beseech God to grant us the honor of the survival of the revolution along with martyrdom for the revolution as a blessing and a favor." [14] On 30 August, President Raja'i was assassinated. This mind-set of marytrdom demonstrates the total dedication of the extremist to the cause.

A second set of characteristics of revolutionary extremist rule focuses upon the actual governmental process. In France, Russia, and England, the extremists governed by committee while at the same time establishing a new and extraordinary system of justice complete with a secret police apparatus. Brinton writes that "the characteristic form of this supreme authority is that of a committee. The government of the Terror is a dictatorship in commission." [15] In Iran, extremist government has

[12] The 13 characteristics have been abstracted from Chapters 6 and 7 in the Brinton book and are as follows: (1) the extremists' fanatic devotion to their cause; (2) their willingness to act ruthlessly to achieve their goals; (3) their strong willingness to follow their leaders; (4) the internecine conflict among the extremists themselves; (5) the emphasis upon centralized power and government by committee; (6) the establishment of a new system of justice along with the creation of a secret police apparatus; (7) the existence of an extremely ineffective and inefficient governmental administration; (8) the relative absence of ordinary crimes of violence, that is, non-politically-related crimes; (9) the sharp and relentness pressure of foreign and civil war; (10) the existence of severe economic crisis; (11) the growing and deepening class conflict that prevails; (12) the revolutionary extremism reflecting the fervor of religious faith; and (13) the very limited number of extremists.
[13] Brinton, *Anatomy*, p. 191.
[14] *Foreign Broadcast Information Service*, 17 August 1981, I, 13.
[15] Brinton, *Anatomy*, p. 171.

been dominated by the *komitehs* and special commissions appointed by Ayatollah Khomeini. In Brinton's words, the old legal system is "supplanted by extraordinary courts, revolutionary tribunals, or are wholly transformed by new appointments and by special jurisdiction. Finally, a special revolutionary police appears." [16] In Russia, France, and England, that special police was the Cheka, the Comité de Sureté Generale, and the independent parish clergy respectively. In Iran, it has been the SAVAMA backed by the *Pasdaran* (Revolutionary Guards).

The Brintonian model also outlines the common revolutionary patterns whereby extremist rule is affected by the pressure of foreign and civil war as well as by serious economic crisis at home. In Iran, extremist politics was only intensified by the war with Iraq as well as continual civil disturbances in the form of rebellion in Kurdistan and terrorism in the urban areas. Also, the economic crisis in post-Pahlavi Iran is seen in the fact that nearly one-third of the labor force has been unemployed, inflation ran at one point as high as 40 percent, and the industrial and technological infrastructure existed in an advanced state of deterioration. Finally, the extremist stage of revolution is dominated by a religious zeal that is the major motivating force of the ruling elite of the time. Brinton may just as well have been describing the role of Shi'ism in Iran when he wrote, "Religious aims and emotions help to differentiate the crises of our revolutions from ordinary military or economic crises, and to give to the Reign of Terror and Virtue their extraordinary mixture of spiritual fury, of exaltation, of devotion and self-sacrifice, of cruelty, madness, and high-grade humbug." [17]

The one generalization about the extremist stage of the revolutionary process that does not stand with respect to Iran is Brinton's assertion that the extremists are few in number. In Iran, the cleric-style extremism involves a large block of lower-middle-class and lower class adherents who are completely committed to the goals and ideas of their religious leaders. Also, the

16 *Ibid.*, p. 172.
17 *Ibid.*, pp. 202–203.

Iranian version of the Terror reflects a two-winged system in which fanaticism prevails on the left and the right. The guerrilla fighters of the Mujahedin-i Khalq have been just as zealous and dedicated to their cause as the ideologues of the Islamic Republican Party. They also have been willing to sacrifice their lives for their beliefs. On 11 September 1981, for example, Khomeini's personal representative in Tabriz, Ayatollah Assadollah Madani, was assassinated by a young guerrilla who lost his own life in a suicidal grenade attack. Similar events took place on 2 July 1982 and 15 October 1982,. when Khomeini's representatives in Yazd and Bakhtaran (Kermanshah), Ayatollah Muhammad Sadduqi and Ayatollah Haj Ataollah Ashrafi-Isfahani respectively, also were assassinated by suicidal acts of young members of the Mujahedin-i Khalq. The fact that neither side has the coercive power to completely destroy the other promises a particularly brutal and extended period of extremism in Iran. Although it is inevitable that the Iranian Thermidor must one day arrive (perhaps after the death of Ayatollah Khomeini), events both internal and external to Iran seem to dictate that extremist politics will prevail for some time to come.

In the face of all of these problems and difficulties, the Iranian revolution continues to prevail and persist. The extremist religious leaders dominate the political machinery of the country, and the regime has prevailed both in a brutal internal war and in a massive confrontation against an outside invading army. Why has the Iranian revolution continued to persist, and how has the post-Pahlavi leadership managed to survive and to govern? What have been the strengths of the Islamic Republic of Iran?

There are six major factors that combine to explain the resiliency and survivability of the developing social and political systems in Iran after the fall of the Shah. These are (1) the leadership of Ayatollah Ruhollah Khomeini; (2) the support of the lower-class masses (the *mostaza'fin*) for the system; (3) the strength of Shi'i Islam as an ideology; (4) the continued support of the military for the regime; (5) the growing experience of the clerics as statesmen; and (6) the outside forces, which promote internal unity by their attacks on the revolution.

Despite outside charges of heresy, lunacy, and conspiracy, Ayatollah Khomeini acted as a shrewd and effective political tactician in the context of revolutionary Iran. As the charismatic symbol of the revolution, Khomeini placed himself above the everyday infighting and from there he balanced the various extremist and radical groups off against one another. In the process, he lived a simple life style, refused to compromise with what he considered Islamic principles, and presented himself as the champion of the downtrodden and the oppressed. By constantly stressing an Islamic populism, he stole the appeal from both the Marxist left and the moderate center of the political spectrum. As the somewhat grim Robin Hood of Shi'ism, Khomeini never ceased his attacks against the superpowers of East and West.[18]

While devouring significant groups of its own initial supporters (that is, the middle classes), the revolution still maintains a solid and broad base of popular support. The Shi'i leaders recognize the *mostaza'fin* (the dispossessed, downtrodden) as their major constituency and seek to meet the demands of the masses before all others. In continuing to take (often brutally) from the rich in order to give to the poor, the Shi'i political elite works hard to ensure the support of the masses. It is from the masses that the regime has recruited the young people who have fought and died for the revolution on the Western front. In this context, Khomeini himself has regularly spoken in class terms about the commitment of the *mostaza'fin* to the revolution. "To which class of society do these heroic fighters of the battlefields belong? Do you find even one person among all of them who is related to persons who have large capital or had some power in the past? If you find one, we will give you a prize. But you won't." [19] On the third anniversary of the revolution, Khomeini warned high-ranking government officials that "whenever the people consider that one of you is climbing to the upper rungs from the middle classes or are seeking power or wealth for yourselves, they must throw you out of their

---

[18] For a detailed analysis of Ayatollah Khomeini as a political tactician, see James A. Bill, "Power and Religion," especially pp. 41–45.

[19] *Tehran Times*, 10 February 1982, p. 6.

ranks." He went on to say that "it was Hezrat-i Ali who said that his torn shoes were more valuable than a position in government." [20] As long as the leaders of revolutionary Iran are able to meet the demands of this large base of popular support, they have an extremely important foundation of power.

The ideology of Islam permeates revolutionary Iran. All programs and policies are justified in terms of Islam as the official name of the country, Islamic Republic of Iran, indicates. This ideology is extremely potent both in the breadth and depth of its appeal. All systems by which an Iranian organizes his life are guided and influenced by Shi'i Islam. All Iranians, regardless of class membership or tribal affiliation, must come to grips with Islam. Since Shi'ism carries within itself the flavor of martyrdom, many of its adherents are often willing to make the ultimate sacrifice in defense of their country, their religion, and their revolution. Since January 1978, there have been thousands of examples of this commitment, most dramatically revealed perhaps during the fighting in the war with Iraq.

The religious revolutionary leadership in Iran has also survived because of the support of the military. With the fall of the Shah, the Khomeini government carried out two major purges of the officer corps, thus decapitating the Shah's military organization. At the same time, the clerics created their own parallel force of Revolutionary Guards (*Pasdaran*) and by the Spring of 1982 had succeeded in blending the two organizations together into one fighting unit. After four years of fighting internal guerrillas and over years of battle against an outside invader, this military force has become battle-hardened and experienced. The victories in the war with Iraq document this record. In the process of this continual conflict, the Iranian military forces have developed a deeper commitment to the cause for which they have fought.

During the years of existence of the Islamic Republic, the clerics have come to a better understanding of the realities of politics. They have gathered some momentum as political leaders. Although their mistakes have been many and the costs thereof very high, there is evidence that they have learned a

20 *Ibid.*

few lessons. One of the most expensive of these was the government's insistence on keeping oil prices unrealistically high throughout 1980, thereby driving away many customers and suffering a loss in market and revenues. In 1981, Iran had to offer sharp discounts and shave prices in the face of economic desperation. A major policy of the cleric-leaders has been their attempts to institutionalize their rule through the construction of a complex political organization network throughout the country. This important attempt is designed to better enable the Islamic system to survive the death of Khomeini by guaranteeing that the clerics will maintain the closest contact possible with their mass constituency. This institutional network includes the following organizations: the many branches of the Islamic Republican Party, the mosque system, the *Pasdaran* organization, the Reconstruction Crusade (*Jihad-i Sazandegi*), the Foundation of the Oppressed (*Bonyad-i Mostaza'fan*), the Foundation for the Martyrs (*Bonyad-i Shahid*), the Welfare Organization of the Country (*Sazman-i Behzisti-yi Kishvar*), the Islamic *Komiteh* system, and numerous other councils, committees, and corps. This overlapping network has served four major functions for the regime: (1) it monitors the needs and receives the demands of the people; (2) it transmits information and policy decisions to the people; (3) it distributes goods and priorities to the masses; and (4) it acts as a complex conduit of information and intelligence to the ruling clerics.

A final factor strengthening the revolutionary system in Iran is negative in character. The Iranian revolution, like many revolutions in history, has found itself consistently attacked and threatened by external forces. Financial, psychological, and political pressure from both the traditional Arab countries and Western nations such as the United States has coincided with direct military invasion by the Iraqis. The activities of counter-revolutionary groups and exile organizations formed by wealthy members of the *ancien régime* are constant reminders of serious threats to the revolution. In the face of this, the various groups in Iran have had to close ranks and to cooperate against a common foe. In this sense, the outside powers who have sought to destroy the revolution ironically have only contributed to its strength and longevity.

In the Spring and Summer of 1982, two events occurred that provided the Iranian revolution with new strength and stamina. Both of these happenings also raised the credibility of the revolution significantly in the region. Besides the attracting features discussed above, the two developments of 1982 invested the Islamic government in Iran with an important surge of respect and appeal. The decisive military actions and victories over the invading Iraqis, which drove their armies almost entirely off of Iranian soil in the Spring, earned the revolutionary regime wide respect in the area. Then in the Summer, when Iran followed its words condemning the Israeli invasion of Lebanon with action by sending a force of Revolutionary Guards to fight with the Syrians and Palestinians, it gained considerable popularity among the Muslim peoples of the area.

The stunning Iranian victories over Iraq began in the Fall of 1981, when the Iranian forces won major engagements in Abadan in September and in the key town of Bustan in November. Then, in two major battles fought in the area of Dezful in March-April 1982 and in Khorramshahr in April-May 1982, Iran completely defeated and demoralized the Iraqi forces. These victories took place despite the fact that the Iraqis had spent months digging themselves into heavily fortified defensive positions.

An example of the scale and enormity of the Iranian military victories can be seen in the battle that took place in the area of Dezful in late March and early April. In this battle, the Iranians organized and coordinated over 100,000 regular troops, 30,000 revolutionary guards, and another 30,000 members of the popular militia. In its offensive, Iran managed to coordinate the activities of five divisions on the battlefield — an extremely impressive undertaking given the conditions. In the process, they destroyed three full Iraqi armored and mechanized divisions and captured over 15,000 Iraqi soldiers. Informed military analysts explain Iran's success in terms of three major factors: (1) the close cooperation and coordination between the Revolutionary Guards and the Regular Army; (2) the high quality of a new cadre of young, courageous Muslim officers who had taken charge of all key command positions over the past two years; and (3) the complete dedication and high morale of the nation and its military forces when faced with the fact of a foreign power occupying Iranian soil.[21]

Despite the threat of the Iranian revolution and the political provocations directed against Iraq, it has been well understood in the Middle East that Iraq had been the aggressor and had attacked Iran at a time when that country was plagued by violent internal political strife and severe economic deterioration. Many expected and desired that Iraq would win a rapid military victory, that the Arabs of Khuzistan would rise against the regime in Tehran, that the cities would erupt into guerrilla warfare, that Khomeini and the clerics would be overthrown, and that the country would degenerate into chaos and anarchy. Instead, Iran resisted the surprise attack with unexpected ferocity, held the Iraqis at bay for a year, and then embarked upon a counterattack. Although this counterattack quickly bogged down and the Iranian forces suffered major setbacks when they attacked into Iraqi territory in July 1982, the Iranians humiliated Saddam Hussein further by forcing the September 1982 summit conference of nonaligned countries to be moved from Baghdad. In the words of a leading scholar of Iraqi politics: "When the Iraqis attacked Iran, they expected to fight a war. Instead, they found themselves fighting a revolution." [22]

In 1983, the Iran-Iraqi war, one of the bloodiest of the twentieth century, continued to drag on despite Iraq's increasing calls for peace.[23] Iran held firmly to its three demands: (1) that Iraqi forces remove themselves from all Iranian territory occupied during the invasion; (2) that Iraq pay reparations for

[21] For the data and analysis presented in this paragraph, we have drawn heavily upon William F. Hickman, *Ravaged and Reborn: The Iranian Army, 1982* (Washington, D.C.: The Brookings Institution, 1982).

[22] Hanna Batatu, Lecture delivered at Harvard-Industrial Bank of Japan Eighth Annual Middle East Seminar, Tokyo, Japan, June 16, 1981.

[23] In the first two years of the war, an estimated 150,000–200,000 combatants on both sides were killed. In October 1982, Iran publicly admitted to the loss of 50,000 members of its regular army. This figure does not include the deaths of members of the Revolutionary Guards (*Pasdaran*) or of the Mobilization Corps (*Basij*) troops, where casualties are believed to be at least as high as those sustained by the Regular Army. See *Iran Times*, 29 October 1982, p. 2. (In Persian.)

all the damage inflicted on Iran; and (3) that Saddam Hussein resign or be overthrown as the leader of Iraq. After an Iraq missile attack on the civilian population of Dezful in southwestern Iran in December 1982, Iranian parliamentary leader Hashemi-Rafsanjani stated that the most important condition for ending the war was "Saddam's punishment for his crimes against the Islamic Revolution." [24] In Iran's eyes, only the issue of the actual amount of reparations was negotiable.

At a time when Iran was just finishing its drive to expel the Iraqis, the Israelis struck Lebanon in a massive offensive beginning 6 June 1982. The goal of the Israelis in this attack was to destroy the Palestinian Liberation Organization once and for all and to make negotiations on the West Bank impossible in the near future. In the face of the overpowering Israeli military might, most of the Arab countries were either unwilling or unable to respond to assist the outmanned, outgunned, and outmaneuvered Palestinian forces. The silence from much of the Arab world was deafening. With the partial exceptions of the Saudis, who attempted to convince the United States to pull Israel off the Palestinians, and the Syrians who crumbled in the face of superior Israeli air power, only Iran made any visible, concrete moves to come to the assistance of the embattled Palestinians. A week after the Israeli attack, the Islamic Republic sent an estimated 1,500 members of the Revolutionary Guards to fight on the side of the Palestinians and Syrians in Lebanon. At a time when most Arab countries did not or could not come to the aid of the Palestinians, this show of support by revolutionary Iran was an important symbolic act.

The message of revolution emanating from Iran will not be carried primarily by military means. Iran has been careful to claim that its military actions against both Iraq and Israel have been defensive in nature.[25] In Iran's eyes, Iraq and Israel

---

[24] *Tehran Times,* 22 December 1982, p. 1. In April 1983, Iraq again launched a devastating series of missile attacks on the Iranian city of Dezful.

[25] Even after Iran counterattacked into Iraqi territory beginning in July 1982, the Iranian leaders stressed that their actions were "defensive." On 6 and 7 August 1982, Khomeini gave public speeches reiterating this point. In his words, "We know that their troops are still holding part of

have been the aggressors. In the words of the Iranian ambassador to Kuwait, "The leaders in most of the Gulf countries are not alien to their people as Saddam is. We are not exporting our revolution to these countries. This is because by definition ideologies don't ask for visas. Other people will learn by our successes and our mistakes." [26]

The continuing survival of the Islamic Republic of Iran, the 1982 victories over Iraq, and the moves to assist the Palestinians provided the Iranian revolution and its cleric-rulers with sharply increased credibility in the Arab world. Now, more than ever before, the Iranian model stood as a serious challenge to the traditional regimes surviving in the Gulf.

THE EXPORTATION OF REVOLUTION IN THE GULF

The Islamic Republic of Iran has based its foreign policy on its leaders' perceptions concerning the level of popular support of a particular nation's government as well as the position taken by that government towards the Islamic Republic itself.[27] There is no Gulf country with which Iran maintains extremely close and cordial relations. Iraq, Saudi Arabia, and to a lesser extent, Oman are countries with which the Islamic Republic has had a definitely hostile relationship. The shaykhdoms of the United Arab Emirates, Bahrain, Kuwait, and Qatar are states with which Iran maintains normal (or correct) relations. In these latter cases, Iran has been much less willing to criticize and condemn in the same way that it has attacked Iraq and Saudi Arabia, for example.

The hostility between Iran and Saudi Arabia is mutual and has intensified with time. The Islamic regime in Iran con-

---

our country and have their own bunkers inside our lands. From outside too they almost daily bomb Abadan and some other cities. As long as the situation continues like this and as long as they do not fulfill our terms which are logical, we will be in a state of war. We do not wish to impose ourselves on anybody; we are not oppressors...." See *Tehran Times*, 9 August 1982, p. 3.

26 *The Christian Science Monitor*, 8 June 1982.

27 For an informative analysis of the foreign policy of the Islamic Republic of Iran, see W. G. Millward, "The Principles of Foreign Policy and the Vision of World Order Expounded by Imam Khomeini and the Islamic Republic of Iran," unpublished paper.

demns the Saudi ruling family as "criminal" and bases its criticism on three grounds: (1) the strong support and generous financial backing that the Saudis have provided Iraq in its war with Iran; (2) the close association that Saudi Arabia maintains with the United States, the country still considered the foremost enemy of the Iranian revolution by the cleric-leaders; and (3) the alleged corruption, repression, and distortion of Islam as practiced by the Sunni Saudi ruling family. The Saudis, on the other hand, view the Islamic Republic of Iran as a force promoting violence and revolutionary upheaval in the Gulf while practicing a perverted brand of Islam at home where bloodshed, repression, and Shi'i superstition are considered to have become the order of the day. The Saudis have been especially concerned about the overt political actions and slogans utilized by the Iranian pilgrims who visit Mecca during the annual Hajj, as well as about the Iranian inspiration that lay behind the coup attempt in Bahrain in mid-December 1981. It was after this event in Bahrain that the Saudi mass media initiated a surprisingly direct and vitriolic anti-Khomeini campaign.

Iran and Saudi Arabia each believe that the other is determined to destroy it. The Iranian regime is convinced that the Iraqi attack of 22 September 1980 was carried out with the full knowledge and support of the Saudis, who saw this as an opportunity to destroy the revolution. In support of this belief, they stress the visit of Iraqi strongman Saddam Hussein to Saudi Arabia on 5 August 1980, where he met with then King Khalid, Crown Prince Fahd, Prince Abdullah, Head of the Saudi National Guard, and Prince Sultan, Minister of Defense. The conclusion of the Iranian leadership: "From the composition of the meeting, it is concluded that it dealt with sensitive military and security matters in relation to the Iraqi Ba'th invasion of Iran less than two months later on September 22, 1980." [28] The subsequent and continuous flow of Saudi financial aid to Iraq along with the strong anti-Iranian position taken by the Saudis within the Gulf Cooperation Council has only reinforced this Iranian mind-set.

[28] *Tehran Times,* 20 September 1982, p. 3.

The Saudis cite the strong propaganda emanating from Iran that has resulted in political upheaval throughout the Gulf, including the incident at the Great Mosque in Mecca and the various violent demonstrations in the Eastern Province. They point to the fact that each year Khomeini appoints the most extreme and politicized mullahs to lead the pilgrimage to Mecca, thus encouraging violence and political incidents that threaten to transform the Hajj into a political event designed to sow the seeds of revolution into the very heart of the Kingdom.[29] In the face of this threat, the Saudis feel that they must fight Iran out of self-defense, and it is in this context that it has been remarked that the Iran-Iraq war is in fact an Iran-Saudi war in which the Saudis provide the finances and Iraq supplies the blood. In the end, the rivalry between Saudi Arabia and Iran resides in the two fundamentally different political styles and Islamic ideologies, the militant revolutionary Shi'i Islam of Iran and the traditional conservative Sunni Islam of Saudi Arabia.

The smaller shaykhdoms of the Gulf — Qatar, the United Arab Emirates, Bahrain, and Kuwait — have had a nervous but diplomatically "correct" relationship with the Islamic Republic of Iran. Since they stand badly exposed before the power of Iran and since Iran has indicated a proclivity to conduct normal relations with these mini-states, there has been a greater willingness to work cooperatively with Iran on the part of the ruling families of these small countries. In this context, in mid-1982 some of them privately began resisting Saudi pressures for the continued unconditional support of Iraq in its war with Iran. Kuwait, which has always pursued an independent foreign policy and is the only traditional government in the Gulf with diplomatic relations with the Soviet Union, considers Iraq

[29] Iran has sent the most extreme and fiery of mullahs to lead the Iranian pilgrims on the Hajj to Mecca. Khomeini himself instructed Hajj leaders like Abdol Majid Mo'adikhah and Muhammad Musavi Kho'iniha to stress the political nature of the Hajj. Kho'iniha, who led the Iranian contingent to Mecca in 1982, was the same individual who coordinated the activities of the students who held American diplomats hostage in Tehran between November 1979 and January 1981. He was arrested and detained by Saudi security forces for encouraging political activities during the 1982 Hajj.

at least as great a threat to its interests as Iran. The United Arab Emirates has maintained very close economic and trade ties with Iran throughout the early years of the Islamic Republic. In fact, the heavy dhow trade between Dubai and the southern ports of Iran is an economic umbilical cord that stretches between the two countries.[30] Bahrain was badly shaken by the coup attempt in late 1981, but by the beginning of 1983 it had become much more sanguine with respect to the future of its relationship with Iran. Bahraini leaders indicated to Iran that they were not supporting Iraq in the war and were themselves somewhat reassured by the visit to Manama of two members of the foreign affairs committee of the Iranian Majlis (parliament) in August of 1982.[31]

Although there is some evident ambiguity and contradiction in Iran's position with respect to the exportation of its revolution, it is possible to determine the general intentions of the Islamic Republic in this regard. Revolutionary Iran seeks to export its revolution throughout the Middle East. It does not intend to do so primarily by force, however, since such action is considered to be counterproductive, unnecessary, and not in accord with the tenets of Islam. In February 1980, Ayatollah Khomeini stated that "we will export our revolution to the four corners of the world because our revolution is Islamic. . . ." [32] In September 1982, he said that "by exportation of Islam we mean that Islam be spread everywhere. We have no intention

[30] Official records show that reexports from Dubai to Iran in 1979, 1980, and 1981 totalled $236, $346, and $191 million respectively. The actual amounts were many times these figures, but the recorded numbers in themselves provide an idea of the size of the trade flows between the United Arab Emirates and Iran. See *The Christian Science Monitor*, 9 December 1982, p. 1.

[31] Bahrain leaders told the Iranian officials that Bahrain sought to cooperate with the Islamic Republic as long as Iran did not continue to engage in unfriendly acts, for example, supporting subversive forces such as the Bahrain Liberation Islamic Front. High-ranking Bahraini officials told the Iranian delegation that if Iran takes a friendly step towards Bahrain, Bahrain will in turn take two such steps towards Iran. Personal interviews, Manama, Bahrain, August 1982.

[32] "Imam Khomeini's Message for February 11 (1980)," pamphlet published by the Ministry of Islamic Guidance, Tehran, 1982 as quoted in Millward, "Principles of Foreign Policy," p. 12.

of interfering militarily in any part of the world." [33] This position was clearly summarized by Majlis Speaker Ali Akbar
Hashemi-Rafsanjani in July 1982 when he indicated that "the
western mass media is trying to frighten the world about the
export of the Islamic Revolution of Iran. We have announced
that we are for the export of the revolution and have explained
what we mean by this. We have launched an Islamic movement and Islam must prevail in the region. . . . We will never
conquer a country through the use of our army, unless that
country commits an act of aggression against us. . . ." [34]

In pursuing the exportation of its revolutionary ideas, Iran
has a surprisingly sophisticated system of information dissemination (what the regime terms *tablighat*), which involves extensive radio and television programming beamed throughout
the Gulf. Radio Iran transmits a strong signal that can be
picked up deep into Saudi Arabia and that can be very clearly
heard in Oman. The Islamic Republic's television programming is easily received in the United Arab Emirates. In Bahrain, special antennae are necessary in order that a clear signal
be received. After the revolution, and especially after the
Iranian victories in the war with Iraq in the Spring of 1982,
the sales of these boosters in Bahrain skyrocketed. In the words
of one Bahraini political observer, "the antennae of the Bahraini people are up and out." [35] The radio programming into
Saudi Arabia and Oman has included particularly biting attacks on the ruling establishments of those countries. The television programming into the Gulf shaykhdoms has been much
more sophisticated and has focused on the transmission of
Islamic messages, the successes of the Iranian war effort against
Iraq, and the commitment of the government to the masses of
mostaza'fin.[36]

Although Iran has no military designs on Saudi Arabia, it
seems committed to bringing down the ruling family there by

[33] *Tehran Times,* 30 September 1982, p. 1.
[34] *Tehran Times,* 19 July 1982, p. 1.
[35] Personal interview, Manama, Bahrain, 19 August 1982.
[36] These observations are based on my [James A. Bill's] own viewing of
the television network of the Islamic Republic of Iran as broadcast on
Channel 3 in Abu Dhabi, 15–16 August 1982.

continuous propaganda attacks. Its position concerning the other Gulf countries (with the partial exception of Oman) is one of uneasy coexistence. The Islamic Republic has continuously gone out of its way to reassure these shaykhdoms that it respects their territorial integrity. At the opening session of the Majlis in July 1982, Speaker Hashemi-Rafsanjani stated that the small countries of the Persian Gulf had no reason to fear Iran, which had no territorial ambitions on other countries. President Ali Hussein Khamene'i has made the same point on several occasions. In November 1982, the Political Undersecretary of the Ministry of Foreign Affairs of Iran, Hussein Shaykholeslam, in an official visit to tht United Arab Emirates stressed publicly that the Islamic Republic did not covet "even one inch" of another country's territory and that Iran would "warmly welcome the friendship of any country which tries to counter the influence of superpowers in the region." He significantly added that Iran would be willing to "forgive past errors and political misjudgments" of such countries.[37] Clearly, he was speaking about the shaykhdoms of the Gulf here and not about Saudi Arabia (or Iraq), whose crimes were considered to be too great to be forgiven — at least as long as the current regimes remained in power in these particular countries. With respect to the other Gulf countries, the Iranian government sought to convince them to cease their support for Iraq while at the same time asking them to cut back in their relationships with the United States.

In the end, there can be no doubt that the Islamic Republic of Iran is currently a strong force for revolutionary change in the Persian Gulf. Although it reserves a special hostility for Iraq and Saudi Arabia and is willing to maintain "normal" diplomatic relations with the other countries, it acts as a catalyst for the fundamental transformation of political systems throughout the region. And it sees such change as inevitable. In the words of leading Iranian ideologues, "Saddam is doomed to be destroyed and after his ouster, the American-sponsored reactionary regimes in the region will one after another follow

[37] *Tehran Times,* 21 November 1982, p. 2.

him under the tremendous pressure of the Islamic Revolution." [38]

While Iran remains embroiled in the war with Iraq, it is not free to turn much attention to the business of revolution exportation to other countries in the region. Once this war is concluded, however, both Iran and Iraq — the two most powerful and revolutionary nations in the Gulf — will be in a better position to promote their respective interests and ideologies in the Gulf. It will be at this time that the message of revolutionary Iran will be sent through the region with a new and greater insistence. In this context, it is important to examine briefly the content of that message.

The revolution in Iran carries three major points of appeal to the middle and lower classes of the traditional countries of the Gulf that have not as yet witnessed major revolutionary upheaval. First, in Iran the masses of people rose successfully and overthrew a venal and repressive traditional patrimonial regime dominated by the Pahlavi family. Second, the Iranian revolution resulted in a system of government whereby the new regime managed to cut its ties of dependence upon outside superpowers and to declare its national independence. The most-quoted slogan of the revolution is "Neither East nor West." Third, the revolution in Iran represented a victory for Islam and a reaffirmation of the strength and relevance of that civilization in the modern world. Well aware of these three facts, the Iranian government has consistently stressed them in its policy pronouncements and in its efforts at *tablighat*. Iranian propaganda emphasizes the alleged corrupt and reactionary nature of traditional ruling regimes and families while championing the cause of the *mostaza'fin* throughout the region. The ruling families are then linked to the United States and are presented as clients of external Western exploitative great powers. Finally, because these traditional governments stand accused of corruption and exploitation on the one hand and subservience to external forces on the other hand, they are labeled as traitors to Islam. On 30 May 1982, Khomeini gave a

---

[38] *Tehran Times,* 27 September 1982, p. 6.

speech directed to the Gulf rulers in particular and in it he stressed these points.

> In this crucial time the U.S. says that it has friends and interests in the region.... We declare here to our neighboring Islamic countries and to their heads, who think of themselves as Muslims, that the interest the U.S. is talking about — which is being endangered by Islam and Islamic Iran — is nothing less than the boundless resources of Islamic lands. Some of you are the friends they are talking about, some of you who are serving them and presenting the wealth of your country to them.
>
> The Iranian nation, the government and its organs want to take this humiliating burden off you. The superpowers should not take your interests and the wealth, which should be employed in the service of your nation and in the construction of your country, for free. They are deceiving you.... Be a servant of your nation and Islam so that you may live as masters. Is it not better than living in isolation from your nations and turning your backs to Islam?
>
> America does not want friends, it wants servants, servants who present them with the interests of their own nations and live in subservience themselves.[39]

Revolutionary Iran also ties the three above points together by emphasizing the Israeli factor. Iranian political leaders constantly and publicly make the point that the ruling regimes in many of the Arab countries are traitors to their people, to themselves, and to Islam because of their failure to adopt a hard line towards Israel. Iran has pointed out that Camp David, the Fahd Plan, and the Fez Agreement were in its opinion "sell-outs." Also, the close American-Israeli association is stressed. The argument is that by associating themselves so closely with the United States, the traditional Arab governments are in fact aiding and abetting Israel. This position was stressed especially during the summer and fall of 1982, when Israeli troops invaded and occupied Lebanon. Iran claimed that the Arabs did nothing to stop this aggression but instead continued to pour billions of dollars of aid into Iraq, which was fighting another Muslim country. Iran also accused Saudi

[39] *Tehran Times,* 31 May 1982, p. 1.

Arabia of turning its troops loose on defenseless Iranian pilgrims during the Hajj instead of on the Israelis, who were in fact attacking Arab lands and peoples. One week after the June 1982 Israeli invasion of Lebanon, Ayatollah Khomeini gave a speech to a group of foreign guests in which he criticized "the reactionary regimes of the region" in the following terms: "What can we say to these deaf, dumb, and blind people? Do these regional governments not consider the Lebanese issue a catastrophe for Islam and world Muslims? If they are not deaf, why do they not hear the cries and mourning of our dear ones in Lebanon, and if they are not blind why do they not see these many people, men, women, and children who are being massacred every day?" [40] Khomeini went on to point out bitingly that "right amidst these problems faced by Iran, a Muslim king in the region is purchasing 24 camels for his modern zoo. The foreign powers are looting everything Muslims have and they are buying camels." [41] On 19 September 1982, Khomeini's chosen successor, Ayatollah Hussein Ali Montazeri referred to the massacre of the Lebanese and Palestinians and said: "Instead of confronting Israel and resisting such crimes, the so-called leaders of Islamic countries unfortunately attack Muslim pilgrims from Iran who have committed no crime other than chanting 'Down with the U.S.' and 'Down with Israel." [42]

To those who are dissatisfied and disaffected in the traditional countries of the Gulf, these are potent messages. Although their appeal transcends Sunni-Shi'i divisions, they carry a special meaning among the large number of Shi'ites who live in the Gulf countries. Despite the Iranian revolution, these Shi'ites continue to make their pilgrimages to the holy Shi'i shrines in Iran and Iraq and are all very much aware of the Shi'i victory over the Shah in Iran. The estimated number of Shi'ites in the various Gulf states follows. Iran, of course, is 95 percent Shi'ite and therefore accounts for approximately 38 million Shi'i believers. In Iraq, the proportion is 55 percent and the total there is about 8 million Shi'ites. Kuwait has an

---

40 *Tehran Times,* 14 June 1982, p. 1.
41 *Ibid.*
42 *Tehran Times,* 20 September 1982, p. 1.

estimated 275,000 Shi'ites, or about 25 percent of its population. In Saudi Arabia, the number is 260,000, almost all of
whom reside in the Eastern Province (there are several extended
families of Shi'ites living in Medina as well). The Saudi Shi'ites
are particularly concentrated in the city of Qatif and its surrounding oasis communities, where the population of 154,000
is 98 percent Shi'ite. At Hofuf, where the total population is
200,000, 45 percent are Shi'ite. In Bahrain, close to 70 percent
of Bahraini citizens are Shi'ites, making a total of approximately 170,000 Shi'ites in that small country. Very rough estimates of the numbers of Shi'ites in the United Arab Emirates,
Qatar, and Oman are 60,000, 30,000, and 30,000 respectively.[43]

The Shi'ites in the Gulf are organized through their mosques
and *ma'tams* (special places of mourning) as well as in the suqs
and bazaars, where large number of the Shi'ites who are of
Iranian origin are extremely active in commerce and trade.
Indications of the social and political restlessness of the Shi'ites
in the Gulf are seen in the various incidents and political demonstrations that have occurred since 1979 in Iraq, Kuwait,
Bahrain, and in the Eastern Province of Saudi Arabia. The
Saudis have approached their "Shi'ite problem" in a rather
heavy-handed way by throwing their National Guard at it —
an approach that has only heightened tensions in the Eastern
Province. In Bahrain, on the other hand, Shaykh Isa has developed a program designed to co-opt the Shi'ites into the
Bahraini political and economic systems. Four of the ministers
in the Cabinet in Bahrain are Shi'ites. In contrast, Saudi
Arabia has never had a Shi'i minister. In the end, the existence
of large numbers of Shi'i believers in the Persian Gulf region
provides a slightly more fertile ground for the revolutionary
seeds being sown throughout the area by the Islamic Republic
in Iran.

The appeal and challenge of the Iranian revolutionary regime cannot be ignored or wished away by the ruling elites of

---

[43] The figures presented in this paragraph are calculated on the basis
of information gathered from a variety of sources, both oral and written.
Most are the results of data gathered during two research trips to the
Gulf in 1982.

these Arab countries. In the face of such a challenge, it is essential that they develop appropriate and prudent policies in response. What are the various strategies available to these regimes? What have been the programs and policies that they have in fact adopted? And how effective have they been?

POLITICAL STRATEGIES AND POLITICAL
DEVELOPMENT IN THE GULF

The leaders of the traditional patrimonial countries of the Gulf can respond to the Iranian challenge by pursuing one of three political strategies: *repression, regression,* and *reform.* The reactive policy of *repression* involves battening down the political hatches and tightening the regime's control over the population of the particular country. The opportunities for dissent and political participation are choked off, and the role of the police and security forces is enlarged significantly. Political development is accorded the very lowest priority in this approach. Those leaders who adopt policies of repression are usually insecure and have faced significant challenges from their own populations.

In a program of *regression,* the political leaders revert to past procedures of crisis management and muddling through. In this response, the regime pursues ad hoc policies designed to address political challenges as they arise. Sometimes they take severely repressive measures; at other times they loosen central control and allow more freedom of expression and open up new channels of political participation. This pendulum-like policy also tends to be a highly reactive one. The leadership chooses to adopt one or another technique based on the events unfolding in the country at the time. During times of sharp crisis, the ruling elite resorts to force; when crises abate, the political leaders may introduce reforms.

Response by *reform* is an enlightened attempt to address the challenges of the day by opening up the system and by providing clear opportunities for individual expression, social mobility, and political participation. Reform strategies place an emphasis upon the need to confront the issue of political development. In particular, it often involves the willingness to expand channels of participation beyond the traditional networks of majlises and to introduce local modes of self-government along with national consultative assemblies. In traditional patrimonial systems in particular, reform strategies include a recognition of the need to spread major decision-making power beyond a small group of individuals in the ruling family. This strategy also usually carries with it serious anti-corruption campaigns as well as loosening censorship policy and reforming the judicial system.

From the perspective of ruling patrimonial elites, all three strategies carry costs and consequences. Policy based on repression can bottle up grievances in the short run but can lead to especially explosive and violent upheaval in the longer run. The violent revolution in Iraq in 1958 and in Iran in 1978–1979 are excellent examples of this principle. Repression only builds social and political pressure. It does not dissipate such pressure. Programs of regression also help to buy time, but owing to their inconsistent and reactive nature, they are often suddenly overwhelmed by new and unpredictable events. To apply force at a time when accommodation and compromise are in order or to open the system suddenly when control is called for are both prescriptions for catastrophe. Regression does carry one advantage over repression: It does allow for some dissipation of pressures building up within the particular society. The strategy of reform is also one that must be administered prudently and delicately. Often political elites decide to introduce reform as a last resort. By then it is too little, too late. Increasingly, the reform alternative in the Middle East in general and the Gulf in particular must take the form of nothing less than revolution from above. Otherwise, it may very well be bloody revolution from below.

With the exceptions of Iraq and Iran, which for quite different reasons and in quite different circumstances have been pursuing heavily repressive policies, the countries of the Gulf have all adopted a policy of regression, a blend of repression and reform. The mixture is quite different from one country to another. In Saudi Arabia, Oman, and Qatar, the emphasis is away from reform and toward control. In Bahrain, the United Arab Emirates, and Kuwait, there has been a relatively greater sensitivity to reform and to the need for some broader modes of political organization and participation. It is important to remember here, however, that the fundamental imperative is that of ruling family political preeminence. Power and authority in the six traditional patrimonial countries of the Gulf are to remain concentrated in the hands of the Al Sauds, Abu Al Saids, Al Thanis, Al Khalifahs, Al Nuhayyans and Al Maktums, and Al Sabahs. With this principle understood, there is considerable room for social and economic change and reform. The governments of all of these countries have stressed major improvements for their populations in the related areas of health, education, housing, and general welfare. This, along with the continuation of the traditional modes of political participation is part of the reform side of the equation.

The presence of the revolutionary message emanating from Iran and the increasing demands of their own populations have caused the political elites of these traditional countries to implement one further policy in the area of development. They have begun to establish national consultative assemblies and advisory councils of one kind or another. In February 1981, Kuwait held general elections and reestablished its parliament, a body that had been dissolved since 1976. Also, in 1981, Sultan Qabus of Oman established a National Consultative Council of 40 members, half from the public sector and half from the private sector. In the United Arab Emirates, there is a Federal National Assembly, while in Abu Dhabi itself there is the Abu Dhabi National Consultative Council, a 50-member body appointed by Shaykh Zayid. Qatar has a 30-member Advisory Council as well. Only Bahrain and Saudi Arabia have no such body, although in both countries there are plans to form consultative organizations. Bahrain is somewhat leery of the formation of such an Assembly, since the one that operated between 1973 and 1975 had to be dissolved in the face of a kind of activism that the rulers felt threatened the country's stability. Although King Fahd of Saudi Arabia has spoken several times about his commitment to establish a National Council one day, the Saud government has chosen to begin its program of cautiously widening participation at the provincial level. In his speech to the nation on July 23, 1982, King Fahd summarized his plans in this way: "... the principles of the basic system of government and the consultative council will, God willing, be in the forefront of the issues of concern to me. . . . This will be accompanied or preceded by moves to bring to completion the necessary measures to put into force the provincial law. . . ." [44]

These measures indicate that there is some sensitivity to the need to broaden political participation in the region. Yet these actions designed to promote wider representation in no way indicate a redistribution of political power. All such organizations exist at the sufferance of the ruling families, which can create and dissolve such bodies at will. With the partial exception of Kuwait, there are no broadly representative policy-making bodies elected from below in the Gulf region. In a quiet understatement, one seasoned observer of Gulf politics has stated that none of the rulers in the Gulf is "wild" about having any kind of seriously representative bodies in their countries.[45] In speaking of the traditional rulers of the Gulf, a former member of the Kuwaiti parliament has stated: "The shaykhs have not learned anything; they believe the people are happy and satisfied. They are convinced they are the best rulers possible. . . . These people have in their blood the morphine of power." [46] Still, what is significant here is the obvious felt need by these rulers to begin establishing consultative councils and assemblies.

Although these sporadic policies of reform are increasingly visible in the traditional countries of the Gulf, the underlying strength of central control is also evident. Police and security forces (often buttressed by experienced outside advisers) are very heavily relied upon to promote political stability. Again, with the partial exception of Kuwait, censorship is extremely severe. Control is tightest in Saudi Arabia, which, although not a police state in the style of the Shah's Iran or Saddam's Iraq, nonetheless leans more heavily in the direction of repression than in the direction of reform. The financial and inter-

[44] Quoted in *Financial Times,* 9 September 1982, p. 12.
[45] Personal interview, Gulf shaykhdom, August 1982.
[46] Quoted in Chris Kutschera, "Democracy in the Gulf," *The Middle East* (July 1980), p. 33.

national power of Saudi Arabia gives it special influence in the region, and its counsel on these important developmental matters carries great weight in the decision-making process of the other Gulf rulers. In the face of Saudi advice, Kuwait, Bahrain, and the United Arab Emirates have been less willing to deepen significantly their programs of reform. Serious discussions and debates of issues such as this one have increasingly been taking place in an organization established in May 1981, the Gulf Cooperation Council (GCC). The GCC itself was formed partially in response to the revolutionary threats that accelerated in the region because of the Iranian revolution.

The Gulf Cooperation Council represents the major political action taken by the six traditional countries of the Gulf and is an attempt to develop some consensus and coordination in view of the political challenges that they all face. Saudi Arabia has been the driving force behind the GCC, whose permanent secretariat is located in Riyadh. Unlike many past attempts by the Arabs to develop schemes of unity, the GCC experiment is not meant to be a "union" but rather to be a loosely organized "cooperative" body. Much of its business has been carried out informally and without official agreements and treaties. Besides a Ministerial Council and numerous committees, including an important defense committee, the GCC seeks to hold Head of State meetings on a regular basis, annually if possible. The first such meeting was held in Abu Dhabi in May 1981, and the second met in Bahrain in November 1982. The leaders of the six member countries intentionally seek to keep the GCC a low-profile organization. In this way, they hope to keep expectations of their people and of outside observers to a realistic level. They also are very sensitive to the need not to alienate unnecessarily the two most powerful countries in the Gulf, Iran and Iraq, neither of which has been invited to join the organization.

In the first years of its existence, the GCC has tended to emphasize matters of mutual defense. Given the impact in the region of the Iranian revolution and its slogan of "Neither East nor West," the Gulf leaders are aware of the need to develop their own defense capabilities and not to have to depend on outside powers such as the United States to maintain a presence in the area. In the words of U.A.E. president, Shaykh Zayid: "Our conception of Gulf security is one in which the countries of the Gulf are allowed to live peacefully and securely without interference from foreign powers, and without the great powers trying to determine the area's fate." [47] Between August of 1981 and November of 1982, the defense ministers of the GCC met on a half-dozen different occasions. Among other things, the discussions here have centered on the possible development of their own Rapid Deployment or Expeditionary Force over the next decade. The major threat to be countered is seen to be that of internal security and the need to coordinate action if serious rebellion or revolutionary upheaval should break out in one of the member states.

In emphasizing mutual defense in the early years of its existence, the Gulf Cooperation Council has stressed crisis management rather than crisis avoidance. Nonetheless, within GCC sessions the members have also begun to discuss political programs and the need to address the problem of political development. The establishment of a defense strategy will be much easier than the creation of some generally accepted internal political strategy. This is, of course, one major reason why the GCC has from the beginning not entertained pretensions of unity. Cooperation, coordination, and the exchange of ideas are the essence of the experiment. Also, the fact that the GCC has been organized is in itself a strong factor countering some of the pressure building among the populations of the member states. It is clearly an important step in the direction of regional independence. Anwar Sadat is reported to have referred to the small shaykhdoms along the Gulf as "those jelly-like entities." With the creation of the GCC, the jelly has begun to congeal.

Of the various challenges carried by the Iranian revolution and described above, perhaps the most serious is the emphasis by the Islamic Republic that its government is of, by, and for the *mostaza'fin*. The revolution is constantly portrayed as a popular movement in which the masses of deprived Iranians rose to overthrow a regime considered to be corrupt and repres-

[47] Quoted in *The Christian Science Monitor*, 26 May 1981, p. 10.

sive. The revolutionary government in Iran stresses the argument that it enjoys mass support and that there is genuine political participation in an Islamic framework in practice in the Islamic Republic. The corruption and subservience of the Shah's regime to the West at the expense of the well-being and dignity of the *mostaza'fin* is also a theme presented throughout the region by the Iranian leadership. It is with this message that the Iranian revolution threatens the political jugular of the traditional patrimonial governments in the Gulf. Huge de fense outlays and skilled security forces cannot erase the impact of this message — a message that speaks directly to the issue of political development.

Despite a growing sensitivity to the need to respond creatively and fundamentally to the demands of their growing middle classes and deeply religious lower classes, the ruling elites of most Gulf countries have yet to implement the basic reform programs necessary to guarantee the survival of their systems in the long run. Instead, they have increased their programs of defensive modernization and have used their oil wealth to buy time. Despite the assertion by one Gulf minister that "we have no *mostaza'fin* here," [48] there is a large visible gap between the "have mosts" and "have leasts" in the Gulf countries. The Islamic tone of the developmental message in the region also means that increasingly there are those whose loyalty and commitment cannot be bought. This is why one ruler in the region has stated that "I would rather deal with ten communists than with one Muslim fundamentalist." [49]

The ruling elites of the Gulf countries have done better than most in providing for the material needs of their people. They have done less well in curbing personal and financial excesses that tend to be endemic to their ranks. And they have yet to respond meaningfully to the growing political demands of their own citizens, whose appetites for nonmaterial goals increase as rapidly as the years of education that their countries

[48] Personal interview with Minister of Information, Gulf shaykhdom, August 1982.

[49] Personal interview with adviser to the ruler, Gulf shaykhdom, 17 August 1982.

give them. Today, the demands are for personal dignity, political participation, social justice, and national independence. Such goals cannot be satisfied by force, repression, and arbitrary rule. A number of enlightened leaders in the Gulf realize this; thus the small but growing sentiment for reform in certain ruling circles. They understand the futility of attempting to stem the twin tides of revolutionary political expectations and resurgent Islam through the application of force. One leading scholar and close friend of the Arab world explains that the ruling elites of the Arab countries had not properly learned from the lesson of the Shah's Iran. "Instead of introducing meaningful reform, they apply more security measures, failing to realize, as did the Shah when it was too late, that when self-preservation becomes the overriding concern of government, repression solidifies into irreversible policy: Coercion leads to more coercion, and contradictions, instead of being overcome, sharpen and become more and more difficult to resolve." [50]

The internal contradictions present in the traditional countries of the Persian Gulf have not exploded into revolutionary violence because the benefits of the processes of modernization fueled by great wealth have been shared to a significant degree by the relatively small populations of citizens resident there. Beginning in 1979, external forces such as the Iranian revolution in the Gulf, and to a somewhat lesser degree, general American and Israeli policy in the Middle East, have placed a sharply increasing strain upon these political and social systems. The response of the ruling families to these gathering and deepening challenges will determine the future of the region.

[50] Hisham Sharabi, "The Poor Rich Arabs," unpublished paper presented at Center for Contemporary Arab Studies symposium, Georgetown University, April 9–10, 1981, p. 3. This presentation was published in *The Christian Science Monitor*, 27 July 1981.

CHAPTER X

Oil, the Middle East, and the Future

To MANY AMERICANS, oil and the Middle East are synonymous and OPEC is a four-letter word. There is no doubt that during the last decade the American economy, based as it has been on petroleum, has suffered from new pricing and production policies from Middle Eastern oil states. In our stereotypes, these producers are invariably in flowing robes, standing by their camels, grinning as they reach down to turn off a convenient spigot. Unfortunately, the situation is enormously more complex than this, and our understanding of it is apt to be painfully inadequate.

First of all, oil is very unevenly distributed in the area that we term the Middle East. West of Libya there is relatively little oil that has been discovered, although Algeria has some petroleum and large reserves of natural gas. Egypt for a long time seemed to have little petroleum, but during the last decade fresh discoveries have given the Egyptians a modicum of oil for domestic consumption and modest export. There is no oil of significance in Sudan, Israel, Jordan, Lebanon, or Syria; and far to the east, the same is true of Afghanistan and Pakistan, although there is natural gas in Afghanistan. It is only in the region of the Persian Gulf that the immense oil deposits are to be found. The distribution — or maldistribution — of petroleum has led to many of the current political problems of the area.

In one way or another the gears of the Middle Eastern social and political systems are lubricated by this precious natural resource. Directly or indirectly, it has become the chief basis for the domestic, regional, and international power currently being used by most Middle Eastern political leaders to achieve their increasingly ambitious goals. The world shifted to petroleum during the First World War to fuel its industrial and military machinery; indeed, this very shift by the British Navy was made possible by the first commercial oil strike in the Middle East, in Khuzistan, Iran, in the first decade of the century. Given the scramble for Gulf oil after the war and the immense reserves that were to be discovered there, it was inevitable that the world would be involved with the Middle East for a very long time to come.

But for the first 70 years of this century, the potentials of Middle Eastern resources were barely realized. Lacking indigenous technological knowledge, economically feeble, and generally subjected to the control of Western colonial powers, the oil-producing states lacked the strength and market dominance to determine the fate of their own resources. In short, they were exploited. The degree to which they were exploited in the early days is almost beyond the imagination of those not accustomed to sitting in the board rooms of the then major oil companies. One instance will suffice: The British government, which owned a majority of the shares of the Anglo-Persian Oil Company in the 1920s, and hence received dividends on the profits, made more money by taxing those profits than did Iran from "selling" the oil. Over the years the distribution of oil and oil products at price levels that were unfairly low not only deprived oil-producing countries of income desperately needed for development but also lured the oil-consuming nations — of which the United States is the standard — into economies and consumption patterns that were in the long run to be dangerous. Even today, as Americans grumble about paying $1 for a gallon of gasoline, they are getting one of the real bargains of the world.

The key decisions concerning exploration, production, marketing, and pricing were made by large Western oil companies or by their parent political systems in Europe or the United States. Here were indeed the seeds of later trials and tribulations.

After the Second World War and coinciding with the strong nationalist movements that swept through the developing world, the petroleum-producing countries began to demand greater control over what they considered their own resources. At first, these demands took the form of insistence on higher prices for petroleum and larger royalties. In short, the political leaders of the oil-rich countries fought in the beginning for better bargains. With the formation of the Organization of Petroleum Exporting Countries (OPEC) in 1960, followed by the succession of meetings in Tripoli and Tehran in the early 1970s and the quadrupling of prices during the October 1973 war, the entire process of international decision making about oil was revolutionized. The producing countries, now no longer content merely to drive better bargains, challenged the entire bargaining system and succeeded in wresting decisional control away from the multinational oil organizations. From then on, the producing countries became the repositories of authority concerning the entire industry of hydrocarbon production and exploitation. It is now the oil companies and the consuming countries who have been put on the defensive. In fact, the international oil companies are now by and large marketing agents for OPEC.

This transformation in the interrelationships of international oil politics and economics has had a profound effect upon the domestic political patterns of all Middle Eastern countries, regardless of whether they are rich or poor in petroleum reserves. It has also changed significantly the interregional and international political scene. And it has affected in new ways the complex interactions between domestic political processes and international politics.

Among the questions that we pose here are the following: How did the dramatic changes in the traditional producer, company, and consumer system in fact come about? What has been the changing political and economic role of the international oil companies? What is the political clout and complex-

ion of OPEC? What have been the politics of the pricing conflict? What are the international political consequences of the
newly developed petroleum power? How does this power affect, for example, United States foreign policy, or the volatile
Arab-Israeli dispute? What are the domestic political consequences of this oil power? How does this power shape the responses of the various countries to the challenges of modernization and political development discussed throughout this
book? Is oil power a conservative or a transforming force? And
finally, what does the future of the petroleum dynamics hold
for the political future of the area?

THE POOL OF PETROLEUM POWER

Many Western observers and leaders of opinion seriously underestimate the extent of Middle Eastern petroleum wealth. It
is often argued that the contemporary international influence
wielded by Middle Eastern governments is a transitory phenomenon, since, with the depletion of their oil reserves, they
will be forced to retreat once again to the backwaters of world
politics. This position is buttressed with emphasis upon the
potential discovery of huge petroleum reserves elsewhere in
the world, the inevitable shift to alternate sources of energy,
the capacity of the Western world to conserve energy, and by
underestimating just how much oil there is in place in the
Middle East. This perspective has to some extent been reinforced by Middle Eastern spokesmen themselves, who have for
years pursued a calculated policy of understating their own oil
wealth.

This position, which was popular in the early 1970s, had
lost much of its credibility by the end of the decade. The social, economic, and technological difficulties involved in the
creation of viable alternate energy sources could no longer be
denied. Among energy experts, a belief in the persistence of
the energy crunch was common, but many people in the United
States continued to believe it illusory and a conspiracy by the
large oil companies or by the Middle Easterners. Nevertheless,
the Western world at least has conserved a bit, probably inspired by the rapid increase in prices in the late 1970s. The
production of monster automobiles has finally peaked, and

some awareness of the problem seems to have penetrated the ultimate consumers. Finally, the oil reserves recently discovered and put into production in the north slope of Alaska, the North Sea, and Mexico, began providing valuable assistance in absolute terms. Still, these reserves are very small indeed when compared to those in the Middle East.[1] Ironically, their very existence has served a negative purpose, since when they came on-stream in 1977 and 1978, they helped occasion an oil glut that only reinforced the opinions of those who continue to argue that there is no energy crisis, that oil is plentiful, that conservation is unnecessary, and that prices are grossly inflated.

The Middle East has steadily accounted for over 60 percent of the world's petroleum reserves. When the reserves of the Communist world are deleted from the equation, the Middle East's percentage of the world's reserves climbs to approximately 75 percent. Petroleum geologists privately estimate that even these figures underestimate the Middle East's share of this resource. It may in fact be as high as 70 percent of the world's supply and 85 percent of the non-Communist world's supply. A study published in the *Scientific American* reports that the rich Middle Eastern reserves "have been found in a region that measures only some 800 by 500 miles. Might such a prolific oil-bearing region be found again? It is not very likely. Many of the remaining possible areas of the world have already been evaluated by seismic testing or exploratory wells and no evidence of a new Middle East has come to light." [2]

The reserves of Saudi Arabia alone are staggering. The figure of 150 billion barrels is a conservative one; some sources put Saudi Arabia's proven reserves closer to 200 billion barrels. An indication of the extent of this wealth can be seen in the

[1] As Daniel Yergin writes, "Alaskan production in a decade or so will only make up for declining production in the lower 48 states. The North Sea oil fields could reach 5 million to 6 million barrels a day by 1985, but, barring some major new finds, their output will then begin to do down. The only major new oil strike of the 1970's was the one in Mexico, and production there is being held back by political and technical problems." Yergin, "The Real Meaning of the Energy Crunch," *New York Times Magazine*, 4 June 1978, p. 99.

[2] Andrew R. Flower, "World Oil Production," *Scientific American* 238 (March 1978):44.

news quietly reported that the Saudis discovered three new fields in 1975, with proven reserves of 7 billion barrels! The estimated total of recoverable barrels in the highly publicized North Sea fields is in contrast only 500 million barrels, although proven reserves are estimated to be as high as 20 billion barrels.[3] Even if one takes the 150 billion barrel figure, the Saudi Arabians still account for one-fourth of the world's proven reserves. Their reserves are five times those of the United States and twice those of the Soviet Union.

Kuwait, Iraq, and Iran also have substantial petroleum reserves. The three of them together have over 160 billion barrels of proven reserves. But even here the figures are misleading. The published figures consistently indicate that Iraq has approximately only half of the proven reserves of either Kuwait or Iran. Again, geologists say otherwise in private. Iraq is generally considered to be the only other Middle Eastern country whose reserves might in fact rival those of Saudi Arabia. This position was lent considerable credibility early in 1978, when a major discovery of a massive reserve near Nasriya in southeastern Iraq was reported. The area was immediately cordoned off by the Iraqi army, and the extent of the discovery is not known. Even Iran, whose reserves are commonly believed to be rapidly diminishing, has approximately 60 to 65 billion barrels of proven reserves of petroleum.

Given these reserves, it is not surprising that production figures have revealed a proportionate share for the Middle East and one that is growing. And this is in spite of the havoc wrought in the Iranian oil industry by the Shah's fall, exacerbated by the subsequent war between Iraq and Iran. Both countries lost significant production, but both continue to produce, Iran at an accelerating rate. The current (1983) world oil glut is caused by many countries outside the Middle East (not all are members of OPEC and OPEC itself contains non-Middle Eastern nations) that have increased their production either to meet their own needs or to raise money to underwrite their developmental plans. (As these words are being written, the British pound stood at $1.53, close to its all-time low. What

[3] *Ibid.* See also *The Oil and Gas Journal,* 17 December 1976, p. 104.

would it have been had the North Sea oil not come on-line?) In spite of a shaky world economy, a frenetic effort everywhere to find and produce oil, and a turbulent political Middle East, the world still depends upon the daily flow of laden tankers passing through the Strait of Hormuz. Middle Eastern oil is essential to the economy of the world.

But the Middle East has more than oil. The area also has one third of all the proven reserves of natural gas in the world.[4] After the Soviet Union, Iran is now the world's second largest repository of natural gas. Algeria, with over 60 percent of all proven reserves of gas on the African continent, is already exporting quantities of this fuel to the East Coast of the United States. As this mineral wealth is converted into cash reserves, the Middle Eastern countries have begun to step up their efforts to explore for other resources. We already know that they possess significant amounts of the world's phosphates, copper, tungsten, chromium, coal, and lignite.

These data indicate that the Middle East has a petroleum base that will guarantee it a privileged and powerful position for many years to come. If it succeeds in its goals of developing its other natural wealth, and if its leaders invest its wealth wisely, then the area may continue to be a critical force in the world well into the twenty-first century. The future depends to a large extent upon the political leaders of the various countries. In the end, the revolutionary shift in power to the oil-producing countries has been a political matter. The resources and economic strength had always been there; it took a series of imaginative political moves to fundamentally shift the control of these resources. A brief summary of this complex story follows.

THE MAJOR OIL COMPANIES AND
THE TRADITIONAL
INTERNATIONAL POWER STRUCTURE

For half a century, the politics and economics of petroleum were largely directed and controlled by a small group of in-

---

[4] This figure is calculated on the basis of data provided in *The Oil and Gas Journal*, 26 December 1977, pp. 98–148.

ternational oil companies. Although the governments of the producing and consuming countries played a part in the overall process, the major companies were easily the dominant force. Today, they are still powerful and influential. The British were the first to move into the area when they began to produce petroleum commercially in 1908 in Iran. Thus, the Anglo-Persian Oil Company (later the Anglo-Iranian Oil Company and today known as British Petroleum) was the first multinational giant to gain a foothold in the region. With the entrance of Royal Dutch Shell into the area, the Europeans gained a tight early grip on oil exploration and production in the Middle East. Much of the history of international oil politics is explained in terms of the struggle between the British and the Americans as United States companies fought to gain entry into the rich Middle Eastern fields.

Although American oil companies had first wedged their way into the Middle Eastern oil business as minority partners in the Iraq Petroleum Company (IPC) and by bringing in their first well in the area in Bahrain in 1931, it was not until 1933 in Saudi Arabia and 1934 in Kuwait that the American companies entered the scene in a major way. In the case of Kuwait, two legendary characters, Frank Holmes and Archibald H. T. Chisholm, representing Gulf Oil of the United States and the Anglo-Persian Oil Company respectively, out-maneuvered each other into a standstill that resulted in the joint concession between the two companies (Kuwait Oil Company).[5]

Saudi Arabia was another story. Here, led by Standard Oil of California (Socal), and subsequently joined by the Texas Company (Texaco) and later by Standard Oil of New Jersey (today's Exxon) and Socony-Vacuum Oil Company (today's Mobil), an all-American group took control over the world's richest oil territory. This operating company in Saudi Arabia is well known as the Arabian-American Oil Company (Aramco).[6]

---

[5] For an amusing account of the Holmes-Chisholm rivalry over the Kuwait concession, see Leonard Mosley, *Power Play: Oil in the Middle East* (Baltimore, Md.: Penguin Books, 1974), pp. 77–86.

[6] For years, Mobil Oil's share of Aramco production was only 10 percent, while the other three partners each controlled 30 percent. In the late 1970s Mobil renegotiated its share of Aramco. Today it is 15 percent,

The four Aramco companies, plus Gulf Oil Company, are the five largest American oil companies; along with British Petroleum and Royal Dutch Shell, they comprise the so-called Seven Sisters.[7]

The seven international majors were the controlling forces of world oil trade for years. Until relatively recently, they accounted for over 80 percent of all oil production outside North America and the Soviet bloc. They also controlled over 70 percent of the refining capacity and 50 percent of the tanker fleet in this area. Although other major companies, such as Campagnie Française des Petroles (CFP) of France and Ente Nazionale Idrocarburi (ENI) of Italy, as well as a dozen other large American companies, have made significant inroads into the territory long monopolized by the big seven, the latter still are far and way the world's leaders among the fully integrated multinational oil corporations.

These companies ruled supreme for so long for several interrelated reasons. First, they were all fully integrated units, that is, they were intimately involved in the exploration, development, production, transportation, refining, and marketing of the product. This provided them with great expertise in all aspects of the business, while at the same time enabling them to shift resources and emphasis back and forth and thus to protect each link in the chain at all times. Second, their very mul-

---

while that of the remaining partners has fallen slightly to 28.33 percent each.

Throughout the 1970s, Aramco and the Saudi Arabian government discussed the participation of the latter in Aramco's crude oil producing operations. The *Mobil Annual Report 1977* explains well the terms of the Saudi takeover: "Currently, the negotiations contemplate acquisition by the government of substantially all of Aramco's assets and the establishment of future arrangements. Under those proposed arrangements, Aramco will provide a broad range of management and technical services, will conduct an exploration program for the government, and will receive a fee. Also, the U.S. owner companies will have access through Aramco to substantial specified volumes of crude oil at a competitive price under a long-term contract." *Mobil Annual Report 1977*, p. 50.

[7] A very readable and informative book analyzing the history, politics, and personalities of these seven huge companies is Anthony Sampson's *The Seven Sisters: The Great Oil Companies and the World They Made* (New York: Viking Press, 1975).

tinational character gave them a flexibility that enabled them to focus their efforts in whatever part of the world was economically and politically most advantageous at any given time. Third, the majors cooperated with one another in a number of subtle and in some not-so-subtle ways. In the Achnacarry Agreement of 1928, the three largest petroleum companies in the world at the time (Jersey-Standard, Royal Dutch Shell, Anglo-Persian) in effect divided up the world among themselves in order to discourage outside competition. In the 1950s, the companies stood together against Iran and Iraq when these countries fought to nationalize the Anglo-Iranian Oil Company and to severely restrict the concessions granted to the Iraq Petroleum Company. In both these cases, the united front of the oil companies successfully thwarted in different ways the demands of these Middle Eastern nationalists. International oil organization unity is also seen in the joint operating companies or consortia in which various combinations of the majors contractually agree to pursue business together. We have seen some examples of such combinations above.

Another cluster of reasons for major-oil-company long-time hegemony resides in the state of the producing countries themselves. Often ruled by weak traditional patrimonial leaders who owed their position to outside powers (primarily the British), the peoples of these countries were in no position to challenge anybody, much less powerful multinational giants. Also, in the case of the European companies, the governments had a direct and controlling interest in the businesses. As late as 1953, a strong nationalist movement in Iran, led by the charismatic Dr. Musaddiq, was suffocated by the international oil companies, backed by the British and American governments. Although Musaddiq's technocracy was able to produce the oil, the international majors made it impossible to market the product.

Throughout this period, the oil companies determined pricing policy. Until about 1950, they simply paid the governments of the producing countries a set royalty that averaged something less than 25 cents per barrel. Following the Second World War, Venezuela and Saudi Arabia led a drive that resulted in taxes amounting to half the net income earned by the companies. This move shifted the emphasis from volume to profits, and throughout the 1950s and 1960s government revenues were based on a posted price.[8] A royalty of 12.5 percent was paid on the posted price. This royalty and the production cost were added together, and this sum was subtracted from the posted price. The result was considered the company's profit, and it was on this profit that an income tax (50 percent until 1970) was paid to the oil-exporting country. These arrangements of the payment process resulted in significantly higher revenues for the producing countries. Yet the rules of the game and all decisions made therein were still essentially determined by the international oil companies. Then, in February 1959 and in August 1960, the major companies unilaterally reduced the posted price of Middle Eastern oil by 8 and 5 percent, respectively. These actions marked the beginning of the end of the old system.

THE POLITICS OF OPEC

In September 1960, the governments of Saudi Arabia, Iran, Kuwait, Iraq, and Venezuela met in Baghdad and founded OPEC. The goals of the organization announced at the time were to coordinate the member countries' policies toward the companies, to acquire a voice in future pricing policy, and to do something specific to restore the recent price cuts. The five founding members were later joined by Qatar, Indonesia, Libya, the United Arab Emirates, Algeria, Nigeria, Ecuador, and Gabon. By 1977, these thirteen countries, eight of which are Middle Eastern, accounted for 82 percent of the non-Communist world's reserves.

The creation and drive of OPEC were an integral part of the wave of nationalistic fervor that swept the world in the 1950s and 1960s. Having only recently broken out of the colonial grasp of several of the greatest Western industrial powers, the leadership of the developing nations fought to develop their

8 The *posted price* is best defined as the price established in principle by the companies as a basis for business and royalty payment. It is compared to the *realized price*, which is the price actually paid for the oil as determined by market conditions. The realized price was usually lower than the posted price during this period.

nations' own identities by destroying their nations' dependence upon Western countries and multinational companies. The two men most responsible for the creation of OPEC were Perez Alfonza, Venezuela's minister of mines, and Shaykh Abdullah Tariki, Saudi Arabia's director-general of petroleum affairs. Both men were ardent nationalists with remarkable intelligence and integrity. They represented the forces of change then sweeping through the world.[9] In the words of George Stocking, the dissatisfaction of the producing countries

> originated in the humus of distrust and suspicion laid down by the abrasive impact of western technology and a business culture on economically underdeveloped countries wholly dissimilar in their political and social institutions and their history and traditions. Once planted, they thrived under a blanket of hostility kept warm by the clash of a corporate quest for profits with the interests of underdeveloped countries as conceived by their politicians and their people.[10]

Little more than a decade after the creation of OPEC, the oil equation had changed. Table X.1 provides a summary of the critical events and specific steps involved in the transformation. Led by the authoritarian-distributive regimes of Libya and Algeria and supported at critical times by the traditional political elites in Iran and Saudi Arabia, the producing countries took control of the world oil process away from the companies headquartered and nourished in the West. Revolutionary nationalism was an important ingredient in the policy of these producing countries. In the case of Iran, the new policy stemmed primarily from the desperate need of the Shah for increased resources to enable his regime to maintain its shaky political control. In Saudi Arabia, elements of nationalism and of regime survival were both involved, but it was also the

---

[9] For a fascinating account of Tariki as "a new man" in the Middle Eastern political and economic context, see Stephen Duguid, "A Biographical Approach to the Study of Social Change in the Middle East: Abdullah Tariki as a New Man," *International Journal of Middle East Studies* I (July 1970):195–220.

[10] George W. Stocking, *Middle East Oil: A Study in Political and Economic Controversy* (Nashville, Tenn.: Vanderbilt University Press, 1970), p. 350.

TABLE X.1   *The Petroleum-Producing Countries' Drive to Power*

Chronicle of Events

August 1960	Major oil companies, led by Standard Oil of New Jersey, unilaterally cut posted price of oil.
September 1960	Representatives of Saudi Arabia, Iran, Iraq, Kuwait, and Venezuela meet in Baghdad and form the Organization of Petroleum Exporting Countries (OPEC).
September 1968	First meeting of the Council of the newly established Organization of Arab Petroleum Exporting Countries (OAPEC). Founding members: Saudi Arabia, Kuwait, and Libya.
September 1969	Traditional monarchy of King Idris in Libya overthrown in coup that brings to power a more radical government, headed by Colonel Mu'ammar Qaddafi.
September 1970	Occidental Petroleum reluctantly accepts agreement with Libyan government after eight months of pressure-packed negotiations. Posted prices raised 30 cents a barrel, with further increases of 2 cents a barrel for each of the next five years; tax rate on profits raised from 50 percent to 58 percent in Occidental's case.
December 1970	Twenty-first meeting of OPEC in Caracas, Venezuela. Producing countries resolve to push forward on all fronts, raising posted prices and increasing tax rates.
February 1971	Tehran Agreement. Posted prices raised 33 cents a barrel with further increases of 5 cents a barrel over the next five years; income tax stabilized at 55 percent. Agreement to remain in effect through 1975.
April 1971	Tripoli Agreement. Posted prices raised 90 cents a barrel with further increases of 5 cents a barrel and income tax rate set at 55 percent. Agreement to remain in effect for five years and Libyan claims for retroactive payments settled.
February 1972	King Faisal of Saudi Arabia in a strongly worded statement supports producing-country participation in petroleum company ownership and operations. Shaykh Ahmad Zaki Yamani, Saudi minister of oil, had been urging participation since 1969.
October 1972	Shaykh Yamani announces formal agreement between producing countries and petroleum companies concerning participation. Countries can purchase an initial 25

TABLE X.1   (continued)

Chronicle of Events

	percent interest in the companies, then further interest until they reach 51 percent ownership.
May 1973	Iranian Sales Agreement. Iran formally completes nationalization of all its resources and facilities and works out a 20-year purchase contract with the consortium, which is assured access to Iranian petroleum. Iran is to receive all of its domestic-consumption oil at cost and is assured its economic benefits are as good as those won by the Arabs.
August 1973	Libya begins nationalizing 51 percent of the assets of the oil companies still in operation there. By September, this action, which was first directed against Occidental and other independents, was expanded to include the oil majors. This represents the beginning of the total takeover of oil companies operating on Arab soil.
October 1973	October War between the Arabs and Israelis. Arab states deliberately curtail production and institute petroleum embargo. Major OPEC members unilaterally decide that they, not the companies, will henceforth determine pricing. Posted price increased to $5.11 per barrel.
December 1973	OPEC members raise the posted price to $11.65, thus quadrupling the price since the outbreak of the October War.
March 1974	Arab OPEC membership lifts petroleum embargo against the United States.

staunch American support for the state of Israel that encouraged the Saudis to develop a tougher stand on oil. And there were other considerations as well, not the least of which was the general desire of weak nation-states to improve their power positions in the international arena.

The basic oil revolution occurred between 1970 and 1974. During these years, the OPEC countries gained the power both to control prices and to determine production policy. They also began acquiring full ownership of the facilities and control over the technical operations within their boundaries.

There is little doubt now that they are also becoming increasingly active in "downstream activities," including transportation, distribution, and marketing. This sharp shift in power, however, has not rendered the major companies obsolete. They remain indispensable technologically and still dominate the critical areas of distribution and marketing. In the end, however, there is little doubt that the petroleum exporting countries have gained primary control over their own hydrocarbons and that both the companies and the consumers have lost most of their leverage.

The economic reasons underlying the success of OPEC were numerous. First, oil was an essential commodity for which there was no immediate, economical substitute. Second, during the 1960s, OPEC's share of world oil exports climbed rapidly, giving the organization greater and greater control of the market. Third, by 1970 all of the excess production capacity resided in the OPEC countries, especially those in the Middle East. Fourth, the international appearance of a growing number of independent oil companies contributed significantly to producing-country power. Fifth, over the decade of the 1960s, OPEC countries had built substantial amounts of foreign exchange, enabling them to confront more comfortably the oil-importing nations of the West.[11]

Ever since OPEC's formation, scholars, journalists, businessmen, and other observers have been predicting its demise. Specialists in econometric modeling and supply-and-demand economics have continually explained why OPEC must shatter and why oil prices must plummet. At every sign of internal dissension within OPEC councils or of a temporary glut of oil on the world market, these prognosticators have come out with their statements that collapse is imminent.

In the spring of 1983 it seemed to many that these dire predictions were about to be realized. The oil glut that matured in 1981–1982 was a very important reality. The success of OPEC in the past in controlling production and elevating

11 These points are discussed in some detail in Hossein Askari and John Thomas Cummings, *Middle East Economies in the 1970s: A Comparative Approach* (New York: Praeger Publishers, 1976), Chapter I.

prices made mandatory a wide search for substitute sources of oil. Some were found, and even if they could hardly substitute for OPEC oil, their marginal contribution made it ever more difficult for OPEC to control the ultimate pricing and production structure. Two points are important. The first is that OPEC is not a cartel of all oil producers, so that it must always deal with the actions of other oil producers. The world oil market is thus affected by not merely OPEC but by others as well. The second point is that not all OPEC members agree, nor can they easily agree, on production figures or final amounts of revenue to be realized from their sale of oil. There is a vast difference between Saudi Arabia, with a small population and huge deposits of oil, and Iran, with a large population and a fragile revolutionary economy. Iran and Nigeria are the examples often offered of countries that have to produce regardless of price level because of the fragile nature of their development programs and the chaotic qualities of their economies. If the glut is going to be erased by OPEC (or other) actions, literally all major producers must lower production. Outside of OPEC some countries will not; inside OPEC some cannot (Iran for example). The natural result of overproduction is a softening of prices, and this has occurred. The situation in early 1983 was viewed with great alarm by both governments and private bankers. Mexico may be offered as an example. As Lawrence Rout and Steve Mufson report in *The Wall Street Journal*,[12]

> According to figures given to bankers by Mexico's Finance Ministry, the country should get slightly less than half of its foreign exchange this year from oil exports. "Mexico's current-account deficit is very sensitive to a drop in oil prices because oil makes up so much of the country's exports," says Vaughan Montes, an economist with the Mexican Project at Wharton Econometric Forecasting Associates. "So, when oil prices change, it changes everything."
>
> Wharton has been predicting a 3% decline in Mexico's output of goods and services this year and a current-account deficit of $3.7 billion. If oil prices fell just $2 a barrel, Mr. Montes says, economic output would drop 3.7%, while the current-

[12] 26 January 1983, p. 1.

account deficit would widen to $4.8 billion. The result would be more unemployment in Mexico and less money to pay import and debt bills.

"That's only after a $2-a-barrel drop," Mr. Montes notes. "If it's a lot more, I'm not sure how Mexico can service its debt." Mr. Montes explains that Mexico's agreement with the International Monetary Fund depends on a certain amount of oil revenue and a certain amount of borrowing from foreign banks. If oil revenue dropped, that delicate balance could be upset. Mexico would then have to slash imports even further or borrow additional funds from foreign banks, if it was to pay the interest on its debt.

Because large international banks have underwritten the financing of developmental programs in such countries as Mexico perhaps too lavishly, the ripple effects of falling prices could render not only countries insolvent but banks too. Together it could mean economic catastrophe for the world. It is only fair to say that not all economists or oil specialists view the situation as quite so alarming. Yet it obviously is serious.

This is currently emphasized by OPEC's inability to stabilize production and pricing. OPEC oil ministers met in Geneva in the latter half of January 1983. An effort was made to cut OPEC's daily production from 18 million barrels to something over 17 million barrels, but Saudi Arabia wanted this cut in production to be coupled with an end to price discounting by such countries as Libya and Nigeria and particularly Iran. The OPEC conference ended in disarray; the expectation was that price cuts perhaps to as low as $25 a barrel might be in the offing. Only weeks later OPEC finally did achieve agreement on price — $29 for Saudi light — and on production. Yet by May Iran had given a discount of $2 on a shipment of oil to Syria and the Japanese claimed that its new agreements with Iran would reflect some discounting. If true the fragile agreement may not last long. There is no way that one can predict the course of events in this highly volatile industry over even a few years. But what seems correct as of early 1983 is that:

1. There is an oil glut that may not quickly go away;
2. OPEC is in some internal disagreement over how to handle the situation;

3. Despite this internal disagreement, OPEC is not likely to disintegrate;

4. The world financial community does not want a collapse of oil prices;

5. In the long haul, an energy crisis remains; the glut will not last forever. Petroleum remains a precious resource.

Eight years after the formation of OPEC, three Arab countries within it initiated the creation of another related organization, the Organization of Arab Petroleum Exporting Countries (OAPEC). A low-profile group that is more politically conscious than OPEC, OAPEC promotes petroleum planning, joint economic projects, and manpower training among its members. Besides the seven Arab countries who are part of OPEC, OAPEC includes Egypt, Syria, and Bahrain. It was OAPEC (not OPEC) that planned and implemented the October 1973 oil embargo. Its sensitivity to political issues is seen in its published bulletin. In a 1977 issue of this publication, for example, European colonialism and economic exploitation were roundly criticized. According to the OAPEC analyst, "In the Arab world, the process of decolonization has been especially harsh. Needless to say, we have been and still are wiping the blood off our wounds." [13] Although OAPEC political concerns obviously carry over into OPEC deliberations, they rarely influence OPEC decisions. One careful study has impressively documented the fact that "there has not been an 'Arab' position on oil pricing at any time during the period that oil prices have been under OPEC control." [14]

THE POLITICAL CONSEQUENCES OF PETROLEUM POWER

The petroleum exporting countries of the Middle East have gained an enormous amount of international leverage as a result of their newly acquired control over their own resources,

[13] George J. Tomeh, "Arab-European Political Relations," *OAPEC News Bulletin* 3 (May 1977):17.

[14] Mary Ann Tetreault, "Petroleum Cartel: The Role of The Arab Nations in OPEC Bargaining" (Paper delivered at the Annual Meeting of the Southwestern Political Science Association, Houston, Texas, 12–15 April 1978), p. 24.

which was quickly translated into vastly expanded revenues. Domestically, the explosion of wealth meant that political leaders suddenly found themselves with new opportunities — the opportunities to pursue new policies and programs. In 1970, the revenue paid into the Middle Eastern oil producing countries approached $6 billion; in 1980, the figure was over $270 billion. The revenues of Saudi Arabia alone in 1980 were over 15 times those received by all Middle Eastern countries in 1970. What about 1983? Forgetting absolute precision, one can multiply OPEC's daily production of 18 million barrels by, say $30 as the approximate price per barrel and then multiply this product by 365 days in a year. One obtains a little less than $200 billion, and this is from OPEC alone and does not count non-OPEC Western oil or the Communist bloc oil. The figures remain staggering; so are the political implications.

The International Impact. The first clear indication of this new international political role occurred during the October 1973 war, when the Arab oil exporting countries implemented the now famous oil embargo. Although every major Arab oil exporting country (except Algeria) had terminated production shortly after the 1967 war began, this first embargo was short-lived. There was plenty of oil elsewhere in the world, and Iraq and Saudi Arabia were reluctant participants in any case. The 1973 scenario was quite different. Under the direction of King Faisal, the Saudis took the lead. On 17 October 1973, all the OAPEC countries announced their decision to cut production monthly by 5 percent of the previous month's sales. On 18 October, the Saudis made public their determination to cut their own production by 10 percent. When President Nixon requested $2.5 billion emergency aid for Israel, Saudi Arabia declared a total embargo against oil exports to the United States. Other Arab countries followed the Saudi lead. Although not nearly as shattering as it could have been, the embargo's impact was felt internationally. Available Arab oil fell from 20.8 million barrels a day in October to 15.8 million barrels by December, although there was some leakage, notably by Iraq. Saudi crude oil accounted for nearly half of this shortfall. Although countries such as Canada, Nigeria, and Indonesia, as well as non-Arab Iran, picked up some of the slack, "in terms of international trade in crude oil, the net loss was quite considerable — about 14 percent." [15] The possibility of another oil embargo has been a concern of world leaders ever since. The effects of the next one could be even more devastating.

This economic reality carries enormous political meaning in international politics. Although the term often used in the American press is *blackmail,* this oil leverage represents the reawakening of the Arab in world politics. There is little reason to believe that the Middle Eastern leaders would hesitate to use their power in what they consider their national self-interest any more than would the leaders of any other nation-state to use its particular resources for its own ends. It is often forgotten, for example, that in the summer of 1973, just a few months before the oil exporting countries resorted to "black-mail," the United States suddenly declared an embargo on soybeans, a temporary policy that threatened to cripple our Japanese allies, for whom we had developed the market in soybeans, now their chief source of protein. Not surprisingly, this and similar programs have been an integral part of American foreign economic and political policy for years. And other countries have made use of similar programs. The Middle East will be no exception; however even the Arab oil producers have found it difficult to agree when to use this potential weapon. Moreover, some, like Iraq, desperately need the revenues from the sale of petroleum. Although the potential for a devastating boycott is there, it is certainly not immediately likely.

The most explosive of the regional problems upon which oil power will have an effect is the Arab-Israeli issue discussed in an earlier chapter. There can be little doubt that economic self-interest is a major factor in Israel's substantial loss of support in the world community of nations. There are other reasons for this loss of support as well, of course. But since 1973, it has become increasingly clear that with the exception of

---

[15] Robert B. Stobaugh, "The Oil Companies in Crisis," *Daedalus* 104 (Fall 1975):180. This is the best article available on the actual implementation of the embargo. See also Jerome D. Davis, "The Arab use of Oil," *Cooperation and Conflict* II (1976):57–67.

support from the United States and, perhaps, the Republic of South Africa, Israel stands quite alone.

In the industrialized West, Middle Eastern oil power has also had a perceptible influence. The Atlantic Alliance cracked under the strain of Arab pressure. In November 1973, the European Economic Community drafted a statement demanding that Israel return to its pre-1967 borders and that the rights of the Palestinian refugees be taken into account in any settlement. In subsequent meetings among Western oil consuming countries, France refused to agree to the recommended multilateral approach and insisted on renegotiating its own arms-oil deals with the Arabs. Even the Japanese, always reluctant to move too far out of the shadow of the United States, took the side of the Arabs in the last weeks of 1973.

In May 1978, the United States Senate approved a controversial arms package recommended by the Carter administration. The package included the sale of 15 F-15s and 75 F-16s to Israel, 50 F-5Es to Egypt, and 60 F-15s to Saudi Arabia. The Israelis and their powerful lobby in Washington chose to oppose the package on the grounds that the sale of F-15s to Saudi Arabia would dangerously shift the balance of power against them in the Middle East. Actually, the showdown was not so much a military issue as a psychopolitical one. The Israelis feared that the Saudi-American connection was becoming so close that their own privileged position with respect to the United States would be jeopardized. In a brutal confrontation between the long-invincible Israeli lobby on the one hand and the Carter administration backed by a developing, but low-key, Arab lobby on the other hand, the arms package was approved by a 54 to 44 vote. Less than a decade ago, Israel could count on an overwhelming, one-sided majority in the United States Senate. Many senators viewed the outcome of the vote as a political watershed in American relations with the Middle East.

The Saudi-American relationship has been a close one for 40 years. The binding resource has been oil. Aramco is an all-American consortium. After October 1973, the Saudi-American connection became especially close. In June 1974, the United States and Sandi Arabia agreed to establish a Joint Commission on Economic Cooperation, which was to promote cooperative programs in all economic areas. Another joint commission was soon set up to promote military cooperation. In short, "It was agreed that Saudi Arabia and the United States will continue to consult closely on all matters of mutual interest." [16] Since 1974, and within the general framework of these joint commissions, the United States and Saudi Arabia have quietly established a number of extremely close economic and military arrangements. They reportedly specify, among other things, that 50 percent of Saudi Arabian annual balance-of-payment surpluses be placed in long-term investments in the United States; that 87 percent of Saudi surplus existing liquid cash be put in long-term bond markets in the United States; that these financial instruments are to carry at least a 7.5 percent rate of interest but are not marketable to third parties; and that the Saudis can draw on the interest payments to pay for military equipment sold by American suppliers. "In return, Saudi Arabia agreed not to increase the posted price of petroleum by more than five percent in any given year for a period ending on 31 December 1984." [17] In June 1978, a leading authority on Saudi economic affairs estimated that out of $100 billion that Saudi Arabia had invested in the world marketplace, $60 billion rested in dollar obligations of various kinds.[18] By 1983, the Saudis had over $200 billion invested abroad.

In 1981 came the AWACS crisis. AWACS is an acronym for Airborne Warning and Control System, electronic surveilliance planes; they can be both offensive or defensive weapons. The

---

[16] U.S., Department of State, "Text of Joint Statement on Cooperation," *Department of State Bulletin*, 1 July 1974. In this agreement, as well as one signed in November 1974 with Iran, the United States indicated that it was not averse to pursuing the bilateral route when it so desired.

[17] This quotation and the other information provided in this paragraph comes from "Secret U.S.-Saudi Pact," *International Currency Review* 9 (13 May 1977):8. This report of the details of the United States-Saudi relationship captures the spirit of the cooperation, if not all the accurate details. The publication of this kind of information throughout 1977 by the *International Currency Review* would seem to reflect the unhappiness of European financiers about the rather exclusive American-Saudi arrangements.

[18] A. J. Meyer, lecture delivered in Tokyo, Japan, 14 June 1978.

Saudis wanted to buy several from the United States. The sale was an executive decision, with the Senate having veto power. So it was in the Senate that the furious lobbying took place and the final vote, approving the sale, marked still another watershed. Some not-so-subtle Saudi economic pressure undoubtedly lubricated the decision.

Although the American-Saudi connection has been a strong one, the Saudis have often complained about how unfeeling American policy makers have been. Regardless of Israeli alarums, Saudi Arabia is unlikely to attack its northern neighbor. But it is worried about other military powers in the Gulf, and it expects American support should crises occur. And to refer once more to the American attachment to Israel, the Saudis feel that evenhandedness is still in the future, that the United States takes the Kingdom for granted, and that the American government is not likely to pressure the Israelis very much. They felt strongly offended by the lack of response to the Fahd plan; in early 1983 they felt that the United States was continuing to let the Israelis "call the tune." Here is a relationship that may not hold up over the long period; and lurking in the wings is the distinct possibility that a new Saudi Arabia may emerge one day, one that may radically alter its relationship with Washington. The power of petroleum remains. The political finesse to influence it, direct it, and combat it may perhaps not be there.

The OPEC countries in general and the Middle Eastern members in particular have not been niggardly in their foreign aid programs. Besides bilateral organizations such as the Kuwait Fund for Arab Economic Development (KFAED), the Abu Dhabi Fund for Economic Development, the Saudi Arabian Fund for Development, and the Kuwait Investment Company, there have been numerous multilateral aid programs. These include the Arab Bank for the Economic Development of Africa (ABEDA) along with its Special Arab Aid Fund for Africa (SAAFA), the Islamic Development Bank, the OPEC and OPEC Special Funds, and the Arab Fund for Economic and Social Development. Between 1973 and 1977, Arab oil producing countries dispensed over $19 billion in soft loans and grants.[19] When aid is figured as a percentage of gross national product (GNP), the Middle Eastern members of OPEC are contributing approximately 3 percent in aid, while the advanced Western countries average below 0.4 percent.[20] This gap is even more marked when one recognizes that several of the major Middle Eastern OPEC countries have a GNP per capita income much lower than that of the industrialized Western societies and that in cases such as Iran, Algeria, and Iraq, funds are badly needed for domestic development programs. The economic assistance given by the less populated Middle Eastern oil producers, such as Kuwait, Qatar, and the United Arab Emirates, has run as high as 10 percent of GNP in recent years. The criticisms of OPEC aid policy that emanate from the Western countries are less than convincing in view of the figures.

The international problem of the rich and poor nations is not a new one. Surely, the oil exporting countries of the Middle East can do more than they already have done to alleviate the problem. But they alone cannot solve the problem. The issue is one that confronts all nations, and only through a worldwide cooperative effort can something fundamental be done about it. As long as the Western industrial powers continue to peg their aid programs well below the 0.7 percent of GNP recommended by the United Nations, there is little reason to believe that their demands that the oil exporting countries contribute even more than they are already giving will be heeded. If the latter should decide for their own reasons to increase their aid programs even more significantly, the problem would remain, since "collectively they are simply too small a part of the world economy to supply most of the funds needed by the LDC's [less-developed countries]." [21] Unless there is effective cooperation among the developed, developing, and oil exporting countries, the tensions

[19] *Middle East Economic Digest*, 14 April 1978, p. 15.

[20] For an interesting analysis of these comparative aid statistics, see Askari and Cummings, *Oil, OECD, and the Third World*, p. 36. In 1978, it was reported that Japan and the United States were spending only 0.21 and 0.27 percent of their burgeoning gross national products on foreign aid. See *Time*, 12 June 1978, pp. 77–78.

[21] Askari and Cummings, *Oil, OECD, and the Third World*, p. 43.

and imbalances in the international system could easily explode into conflict and violence.

Petroleum power has thus influenced international politics in many ways. It has altered the foreign policy of the world's great powers and has juggled alliances and realigned political coalitions. While catapulting a fortunate few of the world's traditionally poorest countries into the ranks of the world's richest, it has deepened the already pronounced divisions between those who have most and those who have least. These transformations have been closely intertwined with domestic political policies, which have themselves been influenced by the economic force of oil.

Domestic Political Patterns and Petroleum. Petroleum power has had a decided influence on the form and substance of Middle Eastern political systems. In the first instance, it has sharply propelled the forces of modernization discussed in Chapter I. In so doing, it has heightened the strain on the traditional political systems, while providing them with new and unprecedented opportunities. Most of the leaders of the oil-rich countries have chosen to enlist the expanding oil power to preserve their own positions of ascendancy. The preservation of patrimonialism has taken precedence over the promotion of political development. As part of this process, and because of their desire to improve their countries' positions in the international political arena, Middle Eastern leaders have tended to stress modernization. There is little doubt that this has improved the living conditions of the peoples of these societies, who now have the best homes, schools, hospitals, and transportation and communication facilities in their histories. In turn, their political leaders have all this besides a near monopoly on national political power, buttressed by the most sophisticated police and military organizations possible.

Oil has fortified the traditional in the Middle East. For years now, petroleum has artificially dampened the fire of revolution in the area. Internally, the royal patrimonial leaders have used its product to buy time and to bribe middle-class challengers. Regionally, the oil-rich countries have provided badly needed aid to the more radical forces, especially the homeless Palestinians. Resources are needed by everyone and every movement regardless of ideology.

In the Middle East, communication channels remain open, alliances fragment, basic ideological divisions are intersected at innumerable points by temporary coalitions, and patterns of cooperation and conflict shift with the political wind. Fundamental differences concerning political form and policies with respect to change are present but are not always a good basis for predicting future developments. In this sense, OPEC is an excellent microcosm of the Middle Eastern political system. It contains important built-in rivalries and natural coalitions; although these are important to understand, the fact that the membership votes primarily on the basis of the issue at hand results in whirling alliances. Thus, only the system is given; its continued existence and style of organization rest to a great extent upon the flexible nature of its internal patterns of cooperation and conflict. The fact that substantial resources are present and that these resources are controlled in a manner designed to further preservation of the system are two further reasons for the continued existence of traditional patrimonialism in the Middle East. In this kind of system, rapid modernization can be accommodated while political development continues to be retarded.

CONCLUDING THOUGHTS

It remains for us to pull together some of the strands from the preceding chapters and to raise a few fundamental and persistent questions about the Middle Eastern political systems and their viability in the present currents of change. The Middle East might once have been studied as an exercise in statics, but in the last years of the twentieth century, it is a dynamic and explosive area. To be dynamic is not necessarily to change or to change in any particular direction. The thesis in this book is that modernization, economic and social particularly, pervades the area. There has always been a gap between such modernization and political development. But events in Iran and Pakistan show how religious leaders in a revolutionary setting can slow modernization and in effect narrow the gap somewhat between modernization and development. To narrow it greatly would mean increased political development. Such political development will have to carry a deep Islamic flavor. The model is only in a state of becoming.

The world itself is in a secular age. Vortexes of reaction and rejection of secularism do whirl out of the congeries of ideological and cultural milieus that once made interesting reading in *The National Geographic*. But cultures have been thrown together by satellite communication, jet planes, videotapes, and TV sets. It has been a jarring experience to a Saudi, for example, who clings to a traditional world view that is immiscible with what is currently being done to his country, courtesy of oil income. Part of that tradition has been religion, which often legitimates other tradition. Many Middle Easterners, confused by what passes for modernization — the newer education embedded in secularism, the critical exegesis of all traditional values, the sexual revolution, the influx of money, the opportunities of new, and untrusted, ways of life — have clung even more tenaciously to the religion of the past, Islam. Is this a passing phenomenon, like a dust devil racing across the deserts of Iran, leaving behind only vestigal traces of its passage? Many believe so. Or is it a fundamental turnaround, which heralds not only for the Middle East but for the world a new emphasis on the normative values of religion? Some believe so.

The Middle East today is gripped by the enthusiasm of a religious resurgence. One cannot blink away what is happening in many parts of the Middle East in this regard, although it is in Iran where most eyes are focused. This collision of values has already stirred up the region so that all other things must be viewed from a newer and different perspective.

Those who have an "asm for isms" (the phrase was Oliver Wendell Holmes, Jr.'s) often set about exporting their newly discovered virtues, or those at least newly energized. Thus revolution that splashes across boundaries. And nothing it seems arouses man's emotional and irrational proclivities so much as the prospect of quarreling with other true believers over the certitudes of religion. Unfortunately, some of the debate is with firearms.

The next few years — by 2000, say — will surely see the end of many traditional authoritarian political systems in the Middle East. New ideological strains will be more resistant than some in the past have been, and the area as a whole will be characterized by movements and ideas that today might be termed radical. The current struggle in Afghanistan may be, from one point of view, even more important in the long run than what is happening in Iran. For in Afghanistan the battle rages over a Marxist menu of modernization. The military struggle is only the surface disturbance symptomatic of deeper antagonisms and rejections.

Much of the political development over the next 15 years is likely to be fraudulent. It may not be actual development but will be labeled as such by political leaders who do not really want an increase in participation. But the pretense will go on, for this, too, is a part of the winds of the late twentieth century.

The Persian Gulf will remain a powder keg, and since so much of the world's oil comes from the Gulf area, the world will be involved in the turbulence there. As the various countries on the Gulf, large and small, attempt to dance to political necessity, new rhythms will have to be learned or at least the old ones altered, from which domestic stress is likely to emerge. In only a few years both Ayatollah Khomeini and his adversary in Iraq, Saddam Hussein, will have departed the scene.

For so many years the Arab-Israeli dispute has dominated the news from the Middle East. At the moment it continues to do so. It too has retarded natural — be it good or bad — political development in the Middle East by siphoning off the radical energies that otherwise might have produced such development. And the machinations of the United States and the Soviet Union have done little to directly promote political development in the area. The United States has consistently supported the authoritarian-traditional systems of Middle Eastern monarchy to the very end, while the Soviet Union has ideologically zigzagged its way through the area — an area upon which it has always had imperialistic designs. Ironically, both the United States and the Soviet Union have, on the other hand, indirectly encouraged political development in the Middle East. In the case of the United States, such encouragement has been the result of several decades of exposure to American values stressing democratic participation and individual liberties. In the Soviet case, it has stemmed from the impressive record of modernization (especially in Soviet Central Asia) that saw Russia transform itself into a major world power only a few decades after its revolution in 1917. This model forced many Middle Eastern leaders to begin social and political reforms in self-defense against the Soviet challenge to the north.

But the Arab-Israeli dispute has a life span too, just as have had so many of its main actors, Ben Gurion, Abdullah, Dayan, Nasser, Meir, Sadat. . . . Whatever happens in the near future, it is highly unlikely that a permanent Israel, as dreamed about by Begin and Sharon, will ever exist. Perhaps much turmoil may occur before this becomes generally evident. Perhaps, too, there will be in the long run no Israel at all. What will have happened is that old Palestine, whatever its political coloration, will remain the gathering ground of a new kind of Sephardim; Israel as we know it, small, courageous, bold, swaggering, tough, and arrogant, may very well be a thing of the past. This will occur only with a change of policy by the United States and by Russia too. But it seems probable.

What of the Palestinians? They will get their state, but probably Reagan will have returned to California by then. At the moment, the midwife is supposed to be Jordan, although King Hussein has painfully little enthusiasm for it. Arafat and the PLO may survive for a time, but post-revolutionary worlds are notoriously unpredictable. The new Palestine will of course include most if not all of the West Bank and Gaza, but eventually it will swallow up Jordan too. This the King knows.

Syria will get Golan back but not immediately. There is no obvious solution for Lebanon, because all of its difficulties are not of foreign origin. Lebanon itself barely has enough glue in its system to keep from flying apart. And perhaps it will disintegrate. In the short run at least, Syria and Israel will play the role of gleaners, picking up what they can.

Today Egypt plays a cautious role under Hosni Mubarak. Egypt is not the easiest country to govern, let alone govern well, but it remains central to the Arab world, not only central geographically, but in terms of population, education, culture, and leadership. Egypt is the natural leader of the Arab world; at least since 1977 it has abdicated that role. Its return will herald some alterations in the petty quarrels of its brethren.

It is likely that Algeria will dominate the old Mahgreb,

which means that Tunisia and Morocco (currently, according to some officials, the staunchest American ally in the Middle East) will be compelled to endorse new slogans. Libya will remain, but Qaddafi may have departed the scene.

The international environment will also change in unpredictable ways. What will be the nature of future American-Soviet rivalry in the area? It need not remain what it is today. What natural political or military ambitions will emanate from within the area? What adventures will tempt future Arab, Iranian, Turkish, or Israeli leaders? We cannot be naïve enough to believe that there will be none. What struggles will ensue between the rich and the poor — between both nations and individuals? (The Palestinians remain the single greatest poor nation of individuals in the Middle East today. And their presence alone has already nearly brought down two Arab states: Jordan and Lebanon.) It is not difficult to imagine the mad scramble for resources, living space, and access to markets by those whose current share of these things is less than that of others.

These struggles may be hastened by ideology. Nationalism is, of course, not dead, even if its Arab variety is much less viable since the year of Nasser's death. But new nationalisms grow quickly to justify struggles against exploiters or imperialists. It is possible to envisage an Egyptian nationalism encouraging adventures in Sudan or perhaps in Libya. It is equally possible to imagine Algerian nationalistic stirrings that might affect its immediate neighbors. Is it impossible to conceive of a permanent Syrian hegemony over Lebanon — a Greater Syria at last — especially one with Israeli blessing? Or, at least in Lebanon, a redistribution of populations along sectarian lines? Again, Palestinian nationalism is going to have to be reckoned with.

In the international environment, the United States and the Soviet Union loom above all. The Soviet Union has already tipped its hand by its brutal invasion of Afganistan. That it has interests in Iran, Iraq, and the corridor of land that would connect it with the Persian Gulf is hardly a secret; the elevation of former KGB chief Yuri Andropov to leadership may speed up or alter Soviet activities in the area. But no one knows in early 1983.

Of the United States, what can be said? It is never had a

consistent policy for the Middle East, and what policy it has had has not been thoroughly connected with a rational statement of its interests. Henry Kissinger, in speaking favorably of the Mainland Chinese as policy makers, had this to say:[22]

> Then there was a difference in the Chinese and American approaches to international relations. China's was in the great classical tradition of European statesmanship. The Chinese Communist leaders coldly and unemotionally assessed the requirements of the balance of power little influenced by ideology or sentiment. They were scientists of equilibrium, artists of relativity. They understood that the balance of power involved forces in constant flux that had to be continually adjusted to changing circumstances. . . .
>
> But the United States possessed neither the conceptual nor the historical framework for so cold-blooded a policy. The many different strands that make up American thinking on foreign policy have so far proved inhospitable to an approach based on the calculation of the national interest and relationships of power. Americans are comfortable with an idealistic tradition that espouses great causes, such as making the world safe for democracy, or human rights. American pragmatism calls for the management of "trouble spots" as they arise, "on their merits," which is another way of waiting for events — the exact opposite of the Chinese approach. There is a tradition of equating international conflicts with legal disputes and invoking juridical mechanisms for their resolution, a view considered naïve by the Chinese, who treat international law as the reflection and not the origin of the global equilibrium. The legacy of America's historical invulnerability makes us profoundly uncomfortable with the notion of the balance of power, and with its corollary that encroachments must be dealt with early (when they do not appear so clearly dangerous) lest they accumulate a momentum stoppable only by horrendous exertions, if at all.

Harold H. Saunders, long-time Middle East specialist in the State Department has this to say in a recent publication:[23]

---

[22] *Years of Upheaval*, p. 50.
[23] American Enterprise Institute *Conversations with Harold H. Saunders. U.S. Policy for the Middle East in the 1980s* (Washington, 1982), p. 10.

How do we approach an area where our interests are as complex, and sometimes conflicting, as they are in the Middle East...? How do we order our priorities within an area like this? These are not just abstract questions. The answers, in the end, can govern action in the most concerted ways. The answer can generate heated public debate, sometimes over unspoken issues.

Today in the United States there is no consensus. There is not even a common view of what the main problems are.

Saunders himself bravely attempts to state American interests in the Middle East. He finds five main ones:[24]

1. The "independence, stability, and political orientation of the key states in the area."

2. The prevention of Soviet predominance in the area.

3. "[A]ssuring the security and prosperity of Israel."

4. Maintenance of "the steady flow of oil...[and] Arab economic power derived from substantial financial reserves."

5. Controlling arms sales and "imbalances" in the area.

Saunders's view of America's interests in the Middle East may not be unreservedly endorsed. But it serves to remind us of what a foremost Middle Eastern planner in the U.S. government thought American interests to be. Readers of the present volume may try their own hand at the game of identifying interests and policies. It is not easy.

Saunders's interests are not strictly easily reconciled. And when administrations change every few years or so — only Wilson, Roosevelt, and Eisenhower have served as many as two terms in the twentieth century — along with support personnel, policies and interests change also. It is inevitable that we turn a perplexed face to the Middle East, read by the peoples there as insensitive, uninformed, and foolish. America has had a big hand in making some of the Middle Eastern problems that it now seeks to solve. Both the United States and the Soviet Union are part of the burden that the modern Middle East must bear.

Despite this litany of problems and failures, there is much

24 *Ibid.*, pp. 6–9.

that holds promise for the future of the Middle East. Vast natural resources are available, and they have finally come under the control of the indigenous leaders, who now sometimes direct their utilization in what is considered to be the best interests of the peoples of the area. Partially because of this, the Middle East is moving back toward the center of the world stage. The new generation of political leaders that is taking power in the area is not as ideologically radical as is often thought. Nor are all the traditional leaders as reactionary as their public images sometimes suggest. Leaders from all political camps in the Middle East have exhibited as much international responsibility as have those from any other region on the globe.

The Middle East is vibrant and alive. It is today a restless, turbulent area at the threshold of enormous alterations in its philosophies, its lifestyles, and its distributive justice. It is filled with political fault lines that can give way to violence as easily as to constructive cooperation. At the center of the struggle are the persistence of continuity and the inevitability of change. The social, economic, and political issues that this book analyzes reflect this conflict between continuity and change in every facet. And its consequences increasingly affect all our lives.

Selected Bibliography

CHAPTER I: POLITICAL DEVELOPMENT AND THE CHALLENGE OF MODERNIZATION

Almond, Gabriel A., and G. Bingham Powell, Jr. *Comparative Politics: System, Process, and Policy.* Boston: Little, Brown and Co., 1978.

Antoun, Richard, and Iliya Harik, eds. *Rural Politics and Social Change in the Middle East.* Bloomington: Indiana University Press, 1972.

Bill, James A., and Robert L. Hardgrave, Jr. *Comparative Politics: The Quest for Theory.* Washington, D.C.: University Press of America, 1982, ch. 2.

Borthwick, Bruce. *Comparative Politics of the Middle East.* Englewood Cliffs, N.J.: Prentice-Hall, 1980.

Damis, John. *Conflict in Northwest Africa: The Western Sahara Dispute.* Stanford, Calif.: Hoover Institution Press, 1983.

El Fathaly, Omar I., and Monte Palmer. *Political Development and Social Change in Libya.* Lexington, Mass.: Lexington Books, 1980.

Halpern, Manfred. "Four Contrasting Repertories of Human Relations in Islam." In *Psychological Dimensions of Near Eastern Studies,* ed. by L. Carl Brown and Norman Itzkowitz. Princeton, N.J.: The Darwin Press, 1977, pp. 60–102.

————. *The Politics of Social Change in the Middle East and North Africa.* Princeton, N.J.: Princeton University Press, 1963.

Hudson, Michael C. *Arab Politics: The Search for Legitimacy.* New Haven, Conn.: Yale University Press, 1978.

Ibrahim, Saad Eddin. *The New Arab Social Order.* Boulder, Colo.: Westview Press, 1982.

Kerr, Malcolm, and El Sayed Yassin, eds. *Rich and Poor States in the Middle East.* Boulder, Colo.: Westview Press, 1982.

Leiden, Carl, ed. *The Conflict of Traditionalism and Modernism in the Muslim Middle East.* Austin: University of Texas Press, 1966.

Moore, Clement Henry. *Politics in North Africa: Algeria, Morocco, and Tunisia.* Boston: Little, Brown and Co., 1970.

Palmer, Monte. *Dilemmas of Political Development.* Itasca, Ill.: F. E. Peacock Publishers, 1980.

Peretz, Don. *The Middle East Today.* 4th ed. New York: Praeger Publishers, 1983.

Stookey, Robert W. *South Yemen: A Marxist Republic in Arabia.* Boulder, Colo.: Westview Press, 1982.

Szyliowicz, Joseph S. *Education and Modernization in the Middle East.* Ithaca, N.Y.: Cornell University Press, 1973.

Tachau, Frank, ed. *The Developing Nations: What Path to Modernization?* New York: Dodd, Mead and Co., 1972.

Waterbury, John, and Ragaei El Mallakh. *The Middle East in the Coming Decade.* New York: McGraw-Hill, 1978.

Weinbaum, Marvin G. *Food, Development, and Politics in the Middle East.* Boulder, Colo.: Westview Press, 1982.

CHAPTER II: ISLAM AND POLITICS

Akhavi, Shahrough. *Religion and Politics in Contemporary Iran.* Albany: State University of New York Press, 1980.

Algar, Hamid. *Religion and State in Iran, 1785–1906.* Berkeley: University of California Press, 1969.

Arberry, A. J., ed. *Religion in the Middle East.* 2 vols. Cambridge: Cambridge University Press, 1969.

Ayoob, Mohammed. *The Politics of Islamic Reassertion.* New York: St. Martin's Press, 1981.

Enayat, Hamid. *Modern Islamic Political Thought.* Austin: University of Texas Press, 1982.

Esposito, John L., ed. *Islam and Development.* Syracuse, N.Y.: Syracuse University Press, 1980.

———. *Voices of Resurgent Islam.* New York: Oxford University Press, 1983.

Hodgson, Marshall G. S. *The Venture of Islam.* 3 vols. Chicago: University of Chicago Press, 1974.

Jansen, G. H. *Militant Islam.* New York: Harper and Row, 1979.

Keddie, Nikki R., ed. *Scholars, Saints, and Sufis: Muslim Institutions in the Middle East Since 1500.* Berkeley: University of California Press, 1972.

Kerr, Malcolm. *Islamic Reform: The Political and Legal Theories of Muhammad 'Abduh and Rashīd Ridā.* Berkeley: University of California Press, 1961.

Khomeini, Imam. *Islam and Revolution: Writings and Declarations of Imam Khomeini.* Translated and annotated by H. Algar. Berkeley, Calif.: Mizan Press, 1981.

Ibn Khaldun. *The Muqaddimah: An Introduction to History.* Translated by Franz Rosenthal. Princeton, N.J.: Princeton University Press, 1967.

Mortimer, Edward. *Faith and Power: The Politics of Islam.* New York: Vintage Books, 1982.

Nasr, Seyyed Hossein. *Ideals and Realities of Islam.* London: George Allen and Unwin, 1966.

Piscatori, James P., ed. *Islam in the Political Process.* Cambridge: Cambridge University Press, 1983.

Pullapilly, Cyriac K., ed. *Islam in the Contemporary World.* Notre Dame, Ind.: Cross Roads Books, 1980.

Voll, John O. *Islam: Continuity and Change in the Modern World.* Boulder, Colo.: Westview Press, 1982.

Watt, W. Montgomery. *Bell's Introduction to the Qur'ān.* Edinburgh: Edinburgh University Press, 1970.

Williams, John Alden, ed. *Themes of Islamic Civilization.* Berkeley: University of California Press, 1971.

CHAPTER III: THE GENES OF POLITICS:
GROUPS, CLASSES, AND FAMILIES

Azoy, G. Whitney. *Buzkashi, Game and Power in Afghanistan.* Philadelphia: University of Pennsylvania Press, 1982.

Barth, Fredrik. *Political Leadership Among Swat Pathans.* London: The Athlone Press, 1959.

Bates, Daniel, and Amal Rassam. *Peoples and Cultures of the Middle East.* Englewood Cliffs, N.J.: Prentice-Hall, 1983.

Beck, Lois, and Nikki Keddie, eds. *Women in the Muslim World.* Cambridge, Mass.: Harvard University Press, 1978.

Bill, James A. *The Politics of Iran: Groups, Classes, and Modernization.* Columbus, Ohio: Charles E. Merrill, 1972.

———. "Class Analysis and the Dialectics of Modernization in the Middle East." *International Journal of Middle East Studies* 3 (October 1972): 417–434.

Brown, Kenneth L. *People of Salé: Tradition and Change in a Moroccan City.* Manchester: Manchester University Press, 1976.

Bulliet, Richard W. *The Patricians of Nishapur: A Study in Medieval Islamic Social History.* Cambridge, Mass.: Harvard University Press, 1972.

Cantori, Louis J., and Iliya Harik. *Local Politics and Development in the Middle East.* Boulder, Colo.: Westview Press, 1983.

Eickelman, Dale F. *The Middle East: An Anthropological Approach.* Englewood Cliffs, N.J.: Prentice-Hall, 1981.

English, Paul Ward. *City and Village in Iran.* Madison: University of Wisconsin Press, 1966.

Farah, Tawfic E., ed. *Political Behavior in the Arab States.* Boulder, Colo.: Westview Press, 1983.

Fernea, Robert A. *Shaykh and Effendi: Changing Patterns of Authority Among the El Shabana of Southern Iraq.* Cambridge, Mass.: Harvard University Press, 1970.

Gellner, Ernest, and John Waterbury, eds. *Patrons and Clients in Mediterranean Societies.* London: Duckworth, 1977.

Gubser, Peter. *Politics and Change in Al-Karak, Jordan.* New York: Oxford University Press, 1973.

Hussein, Mahmoud. *Class Conflict in Egypt, 1945–1970.* Translated by Michel and Susanne Chirman, A. Ehrenfeld, and K. Brown. New York: Monthly Review Press, 1973.

Khuri, Fuad I. *From Village to Suburb: Order and Change in Greater Beirut.* Chicago: The University of Chicago Press, 1975.

Levy, Reuben. *The Social Structure of Islam.* Cambridge: Cambridge University Press, 1957.

Nieuwenhuijze, C. A. O. van. *Commoners, Climbers and Notables.* Leiden, The Netherlands: E. J. Brill, 1977.

Patai, Raphael. *Golden River to Golden Road: Society, Culture, and Change in the Middle East.* 3rd ed. Philadelphia: University of Pennsylvania Press, 1969.

Peristiany, J. G., ed. *Mediterranean Family Structure.* Cambridge: Cambridge University Press, 1976.

Springborg, Robert. *Family, Power, and Politics in Egypt.* Philadelphia: University of Pennsylvania Press, 1982.

CHAPTER IV: THE POLITICS OF PATRIMONIAL LEADERSHIP

Andrae, Tor. *Mohammed: The Man and His Faith.* New York: Barnes and Noble, 1935.

Dekmejian, R. Hrair. *Patterns of Political Leadership: Lebanon, Israel, Egypt.* Albany: State University of New York Press, 1975.

Frey, Frederick W. *The Turkish Political Elite.* Cambridge, Mass.: M.I.T. Press, 1965.

Gellner, Ernest. *Saints of the Atlas.* Chicago: University of Chicago Press, 1969.

Guillaume, A. *The Life of Muhammad: A Translation of Ishaq's Sīrat Rasūl Allah.* London: Oxford University Press, 1955.

Khadduri, Majid. *Arab Personalities in Politics.* Washington, D.C.: The Middle East Institute, 1981.

Khuri, Fuad I., ed. *Leadership and Development in Arab Society.* Beirut: American University of Beirut, 1981.

Lenczowski, George, ed. *Political Elites in the Middle East.* Washington, D.C.: American Enterprise Institute, 1975.

Margoliouth, D. S. *Mohammed and the Rise of Islam.* 3rd ed. New York: G. P. Putnam's Sons, 1905.

Rustow, Dankwart A. *Philosophers and Kings: Studies in Leadership.* New York: George Braziller, 1970.

Tachau, Frank, ed. *Political Elites and Political Development in the Middle East.* Cambridge, Mass.: Schenkman Publishing Co., 1975.

Vatikiotis, P. J. *The Fatimid Theory of State.* Lahore, Pakistan: Orientalia Publishers, 1957.

Waterbury, John. *The Commander of the Faithful: The Moroccan Political Elite — A Study in Segmented Politics.* New York: Columbia University Press, 1970.

Watt, W. Montgomery. *Muhammad at Medina.* Oxford: The Clarendon Press, 1956.

————. *Islam and the Integration of Society.* London: Routledge and Kegan Paul, 1961.

Zartman, I. William, ed. *Political Elites in Arab North Africa.* New York: Longman, Inc., 1982.

CHAPTER V: THE POLITICS OF LEADERS AND CHANGE

Abdel-Malek, Anouar. *Egypt: Military Society.* Translated by Charles Lam Markmann. New York: Vintage Books, 1968.

Abu Izzeddin, Nejla. *Nasser of the Arabs.* Beirut: Imprimerie Catholique, 1975.

Bill, James A. *The Politics of Iran: Groups, Classes and Modernization.* Columbus, Ohio: Charles E. Merrill, 1972.

————. "Iran and the Crisis of '78." *Foreign Affairs* 57 (Winter 1978/1979): 323–342.

Binder, Leonard. *In a Moment of Enthusiasm: Political Power and the Second Stratum in Egypt.* Chicago: University of Chicago Press, 1978.

Burrell, R. Michael, and Abbas R. Kelidar. *Egypt: The Dilemmas of a Nation, 1970–1977.* Beverly Hills, Calif.: Sage Publications, 1977.

El-Sadat, Anwar. *In Search of an Identity: An Autobiography.* New York: Harper & Row, 1978.

Heikal, Mohamed. *The Cairo Documents.* Garden City, N.Y.: Doubleday and Co., 1973.

Hirst, David, and Irene Beeson. *Sadat.* London: Faber and Faber, 1981.

Hopwood, Derek. *Egypt: Politics and Society 1945–1981.* Winchester, Mass.: Allen and Unwin, 1982.

Karpat, Kemal, et al. *Social Change and Politics in Turkey.* Leiden, The Netherlands: E. J. Brill, 1973.

Kazancigil, Ali, and Ergun Özbudun, eds. *Atatürk: Founder of a Modern State.* Hamden, Conn.: Archon Books, 1981.

Kinross, Lord. *Atatürk: The Rebirth of a Nation.* London: Weidenfeld and Nicolson, 1964.

Leder, Arnold. *Catalysts of Change: Marxist versus Muslim in a Turkish Community.* Austin: University of Texas Center for Middle Eastern Studies, 1976.

Mayfield, James B. *Rural Politics in Nasser's Egypt.* Austin: University of Texas Press, 1971.

Özbudun, Ergun. *Social Change and Political Participation in Turkey.* Princeton, N.J.: Princeton University Press, 1976.

Pfaff, Richard H. "Disengagement from Traditionalism in Turkey and Iran." *Western Political Quarterly* 16 (March 1963):79–98.

Philby, H. St. John. *Arabian Jubilee.* London: Robert Hale, 1954.

————. *Sa'udi Arabia.* London: Ernest Benn, 1955.

Tamkoç, Metin. *The Warrior Diplomats.* Salt Lake City: University of Utah Press, 1976.

Waterbury, John. *The Egypt of Nasser and Sadat: The Political Economy of Two Regimes.* Princeton, N.J.: Princeton University Press, 1983.

Zonis, Marvin. *The Political Elite of Iran.* Princeton, N.J.: Princeton University Press, 1971.

CHAPTER VI: VIOLENCE AND THE MILITARY

Barakat, Halim. *Lebanon in Strife.* Austin: University of Texas Press, 1977.

Be'eri, Eliezer. *Army Officers in Arab Politics and Society.* New York: Frederick A. Praeger, 1970.

Bullock, John. *Death of a Country: The Civil War in Lebanon.* London: Weidenfeld and Nicolson, 1977.

El-Edroos, Sayed Ali. *The Hashemite Arab Army, 1908–1979.* Amman: The Publishing Committee, 1982.

Feldman, Shai. *Israeli Nuclear Deterrence: A Strategy for the 1980s.* New York: Columbia University Press, 1982.

Haddad, George M. *Revolutions and Military Rule in the Middle East.* 3 vols. New York: Robert Speller and Sons, 1965–1973.

Harris, George S. "The Role of the Military in Turkish Politics." *Middle East Journal* 19 (Winter and Spring, 1965):54–66, 169–176.

Havens, Murray C., Carl Leiden, and Karl M. Schmitt. *The Politics of Assassination*. Englewood Cliffs, N.J.: Prentice-Hall, 1970.

Horne, Alistair. *A Savage War of Peace: Algeria 1954–1962*. New York: Viking, 1978.

Hurewitz, J. C. *Middle East Politics: The Military Dimension*. New York: Frederick A. Praeger, 1969.

Leiden, Carl, and Karl M. Schmitt. *The Politics of Violence: Revolution in the Modern World*. Englewood Cliffs, N.J.: Prentice-Hall, 1968.

Vatikiotis, P. J. *The Egyptian Army in Politics*. Bloomington: Indiana University Press, 1961.

———. *Politics and the Military in Jordan*. New York: Frederick A. Praeger, 1967.

CHAPTER VII: THE IMPRINT OF IDEOLOGY

Abu Jaber, Kamel S. *The Arab Ba'th Socialist Party: History, Ideology, and Organization*. Syracuse: Syracuse University Press, 1966.

Ajami, Fouad. *The Arab Predicament: Arab Political Thought and Practice Since 1967*. New York: Cambridge University Press, 1982.

Antonius, George. *The Arab Awakening*. Beirut: Khayat's, 1955.

Binder, Leonard. *The Ideological Revolution in the Middle East*. New York: John Wiley and Sons, 1964.

Cleveland, William L. *The Making of an Arab Nationalist*. Princeton, N.J.: Princeton University Press, 1971.

Cottam, Richard W. *Nationalism in Iran*. Pittsburgh: University of Pittsburgh Press, 1964.

Donahue, John J., and J. L. Esposito, eds. *Islam in Transition: Muslim Perspectives*. New York: Oxford University Press, 1982.

Haim, Sylvia G., ed. *Arab Nationalism: An Anthology*. Berkeley: University of California Press, 1962.

Hanna, Sami A., and George H. Gardner. *Arab Socialism: A Documentary Survey*. Leiden, The Netherlands: E. J. Brill, 1969.

Harris, George S. *The Origins of Communism in Turkey*. Stanford, Calif.: The Hoover Institution, 1967.

Ismael, Tareq Y. *The Arab Left*. Syracuse: Syracuse University Press, 1976.

Karpat, Kemal H., ed. *Political and Social Thought in the Contemporary Middle East*. New York: Frederick A. Praeger, 1968.

Khadduri, Majid. *Political Trends in the Arab World: The Role of Ideas and Ideals in Politics*. Baltimore, Md.: Johns Hopkins Press, 1970.

Quandt, William B., Fuad Jabber, and Ann Mosely Lesch. *The Politics of Palestinian Nationalism*. Berkeley: University of California Press, 1973.

Said, Abdel Moghny. *Arab Socialism*. New York: Barnes and Noble, 1972.

Sharabi, Hisham. *Nationalism and Revolution in the Arab World*. Princeton, N.J.: D. Van Nostrand Co., 1966.

Tütsch, Hans E. *Facets of Arab Nationalism*. Detroit: Wayne State University Press, 1965.

Yamak, Labib Zuwiyya. *The Syrian Social Nationalist Party: An Ideological Analysis*. Cambridge, Mass.: Harvard University Press, 1966.

CHAPTER VIII: THE ARAB-ISRAELI CONNECTION

American Friends Service Committee. *A Compassionate Peace: A Future for the Middle East.* New York: Hill and Wang, 1982.

Ben-Sasson, H. H., ed. *A History of the Jewish People.* Cambridge, Mass.: Harvard University Press, 1976.

Childers, Erskine B. *The Road to Suez: A Study of Western-Arab Relations.* London: MacGibbon and Kee, 1962.

Curtiss, Richard R. *A Changing Image: American Perceptions of the Arab-Israeli Dispute.* Washington, D.C.: American Educational Trust, 1982.

Elon, Amos. *Herzl.* New York: Holt, Rinehart and Winston, 1975.

Freedman, Robert O., ed. *World Politics and the Arab-Israeli Conflict.* New York: Pergamon Press, 1979.

Golan, Matti. *The Secret Conversations of Henry Kissinger: Step-by-Step Diplomacy in the Middle East.* New York: Quadrangle/The New York Times Book Co., 1976.

Halpern, Ben. *The Idea of the Jewish State.* 2nd ed. Cambridge, Mass.: Harvard University Press, 1969.

Herzog, Chaim. *The Arab-Israeli Wars.* New York: Random House, 1982.

Hirst, David. *The Gun and the Olive Branch: The Roots of Violence in the Middle East.* London: Faber and Faber, 1977.

Khalidi, Walid. *Conflict and Violence in Lebanon.* Cambridge, Mass.: Harvard University Center for International Affairs, 1979.

Khouri, Fred J. *The Arab-Israeli Dilemma.* 2nd ed. Syracuse: Syracuse University Press, 1976.

Lilienthal, Alfred M. *The Zionist Connection: What Price Peace?* New York: Dodd, Mead and Co., 1978.

Lustick, Ian. *Arabs in the Jewish State: Israel's Control of a National Minority.* Austin: University of Texas Press, 1980.

Peretz, Don. *Israel and the Palestine Arabs.* New York: AMS Press, 1981.

Quandt, William B. *Decade of Decisions: American Policy Toward the Arab-Israeli Conflict, 1967–1976.* Berkeley: University of California Press, 1977.

Rodinson, Maxime. *Israel and the Arabs.* Baltimore, Md.: Penguin Books, 1973.

Sachar, Howard M. *A History of Israel from the Rise of Zionism to Our Time.* New York: Alfred A. Knopf, 1976.

Safran, Nadav. *Israel: The Embattled Ally.* Cambridge, Mass.: Harvard University Press, 1978.

Sheehan, Edward R. F. *The Arabs, Israelis, and Kissinger.* New York: Reader's Digest Press, 1976.

Stookey, Robert W. *America and the Arab States: An Uneasy Encounter.* New York: John Wiley and Sons, 1975.

Timerman, Jacobo. *The Longest War.* New York: Alfred Knopf, 1982.

CHAPTER IX: THE CHALLENGE OF REVOLUTION AND THE PERSIAN GULF

Abrahamian, Ervand. *Iran Between Two Revolutions.* Princeton, N.J.: Princeton University Press, 1982.

Anthony, John Duke. *Arab States of the Lower Gulf*. Washington, D.C.: The Middle East Institute, 1975.

El Mallakh, Ragaei. *The Economic Development of the United Arab Emirates*. New York: St. Martin's Press, 1981.

Fischer, Michael M. J. *Iran: From Religious Dispute to Revolution*. Cambridge, Mass.: Harvard University Press, 1982.

Heard-Bey, Frauke. *From Trucial States to United Arab Emirates*. New York: Longman, 1982.

Hickman, William F. *Ravaged and Reborn: The Iranian Army, 1982*. Washington, D.C.: The Brookings Institution, 1982.

Holden, David, and Richard Johns. *The House of Saud: The Rise and Rule of the Most Powerful Dynasty in the Arab World*. New York: Holt and Rinehart, 1981.

Hooglund, Eric J. *Land and Revolution in Iran, 1960–1980*. Austin: University of Texas Press, 1982.

Ismael, Jacqueline. *Kuwait: Social Change in Historical Perspective*. Syracuse, N.Y.: Syracuse University Press, 1982.

Ismael, Tareq Y. *Iraq and Iran: Roots of Conflict*. Syracuse, N.Y.: Syracuse University Press, 1982.

Keddie, Nikki R. *Roots of Revolution: An Interpretive History of Modern Iran*. New Haven, Conn.: Yale University Press, 1981.

Khalifa, Ali Mohammed. *The United Arab Emirates: Unity in Fragmentation*. Boulder, Colo.: Westview Press, 1979.

Khuri, Fuad. *Tribe and State in Bahrain*. Chicago: The University of Chicago Press, 1980.

Lacey, Robert. *The Kingdom: Arabia and the House of Saud*. New York: Harcourt Brace Jovanovich, 1981.

Marr, Phebe. *The Modern History of Iraq*. Boulder, Colo.: Westview Press, 1983.

Quandt, William B. *Saudi Arabia in the 1980s*. Washington, D.C.: The Brookings Institution, 1981.

Ramazani, Rouhollah K. *The Persian Gulf: Iran's Role*. Charlottesville: University of Virginia Press, 1972.

Shaw, John A., and David E. Long. *Saudi Arabian Modernization: The Impact of Change on Stability*. Washington, D.C.: Center for Strategic and International Studies, Georgetown University, 1982.

CHAPTER X: OIL, THE MIDDLE EAST, AND THE FUTURE

Abir, Mordechai. *Oil, Power and Politics*. London: Frank Cass, 1974.

Askari, Hossein, and John Thomas Cummings. *Middle East Economies in the 1970s: A Comparative Approach*. New York: Praeger Publishers, 1976.

Conant, Melvin A. *The Oil Factor in U.S. Foreign Policy*. Lexington, Mass.: Lexington Books, 1982.

Dawisha, Adeed, and Karen Dawisha, eds. *The Soviet Union in the Middle East*. New York: Holmes and Meier, 1982.

El Mallakh, Ragaei. *OPEC: Twenty Years and Beyond*. Boulder, Colo.: Westview Press, 1981.

Fesharaki, Fereidun, and David T. Isaak. *OPEC, the Gulf, and the World Petroleum Market*. Boulder, Colo.: Westview Press, 1983.

Freedman, Robert O. *Soviet Policy Toward the Middle East Since 1970.* New York: Praeger Publishers, 1975.

Kerr, Malcolm H. *The Arab Cold War.* 3rd ed. London: Oxford University Press, 1971.

Mabro, Robert, ed. *World Energy: Issues and Policies.* Oxford: Oxford University Press, 1979.

Magnus, Ralph H., ed. *Documents on the Middle East.* Washington, D.C.: American Enterprise Institute, 1969.

Mikdashi, Zuhayr. *The Community of Oil Exporting Countries: A Study in Government Cooperation.* Ithaca, N.Y.: Cornell University Press, 1972.

Mosley, Leonard. *Power Play: Oil in the Middle East.* Baltimore, Md.: Penguin Books, 1974.

Rustow, Dankwart A. *Oil and Turmoil: America Faces OPEC and the Middle East.* New York: W. W. Norton and Co., 1982.

Spiegel, Steven L., ed. *The Middle East and the Western Alliance.* Winchester, Mass.: Allen and Unwin, 1982.

Tillman, Seth P. *The United States in the Middle East: Interests and Obstacles.* Bloomington: University of Indiana Press, 1982.

Waterbury, John, and Ragaei El Mallakh. *The Middle East in the Coming Decade.* New York: McGraw-Hill, 1978.

Index

458 *Index*

Class, 110–131
  defined, 111, 116
  -group interaction, dynamics of, 127–131
  and power in Middle East, 112–116
  professional middle, 122–127, 175
  structure, 111, 112–113
  system, Middle Eastern, 116–122
Cliques, 15, 28, 65, 74, 76, 77, 78, 82, 84, 89, 90, 94
Communism, 319–322
Conflict, balanced, 166–169
Conventional arms transfers, 282–284
Copts, 38–39, 72–73, 293–294
Cottam, Richard W., 303
Coups, 262–270
Cyprus, 236, 253, 347

Dayan, Moshe, 343, 441
Demirel, Süleyman, 194
Democratic party (Turkey), 191, 192
Destourian Socialist Party (Tunisia), 28, 35
Dhofar, 179, 246
Diamant, Alfred, 6–7
Diwaniya, 84
Druze, 38, 325
Dubai, 109, 374, 380, 398
Dulles, John Foster, 216

Eban, Abba, 356–358
Ecevit, Bülent, 194
Ecuador, 423
Education, 4, 16–18, 25
Eghbal, Manuchehr, 210
Egypt, 13, 14, 16, 18, 22, 25, 28, 29, 32, 33, 34–35, 38–39, 46, 54, 55, 57, 60, 69, 72, 83–84, 87–88, 91, 94, 108, 124, 130, 213–233 *passim*, 236, 237, 242, 248, 249, 251, 258–264, 269, 278, 284, 287, 291, 293, 301–302, 308, 309, 313–314, 316, 322, 327, 335–355 *passim*, 359, 360, 361, 362, 364, 368, 370, 413, 430, 433, 441, 442
Eickelman, Dale, 90
Eisenhower, Dwight D., 347, 361, 444
Eisenstadt, S. N., 7
Eitan, Rafael, 284, 365

"Emanation," 150–152, 154, 155, 156, 162, 203, 204, 211
England. *See* Britain
Enver Pasha, 184
Eshraqi, Ayatollah, 96–97
Ethiopia, 23, 259
European Economic Community, 433
Evren, Kenan, 30, 194

Factions, 76, 77, 78, 82, 84, 89, 90, 94
Fahd, King (Saudi Arabia), 47, 133, 181, 182, 364, 396, 407–408, 435
Faisal, King (Saudi Arabia), 182, 237, 266, 278, 305, 374, 431
Family, 90–98, 115, 129–130, 157–158
Farid, Muhammad, 302
Farouk, King (Egypt), 87, 92, 94, 162, 178, 214, 222, 225, 263, 287, 308, 361
Fatah, al-, 240
Fatima, 101, 146
Fatimids, 48
Fazl, Yahya al-, 120–121
Federation of Arab Republics, 309
Fidayan-i Islam, 58
France, 14, 107, 216, 236, 243–244, 248, 249, 282, 305, 330, 347, 433
Frankel, Zacharias, 70
Free Officers, 87, 213–214
Friedmann, Georges, 56, 71
Front for the Liberation of Occupied South Yemen (FLOSY), 241
Fuad, Ali, 193
Fundamentalism, Islamic, 67–69, 110, 127, 379

Gabon, 423
Gallipoli, 184
Gaza Strip, 333, 337, 339, 346, 349, 355, 362, 364–365, 368, 370, 441
Geertz, Clifford, 78
Geiger, Abraham, 70
Gemayel, Amin, 87
Gemayel, Bashir, 87, 275
Germany, 70–71
Gibb, H. A. R., 298
Gibbon, Edward, 134, 144
Glubb Pasha, 237, 265
Gökalp, Ziya, 300